Jewish Women in Pre-State Israel

HBI SERIES ON JEWISH WOMEN

Shulamit Reinharz, General Editor
Joyce Antler, Associate Editor
Sylvia Barack Fishman, Associate Editor

The HBI Series on Jewish Women, created by the Hadassah-Brandeis Institute, publishes a wide range of books by and about Jewish women in diverse contexts and time periods. Of interest to scholars and the educated public, the HBI Series on Jewish Women fills major gaps in Jewish Studies and in Women and Gender Studies as well as their intersection.

For the complete list of books that are available in this series, please see www.upne.com and www.upne.com/series/BSJW.html.

Ruth Kark, Margalit Shilo, and Galit Hasan-Rokem, editors, *Jewish Women in Pre-State Israel: Life History, Politics, and Culture*

Tova Hartman, *Feminism Encounters Traditional Judaism: Resistance and Accommodation*

Anne Lapidus Lerner, *Eternally Eve: Images of Eve in the Hebrew Bible, Midrash, and Modern Jewish Poetry*

Margalit Shilo, *Princess or Prisoner? Jewish Women in Jerusalem, 1840–1914*

Marcia Falk, translator, *The Song of Songs: Love Lyrics from the Bible*

Sylvia Barack Fishman, *Double or Nothing? Jewish Families and Mixed Marriage*

Avraham Grossman, *Pious and Rebellious: Jewish Women in Medieval Europe*

Iris Parush, *Reading Jewish Women: Marginality and Modernization in Nineteenth-Century Eastern European Jewish Society*

Shulamit Reinharz and Mark A. Raider, editors, *American Jewish Women and the Zionist Enterprise*

Tamar Ross, *Expanding the Palace of Torah: Orthodoxy and Feminism*

Farideh Goldin, *Wedding Song: Memoirs of an Iranian Jewish Woman*

Elizabeth Wyner Mark, editor, *The Covenant of Circumcision: New Perspectives on an Ancient Jewish Rite*

Rochelle L. Millen, *Women, Birth, and Death in Jewish Law and Practice*

JEWISH WOMEN IN PRE-STATE ISRAEL

Life History, Politics, and Culture

Edited by

Ruth Kark, Margalit Shilo, and
Galit Hasan-Rokem

Brandeis University Press
Waltham, Massachusetts

Published by University Press of New England   Hanover and London

Brandeis University Press
Published by University Press of New England,
One Court Street, Lebanon, NH 03766
www.upne.com
© 2008 by Brandeis University Press
Printed in the United States of America
5 4 3 2 1

Library of Congress Cataloging-in-Publication Data
'Ivriyot ha-hadashot. English.
Jewish women in pre-state Israel : life history, politics, and culture / edited by Ruth Kark,
Margalit Shilo, and Galit Hasan-Rokem. — 1st ed.
   p.   cm. — (HBI series on Jewish women)
Includes bibliographical references and index.
ISBN 978–1–58465–702–6 (cloth : alk. paper) — ISBN 978–1–58465–703–3 (pbk. : alk. paper)
1. Jewish women—Palestine—History—Congresses.   2. Jewish women—Israel—His-
tory—Congresses.   3. Feminism—Palestine—History—Congresses.   4. Feminism—Is-
rael—History—Congresses. I. Kark, Ruth.   II. Shilo, Margalit.   III. Hasan-Rokem,
Galit.   IV. Title.
HQ1728.5.I9513 2008
305.48'892400904—dc22 2008007648

Contents

Shulamit Reinharz, Ph.D.

Foreword

You may not be able to judge a book by its cover, but you probably won't go wrong judging an anthology by its editors. The three editors of this particular collection — professor of historical geography, Ruth Kark; professor of history, Margalit Shilo; and professor of folklore, Galit Hasan-Rokem — are stars of the Israeli academic scene. Their subject matter is pre-State Israel, i.e. the Jewish community that lived in what was to become Israel in 1948. Within that community, about which so much has been written, there is one group that has garnered less attention than it deserves. That group is women. The relative lack of attention paid to the study of pre-State Jewish women stems from the same problems that are true around the world. There is no special archive to collect papers on this group; there are no special chairs at universities; and there is very little research support in Israel devoted to this topic. Thus, the work is difficult to undertake and funding is hard to come by.

The Hadassah-Brandeis Institute, founded (under a different name) in 1997, was created to address these specific problems. The following year we partnered with the Lafer Center for Women and Gender Studies at Hebrew University (and the Tauber Institute at Brandeis University) to hold a conference on a topic never previously discussed in a large public forum — the contribution of Jewish women to the creation of the State of Israel. Held at the Hebrew University, the conference was organized under the title "We Were Here, Too!" and received a lot of media attention. The papers in this collection stem from that early conference. The next year we held a complementary conference at the Hadassah-Brandeis Institute, focusing on the American counterparts of these Jewish women in pre-State Israel. This second conference resulted in the volume, *American Jewish Women and the Zionist Enterprise*, edited by Mark A. Raider and myself, and published in this series.

Since then, many other conferences have been held, and many new research projects initiated. And yet, the contributors in the current volume were the earliest ones, and their research was truly groundbreaking.

To make this extremely broad topic manageable, the editors chose three foci: life history, politics, and culture. They also chose only Israeli academics, both women and men, all of whom are very well known in their fields. The book begins with historiographic reflection, i.e., how should historians and other researchers deal with the study of women. Two initial contributions, by sociologist Deborah Bernstein and historian Yossi Ben-Artzi, start this discussion. To counterbalance the previous nearly exclusive focus paid to Ashkenazi Jews, several of the next contributions (by Henriette Dahan-Kalev, Michal Ben Ya'akov, and Esther Meir-Glitzenstein) deal with Mizrahi women, North African women, and Iraqi women. Joseph Glass, an expert on immigration to Palestine from the United States and Canada, offers a chapter on this topic in the interwar years. Penina Morag-Talmon discusses women immigrants not in terms of individual adjustment and choices, but as parts of social networks.

Another group of chapters deals with ideas rather than behaviors. Einat Ramon, for example, brings the ideology of key Zionist theoretician A. D. Gordon to bear on the feminist concerns of women in the Second Aliyah. The image of pre-State Israel is still very much rooted in the unusual communities of kibbutz and moshav, rather than the city. And in this book, as well, we find an emphasis on the kibbutz. The contribution by Henry Near takes up once again the question of why women did not find in the kibbutz the utopian society of which they had dreamed.

The story of Jewish women's political activity in pre-State Israel is not so much one of elected office but rather of creating new organizations. To achieve this objective required considerable political skill. The examples in this volume are Margalit Shilo's study of girls' schools in Jerusalem; a study by Shifra Shvarts and Zipora Shehory-Rubin of the unique institution called Tipat Halav (maternal and infant welfare centers); Nira Bartal's study of the nursing school in Jerusalem; and Bat-Sheva Margalit-Stern's examination of the women's workers movement.

Cultural products of Jewish women in pre-State Israel are discussed in a book section entitled "Creativity in Word and Music." There we can find chapters on poetry, fiction, and music. The book concludes with a discussion of memory, with contributions by Billie Melman and Judith Baumel-Schwartz. Studies of memorialization and the creation of legends form an appropriate bookend to contrast with the opening section on historiography.

Collective memory is the process and product of a society's defining of its past; historiography is the analogous phenomenon on the part of professional historians.

As anyone who has done work in the field of women's studies knows, conducting research and publishing one's findings are only the beginning. The next step is equally significant, and that is to incorporate this work into the general record. If the work is not integrated into the studies conducted by people working in fields other than women's studies, then it will remain marginal. Nor is the point to have research on women sit side-by-side with that of research on men. Rather, our goal should be to take work such as appears in this volume and integrate it into a larger whole. Then we can ask more sweeping theoretical questions that will help us uncover the meaning of gender in society.

As director of the Hadassah-Brandeis Institute, I am pleased that we are able to contribute to progress on all the steps along the way to this greater goal. We offer research grants to scholars around the world who do work in the field of Jewish women's studies; we sponsor conferences; we invite scholars-in-residence to spend time at our headquarters at Brandeis University; we publish *Nashim: A Journal of Jewish Women's Studies & Gender Issues* (in partnership with the Schechter Institute of Jewish Studies in Jerusalem and Indiana University Press); and we publish the HBI Series on Jewish Women, of which this excellent volume is the latest publication. It is our sincerest hope that all of these efforts will contribute to a change in historiography and memory. And that as the field of Israel Studies develops on campuses in the United States and elsewhere, books such as this one that deals with half the population will become central to the curriculum.

Jewish Women in Pre-State Israel

Introduction

This collection was prompted by a search for the concealed identity of women in the history and culture of the *Yishuv*, the Jewish settlement in pre-state Israel, and by the call for a new national discourse. Issues regarding women and gender have been largely ignored in the historiography of the Jewish community in Palestine and research into its culture.[1] Even today the discourse is overwhelmingly male dominant.[2] This exclusion of women is the direct continuation of women having been barred from public life in Jewish communities in the past.[3] The attempt to establish a new society based on ideological foundations of equality did not succeed, and its lack of realization created frustration and anguish.[4]

The fiftieth anniversary of the founding of the State of Israel was the catalyst for convening a multidisciplinary interuniversity conference on the topic "Women in the Yishuv and the Early State of Israel," which was held at the Hebrew University of Jerusalem. It was co-sponsored by the Leifer Center for Women's Studies at the Hebrew University as well as The Hadassah-Brandeis Institute and The Jacob and Libby Goodman Institute for the Study of Zionism and Israel, both affiliated with Brandeis University, Waltham, Massachusetts. The participants, from universities in Israel and the United States, addressed a wide range of topics: history, sociology, historical geography, political science, literature, anthropology, folklore, musicology, history of philosophy, and cinema studies. The forty or so lectures given in the course of three tightly packed days stimulated considerable interest. This peer-reviewed multidisciplinary anthology in English comprises a selection of articles based on the conference presentations.

Reverberations of the second wave of feminism, which also reached Israel, prompted there, too, the desire to reveal the feminine voice and the genderization of the past. Over the last two decades, we have been fortunate to see pioneering initial studies responding to the invocation "to seek, tell and write new narratives that will give expression to woman's life, to the story of her activities, to her contribution, and to her naturean the authentic multi-faceted Hebrew-Israeli voice."[5] Postmodern contemporary research permeated by concepts of cultural pluralism serves as a catalyst for a revised national discourse, one that also expresses the world of women and issues of gender.

Intense preoccupation with the myth of the equality of the sexes in Eretz Israel, an ethos that has been scrutinized and smashed in extensive research, led to a number of basic questions: What was the reality of life for women in Jewish society in Eretz Israel in the early years? What was the contribution of women to the renewal of Israeli society and culture? What is the place of gender perceptions in the study of the new Eretz Israel identity?

In a stimulating, challenging programmatic article, Billie Melman has called for not being satisfied with seeking out and exposing the hidden half but rather for applying new insights derived from feminist research to create a new historical-cultural narrative.[6] Her evaluation that "Zionism was perhaps the most conscious and intensive attempt to change the concepts of gender against the background of national realization," presents the study of "Israeliness" as a gender test case of unique importance.[7]

The original articles in this anthology, each in its own way, forge an innovative response to one or more of the questions presented above and can be viewed as a representative sample, reflecting the state of research in the field. Analysis through the prism of gender should greatly enhance our understanding of the key issues for Israeli society.

This volume is divided into six sections, each chronologically presented.

In the first section, "Constructing the Historical Narrative," Deborah Bernstein, Yossi Ben-Artzi, and Henriette Dahan-Kalev address issues of methodology and historiography. The first two authors propose a map for future research in this field, while Henriette Dahan-Kalev focuses on the study of Oriental women and informs us of the special problems involving the "other."

The articles in the second section, "Women and Immigration," deal with four different groups of immigrants. Michal Ben Ya'akov elucidates immigration patterns of traditional women from North Africa who headed for Eretz Israel in the nineteenth century. Joseph Glass assesses the contribution of women immigrants from the United States to the *Yishuv*. Esther Meir-Glitzenstein sensitively depicts the encounter of young Iraqi women with their new homeland and the influence this meeting had on their gender identity. Penina Morag-Talmon gives a new reading of the experiences of young women who immigrated to Jerusalem upon the founding of the State and depicts their support systems.

The topic of the third section is "Pioneers and Defenders." Einat Ramon offers fresh research into A. D. Gordon's perception of the status of women in Eretz Israel. Henry Near confronts the weighty issue of why the discrepancy between the ideal of equality and the reality in the kibbutz was so disturbing for the female members. Smadar Shiffman's discussion revolves around the mutual fashioning of the image of the "*halutz*" (male pioneer) and "*halutzah*" (female pioneer). Hagar Salamon weaves a thread from present to past through the Mandate period to the Ottoman era by analyzing the image of a complex feminine figure (Zohar Wilbush), who played a central role in preserving the heritage of Eretz Israel material culture.

The fourth section articles deal with "Education, Health, and Politics" and exposes female activity in these arenas. Margalit Shilo presents the model of the new woman as fashioned in the first school in the country for young Jewish women, the Evelina de Rothschild School, at the turn of the twentieth century in Jerusalem. The studies by Shifra Shvarts and Zipora Shehory-Rubin and by Nira Bartal examine the organized involvement of women in the field of health during the Mandate period. Shvarts and Shehory-Rubin delved into the establishment of the *Tipat Halav* (Mother and Child Health Clinics) and their influence on society, while Bartal focused on the first nursing school in Eretz Israel. The discussion by Bat-Sheva Margalit Stern of the women's labor movement within the Histadrut is also a study of the obstacles and limitations that faced female political activity, revealing that barriers persist to the present. Hannah Safran wrote about women's suffrage in the *Yishuv* and the unique contribution of Dr. Rosa Welt Straus.

The fifth section, "Creativity in Word and Music," is devoted to articles in the fields of literature and music. Orly Lubin provides a new, feminist reading to the writings of the First Aliyah author Nehama Pohatcevsky (Puhachewsky). Tali Asher addresses the masculine and feminine images in Rachel's poems and their cultural implications. The study by Yaffah Berlovitz presents the biblical narratives incorporated within the poetry of the poet Anda Amir-Pinkerfeld, thereby placing her more centrally in the Hebrew literary map than to date. Hannan Hever proposes a feminist interpretation for *Shirim la-Geto* (*Poems to the Ghetto*) by Yocheved Bat-Miriam, an explication that renders feminist poetry as an authoritative voice in the new reading of national history. A musicological contribution by Yael Shai and Rachel Kollender considers the role of women in the preservation and transmission of musical traditions in Israel.

The sixth and final section in this anthology is devoted to a discussion of the topic of "Shaping the Collective Memory". Billie Melman examines transformations in the image of Sarah Aaronsohn and the historical significance of these changes in meaning, tracing them from the past through to the present. The article by Judith Baumel-Schwartz, in which she analyzes commemoration of women in memorials in the State of Israel, concludes this collection.

The editors of this anthology see it as an appetizer and not as a definitive collection; they hope it will spark new research. As alluded to above, many topics await illumination through gender studies. Some topics need preliminary gender examination, while others are already at a stage that allows the execution of more advanced feminist research evolving from existing findings. The aim of this collection is to indicate research challenges and to act as a catalyst for a great deal of multidisciplinary activity in the future.

The appearance of this volume provides the opportunity to thank all those who supported its translation from the Hebrew: The Hadassah-Brandeis Institute, Brandeis University; Prof. Shulamit Reinharz, its director, Prof. Sylvia Fox Fried, and Helene Greenberg; Mrs. Rachel Pollack and The Edith and Israel Pollack Fund; The Scheine Center at the Hebrew University of Jerusalem; the Fanya Gottesfeld Heller Center for the Study of Women in Judaism at Bar-Ilan University, and to the Yad Ben Zvi Press and to Dr. Zvi Zameret, the Director of Yad Ben-Zvi, who gave permission for the publication in the English language.

Special thanks are due to Fern Seckbach for the translation of the Hebrew volume into English and for the preparation of the glossary and index, to David Louvish for the translation of the article by Margalit Shilo, and to Keren-Or Schlesinger for her efficient organizational assistance.

Finally, the editors wish to thank Prof. Shulamit Reinharz and Dr. Lilach Rosenberg-Friedman for reading and improving the English manuscript, and University Press of New England for its help in publishing the volume.

Prof. Ruth Kark (The Hebrew University of Jerusalem)
Prof. Margalit Shilo (Bar-Ilan University)
Prof. Galit Hasan-Rokem (The Hebrew University of Jerusalem)
October 2007

The Hebrew transliteration in this volume is based, in general, on the system of the *Encyclopaedia Judaica*. Authors were permitted to use alternate spellings.

❧ Constructing the Historical Narrative

✾ *Deborah Bernstein*

The Study of Women in Israeli Historiography
Starting Points, New Directions, and Emerging Insights

Feminisms are never autonomous but bound to the signifying networks of the contexts which produce them. — Deniz Kandiyoti[1]

For about twenty years now, since the mid-1980s, the story of women has begun to seek its place as part of the general story of Jewish-Zionist settlement in Eretz Israel. We have come a long way since then. Male and female scholars turned, simultaneously, to a number of channels, and by uncovering voices and images, set the foundation layers in various historiographic directions: the stories of female leaders, the development of the movements and institutions that women established to promote their issues, and the daily life of the "ordinary" women. During this period, our historiographic world began to be one of foment and ferment. The "general story" fell apart and is still going to pieces; debates took its place: debates over the starting point of the new "story," and at the same time, the voices and claims of the other stories, which are trying to assume their rightful place on the agenda of the past and the present. These controversies and others were echoed in women's studies and raised new questions: Will we — and how will we — continue to bring to light the women's stories as yet untold — and they are legion? How will we integrate their stories in the new narratives that are coalescing, and how will we fit in with the fashioning of the starting points of the new general story or the many, bustling-inchoate stories around us?

This article will attempt to survey the distance we have come, the milestones we have passed, the directions in thinking and research that have opened, and other channels that deserve investigation.

The Sociological-Historical Search

Historical study of women in the *Yishuv* period, the formative time of the new Israeli society, began as a feminist project, as a compulsion of female scholars to get to know and to illuminate the story of women, which was missing — almost completely — from the historical story of the society as it took shape. We wanted to fill in what was missing, to tell what had not been told, to let the mute voices speak. Article after article began by describing what was missing in the hegemonic story: the absence of the figures of women as leaders, heroines; the absence of women's writings; the absence of any awareness of the women's contribution to the community in formation, and the lack of recognition of their unique, different experience. Like many feminist researchers in other societies, we sought "roots," what preceded our current routine life, what preceded our social inferiority, what preceded our attempts at struggle and organization. As time passed, the study of the past began to crystallize. It can serve as compensation for the silencing and as a source for answers to some of our questions.

Yet, the importance of this first stage went far beyond filling in what was missing. Putting women into the picture changed it completely; at first, only in the eyes of a small circle of scholars (male and female) and readers (male and female), but in time, in the eyes of ever-expanding circles. Integration of women through analysis of their subordination on both institutional and personal levels shed light on the inequality of the society-in-the-making. Thereby, the study of women was unavoidably intertwined, from the outset, with the critical analysis of Israeli society. This analysis gathered momentum at the end of the 1970s, and in the 1980s took its place alongside other icono-clastic projects, and became part of a re-examination of Israel society — its nature, its past, and its messages. At the same time, women's studies gave the first impetus toward social history in place of the exclusivity of political and institutional history.

The study of women in Israeli historiography clearly parallels the initial stages of the study of women in other societies: inserting women into the historical story, making them no longer "hidden from history," and telling "herstory" — as shown to us, among others, by Joan Wallach Scott regarding the history of women in the west and by Deniz Kandiyoti in the study of women of the Middle East.[2] But this step, which seems so obvious on the surface, was complex and had further repercussions. We integrated new actors — actresses — into a story that seemed to have been told already, and by doing so we added a new perspective to the entire story. We added the "missing sex" to the community-in-the-making, and thereby uncovered a new community, a community composed of women and men, a community whose masculinity was no longer merely an aspect of national renewal but also a pattern of dominance. We traced the root of the inequality between women and men, contributing to the challenging of the myths of Israeli society in general. We moved some distance away, but not a great one, from the institutional, political, public sphere toward the private sphere, toward daily life. These were imperative steps that had to be taken to illuminate vital aspects in the life of women, and while doing so we revealed the almost total absence of social history in the historiography of Israeli society at large. But most important of all: We began — even if it were the most modest of beginnings — to lay a foundation for getting to know the lives and experiences of women, at least of certain groups of women, in the formative period that preceded the establishment of the state.

Informative and Enriching Debates

The historical study of women in Israel, and for the purposes of this article — academic-feminist research — emerged in the late 1970s and in the 1980s out of sociology and history, in a calm, intellectual atmosphere. Israeli sociology was, indeed, tempestuous in those years, but the eye of the storm centered on the power structures that came into being after the establishment of the sovereign state, and the feminine-gender dimension was marginal to the salient issues of ethnic group and class. The pre-State period, at that time, remained outside the eye of the storm, and with it also the study of women in that period. To be sure, this research was accompanied by iconoclasm, but this did not shatter any foundations. Research showed that women had not enjoyed equal rights, as usually claimed, but it seemed that the putative claim of equality had no deep significance, and undermining it was not taken as detrimental to any weighty factor, or hallowed symbol, within academia or outside it.

This relatively serene attitude to the historiography of the *Yishuv* period changed radically in the past decade, from the end of the 1980s. In the stormy, polarized years of the *intifada*, and afterwards of the peace process, understanding of the pre-State period turned into a no less fiery arena than the controversies of the present and the more recent past. The arguments about the nature and character of Zionist settlement went beyond internal academic debate. These debates occupied public figures and authors, journalists and academics, and created a stimulating, thought-provoking intellectual atmosphere leading into new venues in academic-feminist research as well.

The debates became more diversified. Soon there was a relative decline in the study of historical issues and events, and the discussion expanded into historiography itself, its suppositions, its concepts, its methods, and its conclusions. These debates can be divided into two main categories. One revolves around the group that earned the sobriquet of the "New Historians" and around its arguments on the essence of Zionist settlement, while the other category concentrates mainly on arguments derived from social history and from multicultural analysis. The first type — the New Historians' debate — revolves around historical writing and historiographical discussion that examined and challenged Zionist settlement. The writers focused on examining Zionist settlement through international comparisons, and they particularly discussed Zionism as compared to other national movements and various types of colonial settlement. The New Historians devoted most of their attention to the Jewish-Arab conflict, considering it the central formative factor of Zionist settlement. In the course of doing so, they posed penetrating questions about the very legitimacy of Zionism and its new national identity. Yet, these radical arguments focused almost exclusively on the political elite, the institutional system, and the dominant ideology. Absent from the New Historians' discussion is any gender aspect at all, and of women in particular, no less than in the hegemonic historiography that they were challenging.

Alongside the claims by this group of historians, much wider-ranging historiographical debates took place. They expressed the aspiration for multiculturalism, that is, for viewing the past (and hence the present) from different perspectives reflecting the separate experiences of groups with different social status, different interests, and different culture, perspectives that send the researcher to the many, varied groups located outside the *Yishuv* society elites.

Some tried to link these two categories of historiographical debate, but the adoption of the multicultural and the historio-social arguments by the New Historians remained, to a great extent, wishful thinking or a declaration of intent.

To sum up, one may point out a number of primary results and conclusions that crystallized in the historiographical debates carried out largely by the New Historians.

- Challenging the ethos and myths of Israeli society, not only in the sense of certain concrete elements of this ethos but through touching upon the nature of the legitimization of Zionist settlement — not only refuting the claim of equality in *Yishuv* society, but placing question marks on the reasons for immigrating to Palestine and inserting exclamation points on the repercussions that our coming had on others.

- Placing the discussion of the past on the social agenda, not in a concealed, imperceptible manner, but openly and declaredly. As a result, it was possible to begin examining various narratives of the past, comprehending the way in which these narratives took shape and tussled with each other and their significance for the current politics of identities.

- Turning to comparative research in search of similarities and differences between Zionism and national movements and settlement movements in other times and places.

- Preferring the colonial point of view over others as a way for comprehending Zionist settlement; or alternatively, presenting this point of view as one among other vantage points, which provide — in combination — complex explanations for the existence and development of the Jewish-Zionist *Yishuv* in Eretz Israel/Palestine.

- Calling for multiple points of view, multiple narratives, "multiple voices." Accepting the fact (and even glorifying it) that there are different ways to be integrated into the national, Jewish, or Zionist narrative and that there are other ways to experience the local story — the story of this space, with its cultural, social, and political definitions, and not necessarily through Jewish nationalism.

- Understanding the inadequacy of historiography that does not go beyond the borders of the elites and the boundaries of their endeavors and interests, historiography that focuses almost exclusively on the institutional system, on the relations between the different elites, and on ideological perceptions, and ignores the private sphere and mundane daily life.

The historiographical debates, and the ferment that accompanied them, constituted a productive, inspiring intellectual context for the development of the historical-feminist discussion. At the same time, this discussion itself nourished and enriched the search for alternatives in historical writing. Reference to gender aspects was not uniform. Most of the facts and claims of the New Historians continued to focus on the political elites, in the formal, institutional sense of this concept, and on the political and ideological history, while completely ignoring any gender aspect. Only at a much later stage did scholars begin to apply a gender view to the Zionist movement, its leaders, and their attitudes (as in the works by Boyarin, Gluzman, and Biale), to the Jewish-Arab conflict (in the works by S. Katz, T. Mayer, and J. Peteet), or

Israeliness that takes shape with the beginning of the Zionist *aliyot* (as in the study by Billie Melman).[3]

The situation is totally different from the second perspective of the historiographical debates, the call for multiculturalism and for "history from below" moving away from the elites. Here, feminist historiography is an inseparable element and from the outset played a central role in the development of this point of view.

Women's history, like women's studies in general, took its inspiration from the women's movement and from the new feminist agenda. Thus the theoretical-academic dimension and the political dimension were interwoven. Interlinked from the beginning were empirical questions, theoretical questions, and political questions, and the discussions of the aims of women's history dealt, simultaneously and in combination, with these three dimensions. The main aim in women's history was to integrate women into the historical narrative, or — with slightly different emphasis — to bring their history to light, focusing on the special feminine experience in different places and different times; what women did, what they felt, what they created, how they reacted to their condition, and how they tried to cope with it and change it. The aim, as expressed by Joan Wallach Scott, was "to give value as history to an experience which has been ignored and thus devalued and to insist on female agency in the 'the making of history.'"[4]

Some of the researchers shed light on women who were active alongside men, or by themselves, in the organized political and social arena. They added women into the historical narrative that had been accepted until then. Others approached ordinary women, daily life, and the nature of the women's sphere and feminine consciousness. The main theme is this approach was the presentation of women as agents of action. Many studies presented the ideas, expressions, and activities of the women, as individuals and as a collective. The explanations and interpretations developed by these scholars were taken from the area of the feminine experience. That is, they based themselves on the same factors that research had shown were of particular importance in the lives of women — the private sphere alongside the public sphere, personal experience, the family and domestic systems, and both the emotional and physical support systems that women developed among themselves.[5]

This research into women's history led to the creation of a wide-ranging, rich, and varied literature. The study of women developed to an impressive extent, yet remained a distinct field on its own — new topics, new questions, new conceptualizations, a stirring, provocative, stimulating discussion — but still it seemed that women spoke mainly among themselves. Women's history led the scholars in this field to examine critically the existing historiography in general but did not result in great changes in that historiography, or—as Scott puts it—did not lead to a rewriting of history. The dominant perceptions held sway, with the addition of a new field, alongside the other fields. The isolation, or "ghettoization," dulled the theoretical sting and the political message in the study of women, a message of changes in thought patterns, which was vital when feminine-feminist history was just starting out.

Toward the end of the 1980s, this internal criticism led to a shift of emphasis from women's experience to an examination of femininity; not femininity alone, but femininity and masculinity, an examination of the social construction of sexuality. In other words, emphasis passed from women to gender, and from the story of women to the gendering of society. Focusing on gender will make it possible to go beyond the limits of the separate feminine story. Gender studies link sexuality, the social definitions of femininity and masculinity, and the structure of power, strength, and wealth in society, which influence the formation of these definitions, their production and/or their change. Thus, sexuality goes straight to the heart of political history, the field that has thus far dealt, almost exclusively, with the public activity of the masculine elites. The essence of feminist history, according to Scott, is in the gendering activity, in the terms of the forces frequently hidden and unseen, which through construction of femininity and masculinity, organize social action and structure.[6]

Most of the researchers welcomed the political, theoretical, and intellectual challenge found in the concept of gender and in its linkage to all social processes. Other female researchers warn of the limits of the "gender" approach. J. Bennett, for example, argued that gender study as proposed by Scott, ignores the study of women as women, moves away from the material reality of women's lives while giving preference to representations and metaphors, leading to excess intellectualization and abstraction of the inequality between the sexes. Bennett summarizes the issues with the claim that "The hard lives of women in the past; the material forces which shaped and constrained women's activities; the ways that women coped with challenges and obstacles—all of these things can too easily disappear from a history of gender as meaning."[7]

And for Us in Israel

And what can we learn from these developments for the historiography of women in Israeli society?

There are many points in common. The isolation of the study of women in *Yishuv* history is striking and blatant. To be sure, initial steps were taken to integrate this research into the forums dealing with Israeli society and its history in a general manner, with the journal *Cathedra* serving as an example, but this integration is still spotty. It was precisely the jubilee year of the establishment of the State of Israel (1998), a year that saw the production of a plethora of anthologies and conferences, that revealed the scant influence of women's studies on the overall historiographic discourse. Besides a number of highly interesting conferences in the field of the study of women in new Israeli history, the "general" meetings continued to deal with the public sphere and the activity of the elite groups, with no mention of women or gender; as if no new insight or any new, vital information had accumulated for integration into the historiographical discourse in order to consolidate a slightly more "general" picture. Is there room to argue, as Billie Melman does, that this relative isolation and disregard derived from the female researchers limiting themselves solely to the history of women, with no attempt at interpolating women's experience into a more inclusive analysis of formative processes in society at large? Or as she writes:

> Instead of focusing on the course of the exclusion and marginality, it seems it would have been more fitting to emphasize gender as a principle element in the Eretz-Israel identity and the Eretz-Israel experience as well as a factor that is leading toward change in social organization and in political and cultural modes of organization. The use of gender as a "useful historical category" does not, of course, have to diminish research into the relevant historical sources and their interpretation. Such empirical research is the heart of history — all history — as a discipline. Yet, the use of gender as a topic for research, and particularly as an analytical tool for investigating historical changes, is vital for dynamic historical investigation of the *Yishuv*. This way one is not forced to discuss the story of the "*Yishuv* women's" experience separately or simply as a narrative of discrimination and lack of equality.[8]

I have no doubt that the concept of gender and the way it is used, as Scott and Melman have proposed, can enrich the historiography of women in Israeli society in particular and of Israeli society in general. It will permit us to anchor women's condition within a wider social context and to examine their activities in light of the systems of relations between women and men and between female and male institutions. It will be possible to understand women's perspective, among other things, as a reaction to the attitudes and perceptions that surrounded them, the perceptions of men regarding women, femininity and masculinity. Another analytical direction to which the concept of gender may be applied is in the examination of the mutual relations between gender and other formative factors such as class, nationality, religion, and ethnic group; and in the case of Israel, for example, the mutual relations between the construction of femininity and masculinity and the feeling of national belonging, Jewish or Israeli, Arab or Palestinian, or the construction of femininity and masculinity through the encounter of different Jewish publics from Central and Eastern Europe, from Yemen, Turkey, and North Africa. On a more innovative level, it will be possible to employ the concept of gender as an organizing principle for the analysis of central processes, institutions, and structures in Israeli society, which thus far have been totally disconnected from the concepts of femininity and masculinity. These varied applications of the concept of gender do, indeed, appear in the literature of the past few years. For example, a number of researchers have dealt with the gender aspect of the perception of the national revival in the Zionist movement. They stressed the Zionist identification of Jewish existence in the Diaspora with weakness, femininity, and distorted masculinity and the identification of national revival with the revival of Jewish masculinity, and the creation of the new Judaism, "muscular Judaism." As Daniel Boyarin writes: "The Zionist endeavor was to a great extent the turning of the Jewish male into the masculine type they admired — the ideal 'Aryan' man. If Zionism's political mission was to turn the Jews into a nation like all other nations, then the change in the spiritual dimension was expressed in the attempt to turn the Jewish male into a man like all other men."[9]

Nira Yuval-Davis deals with citizenship and gender, exploring the dual way in which women are included within general citizenship while also being excluded from it, and on how they serve as the indicators for the limits and continuation of the national collective.[10] Sheila Katz has brought the gender viewpoint to an analysis of the Jewish-Arab conflict while illuminating the way that the imagery of femininity and masculinity and metaphors for femininity and masculinity, openly and covertly, were used in fashioning the national discourse in the Arab national movement and the Jewish national movement, and in the obstreperous discourse between them.[11]

The significance of the new insight that the concept of gender provides for the study of social structures and the reproduction of patterns of dominance mark new directions for the study of women in Israel. Important to remember, however, is that gendered analysis was taken up in the United

States and other countries in which a wide-ranging, rich, varied body of scholarly literature in women's studies had been written a few decades earlier. The situation in Israel is completely different: the research literature surveyed above should be considered initial steps, only the beginnings of "letting the voice be heard," the beginnings of "institutional history," of mundane life and social history — but only the start; a great many areas have not been investigated at all. I will point out a few such directions.

- Life cycle and accompanying aspects: As yet scholars are only beginning to examine basic patterns of women's life cycle and the social perceptions connected to them, such as childbearing and limiting it, marriage and divorce, childhood, widowhood and singleness, sexuality and the concepts of morality, and social institutions that organize and fashion these patterns.
- Beyond the dominant public women. Research has yet to begin to examine women outside the hegemonic groups: members of the petite bourgeoisie or the urban upper class, largely Ashkenazi, members of the veteran Sephardi public, and members of the many oriental ethnic groups — Yemenites, Moghrabi, Bukharan, and others. Few studies have highlighted their way of life, their relations with their environs, with the men around them, and with the other women in the family, in their own community and outside of it.
- Beyond the "*Yishuv* period." Feminist historical research has not begun to shed light on women's experience that underwent far-reaching changes with the establishment of the State of Israel in 1948 — and as a consequence of it. This applies to the Palestinian women whose world changed from one extreme to another — whether they remained in their settlements or became refugees in other settlements in Israel or turned into refugees in camps in the surrounding countries; this is also relevant for the female Jewish immigrants who arrived with the mass immigration from Yemen and Iraq, Romania, Bulgaria, and elsewhere, as they grappled with their life experience as women in Israel.
- Beyond the limits of the discipline. The writing of women's history in Israel grew through a combination of sociological and historical approaches, but these should be linked to other disciplines. A number of anthologies have included articles from various fields of research, thus contributing to an interdisciplinary approach, but we must still strive for methods of analysis, research and writing, which will further develop empirical, theoretical, and conceptual cooperation.[12] Such an interdisciplinary perspective can contribute to a more holistic approach to the topic of our study —

women, their lives and their experience. If we now shift the emphasis in feminist historiography from "the voice of women" to the "gendering of society" without a broad, multifaceted foundation of knowledge about women's lives, experience, perceptions, and consciousness, we can still lose sight of women as "actors" in society with a voice of their own.

One also may wonder whether this conceptual-analytical turnabout is capable of eliminating the isolation of feminist historiography and of abolishing the marginality of the "feminine story." Perhaps so. The gendering investigation deals with a cluster of social aspects and not "only" with one sector — and therein lies its uniqueness and explanatory power. Yet, it seems to me that the marginalization of feminist historiography does not stem only from "reductive conceptualization." Factors that are mainly political — in the broad sense of the term — will determine the impact of the feminist perspective on the public and academic agenda. Cultural, social, and political factors also will define and fashion the context in which we continue to develop the feminist-academic discussion. Feminism, or feminisms, are not autonomous, as in the quote from Kandiyoti cited at this beginning of this article. I hope that we will not just be fashioned by the context in which we are operating, but that we will also shape it.

❦ *Yossi Ben-Artzi*

Have Gender Studies Changed Our Attitude toward the Historiography of the *Aliyah* and Settlement Process?

Background

The aim of this article is to examine to what extent gender studies in Israel have thus far changed our attitude toward the history of the periods of the First and Second Aliyah, and in general, the history of the *aliyah* and Jewish settlement processes in Eretz Israel at the end of the nineteenth and the beginning of the twentieth centuries and to propose directions for research that are likely to make gender a central, different elucidator of known phenomena of these processes.

In general historiography of the First and Second Aliyah periods, significant changes have taken place in the past two decades thanks to joint research projects or individual studies.[1] They certainly have shed new light on the periods themselves, and they have presented new perspectives on each period or for understanding the settlement developments that occurred during them. For instance, the place of the moshavah in settlement history now appears totally different than it did in the previous classic studies.[2]

The roles of the Baron Edmond de Rothschild's administration and of the Jewish Colonization Association (JCA) already are perceived completely differently than the way they frequently had been distorted in historical memory.[3] A more balanced, fact-based picture has been drawn toward understanding the proportional role of private versus public capital in the processes of modernization, settlement, and land acquisition.[4]

All the foregoing are examples showing that in settlement historiography, a new stage has been created that completely changes our appreciation of pivotal phenomena: land purchases, settlement in its various forms, organization of settlements, factors in settlement, and so on. From this, we deduce

that one may achieve fresh insight into central phenomena by using alternative research paradigms for the writing of classic history, such as the historical-
geographic approach, or the economic-historical approach, or understanding
the place of institutions and organizations in historical processes.

It should be stressed that the place of research into women and gender
perception have not been left out of this renewed scrutiny of the early periods of *aliyah*; moreover, in recent years, many studies have focused on the
feminine "voice" and the feminine view of processes and phenomena related to these *aliyot*. These studies have successfully met two important criteria in their own right from the aspect of the gender paradigm: first, an addition to existing knowledge, in the sense of new materials that emphasize
feminine participation in the formation of the *Yishuv* with all its various
characteristics; second, complementing the first, amplifying feminine or
gender exclusion from study of the period. In this way, pioneering studies,
such as those by M. Shilo, D. Bernstein, and D. Izraeli, became the foundation stones for a fresh look at well-ensconced "truths," such as the equality attributed to women of the Second Aliyah and of the labor movement.[5]

Central Issues in the Study of the Period

The central issues related to the history of settlement to which we will refer
in the context of gender in this article are the following:

- Immigration (*aliyot*) as a historical and social process: circumstances,
  characteristics, trends, dimensions, and results;
- Settlement in its extended meaning: land acquisition, settlement distribu-
  tion, forms of settlement, structure of the economy;
- Formation of the social fabric: ethnicity, ages, genders, internal relations;
- Education: institutions, methods, organizations;
- Culture and creativity: language, writing, creativity, and the shaping of
  identity;
- Political and organizational structure: movements, trends, parties, mem-
  bership, and organizations.

All of these phenomena and processes have been studied, of course, by a
wide range of researchers dealing with the study of the history of settlement;

and our goal here is to examine to what extent we would write a book on the history of settlement differently if we scrutinized all these through the prism of gender. Would we just gain additional knowledge, a contribution in the uncovering of new facts about women's "participation" or exclusion, or would we, perhaps, forge new insight into the settlement endeavor in one, a part, or all of the issues listed?

First we will examine in what way existing gender studies have changed our understanding of some of the phenomena mentioned. Then we will offer a list of questions, hypotheses, and topics for research from a gender viewpoint to complete the claim that it is, indeed, possible to write a different book on the history of settlement.

An Examination of Women's and Gender Studies and Their Contribution to the Historiography of the Settlement Process Thus Far

Interestingly, the pioneering gender approach to understanding this important chapter in the formation of settlement society was adopted inadvertently, that is, even before the formation of the gender approach. I am referring to studies dealing with the Hebrew language and the effort to turn it into a spoken, living language. Bar-Adon's work on this topic was a kind of swallow as harbinger of the historiographic spring in this important sector of "building the nation" — the revival of Hebrew.[6]

The emphasis on the role of the "mothers," the women of daily life, in adapting the Hebrew language to the native-born generation and their descendants, created a new, different attitude toward understanding the phenomenon that riveted global attention. It was no longer E. Ben-Yehuda alone, and not even the innovators and others involved in the mechanism for reviving the language, who were spotlighted by history, but simply the mother, she who speaks to her children, who was more influential than any other linguistic factor in this central historical process.

Similarly, the works of Shilo, Bernstein, and Izraeli changed the prevailing historical image of women during the periods of the Second and Third Aliyah.[7] Even if they bound themselves to historical validity, they knew how to present the ongoing longitudinal processes of the attitude to women and their being distanced from the foci of power and influence as powerful explanations for the status of the woman in modern Jewish settlements. Women's struggle to attain positions of influence, to achieve true rather than rhetorical equality, and scholars unbiased illumination of the inequality as opposed to the idealization of "those [wonderful] girls" in historical memory, contributed greatly to becoming familiar with historical reality. This contribution created a more fitting balance between image and reality, between historical discussion and generalization; it drew scholarly attention to the need for a re-examination of conventional truths. Yet, and mainly because of the precedent-setting status of these studies, they made no attempt to present the new settlement narrative differently. That is, if, indeed, the women of the Second and Third Aliyah did not enjoy the equality and cooperation they deserved based upon their class affiliation and their political awareness, how did this affect the settlement process? Did this lead to maneuvering their comrades and spouses in new directions — for example, to the creation of a change in the general aspiration from hired labor to independent settlers?

The breaking into the gender space of the periods of the Second and Third Aliyah that resulted from these studies has been characterized thus far by the expansion of knowledge, in recompense, in supplementation, and in amplifying the exclusion. R. Aaronsohn and Y. Ben-Artzi exploited the breach that was created for a fresh presentation of women's place in putting settlement on a firm footing in the moshavot and for contrasting of woman's images and standing in the moshavah, both the one in memory and in the historical image as well as that of the women in the Second Aliyah and in the cooperative settlements.[8] Their articles are rich in new details, in a fresh illumination of "the missing half" in the scraps of information, and in the attempt to present women's great contribution to the survival of the moshavot under the conditions of those times. Yet, even these works by settlement researchers with a settlement-geographic point of view do not create a new narrative of the history of the moshavot, as these two scholars actually have done in other contexts for this settlement type. A similar place is held by M. Shilo's study about women in the First Aliyah.[9] Shilo attempts in her article to present as a historical dilemma the question of the role of the woman as a full partner ("member") or as a "laborer" in the settlement process, but like her predecessors, she turns out to be a contributor to the learning of many new facts about the place of the woman in "the revival project," in her words, but this revival project receives no different or new historiographical illumination even in this pioneering study. A bit different is the outstanding work by Y. Berlovitz that delves deeper into understanding the place of women in creating the national-Hebrew identity in Eretz Israel during the First Aliyah.[10] Viewed from the discipline of literary (and in effect, cultural) research, Berlovitz demonstrated effectively not only the contribution of women measured in the sense of this or that act, but also specifically: in creating a cultural infrastructure for the invention of the nation. She, thereby, takes a step and a half beyond compensation and explication of participation, but she also calls for another understanding of a rather ignored aspect in the history of settlement — the aspect of written artistic culture and creativity.

In this regard, R. Elboim-Dror provides a material foundation in a tangential field — education and its history.[11] This foundation is not used for a new reading of settlement activity and leaves the schools, teacher training, and curricula as an almost separate text from the broad context of settlement and its characteristics.

An economic methodological view for the aspect of equal employment opportunity is used by Katz and Neuman, but their contribution, too, is at the level of factual analysis of the long-time conventional premise that equality was a ritual never put into effect.[12] In a certain way, they also take a small step forward toward a new explanation of the settlement trends in the 1930s in light of the conclusions that women drew from the inequality they faced, namely, the creation of independent female workers' farms.

So we find that the 1990s were replete with studies and works from a feminine or gender viewpoint that were definitely refreshing and innovative — mainly in the basic meanings of the paradigm: addition to knowledge and information, a different interpretation of an existing text, balance and compensation, illumination of the participation and amplification of the exclusion of women. All of them combine into a new picture of the gender situation in research into *aliyah* and settlement, but all of them together did not coalesce to create a new or different book of settlement history in general, or its main issues in particular.

Suggestions for a Re-Examination

Immigration (Aliyah) *and the Motivation for It*

The motives for the First and Second Aliyah to Eretz Israel have been examined to date mainly from the ideological, economic, and political points of view, and there is no reason to repeat them here. Anita Shapira already has indicated the possibility inherent in the gender aspect of the motive for national revival, by comparing the situation of the nation to that of the woman.

The humiliation of the Jewish people through persecutions and pogroms and the presentation of its physical helplessness were like the disgrace of the woman sullied in those events.[13] Despite the validity of this argument, it does not contribute to the possibility for understanding immigration from a gender-social viewpoint. The aspiration for *aliyah* cannot be explained by unisex Zionist ideology, as if women were dragged against their will to the Zionist idea by their spouses infused with the spirit of national revival.

Until now, the place of the Jewish woman's aspiration in the two Aliyot is missing in most of the studies of immigration and the formation of the Hovevei Zion associations and other Zionist organizations. Should this aspiration be investigated, it may turn out to have two facets: Zionism for its own sake, as with the men, derived as a rational conclusion about the validity of the Zionist idea as a unique escape hatch from the travails of the Jewish people, or — and herein will lie the main innovation — the desire and hope to change her own status. The striving for extrication from her basically inferior status in Jewish society, even in the more modern and certainly in the traditional, is a motivating force that has yet to be examined thoroughly toward understanding the participation of women in the immigration processes in general and in that of Zionism in particular.

The desire to become free of society's ills, of difficulties of subsistence, of the danger of persecutions and pogroms, and the hope to find a new life and better chances in new worlds is common to all the male and female Jewish immigrants to Western Europe and the New World. In that, they are no different than other peoples who emigrated by the thousands to the same destinations. But the latent promise in the Zionist "new world" was also bound with a new social world in which women would find a more fitting, more equal, and free place for effecting her personality and independence. It was this promise, more than anything else, that perhaps captivated the Zionist woman. There, in the new Jewish society, in the land of the forefathers, where the "new Jew" would come into being "ex nihilo," the new "Jewish woman" would be created too. These motives apparently were stronger among families that had begun to go through processes of modernization, (relative) secularization, and education, since in that case the women were more strongly exposed to the shame of their status in Jewish society with its traditional approach. Research into the motives for emigration, *aliyah* to Eretz Israel must, therefore, find new input from this attitudinal perspective. If that does happen, we will be able to construct not only a balanced picture of women's participation in this pivotal historical process, but perhaps also a new understanding of it; and this, of course, is in addition to the accepted historical insights, since it will not be a single, exclusive explanation for this entire phenomenon that will be under discussion.

Settlement and Aspects of It

Studies of the First Aliyah and settlement within its framework have focused mainly on the activities of the organizations, companies, and institutions involved in land acquisition as well as on planning and implementation of settlement. Thus Hovevei Zion, Bilu, Baron Edmond de Rothschild, the Jewish Colonization Association, and many moshavot were the focus of the examination of settlement processes. Only recently have treatments begun to appear of additional aspects, at whose focal point are people as individuals who were the "makers and shakers" of the processes. Land acquisition in Eretz Israel, one of the most widely studied processes in the history of the settlement, in most cases, has been studied from the institutional aspect and with regard to practical measures: locating available land, carrying out the purchase, payments, quantities, contracts, and so on. Also put on center stage by the shift to scrutinization through the personal prism were people like Hankin and Ruppin. M. Smilansky had already specifically pointed out Olga Hankin as the motivating force behind her husband Yehoshua; this was expanded upon in the romantic sense — but based on proven historical evidence — by Kark and Amit.[14] May we now consider Olga the key woman in the large land acquisitions in Rehovot, Hadera, and later the Jezreel Valley and elsewhere? And if so, what was happening in other places, in other organizations? And why should Olga want to try to support her husband — was it because of her Zionism, or as part of her deep understanding of the importance of land ownership as a solid foundation for the hoped-for change in society (and then also in the status of women)? In a similar fashion, close examination of the struggle for survival (mainly) by the early moshavot may reveal new information about women's roles.

Aaronsohn and Ben-Artzi have pointed out women's role in the First Aliyah's version of *tzumud* and we will not repeat here the many examples and details they cited in their articles.[15] But they, too, asked — Why? What connection was there between these women, who came from towns and cities that already had absorbed a bit of the niceties of modern life in Europe, and the sand dunes of Rishon le-Zion, the rocky ground of Zamarin, and the Huleh swamps? What led the Aaronsohns' mother to determine, "even if we eat rocks — we are staying here." Even if she is not the one who made this statement, why is this type of saying attributed specifically to a woman? What stops the mother of the Gluzgial family in Hadera when her husband and infant die? Was it really only the spirit of Pinsker and Ahad Ha-Am pulsating in them? Or, perhaps, the explanation is linked to the same factor cited previously: Only here, in the new society, as part of the rebirth of the nation, society, and culture, may women attain what they longed for: independence, equal status, self-realization. Is there a better explanation for their clinging to the idea, their determination, and their superhuman strength to remain?

From a different angle, the place of the women in settlement planning has physical and economic considerations. Here, too, detailed, innovative studies have increased of late, but they lack examination of the gender aspect. Regarding planning of the moshavot, for instance, the role of women is not used as an explanation for the design of the family farming unit and the suitability of its design to women's needs.[16] An allusion to the possibility for gender observation of this aspect is found in Joseph Klausner, who explains the uniqueness of the moshavah Sejera. There, as we know, the *hakura*, a plot of land next to the home, was in the front yard of the farming unit and not behind it, as was customary. When Klausner visited there in 1914, he noticed this distinctive feature of Sejera and explained it as follows:

> If Sejera is not the most beautiful of the moshavot, it is the most original in its appearance.
>
> A very wide street, unparalleled in its breadth, on the mountain slope. On both sides of the street — very tall, dense trees. Behind the trees — large gardens with all kinds of vegetables and behind the gardens were built the small, simple houses of the moshavah.
>
> So the vegetable gardens were not behind the houses, as usual, but in front of them. This was instituted by the agronomist who founded the moshavah, first, so that the unseen gardens would not be destroyed by Arabs, on the one hand, and the birds on the other. Secondly, so that the women farmers would always keep an eye on them, water them, and nurture them.
>
> . . . No [other] moshavah looks like a village to the extent Sejera does.[17]

Even though this superficial explanation is embedded in a typical, chauvinistic view, it is among the few that lead to a new direction, a gender one, in understanding the planning of the farm and the farmyard of the moshavah.

These three aspects of settlement activity: land, survival, and planning are only allusions to the possibility for a fresh examination of women's part in this activity, and not in the sense of "participation," but rather in that of the motivating, explanatory force.

Relations between the Sexes: Cooperation, Violence, Competition

Many have written about keeping women far away from the sources of power and the main activities of the First Aliyah. In the moshavot, women were not given the status they deserved for their contribution to survival and daily existence, and even independent women among them were not allowed to be elected to committees or key positions. In the organizations of the Second Aliyah, a rare few earned a central position, but precisely because of their tiny representation, one can see proof of the discrimination against the bulk of them: in field work and guard duty — the heart's desire of every male and female belonging to this Aliyah. In the following section, we will address the issue of the consequences and influence of this inequality and nonparticipation in the Second Aliyah, but here we would only like to add another as yet unstudied aspect: violence toward women as a concealed social facet. The only type of violence studied to date for these aliyot has focused on provocations such as robbery and murder against Jewish settlements within the context of relations between neighbors or between nations. Violence as a social aspect has not been studied — or has been ignored within the framework of the various types of historiography. The image of the inhabitants in the settlements of the First and Second Aliyah appears, therefore, as idealistic, free of all social ills. An exception is the issue of the attitude toward immigrants from Yemen — as has been addressed by Nitza Druyan and Yehuda Nini.[18] But violence in moshavah society was not at all an unusual phenomenon; below we offer two examples of its gender aspect.

There is no instance of a historical source mentioning rape or sexual violence against women. "Smirking" hints were heard about Eliyahu Scheid and others among the Baron's clerks who had an eye for the girls in the moshavot. The trouble is that as early as the first weeks of the existence of Rehovot, always cited as the model example of an independent, free, pure Hovevei Zion moshavah, one of the founders raped a colleague's wife. The rape was mentioned in the records of the moshavah and had other repercussions, but even now the incident stands uninvestigated, neither in its own right nor as part of a broader context of violence against women.[19]

Murder and internal violence were not investigated thoroughly enough, if at all, meaning that the issue of women suffering from this type of violence never surfaces. An illustrative example is the application by a woman from among the founders of Yavne'el to the leaders of the settlement who she tried to convene after a meeting in Zikhron Ya'akov in 1903. In her letter, she reveals in full the terrible affair of her husband's murder by a co-resident of their hut in Yavne'el over a trifling. Her desperate cry is that something should be done not only in memory of her husband but especially to help her maintain herself in the moshavah and to not force her to leave it owing to the lack of means to provide a livelihood.[20] This incident, too, attests not only to the uninvestigated facet of internal violence in the moshavot but also to women's aspiration to remain attached to the moshavah and the new way of life they had chosen, even those who had become widowed.

The issue of widowhood has been discussed by Ben-Artzi, but only in the sense of exposure and not in the context of the question: why did they remain?[21] Why did they cling so firmly to the settlements in which they lived? The answer, perhaps, leads us back to the new interpretation of settlement seen in the mirror of gender, bound up with the issue of the women's motivation and influence on the formation of the movement for immigration and settlement in Eretz Israel.

Competition over women, a subject not without use in understanding historical processes, was passed over in most studies of the period. Can one understand, for example, the entire chapter of the relations among the moshavot members and the hired laborers solely against the ideological background as historiography presents it? Were all the farmers opposed to Jewish labor, to the socialist ideas and secularity of the new workers, or perhaps fears and anxieties fanned the flames and exacerbated the inherent distinctions between the Aliyot? Might it not be the fear of their daughters becoming captivated by the itinerant "ragamuffins" or perhaps of their sons becoming ensnared by the "new women" who lacked any obligation to existing traditions and frameworks that led to the creation of clear antagonism? This antagonism is presented by historians as strictly ideological — but might it not be that such an aspect was not at all a motive behind or the focal point for this issue? Might it not be that the competition over the hearts of the moshavot girls is what stood behind the confrontation and rivalry between "Hashomer" and the "Gideonim"?

The Second Aliyah and Its Settlement Process

Two basic issues in the history of the Second Aliyah have not as yet been investigated from the gender aspect: the shift to permanent settlement ("conquest of the soil") and the model of the "mixed farm" that took shape in this settlement period (although actually only after World War I).

The shift to settlement by the members of the Second Aliyah became an essential milestone in its history and in the history of settlement in general.

Four types of settlements developed because of this shift: *moshav ha-po'alim* (laborers settlement; and from the lesson learned from it, the consolidation of the concept of the *moshav ovedim*, workers settlement), the *kevutzah* (commune of pioneers in a small agricultural settlement), the *ko'operatziyyah*, and the different types of farms. The passage to permanent settlement was actually revolutionary for the classical workers' ideas: conquest of labor, conquest of security, creation of a workers' class according to the socialist model they steadfastly adhered to. Researchers of the Second Aliyah have provided many and varied reasons for the permanent settlement of Israel by the laborers in its various forms:[22] Vitkin's call "for conquest of the soil" found a willing audience among the laborers of Petah Tikvah; the enhanced status of permanent laborers who began to earn well and to set aside savings; the aspiration for independence and self-administration; constant competition to sway the employers; the historical connection between the laborers, on one side, and Ruppin and the leaders of the Zionist Organization on the other; the Jewish National Fund rules for land management that called for leasing only, indicating that they were appropriate for people without capital—all of these plus other reasons not listed here were certainly factors accelerating the shift from "conquest of labor" to "conquest of the soil." Two aspects, however, are missing from this historical observation: the woman and the family. The women of the Second Aliyah have been the object of research in more than a few instances, and in every case—as is seen in their memoirs—a rather clear picture emerges of feelings of discrimination, inequity, being held off, and of being kept away from realizing aspirations similar to those of their fellow male immigrants. These feelings apparently intensified, since externally their colleagues espoused cooperation, equality, and the provision of similar opportunities to both sexes. The common lack of confidence on the part of both the laborers and the farmers in the women's physical ability to cope with the various farming tasks understood from Sarah Malkhin's memoirs parallels the women's frustration at not having been accepted as equal members of the *kevutzah*, or at not having been assigned to guard duty.[23] Being shunted off to the kitchen in Kinneret or Deganyah was the same as remaining with the children in Tel Adashim or Mesha when the guards left for their patrols. Added to these affronts were salary discrimination and nonparticipation and nongranting of rights at meetings and gatherings; some of the results of all the foregoing ultimately found expression in the various types of women's organizations.[24]

   I suggest that the frustration, discrimination, and nonrealization of the aspirations and wishes of the women who belonged to the workers' movement are what led them to the conclusion that the only chance for attaining equality, participation, and full utilization of their responsibility would be through permanent settlements in which they would play a full and active role, both as partners and as spouses. If we adopt this as a research hypothesis, and we find contemporary evidence and proof or in sources from that time, we will reach a completely new conclusion that will explain the formation of the *kevutzah*, the moshav, and what derived from them. The passage to permanent settlement instead of the wandering and instability of a work group or as individual men and women was likely to solve their problems of livelihood but in particular to address the feelings of frustration, disappointment, and despair that washed over the women of the Second Aliyah as individuals, spouses, and unequal members of work groups. If we have accepted as fact the results of studies affirming these feelings, and we have turned them into a premise, the next stage is the research hypothesis formulated above. The women were the ones, apparently, who pressed their husbands to change over from paid laborers to permanent settlers. At first it was small, young families in Petah Tikvah who did this, turning themselves into a laborers' moshav, and once the trail was blazed, the system was adapted both for people who favored the idea of the family as "a production unit" and for those espousing economic "collectivity." For both groups, the common denominator was the participation of women, and this time in a different way: as spouses or individual women — but full partners as *haverot* (members) in the *kevutzah* or the cooperative or as possessors of farming units in the laborers' moshav, and afterwards in *moshavei ovedim*.

In both settlement types, women could do away with their previous dependence, their physical inferiority, and their exclusion from participation in activities and prevention from realizing their aspirations, and they could release their pent-up frustration. We must look for and clarify what measures they took, how they applied their influence on their spouses or their colleagues and the laborers' groups; we must examine the validity of the hypothesis proffered here. Should it be found valid, we will be able to write a different history of the shift to settlement during the Second Aliyah. The circumstances of that move as currently known will turn into an ideological shell surrounding a hard gender kernel that is the major explanatory motif. Of course, even then other circumstances contributing to the about-face of the Second Aliyah members remain valid, such as the policy of the Palestine Office, Ruppin's personality and his being enraptured by the workers' spirit, the accumulation of Jewish national land that somehow had to be worked and maintained, but all of these only complement the true motive: the women's desire to change their situation fundamentally. The place of the woman and the family as a principal factor in the Second Aliyah laborers' move to permanent settlement therefore must be re-examined, and an essential chapter in the history of the settlement must be illuminated in a gender light.

Similarly, and as a direct continuation, one must re-investigate the coming into being of the "mixed farm" in what is called "working" settlements, that is, consisting of Second and Third Aliyah laborers and not the type in the moshavot (where they also obviously "worked"). At the end of the Ottoman Period, the farm in the JCA settlements was just as varied and did not depend on growing a single crop as has been commonly thought.[25] In the German villages, too, the farm economy was essentially varied by a combination of orchards and dairy farming and all that involved.[26] The latter model is the one that influenced Yitzhak Wilkansky, who as the director of the *haksharah* at Ben-Shemen had studied closely the German farms at nearby Wilhelma and developed the idea of the "mixed farm" on the basis of them. He expressed his ideas as early as 1913 when he formulated the regulations for the *moshav ovedim* as it developed a few years later.[27] At the center of the "mixed farm" as it took shape, mainly during the 1920s in the *moshav ovedim* — and to a different extent than in the kibbutz — stood dairy farming, and around it field crops related to it. The dairy farm was, indeed, intended to create a stable, long-term economic base, but it was selected as particularly *fitting* for a family farm, that is, a farm in which the wife works as a full partner. Allusions as to the place of the woman in the family farm were voiced by Ruppin in 1913, and quite a few researchers have quoted him for different purposes in their studies.[28] According to Ruppin, a German farmer at Sarona claimed that the Jews would never truly become farmers and live a full village life as long as their wives did not get up for the early milking. Milking, therefore, became a kind of touchstone for the participation of the woman in the burden of farm work. Hence the dairy would be the linchpin on which the farm would revolve if they wanted to effectuate the idea of the new Jew: the worker of the land who lives by the sweat of his — or her — own brow. From here to placing the dairy as the focus of the desired farm model was but a short distance.[29] So it was that Ruppin became an enthusiastic supporter of the "mixed farm" as formulated by Wilkansky, and as time went on, both of them were responsible for putting it at the center of settlement activity in the first *moshavei ovedim*. The participation of women becomes, according to this proposal, not only an important motive for the shift to permanent settlement, but also for understanding the farm adapted to this settlement style.

But How to Carry Out the Research?

The main difficulty facing a person trying to investigate issues in a gender light is methodological, namely, which texts and documents can be located and used for the purpose of proving research hypotheses such as those previously mentioned. B. Melman correctly noted the internal contradiction faced by male and female scholars of gender in the history of Eretz Israel, who tend to invalidate from the outset "individual" or "personal" sources that are not within the purview of classical archival documents. Melman did use for her study "personal" material, such as diaries, letter, testimonies, and memoirs, allowing her to develop a new position regarding the crystallization of the Eretz Israel identity of "the native-born."[30]

To be sure, if we have recourse only to "positivist," classic historical materials, such as the notes from meetings of settlement bodies, reports, contemporary articles, and so on, we will not be able to go far in changing the concept of the role of gender as a motif explaining the history of settlement. At most, we would be able to reach the place where current research stands, that is, a "different" reading of existing text and the inclusion of the woman as a participant in the historical narrative in the sense of "compensation" for her absence from the historiography of the settlement process.

The other way to use existing materials and to read them differently is the use of new materials (and, of course, it is necessary to discover them), such as personal letters, memoirs, diaries, and "dry" material such as account books, analysis of living expenses, and so on. Only with these we will be able to find and expose the feelings of the people who took part in the historical processes, their thoughts, and especially the methods they adopted to influence change in the direction wanted.

In the official reports, no conversations between a woman and her spouse have been found, and we have no way of knowing what methods she used to make clear to him the desperately vital need to change direction, for example. Between the lines of late testimonies and of memoirs, we can read the women's cries, but how the changes actually occurred and how, for example, they switched from life in a itinerant work group to a family in one or another settlement, we can only learn from "personal" material. These items have long been known in archives as "private collections," but most of them are still packed in dilapidated suitcases standing in the dark corners of cellars or stuck up in an attic somewhere. Uncovering this material, analyzing it, and generalizing from it must become an accepted research method, particularly in gender studies.

Beyond that, one must read between the lines in better-known material. A proper combination of the two methods, and particularly enhancing the importance of the "personal" material as reflecting public and general concern, are likely to support research hypotheses of the type proposed in this article.

Conclusion

The aim of this article was to see to what extent the study of women and gender has changed our understanding of the processes and central phenomena in the history of Jewish settlement in Eretz Israel, especially during the periods of the First and Second Aliyah. Currently, we see that gender has changed practically nothing in the understanding of the phenomena and processes but has been able to add much information to it, in the sense of "compensation" and "completion" of accepted history by illuminating the role and contribution of women to sustaining settlement and to the development of the Eretz Israel social structure and cultural texture.

We feel that a real change in the understanding of certain phenomena in the history of settlement can occur if we establish gender as a leading research paradigm, and if we pose new questions, or offer new, alternative hypotheses on the formation of phenomena, such as the motives for emigration and *aliyah* to Eretz Israel, settlement methods (in terms of land acquisition, survivability, and planning), internal relations (violence, rape, competition over women), essential changes in the type of settlement, such as the passage of laborers of the Second Aliyah to permanent settlement, and crystallization of settlement development.

In this article, we have suggested these hypotheses as attainable goals for new research, based on the premise (supported by previous studies) that the inferiority of women in these periods, their frustration, and their despair were their internal goads prompting them to seek changes and to find new ways though which they would be able to realize their aspirations. Equipped with these ways, such as the shift from a struggle for the "conquest of work" to "the conquest of the soil," the women pushed for the historical change that usually is explained in historiography by idealistic, historicist circumstances. This view, which sees the "feminine condition" as the true catalyst for historic changes, is that which will lead — if, indeed, it is proven as correct — to a change in the *understanding* of the history of settlement and to a different way of writing about it. Compensation and filling in the blanks, as has been done until now, will not suffice.

✾ Henriette Dahan-Kalev

Mizrahi Women
Identity and Herstory

Introduction

The wordplay in English involving "history" and "herstory" illustrates the claim that history was written by men about men, and that the role of women is missing. The feminist revolution has penetrated into the ivory towers and begun to trickle into fields of research and to illuminate the absence and marginality of women in history. Gender research in political thought revealed the apparatuses for the separation and exclusion of women. This claim has been investigated by female researchers in various disciplines. Susan Okin found that the inclusive term "man" is not so abstract when it comes to the gender division of labor and to its organization according to spheres.[1] In statements about responsibility and the value of the spheres—the private and the public—thinkers such as Aristotle, Hobbes, Rousseau, and Hegel perceive women in instrumental terms in the private sphere, which is considered secondary to the public. When speaking about political concepts such as freedom, control, or justice, they apply them to the concept "man" that is held as an abstract, as it were, and by allusion the discussion applies also to women and includes them, too. In a discussion about the responsibility for the continuation of the human genus, on responsibility for the home and family and childrearing, these philosophers make a clear distinction and point out that this is the role of women. Okin summarizes her analysis with the conclusion that the Western thinkers' approach can be summed up by the gender distinction according to which they perceive women in a instrumental manner and ask "What is a woman *for?*" while their perception of men is one of essence, that is, "What is a man *like?*"[2] Feminist historical research according to this line of argument from now on must concentrate on the history of women in order to close many gaps.

A large question looms up in this regard on how to investigate this field. If the public sphere and the rules of the game within it were determined by men, and if the private sphere has been perceived as so inferior to the point of its not being mentioned, what then are the sources from which one can learn about it? Feminist scholars have demonstrated the importance of multiple points of view in philosophical and historical research, including the problematics of the concept "objectiveness."[3] Following Foucault, they pointed out the need to dismantle the connection between Knowledge with a capital "K" and power during the process of the creation of knowledge — a dismantling that leads to there being no single ultimate, objective, true knowledge, but rather multiple viewpoints. This calls for expanding the gamut of knowledge so that place will be given to every point of view.[4] This line of thought befits other weak groups, too, which until recently also had been excluded and marginalized. The influence of the colonialist government, for example, constituted a broad base for the study of the politics of identities.[5] The combination of political processes with aims of creating knowledge from multiple different viewpoints undermines the patriarchal monopoly on knowledge inherently challenging knowledge. It carries tensions and dangers deriving from the threat directed towards those who hold hegemony over current knowledge. Moreover, it necessitates the development of new methodologies to reach sources of knowledge that are not attested through the traditionally accepted documentation.

In the Western world, one already may find historical studies that construct "herstory," that is, including the role of women in the stories of the national ethos. Their methodological importance is that beyond the expansion of knowledge as to women's role in the national story of building the nation, they point out the difficulty in illuminating women's story when they are not included in the officially documented ethos in the national pantheon. The situation is even more problematic and complicated when dealing with socially and culturally heterogeneous societies. In cases such as these, where there is an attempt at documenting the role of women in a national, historical endeavor, they are perceived as a homogeneous mass in terms of gender, which hides and represses their links to various groups that are at time in conflict.

This is the situation in relation to Israel and the history of women in Israel. "Herstory," when speaking of Israel, is a story that takes place in a society composed of groups divided by ethnic, national, economic, and religious schisms. The question that must be asked is whether it is possible to learn about the women in Israel even when dealing with a segment of one of society's groups.

In this article, I delineate the research framework needed for the purpose of the story of one of the significant but excluded groups in Israeli society — Jewish women from Arab and Muslim countries of origin. Women who belong to this ethnic group often are referred at as Mizrahim (in Hebrew the meaning is Orientals and literally Easterners). Since this group has not been studied from a political perspective and existing knowledge about it is limited to anthropological-folkloric research, all other issues — their identity as Mizrahi persons, their knowledge, their political point of view, and many others — are virgin territory. In the Israeli context, these questions take on a concrete aspect that touches upon their contribution to the national enterprise, their representation in the public arena, their location on the economic scale, and other facets. My objective, therefore, is to indicate the little that has been done as I sketch a framework in which research into Mizrahi women in Israel will develop. At the focal point of the description will stand the identity of the Mizrahi women, the nature of the connection between the experiences that establish this identity and their history and socio-political status in Israel. Owing to their absence in the historical narrative of Israeli society and their absence in herstory, this paper constitutes a proposal for research and for a political agenda whose focus is on Mizrahi women.

The vacuum that exists regarding the formation of Mizrahi women's identity is particularly prominent when viewed against the development of the process of the empowerment of women in Israel. Those who considered themselves as representatives of all Israeli women actually acted on behalf of a partial and specific agenda. Yet, that agenda does not cover all groups of Israeli women, which include ultra-Orthodox women, women with right-wing views, Ethiopians, Russians, and so on.[6] In the historical narrative of Israeli society, their chapter is absent — they simply do not exist. In 1999, following the feminist annual conference traditionally celebrated in Givat Haviva, a first initiative was taken and the organization Ahoti, For Mizrahi Women was founded by Netta Amar and myself. In the case of the Mizrahi women, such an organization was missing twice, once as women in the way that the story of the entire body of women in Israel is lacking from the patriarchal and historical canon and once as Mizrahi women, similar to the story of Mizrahi Jews in Israel. Also lacking is the story of the community of immigrants from Asia and Africa.[7] In the first study, made twenty years ago, on the topic of women who had come from Arab and Muslim countries dur-

ing the mass immigration of the 1950s, I found that Mizrahi women constitute the "invisible" quarter of the Jewish population of Israel. Even when
concentrating on Jews who came from Arab and Muslim countries, the
Mizrahi women are swallowed up and invisible.

The debate taking place in Israel on the issue of the ethnic rift and the
fact that statistically defining Mizrahim and locating this social category is
becoming increasingly problematic (in light of intermarriage, a policy of denial, and a tendency toward repression on the part of many Mizrahim as
well). The creation of a political and research space in which Mizrahi women
will be discussed as a category becomes difficult, if not even prevented. In
this framework, I will concentrate on delineating the difficulty in the absence of Mizrahi women from the historical narrative. In the course of my
analysis, I shall illustrate directions for research and indicate the recommendations called for in the study of the processes of the construction of the
identity of Mizrahi women.

The State of Research and the Feminist Alternative

When I began to deal with the study of the history of Mizrahi women in the
mass immigration, I found that for three generations Mizrahi women have
constituted a decided majority at the bottom of the Israeli social scale, alongside Palestinian women. I also learned that no works have been devoted to
the history of Mizrahi women in Israel.[8] The little that has been done includes studies that have dealt with dance among the women from Kurdistan,
the singing of Yemenite women, embroidery and weaving in the Tunisian
villages, and women's sayings from North Africa (Harvey Goldberg, Alex
Marx, Esther Sheli Newman, Tsvia Tobi, Galit Hasan-Rokem, Dov Noy,
S. Deshen, A. Weingrod, Ben Refael, Susan Sered, Rachel Wasserfal, Tamar
Alexander). In light of this difficulty, I started from scratch, eking out from
primary data a profile of Mizrahi women in Israel using sources that referred
to Mizrahim in general. Around that time, the first articles appeared on
Mizrahi women: Ella Shohat, as part of her analysis of Israeli cinema, treated
the image of Mizrahi women, and Vicki Shiran, as well as Debby Bernstein,
wrote about Mizrahi women in relation to Ashkenazi women in the division
of labor in Israel by class.[9] In addition, in November 1990 an article appeared
in the journal *Megamot* that looked at "trends of discrimination in the
salaries of Mizrahi women and members of Mizrahi ethnic groups in the
universities, R & D labs, and hospitals in the period 1972 to 1983."[10] Recently,

research has been carried out in the field of the history of groups of women in Arab countries, such as that by Esther Meir-Glitzenstein on Iraqi women in Youth Aliyah (1997).[11] The approach in the great majority of these articles is blind to the issue of the initial location of women in the patriarchal order that places them low on the political and social scale. That is, the theoretical approaches upon which the analysis of Mizrahi women is based do not apply feminist methodology or conceptualization. They continue the lines of argument commonly found in approaches based on the patriarchal point of view. Treatment of the differentiation between the patriarchal viewpoint and the feminist one is discussed in feminist philosophical literature by scholars such as Sandra Harding, Donna Haraway, Lynn Hankinson Nelson, and others.[12] This trend extracts its patriarchal bases from pretension to scientific objectivity, shows that it is steeped in values, and proposes alternative approaches to increasing feminist viewpoints whose main thrust is in the adoption of different levels of scientific reflexiveness.

I hone and dwell upon concepts, instruments, and theoretical approaches that respond to research expectations from a feminist viewpoint in order to construct a theoretical category identifying the "Mizrahi women in Israel," historically and politically.

A connection exists between the processes of constructing the Mizrahi women's identity and their nullification. We have here a process according to which Mizrahi women are a population segment constituting about one-quarter of the Jewish population of Israel, but who are not recognized as a sociological and political category.

The question of identity in general is a main topic in the development of feminist research. It deals with the sense of self and with experiences establishing this sense of self. In this context, Mizrahi women are a social category of women whose identity draws from Arab-Jewish cultural sources, from the experiences of the encounter between them and the Western world, and also from the experiences that turn them into Mizrahi women in distinction from other Israeli women who lack this experiential world. Mizrahi women, in effect, exist only in Israel. Jewish women who live in Yemen are not Mizrahim, and the same is true for Jewish Iraqi or Moroccan women who lived in those countries. One can only be a Mizrahi woman in Israel. Yet, there are no works on the different life experiences of the Mizrahi women whose world is anchored in the heart of the Israeli experience.

In this situation, to start at the beginning means classifying the many channels that nurtured the process of identity construction for women from Arab and Muslim countries, even sources that reflect the canonical Israeli historical viewpoint. Channels from which one may extract such materials might be (1) the Arab experience that Mizrahi women have by virtue of having lived in the Muslim and/or Arab country of origin; (2) the immigration experience and having gone through the absorption process from an Arab country into Israel — Western-colonialist in its attitude to Mizrahim; (3) the experience of the transfer to a Western country; and (4) the experience of shifting from a Jewish way of life as lived in the country of origin to, the influences of Judaism as they took shape in Israel. These four areas are divided by two main axes in the establishment of the construction of identity as women and as Mizrahi women in Israel: the patriarchal axis and the Zionist axis. In this sense, Mizrahi women share partial commonality with the other categories of women in Israel. Additional topics of interest involve the differences between the generation of the mothers and that of the daughters who came as children to Israel or were born there.

In the direction of the patriarchal axis, there is special interest in the study of Mizrahi women, since this constitutes a two-faceted area of the experience of oppression, both in the country of origin (the Muslim Arab one) and continued within the family life of the Mizrahi women in Israel; and as it was experienced in a Western version in Israel, mainly when Mizrahi women ventured into the public sphere and took part in it.

My research on this topic focuses on the socio-economic background, presenting through statistics and data a profile of women from Arab, Muslim, and Far Eastern countries, members of the first and second generation who immigrated to Israel in the 1950s — in the mass immigration; and on the images and identities of the Mizrahi women as seen in Israeli culture, through such sources as children's books, literature, cinema, and theater. An analysis of these topics led to a few conclusions, the two principal ones being: first, until the end of the 1980s, Mizrahi women were one-quarter of the Jewish population in Israel; second, they were located at the bottom of the socio-economic scale, far below the non-Mizrahi women. Their position derived from their being part of a public perceived as inferior and lacking the means to grapple with the challenges the Western world presented them. The ramification of these two conclusions was that this is indeed a social category whose characteristics distinguishes them from the other women in Israel.

The denial and opposition to recognizing the existence of this category derives from a broader denial rooted in Western culture. But in the more limited context of Israeli society, this denial appears in full force when viewed against the background of the election of a female Arab Knesset member that enabled the preening of the left-wing Meretz Party, claiming that it was not only the most liberal party but also the most egalitarian in representing women.[13] The election of Ms. Husnia Jebara, the first Israeli Arab woman, to the Knesset highlighted the problem of the non-being of Mizrahi women even more, since the identity of Arab women is set in the sense of nationality, and it is even easier to indicate its limits owing to the boundaries between the two civilizations, the Arab and the European. Yet, Mizrahi women are torn between the two and are not fully recognized as having a distinct, separate identity because their world draws culturally on both. These cultures and this merger are not recognized politically, and the result is Mizrahi women's nullification. This topic was never investigated and it provides room for a wide range of studies.

In addition, the cultural differences between Western patriarchy and Judeo-Arabic patriarchy provide a wider external circle for looking into the development of women's identities in countries like Israel in which both the Mizrahi and Western experiences have a role in the construction of women's identities. The cultural differences abound, but one of the most prominent is the patriarchal rhetoric in Israel, which as a liberal Western country spouts promises of equality, while almost all of its citizens come from a background lacking in democratic experience, whether Western or Arab. In Arab and Jewish rhetoric, there are no declared promises of equality—neither from the perspective of ultra-Orthodox Judaism nor that of the Arab patriarchal tradition. Against this background, the Mizrahi women, who underwent the process of change and shift from one civilization to another, at times renounced their old world because of the promise of equality inherent in the switching to a Western lifestyle. But the promises proved false, and the women discovered that they had simply exchanged Mizrahi patriarchal relations for Western patriarchal relations. This topic deserves separate research because of its uniqueness in adding a Western patriarchal layer to the one they were familiar with in their Arab-Muslim countries of origin and in their homes as Jews. What does such an experience do to Mizrahi women? This is a question that has not yet been fully explored in research.

The complicated connections, which play a significant role in the establishment of Mizrahi women's identity and in fashioning their story as a group in Israel, have not been examined. Yet, Mizrahi women's texts exist, of which few have been published, and the rest, as part of their non-being, find it difficult to reach the public. Dorit Rabinyan's writing turns this nothingness into reality, since she is the best known. Yet, Mizrahi women's poetry and literature preceding Rabinyan, which made the actual breakthrough, such as by Bracha Seri, Atalyia, Tikva Levy, and others, expresses the melding of the experience of being a women and a Mizrahi in Israel.[14] Few of these works give expression to the influence of the Zionist ethos' on Mizrahi women in Israel. It is presented as replete with experiences of oppression and is connected to the "melting-pot" policy.

As a threat to the Western Zionist ethos, Mizrahi culture (but not the folklore!) was suppressed through aggressive Zionism. This was seen in religious coercion, and other means. In all of these, there is no study focusing on Mizrahi woman.

Engendering the Study of Identity of Mizrahi Women

The adoption of the gender approach is essential for explaining the process of the construction of women's identity. This is not a trivial claim in light of the frequency with which women's studies in the social sciences and history repeatedly use the approaches that continue to ignore their identity as women and their experiences.[15]

In the gender literature, Butler and Benhabib provided a gender interpretation to Hegel.[16] Their discussion of the concepts of woman's "self" and "identity" is anchored in the dialectic approach, that is, in the development of the construction processes of opposing forces culminating in the unification of the opposites. These scholars dealt with the issue of socio-political life experiences, in the dynamic process of social life, in the deconstruction and reconstruction of identity, and also in the moving between objective and subjective, and between particular and universal. The works by the scholars mentioned above discuss genderization of Hegel's definition of the concept identity. "Identity" is discussed in terms of a sense of self and of continuity. The sense is created through a dynamic process of personal and social life-experiences and interactions;[17] in the course of which symbols, models, and values are acquired consciously and unconsciously.[18]

This definition assumes that construction of identity is a dynamic process of constant change influenced by both forces under a person's control and those that are not, which are nurtured by sources extrinsic and intrinsic to the individual's personality. The assumptions behind this definition claim that it is impossible to consider identity an experience of an essentialist nature. Weir analyzes the approaches investigating identity and the tension between those who consider identity a constructive experience versus those who see it as an essentialist experience.[19] She also argues that the process of identity

construction entails a constant search for ways to resolve the internal contradictions and to maintain the individual's sense of self. The perpetual
processes of construction develop along dialectic lines.[20] These scholars'
perception of identity is that the dynamic nature of the process of identity
construction can be harmonious and calm or conflictual and crisis-laden.
Likewise, the process can be intense or moderate.

Applying this definition of identity, Mizrahi women's sense of self is based
on personal experiences acquired consciously and unconsciously, in Arab
and Muslim countries, and then in Israel. These experiences merge with the
gender experiences of being feminine, which changes from one culture to
the other.

Two basic elements in this definition give the Mizrahi women their distinctiveness as a social category: one involves disassembly and construction;
the other, the unique life experiences that distinguish them from other
women. This definition is compatible with Butler's perception of women's
identity as a process of the construction of life experiences.[21]

Another area of research in the study of Mizrahi women looks at the
way the process of identity construction links up with the exclusion of
women and their being pushed to the margins. A look at the particular
sources and content that supplied the processes of identity construction and
at the dialectic relation that prevailed between them provides a good starting point.

A frequently encountered argument is that Mizrahi women — similar to
everyone coming from Arab and Muslim countries — not being equipped
with Western knowledge, found it more difficult than their counterparts who
came from the West to fit into the absorption and fusion processes in the Israeli melting pot. This argument tacitly leaves the onus of responsibility
upon the Mizrahi women and ignores the aspects of an active policy on the
part of the founding fathers, the policy designers, and the women who held
public roles in the absorption of Mizrahi women whereby they shoved them
to the margins and excluded them from public institutions and sources of
power. Pushing them to the periphery was not accidental, it was necessary
for the dialectic process of constructing Israeli identity through its contrast
to the socioeconomic and cultural life experiences of whoever came from
non-Western countries: The Mizrahi women (as did the Mizrahi men) provided these life experiences. This assumption must be supported by historical study within the Israeli context after the establishment of the state. Inherent here is a great deal of material connected to the life experiences bound
up with an aggressive process of estrangement from and expunging of the

cultural heritage of Jewish men and women as shaped over the course of their history in Arab and Muslim countries. The problem is that this material is not to be found. It is simply inconceivable that the canonic research will provide a venue for taking upon itself the responsibility for the invisibility of the Mizrahi women.

Thus, the trends in research that deal with postmodernism, post-Zionism, and postcolonialism provide a methodological conceptualization and structure helpful in analyzing the gender, political, and cultural situation that led to the creation of the circumstances that flung the Mizrahi women to the margins.[22]

Beyond its cultural, political, and economic aspects, the problem is particularly embedded in the identity crisis in which Mizrahi Jews in Israel find themselves, a crisis that in the case of women requires a separate analysis that crosschecks the elements establishing the Mizrahi women's identity, from both the ethnic as well as the gender aspect. Another research facet focuses on how the Mizrahi women coped with the reality of the melting pot from which arose the experience of the effacement their identity, as they have reported it in personal interviews and writing.[23]

The Melting Pot Policy—Erasure of Different Shades and the Demand to Become Ashkenazim

Colonialism was a central element in the melting pot policy, and the absorption policy of the founding fathers drew, as is known, on that concept. The meaning of the melting pot in the case of immigrants from Arab and Muslim countries was the disassembly and reconstruction of identity. This policy even had a name explicitly demonstrating this: de-socialization and re-socialization. It was based on studies and observations by educators such as K. Frankenstein and K. Feuerstein and was planned by establishment sociologists such as S. Eisenstadt and R. Bar-Yosef.[24] The methods for implementing the melting pot concept included aggressive, compulsive policies such as the enforcement of birth control (L. Salzberger), religious coercion (or anti-religious practices like cutting the sidelocks of children at school reported in the investigation public committee—Frumkin), the transfer of children from one school to another with a dry notice to the parents about the backwardness of their children, and directing the children to occupational educational tracks or to frameworks intended for the developmentally disabled.[25] This kind of thinking, according to Said, attributed to the Orient inferiority and backwardness as part of the definition of the Other as a consequence of its defining itself.[26]

As part of this approach, the narrative of Mizrahi women's history is missing. It is sufficient to note that in textbooks, today as in the past, the story of the population that immigrated to Israel from Arab and Muslim countries is told in no more than eleven pages out of four-hundred.[27] And when it is mentioned, the texts stress racial stereotypes such as slowness and backwardness. In this sense, the canonic history books are not a reliable source for the genderization of the story of the Mizrahim in Israel.[28] If I have said that the definition of identity is an issue of a sense of self and continuity of the symbols, values, and patterns acquired through social and personal interactions, then what the Mizrahim were supposed to undergo to be absorbed was the dismantling and the cancellation of the sense of self, to alienate themselves from the values and symbols that had nurtured their identity — in effect, the negation of their concept of the self. The success of absorption was conditional upon a process of alienation from a sense of self, with its Mizrahi content.[29]

Thus, women who arrived from Kurdistan had not been exposed to the experience of being natives (in the eyes of the colonialists), but they did not escape it since they went through it in Israel as part of the melting pot whereas Moroccan women did not escape this fate either in the country of origin or in Israel. Their position as part of the generalized category of "Mizrahi women" effected this with regard to the Moroccan women in the process of their absorption. The degree of exposure to colonialism among those who came from the large cities and those who came from the Atlas Mountains villages was completely ignored.

To sum up, in the shadow of this absorption policy, the chances for immigrants from Arab and Muslim countries to be absorbed successfully remained slim as long as they had not divested themselves of components of identity perceived as inferior and primitive. This explanation by itself is enough to indicate their low placement on the social scale and limited capacity for social mobility. If we add to it the exposure of the patriarchal elements, the research potential for revealing in full force this diverse group of Mizrahi women in Israel *considered as non-being* emerges immediately.

The striving for social homogenization in the Eurocentric spirit suppressed the varied life experiences and the different cultural values and habits of Mizrahi women and in so doing, determined the distance from the hegemonic center as the measure for success in absorption. So women coming from a rather varied social background, distributed over a significant part of the Earth, from Yemen, Egypt, Libya, Tunisia, Iraq, Kurdistan, Iran, Algeria, Jerba, Syria, Lebanon, Turkey, Aleppo (Syria), Morocco, Cochin, and India, were perceived as a single mass. We see that the study of these processes constitutes a chapter in itself focusing on the Mizrahi gender-identity crises. The fruits of such research have the potential for social and political lessons for general society.

Even if the women's narrative is a kind of repetition of a similar story that took place among the men, or if this is a repetition of the story of what took place in the Arab countries, this is herstory and it should be told separately with its unknown chapters, because it is missing from the history books. There is an additional facet to this, too, and it is the fact that the Mizrahi women are also part of the women's population of Israel, for whom the same problem holds when speaking of the canonic Israeli historical narrative. It is worthwhile to stress here that the herstory of Israeli women does not guarantee the exposure of the Mizrahi women's story, and certainly not the story of the relations among them. The material available on this issue deals almost exclusively with observing children and folk crafts even if gently and sympathetically.[30] The results of collecting, sorting, documenting, and analyzing historical materials from the melting pot period, written by Mizrahi women, are now being published little by little.[31] In my study of women who came from Arab and Muslim countries during the mass immigration of the 1950s, I found that where Mizrahi women are mentioned — in official state documents such as reports of the courts; the welfare and employment offices; educational and occupational assessments — their image among the Israeli public (Mizrahi and non-Mizrahi) is one of women whose morals are doubtful and whose ability for economic and social mobility is low (some of these results, such as their limited capability for social mobility, were still valid at the end of the 1990s).[32]

From what little we do have, one may learn that the collection of life experiences of women who came from Arab and Muslim countries, from a way of life in an Arab/Muslim environment that was exposed to varying degrees of colonialism, whether in the country of origin or in Israel, reveals coping and detachment accompanying the life stories of these women. All of them indicate that they were thrown into a situation at the crossroads between the axis of Mizrahi identity and the axis of gender. All of them describe life experiences that turned into leg irons, making their mobility difficult and at times perpetuating their marginality. In any event, what they were required to do was make a decision over dilemmas concerning processes of the construction of their identity, mainly as Mizrahim and only after that as Mizrahi women.

Dilemmas and the Ways that Mizrahi Women Coped with Them

The responses by the female immigrants from Arab and Muslim countries to the demands of the melting pot were varied and derived from factors indicated above, such as exposure to Western culture, urban or rural environments, and cultural differences among the different Arab countries and their influence on the lives of the Jews in them. One may classify these factors according to three sources behind the dilemmas faced by the Mizrahi women: (1) dilemmas deriving from the link to Jewishness as understood within the framework of the Zionist ethos; (2) dilemmas deriving from Eurocentricism as experienced through colonialism; and (3) dilemmas created by the meeting between the Arab Muslim framework from which they came and the Israeli reality that they entered.

The Mizrahi women, by coming from a traditional Jewish world that took shape in a Muslim/Arab environment, were trapped between what they were and what they were expected to be. Clashes between cultural, traditional, ideological, and religious life experiences resulted in confusion and different combinations in which these immigrants were trapped when they had to cope with the dismantling and construction of their identity. Imagine, for instance, the influence of de-socialization and re-socialization processes on women exposed to Western culture in their country of origin, in cities such as Alexandria, Baghdad, or Casablanca, where an *aliyah* activist promised them a brave new world, who upon their arrival in Israel were sent to moshavim in the Adullam or Lachish regions, which at first were nothing more than arid spaces isolated from any other inhabited site; or their encounter with women who had not been exposed at all to the West or to the colonialist experience. And then compare that with what happened to those who were housed on the outskirts of the cities. How did that policy influence women from Yemen or Kurdistan who had never been exposed to Western culture? What happened to them when they were settled in faraway outlying regions or, alternatively, were housed in arid marginal areas planned as development towns? This material has never been investigated. Complexity and confusion became more severe when the women had to make a decision over dilemmas of Jewishness. They could choose the traditional interpretation of religion as they had known it and followed it in their Arab, or Muslim, country of origin, or choose the European interpretation that were exposed to in Israel. Within the European interpretation, they faced another decision: Zionist, or ultra-Orthodox, or even anti-religion as manifested in secular, socialist Zionism, instituted at first mainly in the Mapam and Ha-Shomer ha-Tza'ir kibbutzim. These alternatives presented to Mizrahi women were totally submerged in the various establishment policies: education, welfare, settlement, housing, and employment. Every decision yielded benefits and the allotment of resources but also exacted a cultural, social, ethical price. At times, choosing the melting pot was expressed by the dissolution of the family, feelings of guilt, cultural vapidity, alienation, and loss of a sense of continuity and self. In terms of dialectic analysis, deconstruction of identity is an issue of negation and alienation of the sense of self and continuity. Fanon, who investigated colonial influence on blacks, found that with the strong desire of the non-Europeans to be accepted and Westernized, they went through a process of self-negation that always remains an imitation and is never completely internalized. Toni Morrison described it as internalizing the slave, and seeing the self as inferior in light of colonialist values in contrast to the colonialist who is always originally white and European. Both Morrison as well as Fanon see in this process "whiteness," paralleled in our case by "Ashkenaziness," that is, wearing a white mask on dark skin.[33] Investigation of these processes is likely to shed clear light on the dimensions of the depth or superficiality of the Mizrahim's integration into Israeli society, the ways Israeli and Sabra patterns are adopted, and even on the differences between these patterns and those of the children of Jews who came from Europe and America.[34] Alternatively, the women's rejection of the option of fusion means choosing the option of "otherness." A fairly significant group among the Mizrahim could not even take advantage of these possibilities for dismantling and creating their identity, since its members' external appearance — dark skin — allowed them no way out. Women from Cochin and Yemen, from Iran and Kurdistan, found themselves in the situation that Fanon calls a white mask on black skin, that is, basic otherness that cannot be escaped even by processes of de- or re-socialization.

Considering all this, what turned the women from Arab and Muslim countries into *Mizrahi women* was a combination of four factors: being from Arab or Muslim countries; being Jewish — traditional, religious, or secular; the extent of their exposure to Western colonialism; and the extent of their exposure to Zionism. No matter what combination, all of these types were steeped in oppressive patriarchal patterns even if according to different codes of tradition and culture.

If we link the historical content with the definition of the Mizrahi women's identity and their life experiences in any combination, we will find that a not insignificant portion of the Mizrahi women of the first and second generations were ensnared in an identity crisis, even though between the generations this trap had diverse manifestations that outwardly differentiated between them. Two conclusions can be drawn from this: first, Mizrahi women are not defined as such because of their country of origin, but because they are doubly suppressed in comparison to Mizrahi men and in comparison to non-Mizrahi women. What turns this personal experience into a political experience, and therefore one located at the heart of gender discourse, are its consequences. For, from this point of view, the Mizrahi women become visible and defined as a group separate and distinct from the two social categories mentioned. Second, Mizrahi women were not a homogeneous part of ethnic groups or of the members of ethnic groups. In any event, the results of the crisis they faced weighed down these women like leg irons, weakening their ability to climb higher on the social scale, and this remains the situation with the third generation, too. Thus, the research agenda on the subject of Mizrahi women should center on two focal points: one, raising the category to such a level that it will be recognized as distinct and separate; the other, concentrating on the methods of identity construction, on its being established from cultural content and from passage from Arab to Western civilization, and on the crises and consequences involved in that passage. We must develop goals for the study of the different histories, such that neither the narrative of the women in Israel nor that of the Mizrahi Jews will be lost.

❧ Women and Immigration

✾ Michal Ben Ya'akov

Women's *Aliyah*

Migration Patterns of North African Jewish Women to Eretz Israel in the Nineteenth Century

The pioneering women of Palestine, those Jewish women who joined the Zionist *aliyot* (migration; literally, "ascent"), have been the focus of much current research on gender and Jewish settlement in late nineteenth- and early twentieth-century Eretz Israel.[1] However, these pioneers represented only a small proportion of all Jewish women in the country at the time.[2] Moreover, the exclusion of the traditional women from the historiography of the Jewish settlement in Eretz Israel in the nineteenth century is particularly glaring, considering the demographic imbalance in the population: nearly two-thirds of all adult Jews were women.

The Problem of Sources

Few written sources have been uncovered relating to women in the traditional societies of nineteenth-century Eretz Israel, and those we have are limited in scope. Immigrants from North Africa, both men and women, left almost no written records that shed light on the topic under discussion: there are no known diaries, few personal letters have survived, and communal records relate only indirectly to the process of migration itself.[3] In fact, it is questionable whether those existing documents shed light on the realities of the times, as internal communal "censorship" was strict, lest the Holy Land

I thank the Lafer Center for Women's and Gender Studies at the Hebrew University in Jerusalem for a research grant in 1997–1998 in support of much of the initial research for this article.

be defamed.[4] In addition, most existing documentation was written by men, and from their perspective.

Although few written descriptions remain to shed light on the migrations of North African women, a wealth of demographic information can be culled from contemporary censuses carried out in Jewish communities of nineteenth-century Eretz Israel. At the initiative of Sir Moses Montefiore, a Jewish philanthropist and public figure in nineteenth-century England, a modern census was carried out five times among the Jews of the Holy Land, in 1839, 1849, 1855, 1866, and 1875.[5] In most instances, the Jewish population was enumerated by household, with detailed information relating only to the male head of the household: his place of birth, age, year of arrival in the country, profession, and members of his household. Only the existence of married women is noted, and usually (but not always), their names. However, separate lists were prepared of the numerous widows in each of the communities, with columns for information as noted for the male heads of households (see figure 1). Although we cannot rely on an analysis of the demographic information for women listed as widows at the time of the census to reconstruct a comprehensive picture relating to all women, it does provide a relatively reliable picture, as many of these women immigrated as young girls or married women. More importantly, such an analysis opens new directions for research, reveals areas of Jewish life yet unexplored, and raises pertinent questions regarding traditional Jewish communities.

Together with gender theories culled from a variety of disciplines such as demography, economics, geography, sociology and history, the analysis of the censuses has created the framework from which additional documentation has been examined. A gendered reading of scattered evidence on North African *aliyah* to Eretz Israel found in travelers' journals and diplomatic papers presents numerous examples and graphic descriptions. Oral documentation collected from the descendents of those women immigrants to Eretz Israel (*olot*) has also been integrated into the research. The elderly female informants in particular opened a window into the lives of their mothers and grandmothers. They added "flesh and blood" to the skeletal existence recreated by the statistical analysis. These combined resources have permitted a serious examination of the demographic characteristics of *olot*, their motivations in migrating, and the effects of their *aliyah* on the communities of their destination. This article will limit the discussion to aspects of the migration itself; its implications for Jewish life in Palestine will be dealt with separately.

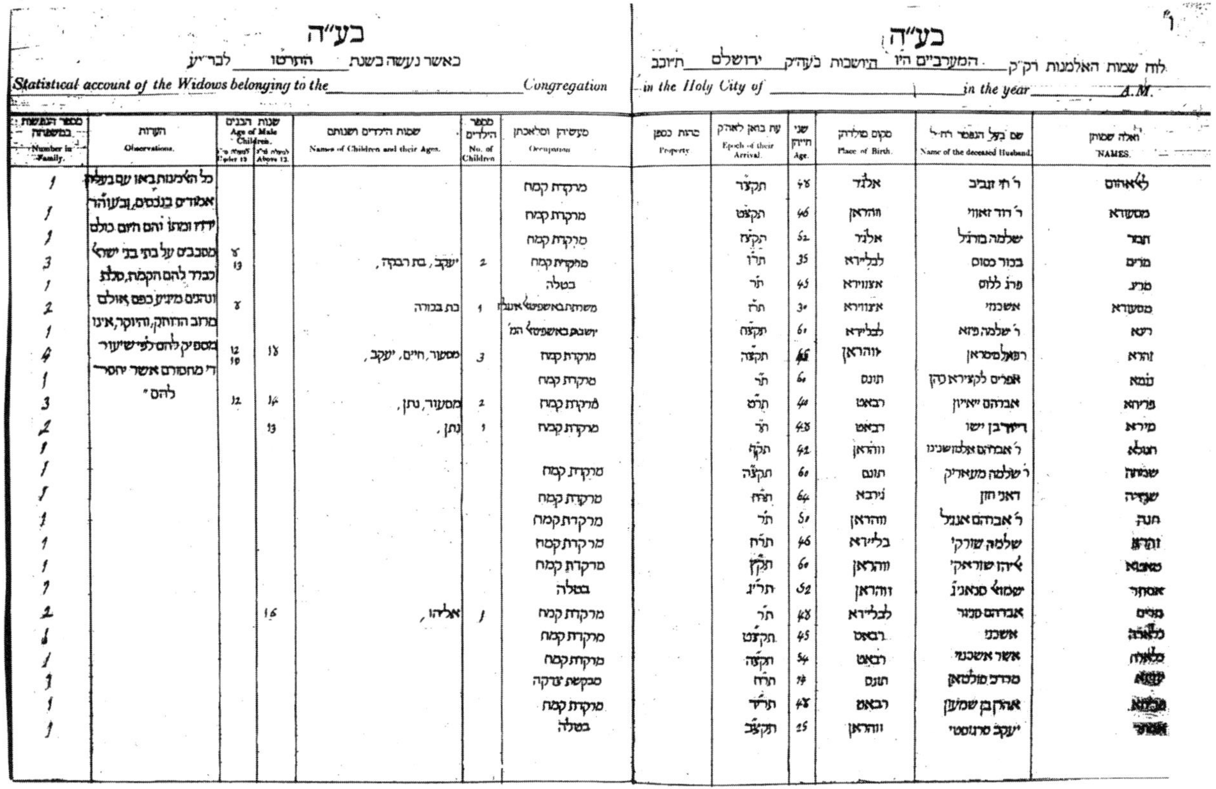

בע"ה

לוח שמות האלמנות רק"ק המערבים היו היושבות בעה"ק ירושלם תובב"א

Statistical account of the Widows belonging to the Congregation in the Holy City of in the year A.M.

NAMES.	Name of the deceased Husband.	Place of Birth.	Age.	Epoch of their Arrival.	Property.	Occupation.	No. of Children.	Names of Children and their Ages.	Age of Male Children. Under 13	Age of Male Children. Above 13.	Observations.	Number in Family.

Fig. 1. *A page from the 1855 Jerusalem census of Maghrebi widows (details are in Hebrew; titles are bilingual English and Hebrew), London School of Jewish Studies Library, Montefiore ms 531 (Institute of Microfilmed Jewish Manuscripts, Jewish National and University Library, Jerusalem, reel 6153).* Reproduced with the kind permission of the Montefiore Endowment Committee and Mr. Ezra Kahn.

Demographic Imbalance of the Population

The high percentage of women within the Jewish population of the Holy Land can be explained by three major factors: first, marriage patterns of North African Jews, both in Palestine and in their communities of origin; second, differential rates in life expectancy between men and women; and third, patterns of *aliyah*, differing for families and singles, the latter primarily widows.

In both the Maghreb and Palestine, the traditional age of marriage for girls was around twelve, and for boys between sixteen and eighteen.[6] High mortality among Jews of all ages resulted in a large number of widows and widowers, as well as numerous remarriages, which traditional Jewish society encouraged to ensure community stability. However, a greater age differential between men and women was common in second and third marriages, with younger girls marrying older men.[7] As a result, many women remained widows, even at relatively young ages of twenty and thirty.[8]

Another phenomenon that seems to be similar in both regions is that of differential mortality rates for men and women, favoring women. During the nineteenth century, natural disasters, disease and epidemics, poor sanitary conditions, deteriorating physical conditions, and a general lack of health services were particularly severe in Eretz Israel, and actually resulted in a natural decrease in population. Although these factors affected both men and women, it seems that the situation for women was somewhat better than that for men. Despite the dangers involved in childbirth, women worked at home — in their homes or in the homes of others — in a relatively safe environment. Men, on the other hand, were exposed to more danger both because of their work in trades and crafts under less protected conditions, and because of their workplace, in the open market or in Arab villages, often among population hostile to them.[9] As a result, many more women were widowed than men, both in the Maghreb and in Palestine. These factors created a demographic imbalance, which in turn resulted in much greater statistical chances for widowed or divorced men to remarry than for the greater numbers of women in the community.[10]

Before examining the gendered patterns of *aliyah*, it is necessary to focus first on the patterns of *aliyah* in general, and those of North African Jews in particular. It is within this context that North African women's *aliyah* will be examined.

During the nineteenth century, a steep increase in the number of Jews arriving in the Holy Land not only balanced the negative growth rate of the Jewish population, but also surpassed it, resulting in a significant overall increase in the Jewish population in the country. The number of North African Jews residing in the Holy Land, for example, grew from some hundreds at the beginning of the century, to nearly eight thousand at the outbreak of World War I.[11] By the mid-1870s, North African Jews comprised approximately one-quarter of the Jewish population in Eretz Israel: in Safed and Tiberias nearly three-fourths of the Sephardi community were of North African descent, as were the Jewish communities as a whole in Haifa and Jaffa. However, in Jerusalem and in Hebron, where the Sephardim of Turkish and Balkan origin dominated communal relations, North African presence was limited: in Jerusalem, they represented no more than 15 percent of the Sephardi community (or 8 percent of all Jews in the city), and only a handful of North African Jews settled in Hebron.

In Eretz Israel, however, there was an exceptionally large proportion of women. This may be explained by the combination of demographic characteristics suggested above — that is, different marriage ages for boys and girls, the prevalence of remarriages with greater age differentiation, and gendered differences in life expectancy — together with patterns of migration particular to Eretz Israel. Traditional Jewish society not only sanctioned *aliyah* for widowed women but may even have encouraged it. Widowed men, as mentioned, generally remarried, and migrated to Eretz Israel as part of a family unit.

Women's Migrations

Various theories and models have been proposed to explain the complex process of migration in general, and *aliyah* to Eretz Israel in particular. Political upheavals, economic changes, and personal safety are among the primary motivating factors noted. Secondary factors generally include ideological and personal aspirations and individual circumstances.[12] An analysis of the demographic characteristics of North African women who immigrated to Eretz Israel, and in particular those characteristics that point to motivating factors for *aliyah*, reveals a gender bias in the organization of the models developed to explain migration. Factors influencing women's decisions to migrate almost all, and not unexpectedly, fall in the private, individual sphere. This stereotyped dichotomy of society brings into question both the terminology used and its gendered view of women's reality. Must these models direct research on women's activities exclusively to the private and family spheres? I suggest that existing categories be utilized, yet re-defined in order to create a broader definition of the phenomenon of *aliyah*, a definition that will be more inclusive (and perhaps more credible?) and therefore applicable to all groups of Jews who immigrated: men and women, rich and poor, the learned and the common people, and to various cultural and ethnic groups. For example, categories such as personal status that influence an individual's response to economic and political change, can be redefined to include wealth, age, and profession, as well as gender. Thus the division between private and public becomes blurred, with gender as a primary variable.

Initial research on women's migrations has mostly dealt with economic aspects, and in particular, those of contemporary women in less developed countries.[13] From these works, it becomes clear that women's positions in their families and communities generally explain and define the limits of their geographic mobility, their motivations for far-distance migrations, and the natural selection of immigrants among the women in their society. However, one must consider not only marriage possibilities or economic factors of the labor market as motivating and influencing the decision to migrate, but also ideological and spiritual factors, and the part of women in migrations that were principally ideological, such as *aliyah* to Eretz Israel. That being said, one also must recognize that it is impossible to ascertain the full range of factors that motivate each individual to migrate. Moreover, as the demographer Everett S. Lee has noted, "The decision to migrate . . . is never completely rational, and for some persons the rational component is much less than the irrational."[14]

North African Jewish Women's Love of Zion

Although we have no direct documentation on factors motivating North African women to migrate to Eretz Israel, one may assume that the main factor is their deep emotional attachment to the Holy Land and their belief in its inherent spiritual qualities.[15] This overriding, deep attachment to the Holy Land and the special virtues that living in the country endows upon its Jewish inhabitants explains the spiritual factors motivating all Jews, and not only women. We will focus here on those aspects of the traditional love for Zion defined specifically by gender.

On the one hand, most scholars have discussed the traditional attachment of North African Jews to Eretz Israel and their legal obligations to migrate there, using terms and forms of expression of the established (male) community: fixed and written prayers, poems (*piyyutim*) written in praise of Eretz Israel, public communal lectures (*derashot*), and rabbinical court decisions that discuss the commandments and their significance as well as financial contributions to the Holy Land and its inhabitants. Men could — and did — elevate their well being in study and prayer while living in their original communities. Women seemingly had no direct part in such activities, all well documented in the writings of communal male leaders and rabbis.

On the other hand, women, as well as men, believed in the special virtues endowed upon those living in the land — atonement of sins, answers to private, individual prayers, health and longevity.[16] The act of *aliyah* itself, of migration to the Holy Land, endowed each immigrant with a special status: Each Jew living in the country became a special envoy of his or her family, community, and the entire Jewish people. These women immigrated ("ascended") to the Holy Land in order to "ascend in holiness," and to strengthen their faith, and not to be part of a social revolution.[17] Upon their arrival in the Holy Land, they prayed fervently and often on the graves of saintly rabbis, they made supplications for their own personal benefit and for that if all Jews.[18]

By broadening the definitions of expressions of the traditional love and attachment to Zion and the religious activities of North African Jews to include those outside of the established rituals of the community, and by including nonformal expressions of religiosity, women's love of Zion and their deep desire for *aliyah* are revealed. During the nineteenth century, for example, the phenomenon of saint veneration grew among North African Jews in general, and among Moroccan Jews in particular. Women as well as men, and perhaps more than men, participated in public celebrations (*hilulot*) and believed in the special powers of saintly men and women.[19] This belief also encompasses a deep connection to Eretz Israel, accompanied by each individual's personal participation in the process of redemption.[20]

Many women vowed to move to the Holy Land to thank God for fulfilling a prayer, to prostrate themselves on the graves of famous rabbis, such as Rabbi Simeon bar Yohai in Meron near Safed, or to "visit" the Prophet Elijah on Mount Carmel. Although the ideological basis for such a vow is deep within traditional Jewish culture and its affinity for Zion, a vow is a very private and individual expression of this attachment. Vows of men attesting to *aliyah* exist in legal contracts and rabbinical court decisions;[21] the vows of women seem to have been much more private and informal, and as such, were not documented in communal records. They are, however, remembered and repeated in stories relayed through generations by family members.

Research that integrates gender with such aspects of saint veneration, vows, and attachment to Eretz Israel may well reveal additional aspects of the folk religion of North African Jews as well as the possibilities for religious self-expression among women, including their decisions to migrate to the Land of Zion.[22]

Aliyah in Family Units

One of the dominant characteristics of *aliyah* from North Africa to Eretz Israel in the nineteenth century is its pattern of family migration.[23] In 1829, for example, Joseph Wolff, a missionary of the London Society for Promoting Christianity among the Jews, reported from Beirut that he saw "fifty Jews besides their wives and children . . . coming from Tunis and Tripoli, for the purpose of residing at Jerusalem."[24] An analysis of the Montefiore censuses shows that almost a quarter (23.2%) of all North African–born men in the Holy Land arrived as children (up to 15 years of age); and over half (57%) were between the ages of 20 and 49. Only about 10 percent of the men immigrated between the ages of 50 and 60 and less than 10 percent (8.6%) were over the age of 60. As mentioned above, nearly all the males were married at the time of their arrival in the country.[25] Associational migration characterized most North African Jewish women traveling to the Holy Land together with their families: their fathers, husbands, and sons.

In addition to immediate families listed in the censuses, it is possible to identify extended families that appear to have immigrated together. Family cohesion and continuity gave support to the immigrants both during their long journey and while adjusting to a new environment and society after their arrival.[26] In 1844, for example, eight families, including many widowed mothers/grandmothers, set out from the Moroccan city of Meknès on their way to Eretz Israel.[27]

Moroccan authorities also seemed to have recognized the fact that Jews preferred to immigrate to Eretz Israel in family units. Jewish men often had to travel for their work in commerce and trade. However, because of their importance to the economy of the country, the authorities tried to supervise their movements outside Morocco. In an attempt to prevent Jewish males from migrating, emigration from the country was prohibited; heavy exit taxes were imposed upon them, or alternately upon their wives, certain to accompany them.[28] The German traveler Baron Heinrich von Malzan wrote of his three years in North Africa during the 1860s and noted that exit taxes could

be exorbitant, especially for an entire family, remarking that women were required to pay ten times that of men.[29] In 1892 it was reported, "To leave the
country, the men used to have to pay $4 and the women $100, and sometimes the departure of the latter is still prohibited."[30]

But what was the part of women in the family decision to migrate to the
Holy Land? At times, women seemed to have encouraged and even initiated
the migration of their families. Rabbinical court decisions, such as that of
Rabbi Raphael Moshe Elbaz (1823–1896) in Sefrou in 1858, show the express
wishes of women to immigrate to Eretz Israel, and in fact, their right to immigrate, even in light of objections from their families.[31]

There are also instances in which women refused to migrate with their
husbands, and postponed or canceled plans for *aliyah*. In the 1870s, for example, the illustrious Rabbi Isaac Ben Naim from Tetuán desired to settle in
Eretz Israel, but his wife objected. In the end, R. Ben Naim made a pilgrimage journey to the Holy Land in 1877, after which he returned to Tetuán.[32]
Court cases, presenting instances of family discord, indicate that the decision to migrate to Eretz Israel was a family decision, in which women were
active participants.

Widows' *Aliyah*

In addition to families, singles — mostly widows — also immigrated to Eretz
Israel. In the early nineteenth century, the American Consul in Algiers,
William Shaler, reported that these were "aged and infirm Jews, sensible
that all their temporal concerns are drawing to a close."[33] However, one must
bear in mind the statistics presented above, showing that the great majority
of *olim* from North Africa in fact were not old at all. These *olim* migrated in
order to live in the Holy Land, to "take pleasure in her stones, and favor her
dust" (Psalms 102:15). More than men, it seems that women, mainly widows,
chose to spend their final years in the Holy Land, after a difficult life in exile.
Although they did in fact die there, the Jews from North Africa do not seem
to have been motivated by the wish to die and be buried there.

As noted above, statistical information is available only for those enumerated as widows at the time of the nineteenth-century censuses. Although
clear conclusions are not possible because of the limitations of the data, it is
still significant to note that twice as many women as men arrived in the
country over the age of 60 (see figure 2). Because of the high mortality rate,
both in Palestine and in the Maghreb, because of the disparity in ages be-

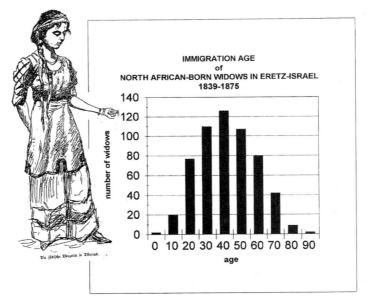

*Fig. 2. Immigration age of North African-born widows in Eretz-Israel,
1839–1875. Statistics compiled from the Montefiore censuses, 1839, 1849,
1855, 1866, 1875. Drawing from Sven Hedin, Jerusalem (Leipzig, 1918), p. 77.*

tween the partners and the difference in life expectancy between men and
women, it is difficult to ascertain who among those widows enumerated arrived as widows and who was widowed after her arrival. One notation
written on the list of Maghrebin widows in Jerusalem in 1855 notes that "all
the widows came with their husbands . . . however much to our distress,
they . . . died"[34] (see figure 1). In 1854, for instance, a caravan of Jews set out
from Meknès for Palestine, and there, in addition to several extended families, were "ten elderly widows, and another of great skill in sewing, and also
of great learning in the Bible and Mishnah . . . and all prayers . . . were
known to her."[35] The 1855 list of widows in the Sephardi community in Safed
enumerates some sixteen widows who all migrated from the Tunisian community of Jerba three years previously, all in their fifties or sixties, leading to
the conclusion that most if not all arrived as widows.[36]

How did widowhood affect these women's decision to migrate to the Holy
Land?[37] Although social conventions generally limited the geographic mobility of women in traditional societies, economic need, family obligations,
and philanthropic activities often mitigated prohibitions.[38] The spatial mo-

bility of women, the motivations for their long-distance migrations, and the selectivity of female migrants are also determined by the position of women within their families and within their communities. *Aliyah* was not only socially acceptable, but seen as a holy act in the eyes of the community. Research using gender as a primary variable in the study of migrations has suggested that certain categories of women are in fact "selected out" for migration, or actually pushed out. Among those are women already at the fringes of society — single women, widows, divorcees, and those with limited means of existence.[39] Although older women often became the matriarchs of their families once widowed, and as such assumed an elevated status, this status should be distinguished from their often-marginal functions in daily life.[40] Jewish families possibly recognized this distinction, and thus accepted the decision of their mothers and sisters to migrate.

After fulfilling their obligations to family and community, many widows were, for the first time, independent. This was the only time in which they could act freely on their own decisions.[41] Thus they could finally fulfill their desires and dreams and migrate to Eretz Israel. However, it must be added that such independence was often limited by their own economic resources or those made available to them by their families. Such may be the case with the sixteen widows from Jerba and the eleven widows from Meknès.

Conclusions

Research focusing on gender in the study of Jewish migrations to Eretz Israel reveals attitudes and patterns of behavior and authority, which previously were barely noted. Although social constraints generally were placed upon women's movements, *aliyah* seems to have been accepted and even encouraged. The ideological-religious factors motivating North African Jews to immigrate to Eretz Israel, their deep love of the Holy Land, and their desire for religious fulfillment were all shared by both men and women. However, the interpretation of these factors and their fulfillment as embodied in actual migration took different forms. The relative independence and freedom of widows enabled many of these women to carry out their dreams, fulfill their vows, and express their own religious aspirations.

Aliyah from North Africa, and specifically the large numbers of women participating in these migrations, not only added to the social weave of the communities, but also changed it. Whether women migrated to the Holy Land as widows or whether they became widows after settling in the country, the communities were blessed with a large number of women. The communal male leadership had to contend with the needs and demands created. Problems particular to them as women and as immigrants in the traditional urban centers of nineteenth-century Palestine were dealt with — or ignored — within the context of the demographic imbalance of the Jewish population in general, and of the widows in particular. The social implications of such patterns and problems will be discussed elsewhere. However, it seems that the same ideals embodied in these women in their decision to migrate continued to fortify them after their arrival and gave them strength to cope with the severe poverty and enormous problems of daily life in nineteenth-century Eretz Israel.

American Jewish Women and Palestine

Their Immigration, 1918–1939

Over five thousand American Jewish women — single and those with their families — migrated to Palestine between the two World Wars.[1] The motivations for their migration reflect their situation as Jews and as women in American society. This study distinguishes between "forced" and "free" migration. Outlined are various motivations for migration in terms of "push" and "pull" factors. Based on their motivations and characteristics and also their settlement pattern, the American Jewish women immigrants are divided into four categories, allowing for a more discerning comprehension of the distinct motivations of the respective groups.

Contemporary discussions of immigrant women analyze their activities within the framework of the models of "threefold oppression" or "double discrimination," namely femaleness, compounded by class (migrant worker) and nationality (foreigner).[2] Uncharacteristically to these models, American Jewish women often gained status as a result of their migration to Palestine. Underlying their motivation for migration was the desire to free themselves of the oppression encountered owing to their femaleness and Jewishness as well as often to their being migrant workers.

A Forced Migration for Women

The migrational movement of American Jews to Palestine is characterized as "free" as opposed to the "forced" migration of most other Diaspora communities. Nearly all waves of Jewish migration resulted from political and economic pressures, and anti-Semitism. Following World War I, Eastern European Jews suffered from the ravages of famine, disease, and civil war.

Aggravated by pogroms in the Ukraine, White Russia, and Poland, all these factors led to a mass migration out of this region. Polish, Romanian, Lithuanian, and Latvian Jewries encountered economic and occupational restrictions and rising anti-Semitism in the early 1920s, a driving force toward emigration. German Jews from 1933 onward left in growing numbers due to increased discrimination that occurred with the rise to power of Adolph Hitler.[3] American Jews, by contrast, were not subject to any large-scale occurrences of anti-Semitism, or economic hardship distinct from the general population that necessitated emigration. Instead, individual American Jews created their own evaluation and constructed their personal credo with regard to migration to Palestine.

Many American Jewish women migrated to Palestine by choice, but dependants of married men are less commonly recognized as forced migrants.[4] Their immigration was the result of a decision usually made by a male family member — husband or father — reflecting patriarchal control exerted over female family members. Most descriptions did not relate to the woman's voice and focused on the man's decision. An article in the Yiddish press "Minneapolis Pioneers go to the Land of Israel" described the Mirsky family's migration in 1921. Mrs. Mirsky's intentions or desires were not discussed; it was her husband who decided. "The travels of the Mirsky family from one land to another recall an old subject from the Pentateuch. 'And Abraham took . . . and he went' and Abraham Mirsky took his wife and his children and he left."[5]

Dorothy Ruth Kahn, an American journalist who settled in Palestine, related to the issue of forced migration in the following story.

> The two smartly attired daughters of Mr. Pearlman could not discard so lightly Brooklyn, Fifth Avenue or Broadway. They were coming to Palestine to fulfill a filial obligation toward their father. . . . They rather wished the boat was heading for Paris instead of Jaffa. . . . It was his cherished hope that the family should settle permanently in Palestine.

In the end, Mr. Pearlman took his daughters' needs into account and decided that they would remain in the United States. "But I'm not sure of the girls. You know how young women are to-day. They like clothes. And there aren't many shops in Palestine. And they like to have a good time. They're accustomed to New York. Perhaps we'll all return to America."[6] In another example, Pauline (Paula) Munweis migrated out of obligation to her husband. "She was not a Zionist. On the contrary, she inclined toward the anarchists and her ideal was their leader, Emma Goldman. She was sympathetic to an anti-Zionist socialist party." Born in Minsk in 1886 or 1887, she immigrated to America in 1904. She married David Ben-Gurion in 1917. He had forewarned Paula that if she were to marry him she would have to journey with him to a small, impoverished country, without electricity, gas, or motorized transport. According to Ben-Gurion's biographer Shabtai Teveth, "Paula was opposed equally passionately to going to Palestine and his enlistment [in the Jewish Legion], but she married him, confident that she could dissuade him, by fair means or foul, from both."[7]

Examples can be found among the Orthodox Jewish population where wives and daughters were obliged to move to Palestine despite their objections. Often they acquiesced to the male family member's desire to achieve religious fulfillment through migration to the Holy Land, finding justification in that they were playing a supporting role in the man's activities.

"Pull" and "Push" Factors

Reasons for American Jewish women to chose to go to Palestine may divided into four general categories: religious fulfillment, Zionism, professional and personal fulfillment, and for the sake of their children. The emphasis is on the drawing power or "pull" of Palestine — the place and its society. These categories overlap and the explanation for these women's migration is often a combination of factors. For many, migration was meant to reduce their sense of oppression resulting from gender, nationality, or class. The triple oppression sometimes experienced by American Jewish women became a substantial "push" factor in their desire to leave America.

Religious Fulfillment

Eretz Israel offered some individuals religious fulfillment. Although there is no clear halakhic requirement for Jews to settle in Eretz Israel, some from the Orthodox community believed that there was a halakhic obligation for *aliyah*. One interpretation of the *halakhah* saw a necessity to migrate to Eretz Israel if their spouse so decided. In general, the Mishnah requires that a wife obey her husband except for the change of residence. In the specific case of *aliyah*, the wife and, of course, the husband are permitted to force the other to make *aliyah*.[8]

The Orthodox population in America provided a disproportionately large number of American immigrants to Palestine. From the mid-nineteenth century onward, many elderly followed tradition to spend their final days in the Holy Land studying Torah. They were members of Kollel America Tifereth Yerushalaym, an organization founded in Jerusalem in 1896 to extend financial support to American and Canadian Jews residing in Palestine. This Orthodox element lived mainly in Jerusalem and the other holy cities of Safed, Tiberias, and Hebron, as well as in Jaffa.[9]

The marital status of women listed as supported by Kollel America Tifereth Yerushalaym illustrates that most of Orthodox Jewish women migrated with their husbands and were financially dependent upon them. Of the 179 adult women, 134 were married, 5 divorced, 19 widowed, 1 was an *agunah*, 2 were orphans, and 18 status unknown.[10] Only eight unmarried women appear to have been employed outside the home.

The Zelig family from Philadelphia migrated to Palestine at the insistence of the mother, Haya Sarah. After the tragic death of her daughter, this devout Orthodox woman became more observant and was convinced that life should be lived in the Holy Land. She feared that if her children remained in America, they would stray from Orthodox practice and assimilate. She, the four youngest of her six remaining children, and her husband migrated in 1934. At first, Kfar Ivri (Mizrachi Hatza'ir of Palestine settlement also known as Neve Yaakov) provided a suitable religious environment. After her husband and two older children returned to America, she moved to the area of the Orthodox Me'ah She'arim neighborhood in Jerusalem and volunteered her time cooking for students at the Neturei Karta yeshiva.[11]

Haya Sarah Zelig appears to be the exception. Most Orthodox women found fulfillment in supporting their spouses' wishes to spend their last years studying Torah. In the end, both man and woman would be buried in the sacred soil of the Holy Land, awaiting their resurrection in the Messianic age. The women quite often improved their status with respect to their Jewishness. They were no longer members of a foreign population in a melting pot society, they were Jews among Jews. In the worst case scenario, they exchanged their foreignness from being Jewish to being an American.

Zionism and the Return to the Soil

The term Zionism, used here in its broadest sense, embraces various nuances of rebuilding the Jewish nation, of being part of the historical process of a people returning to its land, the solution of the "Jewish problem," and under the general headings of nationalism and patriotism. The strength of

Fig. 1. An American couple at Kfar Ivri, 1927 (Original caption: Springtime has come in Palestine: American Jews at Kfar Ivri planting seed in their garden. Every year sees an increasing number of well-to-do Jews from America settling in Palestine.) Source: Palestine Pictorial 1 (April 1927).

Zionist commitment vacillated in response to different events connected to Palestine. The 1917 Balfour Declaration and the liberation of Palestine inspired a large number of American Jews to consider settling there. When World War I ended, some who considered migrating applied for visas to Palestine. Until May 31, 1920, over 5,300 Americans registered for migration. Actual migration fell far below this number; between 1919 and 1923 it totaled 601.[12]

For Golda Mabovitch (Meir), acceptance of Zionism could only be translated into migration to Palestine. In 1971, she explained her migration half a century earlier in simple terms:

I had refused to join the party [Poale Zion] until I had firmly decided to go to Palestine. My ideas of Zionism at the time were quite primitive. I did not understand how one could be a Zionist and not go to settle in Palestine. I had no taste for parlor Zionism. . . . When I joined the party, I knew that I would go to Palestine.[13]

Table 1.

Applicants for Immigration to Palestine from the United States, 1919–1920, according to gender and age group

Age group	Absolute number			Percent		
	Males	*Females*	*Total*	*Males*	*Females*	*Total*
0–13	339	295	634	5.67	4.93	10.60
14–30	610	313	923	10.20	5.23	15.43
31–44	770	698	1,468	12.87	11.67	24.54
45–59	389	323	712	6.50	5.40	11.90
60+	44	30	74	0.74	0.50	1.24
Total	3,245	2,738	5,983	54.24	45.76	100.00

The Fishman family of St. Albans, Vermont, decided to migrate as an expression of their Zionist commitment. It was a joint decision made by the parents, Shmuel and Leah. The eldest son Hertzel explained that "Our family life was oriented to eventual migration to Eretz Israel." Migrating to America in 1923, the couple spent eleven years preparing their family for *aliyah*. They lived, as far as it was possible, in an all-Jewish environment of Hebrew, Yiddish, and Zionist culture. Both parents took an active role in imbuing their children with a love of Zionism and Judaism as Hertzel recalled: "our parents put us to bed each night with Yiddish and Hebrew melodies, and as we grew older, their bedtime stories revolved around the heroes of the Jewish People and great moments in Jewish history — biblical, Talmudic, chasidic, and especially of the era of the modern, idealistic pioneers (*halutzim*) in Palestine."[14] Shmuel worked to amass the necessary funds for migration and in 1934, when their eldest son, Hertzel, reached the age of thirteen, it was time to leave for Palestine.

Miriam, a member of a Zionist youth group, had spent years educating and preparing herself for the eventuality of settlement in Palestine. The description of her departure outlines the collective joy in the migration of this woman.

A delegation of about a hundred spirited young Zionists had bid Miriam a lusty farewell in New York. Miriam was only twenty-three years old but she went forth with the honest conviction that life must be lived in Palestine. Her

Fig. 2. Halutzot *(among them Americans) at Kibbutz Ein Hashofet preparing a meal,* 1937. Source: CZA Keren Hayesod photograph collection.

baggage was slight, her pocketbook thin. Somewhere in her belongings was a labour certificate entitling her to live permanently in Palestine. She had waited long for this certificate. It was the envy of many of her friends who had come to bid her good-bye.[15]

Between May 1925 and December 1942, 5,861 Americans Jews immigrated to Palestine. Thirteen percent of the American immigrants were permitted to enter Palestine with labor certificate visas (Category C — working men and women and their families — under the Immigration Ordinances). The certificates were distributed among Diaspora communities according to the Zionist organization's considerations. The greatest number of certificates was allotted to Polish Jews while the United States had one of the lowest rates. American Jews, it was thought, could find other ways (particularly through capitalist visas) to enter Palestine.[16]

For certain individuals, Jewish Palestine extended opportunities to contribute to the creation of a new society under the Zionist flag. There were different agendas for navigating towards a progressive and enlightened Jewish

Fig. 3. Halutzot (*among them Americans*) *at Kibbutz Ein Hashofet during target practice, December 1937.* Source: CZA Keren Hayesod photograph collection.

society. Deborah Kallen, the renowned educator who settled in Palestine in 1920, expressed her vision in an interview from the 1950s. "I saw an opportunity for creative work. The fact that people thought the Jews were not an artistic people aroused me. I did not support the religious restriction against portraits. In fact I thought it my holy duty to start something which would refute that concept."[17] She introduced this and other ideas through her work at the School of the Parents Education Association in Jerusalem, better known as the "Kallen School."

Under the Zionist umbrella was the desire for a new life and vocation through the return to the soil. The return to a simpler and pastoral life was an important part of the development of a new society in Palestine. In part, it was derived from an underlying religious belief in messianic redemption as described in the biblical passage, "Every man shall sit under his grapevine or fig tree" (Micah 4:4). Most American Jews resided in highly industrialized urban centers; the desire to come closer to nature was a growing motif in American society generally. The return to the soil afforded those party to it a deep sense of satisfaction and pride. Two groups of women migrated with the motivation of settling on the land and engaging in agriculture: pioneers (*ha-lutzot*) in communal settlements and members of the middle class.

American women settled in existing moshavot and moshavim and in new settlements designed for Americans such as Balfouria, Herzlia, Raanana, and Gan Yavne. No examples have been found of individual women identified with the middle class who went to work the land alone. Women, wives and daughters, joined the men to farm the land. Some were partners in the decision, as with the Seletskys of Chester, Pennsylvania. Mordechai explained that "his marriage to Hannah was based on four principles: Judaism, protection, happiness, and friendship [. . .] Foremost in their designs, however, was their shared decision to make *aliyah* to the land of Israel, there to build their true home and 'plant their children.'"[18] The couple purchased a 110-dunam agricultural tract in Balfouria, the American-initiated colony north of Afula. In 1924, the Seletsky couple and their seven daughters left for Palestine. The daughters helped their father in the fields and in caring for the dairy cattle. For over three years while Mordechai was in the United States, Hannah and her daughters ran the farm.[19]

Some *halutzot* were motivated to return to the soil in Palestine. Labor Zionist ideologue Aaron David Gordon outlined the role of agriculture in the process of revival of the Jewish nation and the individual. In a prophetic tone he wrote,

> Your sons and daughters will come to seek the interpretation of their dream in the land of their fathers. They will seek it with all the powers of their hands, with all the strength of their hearts. They will dig it out of hidden places; they will carry on every kind of work in the field and in the vineyard in seeking for it. They will renew the earth and their lives in their search. It will happen that as they search and work, they will grow and wax strong until in the end they will become great, greater than the mountain peaks on the face of the earth; they will see what no man saw before them, and they will become mighty on the earth.[20]

To prepare for their new lives in agriculture and to qualify for a labor schedule certificate, *halutzot* studied at agricultural colleges and trained on *hakhsharah* (training) farms. Women training to be farmers were not a common sight in the American landscape. Tziporah Greenspan explained: "We wonder whether New Jersey farmers will ever get used to us women farmers . . . without fail we are the object of much wonder of these old-fashioned men when we walk into various agricultural meetings."[21]

Fig. 4. The Seletsky family at Balfouria, circa. 1924.   Source: Mordechai Seletsky letters, CZA J33/95.

Chana G. studied at Rutgers University in 1941 and specialized in poultry. She detailed her studies: "The courses in *Lul* [Heb: chicken coop, referring to poultry raising], are quite intensive and since N.J. is an important commercial poultry state . . . The teachers are all specialists in a single field, and are able to carry out their experiments on the farm; this being the state experimental station. We can see the experiments as they take place and are thus informed on the latest developments."[22] She took courses in poultry buildings, poultry crops, poultry products, poultry breeding, poultry feeding, poultry judging, poultry management, types and breeds, miscellaneous fowls, and current problems, preparing her well for an important role in the kibbutz economy she hoped to join. Other women studied different branches of agriculture and gained practical experience at the *hakhsharah* farms.

The *halutzot* were motivated by the desire to improve their status. They would be equal with men in their Zionist utopias. This was expressed by some in their selections of vocations then often deemed exclusively for men. They expected to find gender equality on the kibbutz. Their Jewishness would no longer be an impediment but instead they would be empowered though their newfound nationalist sentiments. The third of their former oppressions, their

Fig. 4. "Esther Shapiro used to be a bookkeeper in Detroit" [*original caption*], *Ein Hashofet,* 1942. Source: CZA Keren Hayesod photograph collection.

class, would be a strength in their battle to create a classless society. It was realized in their kibbutz micro-environment. *Halutzot* expected to gain status as a result of their migration and did so to varying degrees.

Personal and Professional Fulfillment

Another factor in the search for personal satisfaction was connected to the status of women in America and the sense of greater opportunity in Palestine. Despite the success of the American suffrage movement in obtaining the vote for women in 1918, many American Jewish women were still subject to expectations that pointed in one direction—marriage and motherhood. Only a small number combated the inequality between the sexes and the patriarchal expectations placed upon them. Historian of the New York Jewish community, Irving Howe explained:

> Even Jewish girls who had come from Europe as children and were therefore likely to remain fixed in the progression from shopgirl to housewife, found themselves inspired—or made restless—by American ideas. They came to

value pleasure in the immediate moment; some were even drawn to the revolutionary thought that they had a right to an autonomous selfhood [. . .] Feminism as a movement or ideology seems to have reached no more than a small
number of Jewish girls, mostly those who had already moved to rebellion by
socialism.[23]

In Palestine, a revolution appeared to be underway. Marie Syrkin outlined
the atmosphere of the period. "The young women pioneers who came to
Palestine in the early decades of the twentieth century shared the dream of
their male comrades: they would create a new egalitarian society in a Jewish
homeland, reclaimed through their labor. To this they added still another
dimension — the full emancipation of women."[24] The stories of these
women's endeavors reached the American public. *The Plough Women*, first
published in English in 1932, depicted the spirit, trials, and achievements of
pioneer women in Palestine.

From the ranks of American Jewish women subject to discrimination
based on gender in America, a number decided to emigrate. These women
were affiliated with socialist Zionist youth movements such as Hashomer
Hatzair and believed that gender equality could be found on the kibbutz and
maybe in time, in all of society in Palestine.

Palestine became an avenue for personal ambitions and this included
social pioneering as discussed above. A strikingly large number of single
women can be included in this group — Henrietta Szold, Jessie Sampter,
Alice Seligsburg, Bertha Landsman, Yehudit Aaronsohn-Duskin, and Irma
Lindheim — and many were connected to American Hadassah. American-
trained nurse Bertha Landsman of New York City dreamed of living in Palestine and looked to the challenge of working and contributing to the health
and well-being of its inhabitants. Migrating in 1921, she fostered the development of health services and was among the initiators of Tipat Halav (literally,
"drop of milk"), an infant-and-mother welfare program.[25]

Palestine offered certain professional opportunities. American-trained
Jews, proficient in English, were in great demand. In a letter to Lotta Levensohn, Jessie Sampter explained:

> [T]here is such a demand for stenographers and secretaries here, that a
> woman like you, an executive and secretary with the additional advantage of
> understanding Hebrew would quickly find a well-paying job. . . . I don't think
> there are two first rate English stenographers in Jerusalem, to say nothing of
> secretaries with that accomplishment![26]

Levensohn settled in Palestine in 1923. She "ran the gamut from work on the land, to translator, lecturer, author, publicity director and organizer in association with Hadassah, the Jewish Agency, the Hebrew University and others."[27] At one point she considered studying agriculture:

> I decided to make Palestine my home for the for the rest of my life, and to try from an inside knowledge of the new Palestine to win support for our efforts through my writings in the American Jewish and general press [. . .] In order to learn something of the working Palestine [. . .] I feel that I must become one of the workers. That is why I turn to you to ask whether you will receive me as a student in your school.[28]

The demand for American-trained secretaries continued throughout the period of study. Shulamith Schwartz (Nardi) in 1937 explained:

> American business-men with American methods and connections, naturally want American-trained secretaries who can write literate English and not the stylistic atrocities of the average Palestinian secretary who inevitably claims "perfect knowledge" of at least four or five languages. Efficient girl secretaries from any number of American cities form a distinct class in Palestine, for many a young tourist has seen the opportunity to come and work for a year or two — and the news spreads to others. The Imperial Chemicals Industries and the Iraq Petroleum Company alone have harbored many American girls, a goodly percentage of who marry Palestinians — of many origins, to be sure — and stay in the country.[29]

The economic situation and the labor market in Palestine at times offered opportunities for American Jewish women to procure better or better-paying jobs, particularly during the Great Depression. They were immigrant women who did not occupy the lowest levels in the labor force hierarchy (i.e., working primarily as poorly paid domestics, cleaners, waitresses, or sewing machine operators).

Certain individuals experienced discontentment with their lives — in family or personal relations, or employment. In an attempt to institute a change, they believed that another milieu, possibly Palestine, would be more conducive. Poet Jessie Sampter during her first year in Palestine expressed her sense of fulfillment, in contrast to her life in America.

> My feeling now is that I want to, that I must, stay here indefinitely. To go back after this year, which has been really a year of difficult adjustment and prepa-

Fig. 6. Jessie Sampter and her adopted daughter, Tamar Sheleg (no date). Source:
Bertha Badt-Strauss, *White Fire: The Life and Works of Jessie Sampter* (New York, 1956).

ration, would be to leave a job I had just begun. I feel at home here, as I have
never felt anywhere since I was twelve years old [. . .] I love this place; I feel
planted here. If I ever return to the States, it will be to visit, not to go home.
Of course I shall always love the ideal America — but not as much as I love the
real Palestine and the living Jewish people, real and ideal [. . .] there are personal reasons, too. Life has been too hard for me, and I have lived at too high
a tension of spiritual endeavor. Here I can drop all that, and be natural. Mrs.
[Edith Low] Eder agreed with me — I think Miss Szold does, too — that I ought
to stay here for at least a few years to free myself from the past and myself.[30]

Sampter remained for the rest of her life in Palestine. She found personal satisfaction, involving herself in social and educational projects (the founding
of the scouting movement and evening classes for Yemenite women, for example), and building a family by adopting a Yemenite orphan, whom she
named Tamar Sheleg.

Irma L. Lindheim, the second president of Hadassah, considered residing
permanently in Palestine following her husband's death. Following her 1929
visit, she decided to live temporarily in Jerusalem. She explained her strong
attraction to Rabbi Stephen S. Wise: "I went to Palestine in March because

Fig. 7. Jessie Sampter and friends in front of her home in Rehovot, 1927. Source: Bertha Badt-Strauss, *White Fire: The Life and Works of Jessie Sampter* (New York, 1956).

I could not keep away, I am going back in October for the same reason." Lindheim elaborated upon the essence: "Since I have made the big decision I have found my inner peace again. I can no longer be cut off from the source of my life's meaning." She planned a year's experiment for herself and her children. She hoped that after that period, she would find her personal answer. In 1933, Irma settled permanently on kibbutz Mishmar ha-Emek, having been accepted unanimously as a member of the kibbutz. Going by her adopted Hebrew name, Rama was a well-known figure in many aspects of kibbutz life.[31]

Beatrice Magnes and her husband Judah vacillated between Jerusalem and New York. Their decision was based on their fulfillment as a couple, which included ways of cooperation and common interests. Coming out of a period of depression brought on by bouts of malaria that they contracted in Palestine, Judah outlined the following points regarding Jerusalem in his diary: "Common interest in archaeology and history, and religions and churches and libraries — and culture. Work together [. . .] Our primary consideration will be the other — Jerusalem with its cultural riches, the land with its history and places and peoples of interest."[32] New York, on the other hand, offered many rich cultural and social opportunities but not the personal satisfaction the couple hoped to achieve. The couple remained permanently in Palestine.

For the Sake of Their Children

Some Americans were motivated to settle in Palestine to ensure a better life for their children. Parents, as seen above in the example of Haya Sarah Zelig, feared that for their children to remain in America meant assimilation. In the case of the Fishman family, migration to Palestine would provide the children with a meaningful Jewish life. Similarly, the Fish family of Brooklyn found that Palestine could offer their children the opportunity of connecting with Jewish culture and the revived Hebrew language. At the mother's initiative, they settled in Palestine. In 1930, Sarah moved with her three young children to Palestine for a year in order to allow her children to live and learn in a Hebrew-speaking environment. They extended their sojourn, and the family's father, Avraham, joined them. With worsening economic conditions in the United States, the couple decided to seek a new life in Tel Aviv. In 1933, the family opened Pension Fish on Ben Yehuda Street and continued operating hotels throughout British rule.[33]

A sense of dissatisfaction with America can be seen on two levels. In terms of living in the greater society, there was the desire not to live in the Diaspora; a concern about assimilation, the feeling of being the object of anti-Semitism or fear of it. The second level was more personal and included the wish to leave a disliked job, to get away from family, or just to be independent. In these push factors, the emphasis is on the negative. Alienation and persecution, or the sense thereof, are two strong themes in the "push." Author Myriam Harry reported on a meeting with an American woman, probably at Merchavia. In response to Harry's question, "What brought you to Palestine? The Jews are not persecuted, are they, in America?" she explained that Jews were not persecuted and on a personal level her family was materially better off but, "America is too new a country for us. We don't take root there: we are never really 'at home.' We were popular there, but aliens, goyim, while here, as soon as we landed, we felt ourselves in our own land, and it is the non-Jews who are goyim."[34] This response is open to many interpretations, but the strong sense of alienation and being foreign stands out. A more distinct factor is anti-Semitism. Although, "America is Different" as Ben Halpern explained, he elaborated that "American anti-Semitism has never reached the level of an historic, politically, effective movement . . . it has remained, so to speak, a merely sociological or 'cultural' phenomenon."[35] It was this form of anti-Semitism that served as an impetus for migration to Palestine. Anti-Semitism in America was expressed not only in isolated incidents but also through quotas and restrictions in education, employment, and social activities. The fear of anti-Semitism preoccupied many American Jews. Marie Syrkin in her article "The Yellow Badge and Mrs. Grossman" told the plight of this mother's efforts to prepare her son for college and a world, she believed, that was intolerant of Jews. "He has to be prepared for the great day by two amputations: his name and his nose must be foreshortened." To avoid such and other encounters with anti-Semitism, some women decided for themselves and their families to move to an environment where they could live freely without discrimination as Jews. The women motivated by the "push" felt that America was not the "Land of Opportunity" many had hoped it to be.

Return to America

Not all American women who migrated remained permanently. Some found hardship in life in Palestine and returned to "better lives" in America. Others were disappointed by the gap between their expectations and the realities of Palestine. In certain cases, women were forced to return to America by male family members.

The rate of emigration is not known since almost no records were kept differentiating among the citizenship or nationality of emigrants. Yet Americans were stigmatized as having a high rate of reverse migration. Figures, not based on any statistical information, suggested a return rate of one in three.[36]

The American Consulate in Jerusalem reported Mrs. Schneider's emigration in 1921. Apparently the immigration was inspired by the excitement of the period following the Balfour Declaration but the realities of life in Palestine were too difficult for her to bear.

> A widow lady Mrs. Rebecca Schneider came recently from San Francisco to Palestine, imbued with Zionist ideas, and purchased a building lot in the vicinity of Jerusalem upon which to construct a residence, paying therefor the usual inflated price. She complains that the organization (not American) which sold her the land is unable to locate it for her excepting on paper. She wishes now to return to the comforts of her San Francisco home, having

changed her mind about residence in Palestine, and is trying to get her money back. The promoting organization offers a refund of 75% but requires 25% for expenses in encouraging her to assist in building up the new Zion.[37]

A particular difficulty for women was the backward condition of domestic life particularly in the 1920s as Jessie Sampter explained:

> Housekeeping is as primitive as it was in the Adirondacks, in some ways more so. I notice that only those Americans who have had camping experience, like Miss [Sophie] Berger and myself, can adjust themselves to the simple life here. All our water has to be drawn up, with a pail and rope, from a cistern just outside our door. All slop and garbage have to be carried out of doors. Fortunately we have a rather good indoor toilet here, but it is on the upper floor.[38]

Sampter continued by detailing other primitive aspects of domestic life including candles and lamps for lighting, standard oil tins to store water, and cooking on an oil stove. She felt a sense of pride in adjusting to the situation. "Our household is very limited in its goods, partly from principle — one must live simply in pioneering times — but much more from necessity. . . . But we manage to keep our home pretty and clean and warm and inviting, despite the handicaps, and to do it without fuss and worry."[39] Almost all houses were without electricity and plumbing. Gradually, conditions improved with the development of infrastructure and the introduction and wider use of different technologies.

Clearly, not all the reasons for returning to America were connected to domestic life in Palestine. But as American *oleh* Menachem Mendel Freidman pointed out, for women life in Palestine was the most trying. He stressed that for women it was particularly trying with a lack of domestic help, difficulties with the language, and a lack of society. He emphasized that often wives forced their husbands to return to America and that only special women did forgo their personal comfort for the sake of their husbands' dreams. Some were partners to their spouses' Zionist sentiments.[40]

This last example illustrates the difficult gap that existed between dream and reality. Dorothy Ruth Kahn told the story of a young woman from the Bronx:

> In less than a fortnight, Palestine descended upon her with all of its ills, dangers, annoyances, inconveniences, and above all else disappointments. . . . Rachel was a Zionist. . . . She had wept for Palestine. Rejoiced for Palestine. Suffered

for Palestine. Contributed money for Palestine. Prayed for Palestine. Hoped for Palestine. Dreamed for Palestine. But she could not face Palestine.[41]

The rate of return for American women was most probably higher than for women of other nationalities. One obvious reason was that they could return to their country of origin, since they were part of a free migration.

Conclusion: Categorization of American *Olot*

Four different groups of American *olot* may be identified: the Orthodox population, *halutzot* (pioneers), middle-class agriculturalists, and urban professionals.

The Orthodox population for the most part was older. It included families, elderly couples, and widows. The incomes of this group varied from the lower percentiles, needing financial assistance when they lived in Palestine, to a handful of the wealthy. The majority was not American-born, but originally from Eastern Europe.

The *halutzot* were a much younger population, and the majority were single. Most couples in this group did not have children. They were at the beginning of the productive stage of their lives, usually with little capital. Most had graduated high school and some had attended university. Many were trained in agriculture or in skilled professions. In the 1930s, the majority were American-born, some even had American-born parents. Ideologically, they were affiliated with socialism and communism, as reflected in their desire to join communal settlements in Palestine.

The middle-class agriculturalists consisted mainly of families. More often than not, they came from urban centers and lacked agricultural experience but dreamed of owning and farming land in the Holy Land. The couples were in their middle years and their children ranged in age from young to adolescent. These families usually possessed sufficient capital to maintain themselves during their first years in Palestine, and to purchase and cultivate land. For some, the realities of agricultural life was too difficult or the limited amenities did not suit their needs, so they often resided and worked in the city and occasionally visited their rural properties.

The fourth group — urban professionals — is characterized by their vocations or their husbands' vocations and their new place of residence. They had received post-secondary education and were trained as doctors, nurses, educators, social workers, journalists, secretaries, and others. They were single women as well as couples with children. Most were American-born or raised in the United States. They possessed the tools to integrate into mainstream American society but decided to uproot themselves to Palestine.

Many of the over five thousand American Jewish women who were motivated to migrate to Palestine between the two World Wars contributed to the development of its society, culture, and landscape.[42] Their migration stands out when compared to the migration of other groups of women during this period. American Jewish women shook off one or more of their oppressions (gender, nationality, and class) by settling in Palestine.

“⸙” *Esther Meir-Glitzenstein*

Ethnic and Gender Identity of Iraqi Women Immigrants in the Kibbutz in the 1940s

I n the 1940s, a few thousand Iraqi immigrants took their first steps in Eretz Israel among the settlements of Ha-Kibbutz ha-Me'uhad (United Kibbutz movement). For a large part of these *olim*, the kibbutz was only a way station before they moved on to the city; but there were others among them, mostly individuals who had been members of the Hehalutz Zionist movement in Iraq, who wanted to make their home in the kibbutz and even hoped to see large-scale immigration absorbed into it. These *olim* joined the kibbutz within the framework of some twenty settlement training groups (*gar'inei hakhsharot*) and a number of youth communities (educational units of Youth Aliyah) from Iraq. Each training group had between twenty and forty members, one-quarter to one-third of whom were young women.[1] The *haksharot* of Iraqi immigrants, similar to those of other immigrants, were part of an extensive system for training youth in a kibbutz toward the goal of establishing new settlements and reinforcing existing ones.

The *haksharah* members lived on the kibbutz itself, in cabins or tents set aside for them, and they worked together with the kibbutz members in the various branches of the kibbutz. The kibbutz appointed *madrikhim* (counselors) for them who helped with the ideological and social unification of the *hakhsharah* members. In addition, they were eligible to study one day a week or a number of hours each day. Each *hakhsharah* maintained a separate group framework and managed its own independent social life.

Ultimately, the attempt at "Bavli settlement" (these immigrants were called "Bavli" [i.e., Babylonian] to differentiate them from Kurdish Iraqi immigrants) in kibbutzim failed, and by the mid-1950s only a minimal number of these immigrants remained in them. Also, from among the hundreds of young people who came to the kibbutz as part of Youth Aliyah, during the period of mass immigration (1949–1951), few stayed on.[2] For the *olim* themselves, their sojourn in the kibbutz was a formative experience that fashioned their identity as Israelis.

The heroines of this article are the young Zionist women who immigrated from Iraq in the 1940s and who followed the same path to Zionist realization as their male colleagues. In this paper, the process of settlement in the kibbutz will be viewed from the standpoint of these women, while keeping in mind the world of values and culture from which they came as well as the changes in their behavior and identity that resulted from joining the kibbutz. The focus here is on three sets of change:

- The shift from ideological concepts to actual realization: In Iraq the members of the Hehalutz movement had been inculcated in the national and social values of socialist Zionism. But mundane reality in the kibbutz was far less heroic than it had appeared in Iraq. This article will examine the influence of the gap between the ideology and the ways it was implemented in the *hakhsharah* groups.
- The intercultural shift: The ethnic and cultural component in the world of the Iraqi *olot* will be reviewed while examining the shift from the values of a patriarchal, conservative, Eastern society to a society that espoused a utopian, egalitarian, Western ideology.
- The modification in their status as women: In this context, the influence of the change on the immigrants' gender identification will be examined.

To clarify these issues, we will draw a social portrait of the *hakhsharah* members, while focusing on the status of the young women and the factors that enabled their immigration to Eretz Israel and their joining the kibbutz.

A Social Portrait of the Women Immigrants (*Olot*)

The great majority of the *hakhsharah* members belonged to the Hehalutz movement that operated in Iraq from 1942 on. They came from the lower- and middle-middle class, and were sons and daughters of petty merchants, craftsmen, and office workers in civil service or private companies. They were urbanites from Baghdad, Basra, and other cities, and most of them had secondary school education.[3]

These young people joined the Zionist movement in search of an existential solution during a period of national identity crisis and economic and social distress. In the 1940s, the Iraqi Jews' feeling of security had been shaken. The pogrom against the Jews of Baghdad in June 1941 and the policy of discrimination and deprivation in distinctly Jewish fields of the economy, such as commerce and banking, created a sense of ongoing crisis. Moreover, knowledge of the Holocaust of European Jewry undermined their sense of physical security, and the youth sought alternatives to the existing patterns of the Iraqi Jews' way of life.[4]

The solution offered by the Zionist movement was a Zionist-Socialist one that set as the ideal *aliyah* to Eretz Israel and realization in kibbutz. The youth were educated in the values of the Labor Movement with emphasis on self-labor and a communal living framework. The young persons saw themselves as the vanguard whose duty was to be the bridgehead for absorbing the mass immigration from Iraq, and the way to do that, they felt, was by establishing kibbutzim — in which, so they believed, the members of their families and other immigrants would find their place.

This portrait depicts the female movement members as well. The joining of the kibbutz framework by these young women, who had been raised in a conservative, traditional society, obliged them to make a personal revolution, which must be viewed against the background of the characteristics of Jewish society in Iraq and the status of women within it.[5]

The Jewish woman's status in Iraq was determined by the family framework, which constituted a basic unit in Jewish and Muslim society there. A woman was greatly dependent upon her family, particularly on her father and her brothers. Civil and political rights were denied her, and from the time she was born she was educated toward fulfilling the roles that society thrust upon her, those of wife and mother: marriage and running a household, bearing children, nurturing and educating them.[6]

But from the 1920s on, after Britain had conquered Iraq, it was possible to discern cracks in the traditional structure of Jewish society resulting from the penetrating influence of Enlightenment ideas and the beginning of modernization processes. Most noticeable were changes in the field of education. Operating in Iraq was a modern Jewish education system, founded in the second half of the nineteenth century by Alliance Israélite Universelle. Its curriculum equipped the pupils with European languages and educated them in modern values. The Alliance wanted to accelerate the modernization process in Jewish society by educating the girls, in an attempt to replicate among the Jewish communities of Islamic countries the accepted values of conservative, bourgeois society in middle and western Europe toward the close of the nineteenth century. Among other things, it wanted to establish the image of a new woman — educated, homemaker, helpmeet, out-standing in diligence and cleanliness, gentleness, and modesty. They expected her to raise and train a new generation of educated, enlightened people.[7]

At the end of the 1940s, girls made up about one-third of the eighteen thousand Jewish pupils; among the economic and social elite, there were al-ready by that time a number of women who had studied medicine or phar-macology in universities outside Iraq.[8] Yet, beyond providing dignity and prestige, education's influence on the basic situation of the woman was lim-ited, mainly because a young middle-class woman usually was not permitted to go to work. There were few working women among the educated, and when they married, they, too, left their jobs. Most of the young ladies sat at home after completing their studies, waiting for their intended bridegroom.[9]

In this situation, the educated young women were torn between the West-ern worldview along with the set of expectations they had been imbued with in school and the traditional values instilled in them by their families and ac-cording to which they were supposed to behave. These conflicting messages frustrated them. Some of the girls wanted to rebel against the path drawn for them by their families, and part of them found an answer to their personal distress within activities offered by the Hehalutz movement, the only Zion-ist movement operating in Iraq in the 1940s. In the Zionist national and so-cial platform, they saw the way to solve the Jewish problem in Iraq and, at the same time, also the problem of their status as women. Among the fe-male members of the movement were high-school students and high-school graduates as well as illiterate young women from the lower class for whom membership in the movement gave them a chance for evening courses and the acquiring of basic education, in Hebrew. Likewise, there were girls who wanted to escape from social and economic distress or from a family or personal problem, and immigrated to Israel with the help of the Zionist movement.[10]

The active participation of the young women and the responsible roles they filled as group leaders and in the movement's institutions, together with their exposure to education that advocated equality and the special empha-sis placed on the equality of women, led to the cultivation of the members' feminist consciousness, to enhanced self-confidence, and to enhanced rec-ognition of their right to stand up for themselves by waging an internal struggle against traditional, conservation thought. Simultaneously, a change also took place among the young men who belonged to the movement; they were taught to change their patronizing, arrogant attitude to women, to con-sider them equals, and to thereby help them acquire self-confidence and gar-ner strength for the conflicts at home. Internalizing the egalitarian system was difficult for the men, no less than for the women.

The more egalitarian values were internalized among the *haverot*, and the more that equality pervaded movement activities, the greater became the gap between the two worlds in which the young woman lived. After a few years, she had to choose between marriage and *aliyah*. The first route typically was taken by a large part of the *haverot*. The second, rebellious path was characteristic of the activist members and of *haverot* who came from Zionist families. It was not easy to obtain the parents' permission enabling their children's immigration to Israel, and it was especially difficult for their daughters. In some cases, a bitter struggle was waged within the family. In general, however, the girls emigrated with their brothers or other relatives, or followed after them, even gaining a supportive attitude from their parents.

The heroines of this article, who rebelled against the traditional-oriental framework in the name of new social values identified with Zionism and European culture, revolted as both women and as oriental women. Among them was a nucleus of self-aware young women with great stamina and devotion to continuing the struggle to achieve their national and social goals. To lay out a picture of the world of these *haverot*, we will deal with areas that played a central role in their milieu and daily life after they had immigrated to Eretz Israel. We will describe these areas while focusing on the young women's point of view at that time as well as in the memories they drew on in retrospect many years afterwards. With the help of this material, we will attempt to discern what changes took place in the way of life, endeavors, and public involvement of the *hakshara* women in Eretz Israel in comparison to their lives on the eve of their immigration and to see how these changes influenced their identity.[11]

The Shift to Kibbutz Life

Zionist-Socialist consciousness and the perception of the kibbutz as an ideal framework for realizing national and social aims were basic components in the worldview of the *haverot* in the *hakshara*. They greatly admired kibbutz life and the encounter with this lifestyle led them to write enthusiastic praise, such as the following lines that one young women wrote at the end of the *hakshara* year in Giv'at ha-Sheloshah.

> If we look a bit at kibbutz life, it seems that the aspirations we dreamed of for so long are now being fulfilled in this new lifestyle. There is no difference be-

tween poor and rich, pauper and patrician, all live together a life of freedom
and cooperation, with everyone sharing one grand goal — redemption of the
land. . . . I never thought I would live this way: among many fathers and mothers, brothers and sisters who live jointly a cooperative, egalitarian life, on a
large piece of land on which are found Jews from all kinds of countries, who
work by the sweat of their brow in agriculture. . . . By our lives, the lives of a
laborer in the kibbutz, we feel the beauty of nature, the taste of communal life,
the realization of Zionism, and building up the country. . . . One forgets the
difficulties in this type of life through love of nature, labor, and homeland.[12]

The ideological enthusiasm reflects the educational indoctrination process
the immigrant trainees had undergone. The kibbutz was presented as the ultimate and only way for achieving both the national and personal solution.
The longer the young people had been in the movement in Iraq, the deeper
was their attachment to kibbutz life. City life, in contrast, was depicted as
the continuation of Diaspora life and was vehemently disparaged. Special
contempt was poured on the suburbs of Tel Aviv, particularly Shekhunat
ha-Tikvah — which in those years was the first refuge for immigrants arriving
from Islamic countries, among them many people who had abandoned the
kibbutz. This vilification of urban ways was an effort to reinforce the identity
of the young immigrants with the kibbutz, its way of life, and its values.[13]

Egalitarian Labor

As for all other new people joining the kibbutz, for the young *olim*, too, the
physical labor was hard and the initials stages of adjustment were exhausting, but these hurdles were anticipated and perceived as part of the realization process and as a test every pioneer had to go through and overcome.
Working the land was seen as an ideal that embodied something of the
return to nature, purity, and joy of life, and by means of which the personality of the new Jew would be constructed.[14]

Idealization of the life of labor is found in most of the articles by the
young immigrants, young men and young women alike, particularly in essays written during the early stages of *hakhsharah* life. In a letter to her
brother, who had remained in Basra, Shoshana Murad [Mu'allem] described
her feelings on her first day of work in Ashdot Ya'akov:

We weeded and this was the first in my life that I held a hoe in my hand. How
happy was I from the work, from the captivating landscape, and the bright sun
and the fresh air. . . . I worked, singing, for at least two hours, and later my

back ached and I couldn't open the fingers of my hand. I wish you could see me now, you would see my happy face and hear my laugh, since I would be yearning for that time.[15]

Ruth Iliya described working in the tomato field:

"To faraway fields, to work" I went out at sunrise. . . . I live in an egalitarian commune. Before me are distant fields, wide and verdant. And in the middle of this plot, I began to work. This was the day for tomatoes. . . . In the morning I weeded Section A, bent over all the morning hours, destroying the foes of the tomatoes. The tender seedlings need enough nourishment. After the weeding I opened the water. The young seedlings drink their fill and are merry with their bright green color. . . . Working in the garden is not just labor. It is also an ideal and thought and even part of the activity of the world labor movement.[16]

Despite the difficulties of working in the fields, or perhaps precisely because of them, this effort became a symbol of change and of the pioneering, egalitarian outlook of the young women; it is what motivated them to demand their being employed in "masculine" field work. One of the male members of the group explains their motives: "It was the *haverot* themselves who wanted to engage in working in the fields, because in the Diaspora they had been housewives and when they came to Eretz Israel they wanted to make the greatest revolution of their lives. They longed for the field and plain, the trees, the landscape, and the wide open spaces. . . . And in the beginning they did achieve their goal but only for a short time. It so happened that no one wanted to work in the services: sanitation, kitchen, dining hall, laundry, and so on."[17] This explanation informs us of the nature of the relations that coalesced between the men and women in the *hakhsharah:* The men did not mind if the women stepped into the "masculine" jobs, but they were opposed to doing their part in areas defined as "feminine." One of the *haverim* even reported that the dispute over this caused a number of women to leave, because they refused to work in the services.[18] The women's battle was apparently short-lived and ended with the men's victory.

But the young women did not always fight for their right for equal work. At times they simply hoped that they would be made part of it. The process is illustrated in an unpublished essay by Ruth Iliya.[19] This *haverah* tells about taking apart fencing and moving materials out of an army camp located near the kibbutz when the army forces were about to be evacuated from the camp. The narrator saw the *haverim* leaving on tractors and a pick-up with tools in their hands: "I envy them, I said to my friends, why didn't they make us part of it? They don't need the girls, one of them answered. I was heartsick but continued to work." A short while later it became clear that they did need the girls. Apparently by order of the army the evacuation was to be completed by evening, and everyone was called to help with the work. "We were overjoyed," points out the writer, and she describes the joy of labor: "Our hands were scratched, blood flowed, and our faces dripped with sweat. I paid no attention to it," and she sums up: "I will never forget this day, the first day I felt the taste of life in Eretz Israel, the first day we worked outside with the fellows, the first day my friends sensed the responsibility they bore and began to think about their future."[20]

Ruth's closing words reflect the situation that developed in the *hakhsharot* and that also prevailed in the realm of labor in the kibbutz—a gender division of labor between men and women. The "hard" work, the professional, prestigious work with field crops, which was perceived as productive endeavors, efforts that produce a marketable, profitable product, were considered the bailiwick of the men; while the drudgery of the routine, exhausting service jobs—ones the men considered easy—generally were the lot of the women.[21] In the Syrian-Babylonian *hevrat no'ar* (youth community) in kibbutz Bet Oren, the relations between the boys and girls became extremely tense because of this issue. A young women who worked in the clothing supply branch described the situation: "The boys bothered us a lot. They saw [me] sitting on the chair all day and thought I was wasting time, but they did not know how much your back hurts after sitting bent over all day, and how red your eyes get from doing repairs."[22]

The shift to physical labor and to services engendered problems of adjustment particularly for the middle-class girls, since in Iraq they had had little to do with running the household, and the housework usually had been done by the older female family members or maids and servants.[23] Such difficulties are described by Dalya, a *hakhsharah* member in Bet Ha-Shitah: "For the young women the work was harder, and especially for me. No matter where they assigned me I didn't manage to finish a day's work without tempers flaring. In the kitchen I did not know how to wash the floor and the dishes, in the clothing supply shed I was bored from sitting nine hours, in the duck enclosure I had no friends except mother Elkind and the ducks. So they arranged for me to try out in the garden. I was supposed to take the hoe and use it around the cabbage plants. What a sore sight was the row they gave me to do. . . . I finally learned how to hoe, and I liked this work detail . . . the last experiment was the in the laundry. Here I was successful."[24]

Dalya's description reflects the turnabout in the female immigrants' way of life, and set against this background is a picture of the past. Dalya, who had been a teacher in Iraq, remembered longingly: "It was a clear night. I went back to the tent and lay on my pillow. I began to think about what I had to do tomorrow, which classes I would be seeing and what I had to correct and to prepare. I went to the table to take a book and suddenly I drew my hand back: I remembered I was no longer a teacher but just a simple laborer. For a minute I was sad about this change, I thought that then I had been happy: I read a lot, I gave parties, I competed with the others in what I wore, I saw many movies, but the main meaning of life had been missing."[25] It must be noted that the working conditions of the teachers in Iraq were not easy and their salaries were minimal; Dalya's memories, however, were suffused with nostalgia, and we can learn from them mainly about the sharp pangs of adjustment to her new life. In some cases, in response to these adjustment difficulties, the kibbutz refused to place the girls in permanent branches of work, arguing that they did not take the work seriously. This attitude hurt the *haverot* and their motivation.[26] Another difficulty derived from their new social situation, which made it necessary for them to take economic responsibility for themselves: For the first time in their lives the girls had to worry about their livelihood — while in the traditional society, as part of the extended family, their fathers, brothers, or husbands had been responsible for it, and not the women.[27]

So it was that the fight for equality in work constituted the spearhead of the women's struggle for equality in the kibbutz. The way they sought to implement this equality was by conquering the "masculine" type of jobs in their attempt to prove that they had considerable strength even for tasks demanding physical effort. They asked to work in the field and with the field crops, and they considered working in the services, the customary jobs of women in the kibbutz, denigrating.[28] But in the end, the *haverot* of the Iraqi *hakhsharah* achieved no more than the kibbutz women, and they, too, worked in the dairy barn, the vegetable garden, and the chicken coop, but they were found mainly in the services: laundry, clothing supply and repair, kitchen, childcare, and so on.

Social Life

The *hakhsharah* members considered kibbutz society as a lofty cultural model, not only because they had been educated in kibbutz values in the Zionist movement, but also because it symbolized for Eastern immigrants the Western culture that they admired, after having been exposed to it in the modern schools of the Iraqi Jewish community. A member of the *hakhsharah* in Giv'at ha-Sheloshah invoked this concept in an essay printed in the kibbutz newsletter: "To be sure, the physical labor is rather hard, since we have not gotten used to it yet, but the new way of life and *its level of culture* give me the strength to stand firm in the face of all these difficulties."[29] The kibbutz was also aware of this feeling: "The young fellows feel that we are Europeans and they want 'to catch up' to us, to rid themselves of feelings of inferiority."[30]

Yet, despite their education toward life in the kibbutz and their basic willingness to change and adapt and in spite of their preknowledge and preparation for their new life, the immigrants found it difficult to understand the complexity of kibbutz society and to decode the set of internal symbols that molded it. The shift from a closed, hierarchical family structure, in which each member had a set, clear role and standing, to the more open and egalitarian kibbutz framework, whose internal hierarchy was not unequivocal nor obvious, stimulated great admiration along with astonishment and confusion. One of the young women wrote: "In the early days it was hard for me to understand and take in everything. I looked and there was the *mazkir* (chief kibbutz administrator), the physician, the teacher, the laborer—all eating at one table in one dining hall; we were not used to such equality in Iraq. . . . And even more: each member can express his opinion at the general meeting, the young women take part in social life as a complete equal to the young men and other things like these that seemed strange to us."[31] Obviously, the young immigrants wanted to apply the kibbutz way of life to the *hakhsharah* society, including the set of relations between men and women. Moreover, it seems that the immigrants not only wanted to do so but were even asked to do it, by means of the overt and covert messages transmitted to them by kibbutz society through the *madrikhim* and other kibbutz members.

In line with that, the *haverot* of the *hakhsharah* were asked to demonstrate social involvement, to participate actively in the meetings of the *hakhsharah* group, and to volunteer for the various committees alongside the young men. But adjustment to this joint system was difficult, for both the men and the women. The young women found it hard to shed their feelings of inferiority, insecurity, passiveness, and timidity toward initiative in which they had been educated and to adopt assertive patterns of behavior. For most of them, kibbutz life seemed "too free."[32] The boys had difficulty in coping with the girls going beyond their traditional roles and, even so, encouraged them to do so — under the influence of the movement education and the social pressure of the kibbutz, and even the movement's leadership in Iraq.

The changes demanded of these young people affected every aspect of life, including dress, sleeping arrangements, friendship and intimate relations, observing Sabbath and holiday, and more. Implementing them created internal dilemmas. Shortly after they came to the kibbutz, the girls had to replace their clothing, since items had worn out and because the dresses they had brought from Baghdad were unsuitable to their new location.[33] The clothing storehouse offered them blouses, dresses, pants, shorts, and so on, sewn according to the best fashions prevailing in the kibbutz at the time. The shorts troubled and confused the young women who, on the one hand, wanted with all their might to look like kibbutz members, and yet, on the other, were aghast at the extreme abrogation of the rules of modesty in which they had been raised. Naomi, a member of the *hakhsharah* at Gevat, wrote in her diary: "The first second I was taken aback, as if they had dressed me in *sha'atnez* [biblical prohibition against wearing a combination of linen and wool] 'How can I dare show my legs?' I was terribly embarrassed, I asked for a skirt, and only after a long while was I bold enough to wear pants."[34] The reservations of another young woman, Shoshana Murad, were soon shed. The day after she reached the kibbutz she was already wearing shorts. This is how she describes it: "First of all I was embarrassed to leave the room but I made myself do it and went out and no one laughed at me . . . since all the girls were dressed like that and the pants were more comfortable to work in."[35]

In a number of *hakhsharot*, the idea of common sleeping quarters was raised. In Ashdot Ya'akov, a few of the fellows brought up the issue: "We spoke with the young women and young men about arranging to have the men assigned to the same rooms as the women. Many members agreed, so in each room we put two young men and two young women. Some of the women did not agree, so we left them by themselves because we did not want to force them. . . . At first this was hard, hard for young men and for the young women. The members complained, but everything is all right now."[36] From other *hakhsharot*, whose members were younger and had not had any previous Zionist training, came reports of a different set of relations. In the *hakhsharah* at Bet Oren, which was rife with harsh conflicts between the adolescent boys and girls, there were thoughts about dividing the group into two separate ones, but ultimately integration between the sexes was achieved.[37] The case was the same in the Bavli *gar'in* at Ein ha-Horesh; a female kibbutz member who was their counselor tells of the difficulty in incul-

cating them with Zionism and socialism when the system of relations between the sexes had not yet changed, "when it was not yet clear that the
haverot of the *gar'in* who refused (and that was already an achievement) to
clean the boys' rooms did not deserve to be hit, and the girls did not understand that they were allowed to participate actively in the discussions relevant to them."[38] In another example, a *gar'in* member at Sdei Nahum left his
shift because he had been assigned guard duty with a girl.[39]

The issue of sex education also created inner struggles, or as one of the
haverim put it: "Extremely delicate, incisive questions were put."[40] At Ashdot
Ya'akov, a proposal was made to discuss the topic at a general meeting of the
gar'in members, arguing that the fellows were thinking about this issue or that
they did not know anything about how to relate to a young woman or girl-
friend. But the *gar'in* rejected the idea, claiming that the members were not
yet mature enough for a public discussion of this subject and that it was prefer-
able to have a private talk with each of the people grappling with this topic.[41]

The shift from a society in which the norm was complete separation of the
sexes to one in which there prevailed a great deal of sexual involvement was
extreme. It seems that the change among the Bavli members came about in
imitation and obedience to the norm in the kibbutz and not from true self-
awareness, certainly not from organic growth of the idea. Moreover, we can
assume that the relations between the sexes were more intense than the impression given by the newsletter, and even from reports in the *hakhsharah*
journals. In private letters, there are allusions to young men and women who
were expelled from the *hakhsharah* for behavioral problems.[42] We can presume that neither the *madrikhim* nor the group members themselves enjoyed
raising these topics publicly, certainly not in material distributed to the kibbutz members. Even when the issue was raised in the *hakhsharah* newsletters, it was done to demonstrate how the problem had been solved.

An additional problem involved religious observances. Most of the immigrants came from traditional homes where religious customs were observed
but which had a lenient attitude to the weakening of religious observances
among the younger generation. It was accepted that clerks employed in public service worked on the Sabbath, some young people ate nonkosher food
outside the home, and many of them only attended synagogue on holidays.[43]
These secularization processes were not accompanied by opposition in principle to observing tradition and there was no antireligious ideology. In the
Kibbutz ha-Me'uhad settlements, to the contrary, the nonobservance of religion and tradition were an integral part of the fashioning of a secular way of
life and weltanschauung. From the writings of the *hakhsharot* members, and

from talks with them, it turns out that, in general, this issue did not bother them, and they had no complaints about nonkosher food, working on the Sabbath, the lack of a synagogue on the kibbutz, and so on. So, for example, they used the money they earned on the Sabbath to create a common cash pool, and they spent Tisha b'Av dancing and making merry.[44] However, some *hakhsharah* members were distressed by this problem, mainly when they were asked to do something, such as working on the Sabbath; a number of them refused to do it, while others did their duty but were privately tortured by their infraction of religious law.[45] The memoirs of a *haverah* who was asked to cook on the Sabbath tell us: "The decision was very hard, because I tried for as long as I could to not transgress the Sabbath, and here they were forcing me. A decision that it was very hard for me to make my peace with."[46]

The secular, permissive kibbutz lifestyle drew criticism and opposition from the parents of some of the *hakhsharah* girls. These parents, who had immigrated to Eretz Israel in that period, suggested or demanded that the young women join them in the city—anything so they should not continue to live in a framework that shook the foundations of traditional life. Other relatives, too, joined the circle of those applying pressure. The greater the pressure from family members and the more the difficulties and reservations about kibbutz life grew, the greater the dimensions of leaving the kibbutz became. This problem was not directly referred to in the *hakhsharot* newsletters despite its decisive importance for the fate of all the *hakhsharot*. Instead, we find statements by the young women who withstood the temptation and pressure and stayed on kibbutz. So, for example, Tzivyah Nahum went to visit her parents in the city and refused to remain with them: "With heavy heart I got up in the morning and said good-bye to my mother, but not to my father, because I was afraid he would not let me go back to the kibbutz."[47] Shoshana S. headed for Tel Aviv to visit her sister and her cousin who had preferred to live with relatives in the city. Their meeting was full of confrontations, and Shoshana showed great determination: "With my cousin, who did not hold her tongue when trying to influence me to stay with her in the city, I talked harshly. I reviled her as being a hypocrite and a traitor to the cause and to the way we had chosen in common before we immigrated to Eretz Israel and all my speeches to bring her back to the pioneering path and to a life of equality and labor were in vain." Shoshana, too, concluded her visit by secretly leaving the house, without saying good-bye.[48]

From the foregoing, one forms the image of a group of youths who already in Iraq had wanted to cast off many of the traditional customs that they had grown up with. Upon their arrival in Eretz Israel, they were open to assimilating to the cultural, social, and ideological values prevailing in the collective society they wished to join. The first stage of the integration process was characterized by the annulment and cancellation of many of the old values, values of culture and tradition. This is particularly prominent in the status of women, because of the extreme shift from a conservative way of thinking to a socialistic, revolutionary concept.

Most of the written material describing kibbutz life upon which this article is based was produced during the first few months of the young women in the training program, or at the most at the end of a year or a year and a half. Moreover, they written at the request of *madrikhim* who belonged to the kibbutz and under their guidance; they generally reflected the positions expected from the group members. Yet the vast majority of *hakhsharah* members, young men and young women, left within this period or shortly afterwards. After they had gone, few of them continued to write. In the city, they were absorbed as individuals, each one for himself, each one in his own family. Some of them left embittered, others took quitting the kibbutz as a personal failure. None of them explained their motives for leaving, and if they were critical of their life on the kibbutz, they did not express their feelings on paper. They also were not asked to continue to write for the *hakhsharot* newsletters, and apparently did not write elsewhere. If they did, we have not come across the material.[49]

How can one explain the contradiction between their great enthusiasm for kibbutz life and the phenomenon of leaving? Many of the young people left owing to the friction that developed between the *hakhsharot* and the absorbing kibbutz against the backdrop of the nonegalitarian approach the kibbutz applied toward *hakhsharot* members regarding work, studies, and social life.[50] Of note is the fact that this friction was not unique with the Iraqi immigrants and the same complaint was also heard from the *hakhsharot* of European immigrants, who had arrived in Eretz Israel in the same period.[51]

Internal difficulties compounded the causes for leaving. The relatively short period of time the immigrants belonged to the movement in Iraq, and their *aliyah* without training and with insufficient ideological crystallization, together with imbalance between the sexes because of the small number of girls, made it difficult for a pioneering *gar'in* to coalesce in the kibbutz. In addition, the frequent leaving of members and the intaking of new ones did not make social consolidation easy.[52] The *haverim* found it difficult to adjust to the physical labor, communal life, initiative, and responsibility demanded of them, and even to the secular, permissive way of life.

Compounded on top of all that was the influence of cultural differences. Some of the Bavli immigrants felt that the kibbutz members did not understand their mentality and were not relating with a warm and friendly attitude; the kibbutz did not serve as a home for them. Some were insulted by the demand that they speak Hebrew while the kibbutz members spoke Yiddish among themselves in front of the immigrants. Casting a pall over the network of relations were the Ashkenazi veterans' feelings of superiority and the Eastern immigrants' feelings of inferiority, as noted by one of the immigrants: "In the large settlements intimate or social relations are not forged between our members and the kibbutz members, and for the most part they [our members] feel themselves to be strangers, and lower class."[53]

The girls were especially distressed by a feeling of loneliness and alienation, a yearning for the large, protective family they had left in Iraq together with a feeling of strangeness and being cut off in the kibbutz. Their despair was particularly deep, as described in the diary of one of the young women: "I was sad because of the distance from my parents and family. I find myself among strangers, no matter what, and I have not yet been accepted well by the group or by the kibbutz. . . . I was, after all, just an inexperienced girl who had left home for the first time, and with such suddenness I changed my country, way of life, society, and behavior. . . . We were hopeless and did not know what tomorrow would bring. Despite it all, I sometimes took myself in hand and I decided gradually to feel like I belonged to my surroundings. . . . Many were the sighs and the heartache, and I had no one to whom to pour out my anxieties."[54] When this young woman's parents reached Israel, she went to live with them in a ma'barah (temporary settlement transit camp for the mass immigration after 1948) — preferring the familial framework; many years later she continues to wonder if this was the correct choice.

It seems that the willingness to change and accommodate that characterized the initial stage of absorption of the Bavli hakhsharot members in the kibbutz did not persist for the great majority of group members beyond that period. The gap between the cultural, social, and ideological world of the kibbutz and the world of the Zionist immigrants from Iraq could not be bridged.

Conclusion

The story of the Bavli gar'inei hakhsharot in the kibbutzim in the 1940s constitutes a chapter in the attempt of Iraqi immigrants to integrate into Yishuv and Israeli society and in the attempt of that society to assimilate the immigrants and to fashion them in the image of the "new Jews." The model of absorption into the kibbutz was the most absolute, the most demanding of all absorption models in the country, and at times it did not leave the individual any breathing space. Since this model encompassed not only social and national content but also cultural content, its application to immigrants from Muslim countries, despite their fierce desire to accommodate to it, ultimately roused internal opposition to it. What repercussions did the experience of the young women in *hakhsharot* in the kibbutzim have on their national, ethnic, and gender consciousness and identity?

Shortly after their immigration, the Bavli young people discovered that there were other settlement models that coincided with their national approach and still did not oblige them to a revolutionary change in way of life. The city, in which most of the Jewish population in Eretz Israel lived, enabled them to maintain their Zionist-national identity and at the same time to return to an urban way of life, similar to the one they were familiar with from their country of origin.

Moreover, the kibbutz was found to be a closed ethnic unit whose members reacted intolerantly to cultural difference, and the immigrants were required, in both explicit and implicit ways, to integrate into kibbutz society and to be assimilated within it. Of course, the immigrants, too, wanted to integrate with all their heart, but after the first wave of enthusiasm, it became clear to most of them that they were not ready to relinquish their values and customs, and they were not capable of adopting the values of the kibbutz. In the end, they refused to give up their identity. The kibbutz-leaving immigrants went to live in concentrations of oriental population in the cities, the majority in the big city Tel Aviv, especially in and around Shekunat ha-Tikvah. Here they went back to working in fields of commerce and craftsmanship as they had in their country of origin, they kept in touch with their extended families, they observed their religious tradition at one level or another of strictness, they prepared their traditional foods, they spoke in Arabic among themselves, and they listened to the Arab music they liked. All of this diminished the scope and depth of the personal-social revolution demanded of them by socialist Zionism, and they still maintained their national and cultural identity.

As for the gender aspect, we must note that many innovations in kibbutz life attracted the young women: the recognition of their right to equality and their right to decide their own fate, their liberation from the burden of the dowry and forced marriage, the breaking out from the frameworks of the extended family and the reduction of its power to set limits for the family's girls, too. A portion of these young women did develop a deep sense of belonging and obligation to the kibbutz way. And from among them came the founding women of the kibbutzim Be'eri and Neveh-Ur. A few years later, they had to leave the kibbutz, the same as their male colleagues, to help in the absorption of their family members who had arrived in the mass immigration.[55]

But the greater majority of the young women found it difficult to adjust to kibbutz ways and had reservations of one kind or another about abandoning traditional customs, about the free relations between the men and women, about the antireligious attitude, and so on. They felt alienated and estranged from the kibbutz members and the kibbutz way of life; they could not accommodate to it, they did not ask for or want the type of equality accepted in the kibbutz, they did not feel any obligation toward the feminist struggle and they were not prepared to pay the price. They withdrew from the *hakhsharot* within a period of a few days or few weeks to one of a few months. Those who remained in the kibbutz made do with "feminine" jobs and were characterized by passivity in the public-social arena. Sooner or later, they left too.

At the same time, *hakhsharah* membership was a formative period in the fashioning of the gender identity of the young Iraqi female immigrants, those who hastened to leave as well as those who persisted and stayed on the kibbutz. Their experience in a way of life aspiring for equality guided them as they built the next chapter of their lives when they married, for the most part to men from the same ethnic group; and even if they chose to be homemakers and to raise children, as did most Israeli women in the 1950s, many of them did go out to work at that stage or at a later one in their lives, some of them fostered public activity of varying scope, and one of them served as a minister in the Israeli government.

Social Networks of Immigrant Women in the Early 1950s in Israel

Uprooting, immigration, and absorption have been studied and continue to be investigated intensively by sociologists. They have been treated with various types of theoretical emphases. In the 1950s, when sociological research was institutionalized in Israel, the main focus was on integration processes and social uniformity. Little attention was paid to the different, even contrasting roles of those carrying out the absorption and those being absorbed.

The position of women in the absorption processes received scant attention, even though numerically women constituted about 50 percent of all immigrants.[1] Rereading the raw research material and interpreting its results affords some insight into the absorption processes of women.

One of the studies examined during that rereading is the first one dealing with the topic of immigrant absorption, carried out by students of a research seminar in the Sociology Department of the Hebrew University in Jerusalem (in 1950).[2] The students interviewed the first immigrants who settled in the Baqa quarter that had been abandoned by its Arab inhabitants in the wake of the War of Independence.[3] Baqa previously had been an upper-class neighborhood of large homes. However, due to prevailing exigencies, immigrants were packed densely into the neighborhood, at times with several families housed in a single dwelling. The cooking facilities, toilets and bathrooms, halls, living, and dining rooms usually were shared.

Another study was carried out in the Talpiot *ma'abara* (pl. *ma'abarot*; temporary immigrant camps) set up near Baqa in 1957. People in the *ma'abara* were housed in abutting tin huts. Thin dividers inside the hut separated two small rooms, and the edge of the structure served as a cooking corner. The toilets were shared by a number of inhabitants from several huts. A group of cabins in the middle of the *ma'abara* housed public institutions: a clinic, a mother-and-child-health station, a grocery store, an employment office, a social welfare office, branches of political parties, a center for cultural activities, and synagogues. Between the tin huts, *ma'abara* residents set up sheds in which they offered tailoring, shoemaking, diverse utilities, and some grocery products. Between the rows of huts were narrow dirt paths that turned into streams of mud whenever it rained.

The personal journal of a teacher, who documented the experience of working in a neighborhood school at that time, is an additional source of information.

In immigration studies, it has commonly been assumed that women are less exposed to the demands of the absorbing society. Underlying this assumption is the idea that finding a livelihood and providing means for sustenance was entirely — or mostly — the responsibility of the men. Women did continue to function mainly within the family system. Yet, a fresh look at the their daily routine shows that remaining bound to the domestic scene left women with flexibility in arranging the schedule of their working day, and often free time which they used to nurture neighborly relations, visit the various absorption institutions, and build new social connections.

Women's accepted pattern of activity is affiliation through "networks." Network activity is expressed through interactive contacts in which the individual can choose with whom, when, under what circumstances, and for what purposes a person will maintain social connection. A network has no defined borders and can be expanded or contracted according to a change in its goals or needs, and according to the individual's choice. Some networks link members located with a given framework, such as a bureaucratic organization, an extended family, or the like, while others include members from various social frameworks. Networks are distinguished from one another by the nature of the contact, the degree of mutual accessibility among network members, the number of those included, and the frequency of the actual cooperation. Other data such as gender, age, education, profession, and status influence the types of networks' activities.[4]

A fresh look at these studies reveals various numbers of social networks, which assisted in the absorption process of women in Israel in the 1950s: These networks connected neighbors and friends, providers and recipients of services in bureaucratic organizations, and disparate members within the family group.

Neighborhood Networks

The crowded residential patterns contributed greatly to social contacts among inhabitants who shared a hut, a neighborhood, and a *ma'abara*. Privacy was almost nil, and women shared — willingly or not — knowledge, hardships, and suffering and took part in each other's joy and sorrow.

The activity pattern in the female neighbors' network revolved around mutual visits, in pairs or in groups. Neighbors gathered for routine conversations and shared leisure time. These meetings were an important source for passing on information about the absorption authority's services, assistance, and cultural activities.

Through these networks, immigrant women were exposed to the varied ethnic-cultural heritages that they had brought with them from their countries of origin. Newcomers thus encountered a rich, complex socio-cultural mosaic, which did not always lead them on one-way route toward integration into the absorbing society — as shown by one of the interviews:

> I didn't use to go to the *mikveh taharah* (ritualarium), I went there before my wedding, and I went there after I gave birth to my son Abraham. But here some of the neighbors often go to the bathhouse Johanan Ezra near the Market. So I go, too, even if it is not my week [to do so]. . . . My husband is happy and gives me money for the bathhouse. . . . The lady there says that when children come out of the bathhouse, it's like they have the Divine Spirit.

This woman, who did not previously visit the *mikveh*, began to do so because of the influence of her fellow immigrant neighbors. Another example of neighborhood networks was women who took initiative and looked to supplement their housework, mainly as cleaning women in the homes of veteran residents in various Jerusalem neighborhoods. Some worked as seamstresses or hairdressers. They were given these jobs mainly through the help of their female neighbors in the quarter and in the *ma'abara*. To make it possible for them to go out to work, the women were helped by female neighbors — in babysitting, helping with shopping, and in contact with the absorption organizations that operated in the neighborhood and the *ma'abara*. Some women told their husbands little about how much they worked, even to the point of keeping the fact completely secret. As one interviewee put it:

> Mazal brought me to a neighbor of the woman she worked for. I thought I would work there once. I was very frightened. I had never cleaned for some-

one else. I left the baby with Rachel and went with Mazal. I worked hard and the lady was happy. So I went another time. Now I work for her every week. I give Rachel a bit of money. She can't work, she has small children. So now she's the one who watches other children when we go. We go together and we come back together, and we laugh along the way. With some of the money I bought things for the house, and some I leave with the lady to keep for me.

These women who took on part-time work gained economically. To be sure, their income was small, but it gave them a certain degree of independence. Financial help for running the household was likely to influence their standing within the family. Their acknowledged as well as hidden savings gave them a feeling of economic security. As one interviewee said, "Maybe one day I'll buy myself some gold."

In addition, going out to work opened a small window for them through which they could observe the domestic-family way of life of veteran residents — a lifestyle that was usually unknown to other family members, especially to their husbands, fathers, and children.

The information they gained did not necessarily lessen the gap between veterans and immigrants. Even if women were at times exposed to the intimate life of the veterans when they crossed their threshold, they were still serving as maids in the homes of their mistresses. The veteran families dictated the range of social distance and the degree of influence to a great extent. Yet, whatever the women learned by observing and scrutinizing their surroundings, contributed toward their integration.

Women's Networks as Consumers in Bureaucratic Organizations

The "Tipat Halav" health services were intended for treating mothers and children. The examinations and medical care were in the hands of physicians, while nurses were in charge of providing guidance and explanations as well as giving vaccinations and weighing and measuring the infants.

Observations of the meetings between nurses and immigrant mothers reveals a pattern of hierarchic relations, in which many times the superior knowledge and authority of the nurses was demonstrated in relation to the inferiority and neediness of the mothers. Nurses berated the mothers or even punished them by withholding certain rewards if their instructions were not followed, and gave compliments — and sometimes benefits — to obedient women.

The immigrants did not dare to disagree openly with the nurses, but in practice they did not always follow their instructions. To satisfy the nurses, they often demonstrated obedience, since doing what they were told at times earned them certain rewards in kind, such as cans of powdered milk, baby clothes, and other products that were distributed at the health station.

Often, the content of these meetings between mothers and nurses went beyond treatment and guidance. The nurses gave the women advice on educating children and even on spousal relations. It happened that they would tell a woman things like "don't listen to him," or even "divorce him."

The Tipat Halav waiting room served as a meeting place, a kind of club, which the women frequently visited, whether or not they needed advice or medical treatment. This room was heated during the winter, and tea and cookies were served. Occasionally, nurses joined in and sat with the women for a few minutes. These gatherings, accompanied by jokes and laughter, worked to attenuate the authoritative status of the nurses. The formal framework became even more relaxed when a nurse visited in the *ma'abara*. Then the immigrant women would play hostess, offering some delicacies and giving little gifts, usually of their own handiwork. Some women were so bold as to propose traditional medical remedies to the nurses and charms for health and long life.

School Networks

An elementary school was established soon after the immigrants arrived in their neighborhood. The teaching staff exhibited a high degree of volunteerism, and the hours of study were usually longer than allotted for a regular teaching day.

The school left its mark on the neighborhood by mobilizing the pupils for various local activities, such as taking out the garbage, planting a garden, and putting up signs in Hebrew. The school administration and the teachers were in regular contact with the parents and tried to involve them and make them part of different social activities. Festive ceremonies for holidays were opportunities for gatherings of the pupils and their parents. Occasionally, neighborhood residents also joined in.

Primarily the mothers were present in the school: They volunteered to help with various activities, such as maintaining cleanliness and decorating classrooms as well as preparing refreshments for holidays and ceremonies. The mothers gave the teachers small handmade gifts, such as baked goods, scarves, and vests, and sometimes also amulets containing inscriptions and blessings. The teachers visited their pupils' homes in times of joy or sorrow. In some instances, social relations developed between the mothers and the teachers across the defined boundaries between teacher and parent. One teacher wrote in her diary: "The fact that I am single bothers some of the mothers here. But it turns out that even blessings and amulets don't help at this stage. So today Avraham's mother came with a suggestion for a match: a rich merchant from Turkey, who is not so old." The presence of the mothers in the school exposed them to various cultural content and the social substance of the absorbing society. A fringe benefit paid to the mothers for their involvement was the increased attention given to their particular children by the teachers and staff. In practical terms, these mothers also filled the role of auxiliary staff ready to assist the school.

Networks of Mothers and Children

Joining together in the shared spaces of school, neighborhood, and home, mothers and children created exclusive networks of cultural exchange. The mothers absorbed from their children linguistic skills and cultural insights. Owing to their functions outside the home, fathers lacked this same exposure. The children who attended kindergarten and school acquired the Hebrew language within a short time. Hebrew became the common language of discourse between the children, within the family, in the neighborhood, and in the *ma'abara*. Within this context, the language, which served as a cultural mirror of the broader society, penetrated into their parents' culture and way of life. Because of their domestic roles, mothers had more exposure to the worlds their children brought home.

Since mothers were more involved in school life than fathers, a complementary link was forged for them pertaining to activity between these two networks. One example of this is the songs that were learned in school and heard repeatedly at home: A number of mothers became very familiar with these tunes and lyrics.

Still, things did not always go smoothly within these networks. Differences in tradition and culture, varying concepts of discipline and parental honor, preference for the teacher's opinion over that of the parents, and embarrassment over the customs and behavior patterns brought from the countries of origin created difficulties and friction between children and parents. One of the pupils from the *ma'abara* tells that:

> There was tension between what we saw at home and what went on at school. Firstly, the language. Our parents did not know Hebrew. . . . Secondly, the values: What we saw at home was not like what we saw at school, and what we heard at home was not what we heard at school. It wasn't just a generation gap but, in the main, a culture gap. These were two totally different worlds.[5]

Yet, despite the differences in culture and ways of life between themselves and their children and the price paid for the resulting arguments, the mothers still gained from joining the networks that linked them and their children. The fathers were somewhat marginalized, while the mothers were empowered.

Summary

The patterns and routes of immigrant absorption in Israel are not uniform. The difference between land of origin, the variance between types of immigrants, and the period of immigration influence the absorption process and social integration. Differences in the absorption stages are discernible within the same society and even among the same type of immigrant groups. As noted, studies conducted in Israel during the 1950s did not pay sufficient attention to gender differences in the absorption process. A partial explanation of that deficiency may be the reliance upon quantitative and institutional measures as the main characteristics of absorption, with less attention paid to the personal and human factors.

The absorption process of women who are housewives is ostensibly limited, in contrast to husbands, who are integrated into the employment system, and the children, who are integrated into the education system. A housewife draws to a great extent on experiences brought into the home through the mediation of the husband and children. A fresh review of absorption conditions and policy in Israel of the 1950s, however, tells us that the female networks, together with formal absorption institutions, helped women learn about the social and cultural characteristics of their new society. A number of conditions facilitated this absorption.

- For example, the overcrowding in houses, particularly in *ma'abarot* huts, caused physical difficulties, but also contributed to close social contact between inhabitants of the houses and *ma'abarot* dwellers. This connection had two opposing facets: It caused friction on one hand but provided company on the other. The closely packed dwellings served as a pool of resources for women to find female friends and mutual aid as well as for the transmission and receipt of information.

- Additionally, the absorption process in the 1950s was accompanied by the establishment of a comprehensive organizational system that operated in the spheres of welfare, culture, and education. The organizations provided services to the immigrants while at the same time functioning as a means for linking them to the absorbing society. Because of their availability, it often happened that the women were the main consumers of some of these organizations, mainly in the areas of welfare and culture.
- Furthermore, at the beginning of the 1950s, the absorption authorities set up a wide-ranging instructional and educational system aimed in particular at children and youth. The mothers, who were housewives staying close to their children, inadvertently also gained from its fruits.
- Finally, openings in the labor market enabled the women to find part-time work that did not demand professional skills and that matched their housework well.

Homemakers were not usually given the opportunity to become part of formal organizations, which were reserved mainly for men. Yet, it seems that the lack of formal frameworks, and activity in the form of networks, was compatible with the ways that women functioned and contributed toward their absorption. These networks gave women opportunities for choosing and joining social frameworks that were more flexible both with regard to the amounts of time available to them and to their lifestyle.

Place, time, range of activity, and points of emphasis distinguished the networks within the absorption system from one another. Yet, more than once, activity in one framework actually complemented activity in another. Contents stressed in one network were emphasized in another. Retroactive analysis of the networks prohibits a detailed scrutiny of all its structural components. Still, it is clear that the authoritative structure is one of the differentiating marks between the networks and influences of its framework of activity. Networks of women neighbors were built on equality and based on friendship and mutual aid. In the bureaucratic networks, authority and decision-making were in the hands of the service providers, while in the network that linked mothers and children, the ultimate authority was that of the mothers.

The different authoritative structure in each of the networks allowed for different ways of learning and integration. An egalitarian system provides more possibilities for expanding contacts and content. In the bureaucratic networks, authority resides in those responsible for providing the service.

Those who act in accordance with the norms of the organization, and those in need of the organization's services must adjust to these norms and rules of behavior. Despite the flexibility that characterizes activity within the frame of networks, the style of activity in the bureaucratic networks leaves little room to maneuver. The main reward in that type of network is in the benefits the service provides. At times, when the activity pattern exceeds the formal definition of its role, the network members gain additional benefit. In authoritative networks such as that of mother and children, the authority holder can determine the activity pattern of the network. Since it is not bound to organizational authority, she can set the time for activity and its content.

A re-reading of these studies uncovers three types of networks that enriched the women's ability to learn and act in the course of absorption — each network according to its method of operation and the position of the woman-mother within it. Equality, acceptance of discipline, and the status of authority influenced the limits of operation of each network, its scope, and the spheres of its activity. Even with the lack of detailed knowledge about each of the networks, the information elicited from the research material on the manner of their activity helps fill in the picture of the absorption of women immigrants in Israel in the 1950s.

The pattern of absorption is difficult to gauge, because the accepted methods of measurement used as social quantitative measures (place of employment, wages, class mobility, etc.) apply to men but not to women. Those measures are also used to determine family status and the social evaluation of a family's successful absorption.

Analysis of the material cited here highlights a special method of the absorption of housewives, who continue to fill the traditional roles to which they were accustomed in their country of origin. Despite what seemed to be limiting conditions, a small window was opened for women's social and cultural absorption into the Israeli society, namely, by means of the networks described. Further investigation of the integration of these women into society requires an examination of quantitative statistical data, which consistently reveal a striking difference in employment and income between men and women. Beyond the quantitative measures, one may add other measures discussed here, even though they are not necessarily quantitative. One may conclude that the ways that women were integrated in the 1950s possibly alleviated somewhat the absorption difficulties, both for them and their families. Yet, it is difficult to discern just where these absorption paths led. Still, it may well be that the children of the immigrant women of the 1950s reaped the fruits and social benefits of these networks.

Pioneers and Defenders

A "Woman-Human"

A. D. Gordon's Approach to Women's Equality and His Influence on Second Aliyah Feminists

Until the appearance of contemporary Jewish-feminist thought, there was one Jewish philosopher for whom the feminine image was central in his perception of Divinity; it was from this image that his perception of ethics and religion derived. This thinker was A. D. Gordon (1856–1922), one of the first leaders of the Second Aliyah and the kibbutz movement.[1] This article focuses solely on the practical ramifications of a theological worldview: Gordon's social and political perception of women's status in society and in the family and the extent of Gordon's influence on the spiritual world of Second Aliyah women and on their political perception, particularly on that of the women's laborers' movement leaders, such as Rachel Katznelson and Ada Maimon.

Ideological Positions

Gordon's statements on "personality and family closeness" that appeared in the article "Foundations for the Regulations of the Moshav Ovedim," published in 1921 — a few months before his death — illustrate the degree of nebulousness and complexity of his thought on the issue of equality between men and women:

> The entire structure of her soul, like the entire structure of her body and its shape, as well as her role in nature, situate the women's personality as one of the primary components in the creation of the family and the next generation. . . . In this respect the woman's power is much greater than the

man's, since she is the one who carries the baby, gives birth, and suffers through the process of the offspring's formation and raising the child, she is a mother. This is her most supreme freedom and right. However, she has not yet achieved it and, therefore, has not yet found herself. Until today she was, and still is, the man's disciple. She regards man's life as a symbol and a model for her own rights, and she values her rights so long as they resemble the man's, so long as they allow her participation in man's public life. In this attitude one can see to a certain degree the spirit of our time, the wish to instill the spirit of public life into family life instead of introducing the spirit of the family into public life. Nevertheless, in order for the woman to liberate herself from man's tutelage, so that she may know these things for herself from life, from her own experience and failures, one must not deprive her of her complete freedom and right to participate in all aspects of life, private and public.[2]

A similar argument, on the importance of stressing feminine uniqueness in the feminist message, is cited today by many feminists such as Gilligan, Noddings, Irigaray, Kristeva, and others. But Gordon, in contrast to today's feminists, does not indicate how women should be involved in public life after attaining self-awareness.

Apparently, Gordon was the first to recognize the obscurity and complexity regarding the subject in the article itself, which appeared in *Ha-Po'el ha-Tza'ir* in November 1921, while Gordon was in Vienna for treatment for cancer. His correspondence with his daughter, Yael Gordon, at that time attests to his doubts and perhaps even to second thoughts about the article's contents, from the minute the issue reached him. His article appeared, apparently inadvertently on the part of the editor, alongside the piece by Ada Fishman (Maimon), "On the Question of the Woman Laborer." Fishman complained in her article of the sweeping discrimination against women among the laborers in Eretz Israel. She cast historical blame for the discrimination between men and women on the women for not participating in earning a living. She summed up her thoughts as follows: "All of us clearly see (we believe in it) that the fulfillment of our ambition to create a working society without exploiters or exploited can only become possible if the daughters like the sons, the men like the women, will bear the yoke of labor and life to the fullest extent."[3] In a letter to Yael that Gordon sent from Vienna, he wrote that "the remarks in Ada's article are essentially just and her claims are legitimate in the main, in light of today's situation, yet I allow myself to think that a woman who is her own student would express things in a different spirit, with different emphasis, and her demands, too, would then take a different form and tone, and for the sake of unity — perhaps also a different nature."[4]

Gordon's criticism of Fishman's concept of equality involved the passage in the message calling for "instilling the spirit of public life into the family." As Gordon had said, he aspired to instill the spirit of the family into public life. This line of thought came from his overall thinking, which attacks human cognitive and behavioral processes that had resulted in such great alienation between man and his community and between man and himself. In this sense, Gordon saw in the spirit of family closeness hope for the human race, and in the woman, a facilitator and promoter of this spirit. But, he felt that only the women themselves should determine and decide their own fate; society and its institutions have no place in setting limits on them.

This approach led Gordon to support women's suffrage and to attack — in his article "After the Quake" (1920) — the Orthodox groups in the *Yishuv* that in the name of "holiness" intend "to negate human rights from the woman."[5] In the same article, he mentions Deborah the prophetess who was a judge among Israel, and he calls upon the *haredim* (by this term he means all Orthodox Jews) to influence the Israeli national spirit so that it would raise women like her on whom they could also rely. This owing to the fact that they would "not become defective in any way, not in modesty and not in supreme holiness, whether they will not participate or whether they will participate in assemblies with men." Despite Gordon's unequivocal stance compelling the granting of human rights, including suffrage, to the woman, in this article, too, he falls into the trap of ambivalence. He does not realize that it is impossible to bridge the tremendous gap between his basically egalitarian stances and the unequal, stratified perception of mankind in Jewish Law — as perpetuated by Orthodoxy. This unsuccesful attempt to bridge the gap also completely ignores the reservation in the Talmud (Megillah 14b) regarding the overly assertive figure of Deborah the prophetess that is expressed in the Rav Nahman's statement: "Haughtiness does not befit women. There were two haughty women, and their names are hateful, one being called a hornet [Deborah] and the other a weasel." The Talmud grants the title prophetess to women such as Abigail, wife of King David, because of his seduction and faith in the political future of her future husband, but when it turns to discussing women such as Deborah and Huldah who functioned and led the nation as prophetesses, it expresses overt reservations and finds it difficult to accept the fact that they were public leaders. An additional problem that arises from Gordon's plea to the Orthodox to develop women such as Deborah, in his terms, is the nuance of doubt one gleans from these statements concerning the greatness of the leadership of his soul mates the *halutzot* — labor leaders.

The Biographical Aspect — Family Life

Regarding every aspect of Gordon's connections to the women of the Second Aliyah, the term "soul mate" is not a metaphor. At the same time, we should first say something about Gordon's connections with the women in his family. Aharon David Gordon was his parents' sole remaining son, after his four siblings died in childhood. According to the testimony of his friend Yosef Aharonowitz, Deborah Gordon, Aharon David's mother, was a wise, educated woman whom "distinguished people would consult for advice."[6] His closeness to his mother intensified, apparently, owing to the intellectual tension with his father; his daughter, Yael Gordon, explains in a letter to Yosef Aharonowitz that her grandfather, Uri Gordon,

> was not an unrelenting zealot but if, in his presence, someone should transgress one of the mildest commandments, he never held his peace. Sometimes his arguments with his son were very deep and tempestuous when the son [A. D. Gordon] would air his idea that it would be better to annul certain commandments for obvious reasons. At such moments A. D.'s mother would be on guard and trembling from tip to toe with agitation, she would beg them to stop.[7]

Even though A. D. Gordon had observed the commandments when in the Diaspora (in Eretz Israel, too, he kept the Sabbath), he gradually left the rigid Orthodox framework. Gordon was involved in arranging for "modernized" schools and "he was the first," according to Aharonowitz, "to try to place girls' education on a par with the boys'." He taught his daughter Hebrew and Jewish subjects, no differently than he taught his son. Later, Gordon helped Yael, who was a Hebrew teacher, to establish a girls' school in Haschavato, the town where they lived. The foregoing indicates his gradual taking exception to Orthodox Jewish law while he was still an observant Jew.

We know little about Gordon's wife. Surprisingly, she receives scant mention in their daughter Yael's memoirs. Feygle Tartakov-Gordon was Gordon's paternal cousin. From the age of fifteen, while a yeshiva student, he lived in her hasidic father's home, in the town of Obodovka. He became engaged to Feygle and they married about three years later. The couple had seven children, of whom two survived, the daughter Yael and the son Yehiel Michal. In the early years of their marriage, the Gordons lived near the bride's parents, but Gordon's serious controversies over religious issues with his uncle, who was also his father-in-law, prompted the couple to move to the Mohilna farm where Gordon's parents lived.[8]

In a tragic way, Feygle Tartakov-Gordon played a decisive role in her husband's decision to immigrate to Eretz Israel. According to Yael's testimony, after the sale of the farm that was owned by Baron Ginzburg (a relative of Gordon's), the family was forced to return to Obodovka, near the family of Feygle.[9] Gordon, who had kept the accounts for the farm, became unemployed. In the memoirs that Yael Gordon wrote in 1947 (and which have never been published in their entirety), she notes that Gordon first planned to emigrate to America, "but Mother tipped the scales by announcing that she did not agree to go to America but only to Eretz Israel."[10] The fact that Feygle came down on the side of Eretz Israel is very interesting and diminishes somewhat the myth of the elderly pioneer who left everything for his *aliyah* to Eretz Israel. Yet, she was a tragic figure, as we have said, since Feygle Tartakov-Gordon paid for this decision with her life. Gordon preceded the rest of his family by immigrating to Eretz Israel in 1904. Some four years later, he was joined by Yael, and about a year after that Feygle arrived. The son Yehiel Michal stayed behind to continue studying in the Obodovka yeshivah (and eventually died in a typhoid epidemic). The united family almost settled in En Gannim, but only four months later, the mother died of a serious disease not described in anyone's memoirs. Feygle Tartakov-Gordon was buried in the old cemetery in Petah Tikva. As far as we know, Gordon had no intimate relations with any other woman following her death.

The closest person to Gordon in the last twenty years of his life was his daughter Yael; she had been a partner in his educational projects in the Diaspora, in Zionism, in his pioneering, and in his intellectual world, sometimes as the first reader of his writings. In his book *Ha-Yahid*, E. Schweid determined that Yael "sacrificed much of her private life for him. And she also loved and admired him all her life. But truth be told: she was not capable of taking part in his spiritual life, and the demands he made upon her by his very closeness to her were more than she could endure."[11] The indirect evidence provided by Chaya Rutenberg about her talk with Yael Gordon, around 1915, when she worked for Hannah Maisel at Kinneret, indicates that Yael apparently gave up marriage to a man who did not to go on *aliyah* to Eretz Israel because of Gordon's reservations about the match.[12] Yet, in all of Yael's writings there is no evidence that Gordon's closeness to her and his

demands upon her were beyond her endurance. On the contrary, in her letters to him she complained of great loneliness and the lack of ongoing connection with him, and she asked that he write to her more often: "You well
understand how much I need your letters."[13] Her statements to the First
Women Laborers' Convention reflect, on the one hand, the infusion of her
father's expressions and ideas, while on the other, the unequivocal egalitarian aspect she gave to those expressions that her father had coined but had
refrained from making crystal clear:

> We are aspiring to the equality of the woman and to her liberation, which will
> give her the opportunity to fill her roles as both mother and a human beneficial
> to society. And for this we must aspire especially in our young society that is form-
> ing in Eretz Israel through the desire of the nation to maintain its self-concept
> while preserving its "ego" through labor and creativity. The young Hebrew
> women who come here, beside coming to play their national role as daughters
> of our people, want to find themselves here, the "self of the woman-human" for
> which there is no more fitting place in the world to find in it the root of its soul
> and to uncover [it] than in the workers' corner in our land.[14]

The expressions "mother and human," "labor and creativity," and "woman-
human" are all Gordonian concepts that were given feminist meanings in
the words of Yael Gordon. Yet undoubtedly here, too, as in every web of family relations, there was great pain in the father-daughter relationship. Anyone
reading between the lines discerns that in the letters from Gordon to her and
about her one sees a great deal of insensitivity and lack of appreciation of her.
Even in the letter that he wrote in Vienna, with his response to Ada Fishman
(Maimon)'s statements, he demonstrates callousness by saying that a women
is first of all the one who carries the baby and gives birth. Even if motherhood in Gordon's writings is a broad philosophical issue, his very writing
these things to Yael, who never married or gave birth, shows great emotional
insensitivity. She, of course, chose to ignore these nuances of meaning. In
another letter from Gordon, sent from a convalescent home in Safed about
a year earlier, he reveals callousness to his daughter's sensitivities: In the
letter, he quotes what Yael wrote in her letter about "the beauty and blessing
of labor." Instead of praising her feeling or at least ignoring what she wrote if
he found it offensive, Gordon exposed his criticism of her statements in his
public letter to Deganyah: "the beauty and blessing in labor and the harmony among workers are very delicate flowers to which every unnecessary
touch is difficult, for which the coating of words does not always fit."[15]

At the same time, we cannot know why Yael Gordon never married. We may suppose that her fate was similar to that of other Second Aliyah women whose aspirations for equality and agricultural work along with their ideological commitment prevented them from linking up with a spouse, by choice or by necessity. From her letters, we see that she lacked self-confidence, and we may presume this was also expressed in her relations with men. In her letter from Migdal (12 Heshvan 5644 [1913]), she repeatedly complains that she does not have faith in her own abilities.[16] Gordon's letters echo the pain of loneliness that his daughter and some of her friends bore. Scrutiny of their loneliness leads him to ponder the need to change family structure, as part of the yearned-for utopian vision. In his article *"Mitokh Keri'ah"* (From Reading; 1915), he writes: "One of the factors detrimental to the lives of the young [male] laborers is certainly the lack of family life . . . to what extent their remaining bachelors until their hair turns white, brings a blessing to the lives of others, let others judge . . . if there is not some wisdom here — there old age here! Old age in youth . . .[17] Owing to his perception of the heterosexual family as the foundation of human and social life, Gordon could not conceive of the possibility of choosing a life of singleness, for it may have been that some of the unmarried women among whom he lived preferred it. We may assume that a part of them did want to marry and raise a family but had not found the right man. The bulk of Gordon's anger was directed toward his male colleagues, Haskalah writers and their secular-Zionist admirers, in whose statements blaming Jewish tradition for being solely responsible for the discrimination against women, he saw more than a pinch of hypocrisy. "Without family life," he thought, "a nation will not be built." Yet he still admitted that family life, like various aspects of human life in modern times, requires change: "A young man can only see life with the woman he loves and with the entire world, which this life opens for him and instills in his heart. But if new life is sought, then also family life must take on new shape and new character. That is, relations between the man and the woman that are greatly natural."[18]

Biographical Testimony — Gordon's Connections with Pioneering Women

As he saw his readers, they were a public of brothers and sisters.[19] Even in his article on the revival of Hebrew, Gordon stressed the fact that the women had led the language revolution by speaking more Hebrew than the men.[20]

He supported the idea of establishing a Hebrew university (1913) as a solution to the problem of assimilation, and he wrote about its designation as an institution for education of young men and women as obvious; and when writing about the problem of unemployment among the Second Aliyah immigrants, he asks: "Are we not obliged to make sure that each young man and woman who come to Eretz Israel to work, will find work and an environment for a life of labor?"[21]

Evidence of this emotional-ethical stand appears repeatedly as a thread running through the memoirs of the *halutzot* of the Second Aliyah. Tehiya Lieberzohn remembered that Gordon supported her when she persisted in demanding that she be allowed to engage in agricultural work.[22] Hannah Chizik described him reading chapters of the bible to the women while they worked late into the night in the kitchen.[23] The most colorful depiction appears in the words of Eva Tabenkin, reflecting A. D. Gordon's view of the daily life of the *halutzim*, his unique dynamics with them in general and with the women among them in particular:

> What was Gordon for us? . . . For each one who went right from school to this Kinneret, scorching in the *hamsins* (severely hot days), stinging with its mosquitoes on its enchanted evenings, to the harsh conditions next to the bread oven in the deep of the night, to the laundry boiler that blinds your eyes with its non-stop steam of stinging nettles, when Gordon would do laundry with us or bring a lantern to the oven to give us light — then everything turned into an important imperative of life, and confidence that your life is full of meaning, that your strength will be enough, that you, too, are — one arm "in the effort of a thousand arms."[24]

From this we learn not only of Gordon's spiritual strength in his attitude toward the groups among whom he stayed, but also of his working together with the women in the routine maintenance jobs in the kevutzot: in the laundry, the kitchen, next to the oven, and so on.

In light of the foregoing, it is not surprising that at the founding assembly of the Women's Labor Movement at Kinneret, held around the same time as the convention of Galilee Workers in 1915, Gordon was one of four men invited to it (in principle, the gathering was closed to men), with Joseph Busel of Deganyah, Eliezer Yaffe, and Benzion Israeli of Kinneret. The four male invitees were selected on the basis of their sympathy for the women's struggle for equality, or "from among the sympathizers with the woman worker from the beginning" as Benzion Israeli put it in his memoirs (incidentally, he does not mention that he was among those invited to take part); Joseph Busel and his wife Hayyuta were known for their egalitarian marriage.[25] In contrast, there certainly were some men who were disappointed at not having been invited to the assembly, such as Berl Katznelson.[26] Since there are no minutes of this women worker's gathering, we are forced to make do with the testimony of two of the organizers about A. D. Gordon's remarks at it: Rachel Katznelson-Shazar and Ada Fishman-Maimon, who later described his speech in totally different ways. In her essay, Rachel Katznelson expressed her disappointment from his remarks: "This time I saw Gordon in all in his intellectualism and his distancing himself from life. I entered the room and heard his voice. This time his voice was an old one. When Gordon speaks from the heart—his voice is young."[27] Her words corroborate the vagueness and internal tension in Gordon's position on the status of women as expressed in his writings. If, as we may assume, Gordon lectured on his philosophical and religious attitudes and the connection between them and the issue of femininity and family closeness, then it is no wonder that women, who were daily struggling for equality at work and for a reasonable attitude from contemptuous comrades, left disappointed from the lack of practicality in his speech.

Ironically, it was precisely Ada Fishman-Maimon who wrote positively, in her book *Tenu'at ha-Po'alot be-Eretz Israel* (The Women Laborers' Movement in Eretz Israel), about Gordon's appearance before the convention attendees. She describes the same speech to the gathering as follows: "Among those taking part in the convention was A. D. Gordon. In his remarks he asked to reinforce the faith in the heart of the woman worker. Even if now, they do not find enough understanding on the part of their [male] comrades in considering the importance of the woman laborer at work and in society, this understanding, even if it takes time, will surely come."[28] These statements, too, coincide with what we know about Gordon. The essence of his support for all the spiritual, class, and national political struggles was always emotional and personal; expressing emotional support for the women who had gathered sounds natural and apt for the essence of his relations with his [female] friends.

It was Gordon's fate, as perhaps it is for any decent thinker, to be interpreted in contrasting ways. The interesting thing in these testimonies, and particularly in Fishman-Maimon's, is precisely in the way she incorporated Gordon into her egalitarian-Jewish world view—as the daughter of a rabbi, a person well-versed in Jewish law and lore, an upholder of Jewish tradition, and an incontrovertible feminist-socialist all her life. In response to an article besmirching her in the Orthodox daily newspaper *Hatzofe* (31 May 1953), when she was a Knesset member—an article that attacked the fact that she herself had carried a Torah scroll at the ceremony for bringing Torah scrolls into the synagogue at the agricultural school that she had founded, Ayanot—Fishman-Maimon wrote the following:

> I admit that I well understand the bitterness of the author of the article. It has finally become known in our country that Hapoel Hamizrachi and its followers do not have a monopoly on observing Jewish tradition, and that there are institutions and individuals in the Histadrut who actually know how to revere the traditions of their forefathers. And yet [why didn't the writer of the article quote] also the last rows of my article that point out that in Ayanot "prevails the spirit of the late Rabbi Kook and the late A. D. Gordon?"[29]

She goes on to quote the sixteenth-century code of Rabbi Karo, Shulkan Arukh, Sabbath Laws, chapter 282, section 3, that "all go up to be one of the readers of the Torah Portion including a woman or a minor," and she argues: "And if it is permitted according to the Shulkhan Arukh to be one of the readers of the Torah Portion, is it not fitting that she should also have the honor to carry a Torah scroll and to be appointed a *dayyenet* or judge in the rabbinic courts to insure protection for women in issues of marriage and divorce? And are we not obligated at all to educate our children in this spirit of acknowledging equality, for all of us are created in the image [of God]."[30]

Fishman-Maimon's statements are fascinating in themselves for the way she integrates her interpretation of Jewish law in her confrontations with the Orthodox establishment and for addressing the general public in Israel. For our purposes, it is important to see that she saw herself as continuing the way of Rabbi Kook and A. D. Gordon in her methods of interpretation, in her political struggle, and in the egalitarian-Jewish education to which she dedicated her life. Of course, it is doubtful whether Ada Fishman-Maimon was a successor to of Rabbi Kook, whose attitude toward Jewish law was essentially uncompromisingly Orthodox in its unequal approach toward women; but her choice of A. D. Gordon was correct; and this is on the basis of a close reading of Gordon and his non-Orthodox attitude to religion and Jewish law and his anti-hierachical thought. Yet, in contrast to Gordon, Fishman-Maimon strove in her speeches (especially in the Knesset) and in her educational and political activity to adapt Judaism and Jewish Law to a contemporary reality of equality between men and women, since she understood that the confrontation with Jewish heritage was linked to the issue of the woman in Eretz Israel no less than occupational struggles.

Gordon hoped that the Orthodox "would pour some of their national spirit" over the nation by putting women in positions of leadership and that this step would promote justice among the Jewish people. Like him, Fishman-Maimon argued (in her Knesset speech on 21 May 1952) that "I do not come to oppose the Rabbinic Office or the Rabbinic Law Courts. I am not at all certain that a secular court would be more just."[31] To correct the injustice of discrimination against women in Jewish law, she suggested appointing *dayyanot* — judges to the Rabbinic courts — basing herself on the precedents of Deborah the prophetess and the Talmudic stories about Beruriah the wife of Rabbi Meir, for example. Obviously, in theory these ideas are correct, just as theoretically the world of Orthodox Jewish law could take the lead in everything related to equality between women and men, as Gordon had expected. But even in their own time, the women workers had spoken for themselves and in contrast to the optimistic basic premises of both Gordon and Fishman-Maimon.

※ *Henry Near*

What Troubled Them?

Women in Kibbutz and Moshav *in the Mandatory Period*

This study is based primarily on articles written by women members of kibbutzim and *moshevei ovedim* in their movements' periodicals from 1919 onwards. Though not an exhaustive study of the status and feelings of these women, it sheds much light on the concerns and attitudes of the active, literate elite and gives a detailed picture of developments in this, the formative period of the kibbutz movement.

The Kibbutz

The Period of Silence

The periodicals of the kibbutz movements appeared continuously from 1921 onwards. Of almost fifteen hundred articles published between 1921 and 1929, there were only eight on "the question of the woman" [*ba'ayat ha-havera*], three of them by men; and, indeed very few written by women at all — mainly on such matters such as "children and parents" and "the pregnant woman's diet." Only beginning in 1930 was the matter discussed relatively intensely.

In 1936, thirteen years after the foundation of Beit Alpha, the first settlement of the Kibbutz Artzi movement, Meir Ya'ari, the unchallenged leader of the movement, said: "At long last our women are beginning to speak. They have begun to express their bitterness, their aspirations and their efforts. . . . 50% of the members of the Kibbutz Artzi are women, and they have been thrust into a corner."[1] The causes of this silence can be seen best from a broader perspective.

Utopia, Post-Utopia and Gender Equality

Like every intentional society, the kibbutz was a utopian community: It claimed to be the embodiment of a vision shared by a group of people, crystallized well before they reached Palestine, under the influence of the ideology of the pioneering youth movements, fragments of information about the Zionist settlements, and the thoughts and emotions of idealistic youngsters at a formative stage in their lives. This society would be free of discrimination of any sort, including gender discrimination.

Feminist attitudes were part of the mindset of male and female leaders of the labor movement. The work of the liberal and socialist feminists, Russian feminist literature, and other works found their way to the youth movements through many channels. In this literature, the concept of "sexual equality" had four distinct aspects: political equality — women's right to vote and be elected; economic and personal equality — liberation from economic dependence on the husband; equality of occupation — women's right to choose their professions and advance in them according to their talents; and sexual liberation — freedom of speech and action in sexual relationships. The concept of a society in which all these aims would be realized was translated into practical terms in the ideal of the *halutza* (pioneer woman).

> The ideal was the woman who took part shoulder to shoulder with the man in the hardest tasks, created new branches of work, rode a horse, danced, took life by storm. . . . For them, work was a sacred obligation. However bad they felt, unless they had a fever they would go on working to the limits of their strength.[2]

In other words, they strove to be like the male pioneers. Such women fitted well into the early kibbutz, which claimed to be based on equality between men and women. And, indeed, in many respects this claim was not far from the truth. Women's right to participate in general meetings, to speak and to vote, was self-evident from the very beginnings of the kibbutz; from 1920 onwards, women were full members of the kibbutz and did not depend on the men for their living; from the time when Miriam Baratz "conquered the cowshed" by milking the cows without help from a man, women's right to participate in the "conquest of labor" was recognized as legitimate and was often a major factor in the economic planning of the settlement.

With the creation of the communal educational system, the kibbutz came close to the ideal of the family in a socialist society as conceived by Bebel, Engels, and others: couples were united by love alone, while the traditional functions of the woman — child care, laundry, and cooking — were executed by the communal system.

This was exceptional not only in the *Yishuv*, but in the world. The struggle for women's suffrage was not successful in Europe or the *Yishuv* until the mid-twenties, and the woman in town, *moshava*, and *moshav* was entirely dependent on her husband for her livelihood.

Thus, the kibbutz was an egalitarian society par excellence, particularly in comparison with others with which its members were familiar. This is one explanation for the women's silence. The post-utopian syndrome — the belief that current reality matches the original ideal — combined with real and comparative achievements to blunt the critical faculty and stifle protest.

This phenomenon was repeated in every generation. In the early 1940s, Lilia Bassevitz, one of the leading fighters for gender equality in the kibbutz movement, wrote of a meeting with a young woman who expressed feelings similar to her own. "I was so glad that you, the younger generation of kibbutz women, had arrived at the same conclusions as we, the veterans. But I was sorry that you did so only after a long struggle, and much inner turmoil."[3] Apparently Bassevitz did not understand, or did not sufficiently appreciate, a fact that every youth movement graduate knows: In every generation there came to Palestine, and in particular to the kibbutz, young women steeped in a utopian outlook, which they shook off with difficulty, as the result of a process of long, frequently painful, personal experience.

Disillusion and Progress

However, many women were dissatisfied with their lot, and from 1930 onwards their problems were often discussed in the kibbutz periodicals. Their grievances included the small proportion of women in agricultural work, technical underdevelopment of the "services" (kitchen, clothing store), the "insulting" distinction between productive and nonproductive work, and the low level of women's participation in general meetings and administrative positions. Sometimes criticism was voiced in virtually identical terms in articles that appeared fifteen years apart; things changed very slowly, if at all.[4]

Nonetheless, in certain respects the criticism did have some effect. For seven years, from 1935 to 1942, the proportion of women in agriculture increased, reaching almost 40 percent in the early 1940s. "The rule of the third," which laid down that at least a third of each committee be women, was adopted by the kibbutz movements early in the 1930s, and thereafter by the Histadrut. And during the Arab Revolt (1936–1939), women did guard duty side by side with the men.[5] But progress was often followed by a relapse: For instance, after more than a decade of progress in the sphere of occupational equality, Hayuta Bussel said in 1947: "Poultry, dairy, and market-gardening have been taken out of [the women's] hands."[6] At the end of the Mandatory period, the small proportion of women in agriculture was an established fact, and many concluded that it was unavoidable.

It appears that the question of formal political equality did not trouble many women, and it was not mentioned in the literature of the period. The original ideal, that the woman should be as like the man as possible — particularly in the work sphere — still held good. During the 1920s and 1930s, it was reinforced by the influence of educational activities and publications in the youth movements, which tended to emphasize the pioneering ideal rather than the realities of the kibbutz. An outstanding example is the book *Haverot ba-Kibbutz*, first published in 1945 and reprinted twice in the following five years.[7] The first section is a hymn of praise to the women of the Second Aliyah, who pioneered the way to the conquest of labor by women. The rest of the book is devoted to short sections describing life in the kibbutz. Of these forty-five short chapters, thirty-five describe work in agriculture, handicrafts, and the like, and only ten are devoted to the types of work in which most women were engaged. It is small wonder that young women whose education in the youth movement was based on so slanted a viewpoint found it difficult to adapt to the very different reality.

The Second Wave

Whether because of the gap between ideal and reality, or whether because of innate social and psychological processes, other voices were also beginning to be heard. Foremost was opposition to any approach that required women to ignore their special characteristics and imitate men.

To an extent, this approach had always been part of the praxis of the kibbutzim: The "machaism" sometimes to be seen in feminist literature — the contention that women's physical strength is no less than men's — is very seldom to be found in the kibbutz.[8] But the belief that women have, and should have, special characteristics and needs only began to be expressed explicitly toward the end of the thirties.

At the end of 1946, after twenty years of feminist activity, Lilia Bassevitz published a comprehensive article entitled "The Woman in the Kibbutz."[9] The first section, based on a lecture to a non-kibbutz audience, was a song of praise to kibbutz women on their achievements in creating "a reality *different* from that of our mothers and grandmothers." There were, she said, many contradictions in the kibbutz woman's life — for instance, between family life and public activity — but "we know well that through these contradictions we can become whole."[10] Bassevitz enumerated with pride the achievements of the kibbutz woman not only in the conquest of [physical] work but, even more, in "feminine" activities: culture and hygiene, education and child care, "the creation of the national cuisine," and more.

Bassevitz presented these achievements as accomplishments of the woman and kibbutz society in concert. But in the second half of the article, originally presented to a kibbutz audience, she emphasized the price that the woman was forced to pay for these achievements. The woman in the kibbutz

> Is not simply *tired* at the end of her day's work: she is *exhausted*. . . . She is left with little strength, energy and wakefulness to devote to her children, to reading, to voluntary activities. . . . [Moreover], cleaning the room, individual laundry, knitting . . . turn her day of rest into a working day, and add several hours to her working day, especially when her children are young.[11]

This is a significant change from the ideological attitude that Bassevitz herself had formerly accepted wholeheartedly. "Feminine" occupations are no longer incidental or unavoidable additions to the main business of the kibbutz: They are a legitimate and praiseworthy part of kibbutz life, and they should be recognized as part of the labor system. Bassevitz suggested ways of lightening women's burden, but did not go as far as others, who already at this date suggested shortening the women's working day; it was only in the mid-1960s that this idea was adopted by all the kibbutz movements, though not without a struggle.

In Bassevitz's words, women in the kibbutz "create, dream, and struggle." But she now believed that they struggle, not by the side of the men, but against them; and their dreams differed radically in the mid-1940s from those almost universally accepted fifteen years earlier. Others added an ideological note:

> [In many cases] the personality of a women aged between 30 and 40 loses its focus: she does not dare to be a woman, to make the most of her mature femininity. . . . To ignore the fundamental laws of nature leads to the obstruc-

tion of the development of the most vital natural forces, and brings about exhaustion, stagnation, and depression.[12]

"The laws of nature," not always clearly defined, were often invoked in this context. They included the maternal and familial instincts, and the desire for cleanliness, orderliness, and beauty. Recognition of their existence was one of the characteristics of what may be called the second, post-utopian, wave of kibbutz feminism.

The reasons for this development were many and varied. It sprang primarily from the personal experience of veteran kibbutz women. But later waves of immigration, particularly from the German youth movements, brought with them different cultural concepts. They were also influenced by the state of the world feminist movement, now in decline after achieving its primary political aim, and by the eclipse of feminism in the Soviet Union, widely considered to be an exemplary socialist state.

All of these factors combined to bring about a significant change in the way in which the kibbutz woman defined her social outlook and her personal aspirations.

The Moshav Ovedim

The Ideal

In the *moshav ovedim*, the woman worked in agriculture together with her husband, and thereby played her part in the conquest of labor no less than in the kibbutz, according to the ideologists of the *moshav*. In the mid-1930s, a woman in *moshav* Kefar Yehoshu'a explained to a friend abroad why she could not take a vacation. She described her day's work: ten tasks in agriculture (five in the chicken-house, three in the cowshed, two in the orchard), and no fewer household chores — cooking, laundry, child-care. She rose at 5 A.M. and went to bed at 10 P.M. She added: "My work is enjoyable, since I tend the animals, the fields and the orchards. Nobody can take my place, and if I go away for even one month everything will be ruined. . . . I am so happy in my work that I wouldn't give it up for all the money in the world."[13] Despite its clear ideological coloring, this letter expresses basic attitudes and emotions that were current among *moshav* women. The feeling of creative partnership and of freedom to decide on a varied and interesting program each day (within the limits of economic necessity) afforded them a sort of satisfaction different from, but no less than, that of the kibbutz woman.

Reality

In the *moshav,* unlike the kibbutz, the problem of the single woman — unmarried, divorced, or widowed — remained without a fundamental solution for many years. In fact, there was no place on the *moshav* for a single woman who owned an agricultural holding: for instance, Tehiya Lieberson of Nahalal suffered a series of pressures, from ridicule to economic discrimination and the destruction of her farm, as a result of illness during which she received insufficient help. Eventually she was forced to leave the *moshav.*[14] Solutions to specific problems were usually found: neighbors assisted in rotation, laborers were hired, alternative occupations were found. But it was hard to find a permanent solution to the problems of a women who had to look after farm and children without a helpmeet: Most of the women who reached such a state left the *moshav.*

The allocation of functions within the nuclear family in the *moshav* was no different from that in the Diaspora or in the Jewish towns of Palestine. Moreover, until 1936, only the husband was entitled to sign the standard agreement with the settlement authorities; the woman had no rights in the event of divorce or her husband's death.[15] But there were few divorces, and few couples left the *moshav* after the first critical years of its existence.

In the sporadic discussions on the woman in the *moshav* that appeared in the movement periodicals, one problem recurred again and again: women's fatigue, and the consequent danger to their health. Mutual aid provided a partial solution: In periods of illness, and after childbirth, other women did the necessary work in the house and on the farm. But, even so, there could be no institutional solution to this problem, as there was in the kibbutz (release from extra duties, longer vacations, shorter working hours, etc.). Some families eased the woman's lot by abandoning the principle of self-labor. But the woman's life was hard and subject to much strain, particularly in times of economic difficulty.[16]

The Accepted Ethos

Two matters were not discussed in the movement periodicals. First, there was virtually no opposition to the existence of the nuclear family within the kibbutz framework, although its influence was minimized in various ways, such as (voluntary) separation of married couples at public events, and allocation of resources to individuals rather than families. There is no reference at all to sexual freedom ("free love"). The accepted ethos was summed up years later as follows: "In relations between the sexes we had very many inhibitions. In fact, we still had the mentality of the shtetl: subconsciously, we wanted to be like people the world over. Every girl looked for a boy to marry, even if there was no official wedding."[17]

The second issue never raised in contemporary periodicals was the fact that, in neither the kibbutz nor the *moshav*, was there any protest against the traditional division of functions within the family. The feminine activities listed by Bassevitz seemed perfectly natural, and it was not thought necessary to transfer any of them to the men, or to the public sphere — for instance, by a rota system. And the demand to employ males in the system of communal child-care was voiced very rarely, and then most tentatively. It was generally ignored.

Conclusion

What, then, troubled the pioneer women? At an early stage, kibbutz women were troubled by the contrast between the ideal of an egalitarian society and the reality: for, as well as the undoubted achievements of the kibbutz in this sphere, there were striking inequalities in matters of work and of political activity and power. These utopian aspirations were not abandoned, and remained an integral part of kibbutz ideology; but toward the end of the 1930s, other voices began to be heard, voices that emphasized the special characteristics of the woman and demanded social and physical conditions for their expression.

Just as the kibbutz preceded the rest of the world in realizing the first stage of gender equality, the women in the leadership of the kibbutz movement preceded the "second wave" of feminism, with its aspiration to express the "other voice." But kibbutz women had to wait fifteen years for this approach to receive partial legitimization, backed by awareness of the revitalized feminist movement in Europe and the United States.

In the *moshav*, there were no parallel utopian aspirations, and the *moshav* woman did not demand gender equality. But in both forms of settlement, the physical difficulty of village life in Jewish Palestine cast a shadow over their lives, and the need for constant physical effort emphasized their dependence on men.

The changes in the concept of the role of women in the kibbutz can be interpreted either as a failure to realize accepted and desirable aims, or as a successful adaptation of those aims to the nature and desires of the women themselves. But there can be no doubt that women in kibbutz and *moshav* alike paid a heavy price for being women, and, in particular, for being pioneers.

Smadar Shiffman

Forging the Image of Pioneering Women

The Zionist movement was, from its outset, a masculine one; from Herzl, Nordau, and onwards, the Zionist utopia was formulated as a project intended to return to the Jewish man his lost masculinity. Biale, Boyarin, Gluzman, and others have shown how the Jewish national movement is closely connected to the image of the masculine, fighting pioneer, with Aryan physique and appearance, freed from "Diaspora," that is, "feminine," characteristics. The lost "Jewish muscles," for which Max Nordau yearned, characterize that type of Judaism that Zionism would stir to new life "for the first time after the war of desperation of the great Bar-Kochba"; this is, of course, "masculine Judaism," in which women have no part.[1] In the world of Herzl and Nordau, the only role a woman can play is that of a wife, a mother, and a homemaker.

The literature and press of the early twentieth century (the First Aliyah) tend to identify the man with the public sphere and the woman with the private. "In the Hebrew literature of the beginning of the century," says Dan Miron, "the life-experience of the young female Jew is usually interpreted as a personal or private experience while that of the young male Jew is presented as a metonymy for the national experience . . . the severance [of the young Jewish women from their parents' traditional home] is shaped — from the aspect of their subjective experience — as a private event, while the quarrel of the young man with his father or grandfather and his cutting himself off from his home are a symbolic national drama."[2]

The literature of the 1940s and 1950s, the literature of the "Palmach generation," identifies the "new" man with the national revolution and tends to hide his partner in the revolution in the shade; the figure of the *halutza* or the Palmachnikit (female Palmach member) in this literature is a support-

ive, "motherly" one, far from being "new" in its images and its roles. Miron
stresses the uniqueness of the artists of this generation as men and creators
who "were born into a world of war and its signature is imprinted on their
personality."[3] Shaked identifies in their work the stamp of the Zionist meta-
narrative. Shaked notes that the redemption of the nation through redemption of the land is the Zionist myth that most of the works of the members
that generation contended with, and this myth is basically a masculine one.[4]

Thus, we can say that the place of the woman in the pioneering-socialist
world of the Palmach generation authors is not essentially different from her
place in Herzl's liberal-bourgeois world. In a world where one's contribution
toward the national goal is measured mainly by fighting ability, or hard,
physical work in agriculture, woman turns almost per force into the "other":
the one whose characteristics are those rejected by the new Hebrew man.

Against this background, the novella *Kirot Etz Dakim* [*The Other Side of
the Wall*] by Nathan Shaham is a refreshing surprise.[5] Of course, the novella,
which takes place in the early 1940s, was written in the 1970s, but the centrality of the woman in this work stands out both when compared with the
works of the Shaham's contemporaries, Shamir and Yizhar, and when contrasted with later works or studies.

One may say that *Kirot Etz Dakim* is a harbinger of a certain change that
took place in the public and literary atmosphere in Israel about a decade
later. Even if in Europe and the United States the late 1970s were a period
already bearing the marks of the first wave of the feminist revolution, in Israel these were years in which the masculine experience was still the central
experience in literature. One could mention, for example, one of the important novels of the late 1970s, *Zikhron Devarim* [*Past Continuous*] by Yaakov
Shabtai. It may or may not be a coincidence that both *Kirot Etz Dakim* and
Zikhron Devarim appeared in 1977. Shabtai's novel is decidedly masculine.
The protagonists in his novel, the focus of both plot and point of view, are
three men, while the women in it are secondary and seen through the eyes
of the men. In contrast, the main consciousness in Shaham's novel is the
woman's consciousness. One might argue that if the novella was written
today, or even at the end of the 1980s, the central consciousness would be ap-
preciated differently, but in the literary world of the 1970s, what we have here
is quite a surprise.[6]

Looking back, to the 1940s, while adopting a feminine viewpoint, is far
from being obvious. When Oz Almog writes, in the late 1990s, of the process
fashioning the portrait of the *tzabar* of the 1940s and 1950s, he succeeds in
excluding the *tzabarit* (female native-born Israeli), by including her in the

masculine concept *"tzabar."*[7] It might seem that there is no connection between an academic work published in the late 1990s and a novella that appeared twenty years earlier. But the 1940s, the years in which the image
of the *tzabar* was being shaped as the embodiment of native Israeli culture,
is the period both Oz Almog and Nathan Shaham look back upon. Apparently, this retrospective glance causes Almog to exclude the *tzabarit* from his
research, even in the late 1990s.

Placing a female character at the center of a novella that takes place in
the 1940s is exceptional not only when compared to the members of Shaham's generation. In light of women's status in the ideology and literature
that fashioned the image of the "new Jew" and the *"tzabar,"* the shift to a
story told through the consciousness of a woman is a revolutionary one, especially when we remember that Shaham is a male author who came from
the center of the cultural system of the 1940s.[8]

Thus, one could assume that the novella *Kirot Etz Dakim* represents an
improvement in the status of the main female character in Shaham's work.
It would seem reasonable to assume that the Shaham of the late 1970s could
take the impressive step of writing an entire novella whose main character is
a woman; furthermore, that woman's consciousness dominates the text. Apparently, the move that Shaham makes is so extraordinary that it only becomes possible in the late 1970s. Not until the early 1980s could Shulamit
Lapid make a corrective reading, as it were, of the story of the First Aliyah,
in her novel *Gei Oni.*[9] In this period, so it would seem, it also became possible for Shaham to award centrality and substance to the figure of the *halutza*, the partner of the kibbutznik and palmachnik of the 1940s.

Nathan Shaham's novella takes place on a kibbutz in the early 1940s. The
characters in the novella are fulfilling the Zionist-socialist vision of communal life and equality. The public status of the *Yishuv* as a "state before a
state," or "a state-in-the-making," is highlighted by the fact that the protagonists in the novella toil at backbreaking physical labor, participate in the
military activities of the Palmach and the Haganah, or at least in the acts of
hiding weapons and smuggling them, and are keenly aware of the groundbreaking, conceptual status of their daily life.

The central female protagonist's background could have been very impressive. Not only does the heroine live in a young, poor kibbutz, but she has
come to it alone, by choice. This farmer's daughter chose the kibbutz for ideological reasons, and arrived there despite — and not because of — the circumstances of her life and her education: "She used to be proud of the fact
that she came to the kibbutz through the strength of her own decision and

nothing else. Without the youth movement, without the training camp, without close friends."[10]

Precisely because Shaham's heroine is given such an impressive starting point, and is so clearly placed at the center of the novel, it is ultimately even more disappointing to find out that Shaham's idealistic *halutza* has remained a woman who thinks only about her love life, who is easily filled with what she herself calls "self pity, worry about the morrow, miserable fear for her own existence, and yearning for a male."[11] Neither ideology nor creative self-realization fill the emptiness of the heroine's life, but rather spying on her pretty neighbor's love life.

Throughout the entire novella, Shaham's unnamed heroine is occupied with what the text calls "the private arena." As early as the first page of the text, she is described as someone who prefers to read "belles letters," in contrast to the people who gather in the dining hall "to listen to the news and to analyze the situation as reflected in the different war fronts," and as opposed to someone who reads books concerning the public arena. The young woman, who has left her rich father's home and opted for a life of national and socialist realization in the kibbutz, is gradually depicted as someone who is only searching for a bit of love: "After the war it may not be necessary to keep such a stiff upper lip. Maybe then her sensitivity, her generosity, the great power to love welling up inside her will be noticed."[12]

The book's heroine is not the only lonely person on the kibbutz, but while the lonely men keep themselves busy with public affairs, she occupies herself with her [female] neighbor's secret romance. For her lonely [male] neighbor, "For Meir Avrahami — the movement is everything. Without it he doesn't exist."[13] In an argument with the heroine about a novel written by a kibbutz member he, of course, holds the opinion that the interest of the community takes precedence over personal problems, and says "A personal belly ache, who cares about it?" and she, "'What's wrong with that?' she retorts."[14] Even Shmuel B., the lover whom the heroine calls "Theo," cloaking him in her imagination with a romantic mantle, is thoroughly involved in ideological issues. Moreover, he sees himself as the opposition fighting against the movement's institutions and always supports the minority opinion, while our heroine "listens to a long, inflammatory speech and goes away brimming with symbols whose meaning she does not entirely fathom, but which strike her as shimmering truths."[15] One might say, a bit bluntly, that whereas the male pioneers in Shaham's novella act out of ideology and abate their loneliness through taking social and ideological stances, Shaham's *halutza* acts out of "yearning for a male," is impressed by the discussions of social and ideological issues in a hazy, emotional way, "whose meaning she does not entirely fathom," and abates her loneliness by peeping into her [female] neighbor's life.

This means that even in 1977, even in Shaham's novella, whose protagonist is a woman who has chosen socialist pioneering self-realization — at the end, "her world is as narrow as that of an ant" (phrase from a poem by Rachael). Not only is involvement in the main, meaningful, absorbing events of existence reserved for men, but even interest in them belongs to them.

The intellectual stance, reserved for lonely men, who are impressive farmers or amazing underground fighters — such as Meir or Shmuel B. — is not for women, or at least not for our heroine. Even when she does take an independent position, it is a stance based on personal embarrassment rather than on real principles. When she gets riled over the bakery workers' cheating the English corporal while weighing bread, she is not standing for honesty but is embarrassed because her comrades are exploiting his attraction to her in order to cheat him.

When she discusses ideological issues with Theo, her neighbor Raheli's lover, she is aware of his extending her intellectual credit that she is not sure she really deserves. Moreover, Theo extends to Shaham's heroine a broader credit line than she receives from the narrator: "To Theo's way of thinking, she is a little, bourgeois brat who has been taught French, and eurhythmics and playing piano in order to suitably grace the home of a doctor. He takes pride in the change that kibbutz living has wrought in her values. *She has no objection to assuming the role his imagination has assigned her,* even though *she senses no change whatsoever* within herself."[16]

Shaham's narrator could have intervened here or hinted that the heroine unjustifiably underestimates herself. But the narrator maintains his silence: He neither tries to convince us of the heroine's worth, nor does he expose the "principled" lover for even a bit less than the heroine takes him to be. When the heroine imagines Theo's character, when she "wants to fill him with characteristics," we do not spot any reservations at all on the part of the narrator nor on the part of the hero from the range and specifics of the characteristics attributed to him. When a *halutz* imagines a *halutza*, she is a little bourgeois brat. When a *halutza* imagines a *halutz*, his wretched physical appearance is surprisingly unimportant, and it is unthinkable that he does not have his own opinion and ideology.

The woman's status in the kibbutzim of Hashomer ha-Tza'ir is reflected in the words of Meir Ya'ari, written in 1936:

Some people find justification for the *havera*, who is not interested in politics. The woman, apparently, was not created for that. A song of praise is sung to the *haverot*'s thorough understanding of educational issues and skills in establishing comradely and friendly relations in the kibbutz. In this sphere of members' relations it is customary to draw a line between the natural characteristics of men and women. The men's strength is in relations in the public arena, as it were, while the women's is in intimate friendly relations. . . . I do not accept any ifs and buts in this domain. Socialism cannot make do with partial solutions on the issue of women's equality, as well as on the agrarian question. We must demand complete, unlimited equality.[17]

Shaham's novella, set a few years after Ya'ari's statements, reflects the kibbutz members' approach that distinguishes "between the natural characteristics of men and women" more than it does Ya'ari's basic support of full equality. It seems that not only the heroine and the men surrounding her but the narrator too, and perhaps even the writer in the 1970s, bear the "psychological burden of the school of Weininger, Freud, and Nietzsche," as Ya'ari puts it. "In this anti-feminist literature," he adds, "the woman appeared as a passive absorbent receptacle, fettered to the specific time and place. As an unimaginative creature, hindering the conquering assault of the fighting men."[18]

Shaham's men are occupied with public needs and national issues. Even the superficial or vulgar ones among them, such as Big Isaac, Raheli's husband, contribute to the national needs, since they are recruited into the struggle of defending the *Yishuv*. Raheli, on the other hand, is totally occupied with her love affair and is not even touched by the news of the fall of Tobruk. Even our heroine, who is anxious about the fall of Tobruk and the imminent German threat to the Eretz Israel *Yishuv*, again sees things in proper "feminine" proportions the morning after. On the night she learns of the German conquest of Tobruk, the heroine also finds out that Raheli has a lover; come morning, the love affair is the sole focus of her interest and excitement. Tobruk fades into the monotonous background, and the heroine is titillated by her secret piece of gossip.

Even if we managed to ignore the meagerness of the heroine's world, at the end of the novella it is crystal clear that her world has become void with the conclusion of the secret love affair that she had been tracking: "Her life seems to have been emptied of its content. . . . At night she misses the voices on the other side of the wall and during the day the accidental meetings with Theo. Life is boring without the secret that was guarded like a sacred trust. Now, as she goes from place to place in silence, her silence is utterly empty."[19]

Shaham does not really imagine a *halutza* who plays an active, meaning-ful role in the settlement and defense endeavor. Maybe this should not come as a surprise, since "the young Shaham is, perhaps, the most definite succes-sor of the mainstream Hebrew fiction written between the two World Wars, adept in the implementation of the Zionist meta-narrative" as Shaked puts it.[20] Shaham is placed well within the hegemonic center, and even his ver-sion of the Zionist meta-narrative, when all is said and done, is merely a nuanced version of the hegemonic view of the woman: her world is narrow, domestic, and bereft of any real interest.[21]

Shulamit Lapid's portrait of the *halutza* in her novel *Gei Oni* is more of a surprise. Lapid's point of departure differs from that of Shaham not only be-cause she is a woman, and even not merely because she is writing about a more distant period. Shaham writes about the 1940s, about a period he was a part of, from a distance of about thirty years. Lapid, in contrast, harks back to the First Aliyah, which is much more distant in time and less documented in our common cultural corpus. Moreover, Shulamit Lapid's *Gei Oni* is al-most an explicit attempt at reclaiming women's rightful status in Zionist his-tory. The back cover of the novel states that its heroine "Fanya is one of those women-giants whose name is absent in the history books, since only the names of men appear in the lists of farmers who redeemed the land of Eretz Israel."[22]

Fanya, the heroine of Lapid's novel, is a strong woman, who is capable of providing for herself and her family and of making her own decisions. It would seem that Lapid characterizes a feminist heroine, aware of her place and status as a woman. Even as an adolescent, Fanya thinks that "when the time comes she would prove that she is no less than the men," and "indeed, now, as a adult, she has proven the equality of the sexes with a broken back, with unbearable suffering, with unrewarded work."[23] Lapid presents her heroine as a kind of intuitive feminist, "I saw the regulations that the Rosh Pina committee had prepared [says Fanya]. Only men have signed it. Who-ever will read the regulations a hundred years from now will think that there were no women here at all. And it is precisely they who are the true heroines of Rosh Pina."[24]

Yet, even Lapid's heroine takes an interest mainly in "intimate relations." Her motives, in contrast to those of the men in the novel, almost always be-long to the private arena, and she sees her freedom of action as something granted to her by the men, or more precisely, by her husband: "*He gave* her complete freedom. She was free to conduct business, to travel on the roads, to be away from the house. He respected her right to realize her life separately from his. None of the women she knew, even Helen Leah, behaved like she did. And Yehiel never hinted that *she had been given this freedom by him* or that she should act in the accepted manner."[25]

Contrary to what one might expect from a novel with a feminist point of departure, the main line of the novel's plot indicates a woman driven by the will of others. Fanya cannot remain home in Lisabetgrad after the pogrom in which her parents were killed and she was raped. She immigrates to Eretz Israel and does not join her sisters in America, because her father's dream was to go to the land of his forefathers. She is even aware that she is not fulfilling her own dreams but rather those of the men in her life. She stays in the country because it was her father's dream, she fights to stay in Gei Oni — that is, Rosh Pina — because it is her husband's dream, and even that emotional and practical role, ostensibly reserved for women in their own right, motherhood, is emptied of content when her husband dies: "Her house was not a home. It was a place to eat and sleep. Besides a roof over their heads she could not give her neglected children warmth or joy since her heart was as silent as a grave."[26]

Despite her inherent strength, despite her ability to manage affairs and make decisions, the course of her life is dictated by fortuitousness and by men. Fanya's definition as someone's wife is particularly prominent at the novel's conclusion. At the end of the novel, we meet the new man in Fanya's life who has come to redeem her from her desolation. Despite all her capabilities, Fanya does not manage to support her children or maintain her husband's house in Rosh Pina. She is forced to sell the house, only to find out that the buyer is the person who is intended to be her new husband: "I am a person with a profession. My livelihood is guaranteed. That means . . . I need you Fanya! Will you allow me to help you?"[27]

Like Shaham's heroine, Fanya is occupied mainly with love life.

The division between the private-feminine sphere and the public-masculine sphere is further reinforced in *Gei Oni*. "The vision of the redemption burned around them [the women] like a fire in people's bones, while they [the women] took pleasure in idle chatter!"[28] Fanya and Helen Leah are busy with idle chatter, with gossip, and with everyday needs, while the men redeem the homeland. The division of the areas of endeavor and interest between the men and the women is mentioned again in Lapid's novel inadvertently, as it were, as if it were obvious. "The men don't miss us, girl. Redemption of the soil burns like fire in their bones. Everything else is — nonsense!" said Fanya.[29] On the same page in which Fanya notes the importance of women in reclaiming the land, their being the true heroines of Rosh Pina,

Helen Leah, her good friend, brings us back to reality: "'My Moinshtims only talk about redeeming the soil and national revival! Sure, that's the most important thing and that's the reason we're here, but . . .' Helen Leah waved her hands in mock desperation. But then she became serious and asked: 'But isn't he worth the struggle, trying to win his heart?'" — that is, the thing that really matters to Lapid's heroic, feminist heroines is the fight for the husband's heart.[30] True, we are here for the purpose of national revival, but — one gleans from the words and behavior of the heroines — in the end this is a matter for the men.

Both Shaham's novella and Lapid's novel were written in hindsight, from the late 1970s (or early 1980s) to the 1940s and even further, to the beginning of the twentieth century. The differences between the two texts are greater than their similarities. Shaham's perspective is that of someone who lives and writes from the center of the cultural system but who is trying to adopt the viewpoint of the "Other."[31] It is also worth noting that the system from within which he writes pretends to support equality and socialism and its concepts are supposed to include equality between the sexes.

Shulamit Lapid is looking backward, to the First Aliyah. She is writing from the margins of the system, from a woman's point of view and with the rather express intent of presenting an alternative narrative to the Zionist meta-narrative. Lapid's point of departure is more revolutionary than Shaham's, since she is trying to change the prism and not only offer an additional viewpoint, a slightly different one. Yet Lapid's historical starting point places her heroine in a more extreme position of inferiority than that of Shaham's. The people of the First Aliyah did not even pretend there was equality, the way the members of the Second Aliyah did. Despite prominent differences, the status of both women protagonists is fairly similar. Unfortunately, women's status in both the novella and the novel is not much more than a reflection of the socio-cultural norms of the two periods.

Even if we allow for the influence of "reality" on the literary text, it is difficult to ignore the fact that the status of the heroines in Shaham's novella and Lapid's novel attests to the influence of the dominant cultural discourse on literature. Obviously, national literature in general, and Zionist literature in particular, shape the dominant cultural discourse. Yet, one must keep in mind, too, that the dominant cultural discourse shapes the national literature; these are relations of mutual nourishment and mutual formation. Even those acting from the margins of the system are influenced by its center more than it seems at a first glance. Nathan Shaham, who adopts the woman's viewpoint, presents it as peripheral to the main plot of Zionism, and as a rather boring one due to its focusing on the less significant, personal aspects of the plot. Shulamit Lapid ostensibly tried to present an alternative narrative of Zionism; she chose a woman protagonist, an independent and feminist-like one, and set her story not in the clichéd framework of the Second Aliyah but rather in the context of the First Aliyah, the one whose story has not been told countless times and has not, perhaps, become firmly fixed as an ultimately defined and shaped cultural myth. Yet, Lapid, too, does not actually depict a woman who will play an active role in the national narrative, who will take an interest in the public discourse and not only in her "personal belly ache."

Both Shaham and Lapid leave their heroines on the margins of the national revolution. The men are transformed in both works, becoming "new Jews," farmers, fighters, revolutionaries. The women are occupied with the nonrevolutionary aspects of settling the country. They maintain their traditional roles: We were there, too, involved in the personal arena, in cooking, laundry, raising children, and capturing the husband's heart. The Zionist revolution remains a revolution of men, for men, in which women play only a passive, marginal role.

One might have expected that in a period in which some of the influences of the international feminist movement penetrated the country, in the late 1970s, the literary images of the *halutzot* would be a bit different. One might have hoped for an independent woman, a fighter for her opinions and her world, who sees herself as part of the social change taking place in the country. But the difference between the women of the First Aliyah and those of the Second turns out to be a myth. Furthermore, it seems that the alternative view of the past is merely a slight variation of the dominant view. Regretfully, the *halutzot* of Shaham and Lapid are willing, perhaps even desirous, of acting the part the *halutzim* have cast them in.

❦ *Hagar Salamon*

A Woman's Life Story as a Foundation Legend of Local Identity

At every lecture appeared a woman, bejeweled, tall, impressive, and at every lecture she disturbed. She disturbed every lecturer. Every foreign word she thunderously corrected immediately, and she immediately had a parallel word in Hebrew. And afterwards that woman would give a lecture on Arab dresses. And I sat there with my eyes actually rolling, actually, from all this course and from this personality . . .

This was the description given by a participant in a Jerusalem women's embroidery group of her meeting with Zohar Wilbush, whom the embroiderers consider the "founding mother" of a female dynasty organized into embroidery groups in various places in Israel.[1] The centrality of the figure of Zohar Wilbush, the conundrum of her age, and the mythological characteristics relating to her past stood out starkly in the embroidery group's discourse. The women in the embroidery group drew a connection between her and the heroic past and struggle for independence in the pre-state period. This stemmed from her family tree bearing famous figures from the history of the *Yishuv* along with Zohar's rhetorical demonstration of her knowledge, which made her, in these women's eyes, an actual, visual representation of feminine knowledge binding identity and history, the object of attraction, and a threat, all at the same time.

This article is based on Zohar Wilbush's own life story, as told in her Je-

I wish to thank Megina Shlein, whose special connection to Zohar Wilbush constituted the inspiration for this article; to Sharon Agur, who assisted with the field work; to Galit Hasan-Rokem, to Miriam Salamon, and to anonymous readers for their important comments, and especially to Zohar Wilbush for the many hours she devoted in her largesse and for her wisdom.

rusalem home to two women, one in her twenties, the other in her thirties, during long evenings in winter 1997.[2] Zohar Wilbush (1908–2005), defined herself at the outset of her narrative as a "non-typical" woman. The story of her life spans over ninety years and moves in Eretz Israel between Hadera, Haifa, Deganiah Bet, and Jerusalem, and in the Middle East region and Europe — to Damascus, Alexandria, Constantinople, Athens, St. Petersburg, Paris, and Germany.

Her overflowing story is characterized by authoritative, declaredly antifeminist rhetoric within which pulses Orientalism. Authoritativeness suffuses both the plot-content dimension and the formal-rhetorical dimension that integrates questions of knowledge that the listeners are supposed to answer, the use of concepts and sayings in every language of the region, and ethnographic "explanatory snippets" from Eretz Israel society. Knowing the Oriental Other, a definite component of Orientalism, dominates her biography both in content and rhetoric. Thus, when she collects traditional local embroideries and conducts groups for the study of folk embroidery, she again explains: "One must know the embroidery of nations. One must understand what *they* are thinking. Because when you want to know the country's climate and the nation's way of thinking, you only get to know this through material." The rhetoric of her story is an unchallengeable rhetoric of knowledge. There is no question Zohar does not respond to, and her answers show no hint of hesitation. The Oriental axis, with its decidedly colonialistic characteristics, relies upon the special place of the female narrator within the Eretz Israel *halutziyyut* — as the daughter of a local family of industrialists with a prestigious family tree (related on her maternal side to Avshalom Feinberg; on her paternal side to Manya Shohat); she links her childhood with village life, closeness to the earth, to animals, and Arab villagers in the area; and presents her life wisdom as flowing from her location on the seam *between* the cultures and *between* the genders.[3]

For Zohar, this special position is the source of cultural and political insights that reveal multidirectional characteristics of the concept "culture" as Pierre Bourdieu proposes in his theory of practice.[4] Culture, according to his approach, is rooted in *experience* in the sense of the merging between the axis that stresses the understanding that culture constructs practice (as in Geertz's conception) and the complementary axis, the one that stresses a reverse, parallel process in which practice constructs culture. This dynamic, circular direction, which Bourdieu embodies in the idea of the "habitus," passes like a scarlet thread through the unique Orientalist experience of the narrator.[5] In her life story, Zohar looks backward to the past and the present, through decoding and processing by means of a system of opposites shaped by body and practice.[6] The design of this system is focused on thematic nodes considered definitely feminine, prominent among which are embroidery and cooking. These differentiate between contrasting pairs of femininity and masculinity, emotion and logic, East and West, and are duplicated by additional, definitely asymmetrical contrasts, that are presented all through Zohar's life-story in varying relationships that are not subject, as it were, to uniform organizing authority. By that Zohar Wilbush's private voice is striving to become a multivocal, gender-transcending text, that merges opposites into a local, Eretz Israel culture to which the title "feminine Orientalism" attempts to allude.

Edward Said's highly influential book *Orientalism* examines the districts of Western discourse that presents the Orient and Islam as an object for research and domination, imagination and romanticization.[7] The book examines a wide-ranging textual world characterized in rhetoric and images that construct imaginary geographical borders between West and East. These borders serve as the West's set of coordinates for representation and knowledge of the Orient and the Oriental. Thus, Orientalism is the dynamic discourse by means of which the Other is fashioned as an object — and specifically, through which the Orient is shaped by the West. On the overt level, the Orientalist discourse is linked to the cultural and political, and is the means by which the West turns the East into "Oriental" and Eastern. The East became a cultural fact in the view of the West by means of "knowledge," that which was obvious in the Orientalism produced by the West itself and was common knowledge among nineteenth-century Europeans. This "knowledge" constructed, on its own, the very object that it wanted to know, and with its help the borders of the East and of the West alike were indicated.

Said's Orientalist mold raised theoretical and political issues that became central in various disciplines. Analysis of the Orientalist discourse became a focal point for dealing with — to mention just some of the topics — the representation of sexual and cultural differences, overt and covert dimensions of the discourse on Otherness, discursive construction of Other and Self, and the expressions of this construction in the links between culture, knowledge, and power as illuminated by Foucault.[8]

The arena of the discussion, nurtured by Said's analysis in such varied ways, includes the opening of the systematic, closed model that he presented toward the development of complex models of mutuality, or deconstruction, or such as the one that developed within the framework of Lacanian thinking (which leads the discussion in which Bhabha took part), that attempts to decode racial discourse, the systems of connections between representation of Self and Other in psychoanalytical terms.[9]

It is possible to conceputalize the Orientalist discourse from yet another angle, the representation of Western identity to itself by means of the Oriental Other. In such an analysis, emphasis is placed not only on the construction of Otherness, but a no less pivotal construct — that of the Western subject as having hegemonic status, knowing, discerning, and investigating the object of study.

In this sense, its mechanism of action is similar to other fields of identity clarification, which are related to the construction of hierarchical relations of knowledge and control. Such a link is the one between culture and sexuality and between cultural identity and gender identity. The connection between the Western cultural representation as masculine and the Eastern representation as feminine had been raised by Said but developed in detail only recently by Yeğenoğlu.[10] She focuses on the veil through which she attempts a feminist reading of Orientalist and colonialist discourse. The discussion in her book buttresses the concept that cultural representations and gender differences reinforce each other and that the discursive structuring of Otherness is achieved simultaneously by marking cultural and gender differences.

The life-story of Zohar Wilbush moves between masculine and feminine identities and between varied occidental and oriental cultures, whose definition is based on detailed ethnographic knowledge that she attributes to her unique life experience. This article examines the way in which Zohar Wilbush interweaves the contrasts and the national historical events along with routine daily endeavors. Characteristics of a mixture of areas, and the creation of new structures, in the course of her life story, repeatedly break down categories and unite them.[11] Her life story deals time and again with actual cultural representations in which food and handicrafts are prominent — areas also chosen by the "Oriental Others" to represent themselves and their culture in different contexts.[12] The analysis in this article presents a theoretical model that integrates Orientalist discourse and Bourdieu's approach to practice, which attempts to decipher the connections between the routine and the ideological. This analysis is a kind of dialogue, just like the life story told to us, between the narrator's viewpoint and rhetoric and that of the writer of this article, who discerned this model and gave it prominence over other possible models.[13]

. . .

Zohar Wilbush is a woman of striking presence even at her advanced age. From her embroidery-adorned clothing and her ethnic jewelry radiate the detailed attention she gives to her fields of interest and knowledge and combine a gender declaration with an ethnic-colonialist declaration. She told us her life story in the living room of her modest apartment. The room is furnished in pleasant simplicity and decorated with ethnic crafts, particularly local traditional textiles (figure 1). Above a large desk hangs a map of the Ottoman Empire, which we will discuss below. In her life story, the narrator does not follow a general chronological framework; this is a recruited, conscripted text, in which personal life experience is fashioned into an authoritative, didactic text, during the course of which the narrator moves among different events in her life unbound by rules of time.

Despite the lack of the chronological dimension in the life story unfurled before us, our accepted cultural discourse requires a chronological construct. We glean from her story biographical details. Zohar was born in Jaffa in 1908 with the name Sarah Zohara Wilbushewitch, which she later changed to Zohar Wilbush. Her early memories are connected to the *moshavah* Haderah, where her grandfather and grandmother lived, parents of her mother Shoshana and her uncle Avshalom Feinberg (figures 1 and 2). She was raised as an only child until she was ten years old, when her younger brother Yoel was born. Her father, Nahum Wilbushewitz, the brother of Manya Shohat, was a far-seeing engineer and industrialist who traveled widely throughout the Middle East and Europe, each time for a number of months. In her childhood, Zohar spent time in many countries and was raised by private nannies hired for her in each place. Her mother, to whom's Zohar's attitude is overtly ambivalent, was an embroidery teacher who taught her pupils to sew delicate European embroidery. Zohar describes her as a pretty woman, always dressed in the highest European fashion, delicate, fragile, and "spoiled," in Zohar's words. For high school, Zohar studied at Reali School in Haifa, and for a time was the "leader of the [female] scouts" there. After her studies, she moved to Deganyah Bet, and later on traveled to Germany, about the time of the Nazi accession to power, to pursue academic studies that she never completed.

In 1946, Zohar moved to Jerusalem, working first as an arts and crafts teacher and then for Tahal (Water Planning for Israel) for many years. From the age of sixty, for some twenty years, Zohar worked in the Israel Museum Ethnography Department; she specialized in the textile crafts and material culture of the Middle East. For many years, Zohar has held women's groups

Fig. 1. Zohar aged two.

in her home for learning embroidery and its origins as well as ethnography of the area. Her students describe these meetings as a source of tradition for many groups of embroidering women throughout the country (fig. 7). Zohar was married, but she never mentioned her husband's name during the telling of her story; she divorced after a few years of marriage, during which she gave birth to a son who was only alluded to in her story.

"Even at Six or Seven You Can Ride a Horse"

In an authoritative tone, basing herself on examples taken from local folklore, Zohar sketches a hierarchical cultural system, suffused with emotions. The Arab inhabitants of the country represent for her a "natural," authentic, culture whose customs and "way of thinking" are actually known by only a few

Fig. 2. Zohar at the age of five.

of the country's Jews. As a native of the land whose earliest recollections go back to life in the *moshavah*, Zohar considers herself an authority of cultural knowledge and understanding. She recollects: "We used to go hiking everywhere. And for each trip we had an excuse. So the excuse might be to pick a certain species of flowers, or to see a certain type of Arab tribe, since there are different kinds of Arabs in each place." Museological Orientalism — a concept I wish to propose from the current reading — that creates such a crude parallelism between species of flowers and types of Arab tribes accompanies Zohar's life story and is well known from other colonialist ethnographic contexts. She sees herself as someone who received European education combined with primary, "natural" familiarity with the local Arabs:

> When I was at Grandmother's, what would we do? Grandmother would sit me on the big donkey. There was Hmār, and there was Jakhsh, that was the little Arab donkey. Hmār, this was the big one that came from Lubnan (from Lebanon), he was not local and he had saddle bags, *khurj*, so Grandmother would sit me down on Friday morning or Thursday afternoon and say, "Go to Buzaburah" and go to this or that fisherman [. . .] How many kilometers is it from Haderah to the sea? [. . .]' so I would go to him, "Tefadli, tefadli" [. . .] and he would wrap the fish for me, put them in the *khurj*, in the saddlebags, and I would go back. I was not at all afraid. Then, not everyone would send a child alone. I said I was not afraid.[14]

Fig. 3. Zohar's mother, Shoshana Feinberg-Wilbush.

Fig. 4. Zohar's father, Nahum Wilbush (Wilbushewitz) standing next to his older brother, Gedalya, 1913.

Fig. 5. Zohar at age twenty, while in Degania Bet.

In many other places over the course of her life story, Zohar emphasizes her lack of fear of local nature, which includes, as she sees it, the local residents, too. So, for example, she claims that she was never afraid of animals, that dogs would sniff her from afar and "identify" through the smell of her body that she was part of the authentic local experience. As she tells it:

> In Grandmother's yard there were dogs. In the house there was a small dog, but in the yard was a boxer, a real boxer, if you know. Well, now dogs are decoration. Instead of giving love to a child, they give it to a dog. But a boxer, I don't suggest you meet a terrifying boxer, because he won't do anything to you, he won't bark. He'll only take a piece of shnitzel from your body. But I was not afraid. I was a girl of six, five-six-seven. I was not afraid of him or of horses. I said to my uncle Avshalom — "I want to ride, too, everyone's riding, and I'm not." Then he said to me, "But you can't sit here on the saddle, and the horse's head is here." Then I said, "Put me on it." So Avshalom taught me that you can sit on the horse's neck, but hold very, very tight to his mane, not only to the reins. So I would get up [there], and if you give a light tap, he runs. You don't need any saddle with all its stuff, so I rode. Then, you see, even at six-seven you can ride a horse.

Horseback riding—featured prominently among the elite women of the *Yishuv* in those days—is a subject Zohar returns to again and again in her life story. Riding among the *Yishuv* aristocracy is characterized by a decidedly English charm, while Zohar describes it as a different type of riding than that associated with the life of the *moshavah*:

> It was the fashion then to ride horses. But not all women rode. For example, the mother of Ezerke [using the diminutive to refer to the president of Israel, Ezer Weizmann, when she told her story]. So Ezerke's mother and three other women would get together in Haifa. In Haifa there are horses. In Tel Aviv, they apparently drove the horses out. I remember that as little girls we always used to look at them, how they were riding. Because then there was Krichevsky, one of them was Hadassa Samuel. For then the English high commissioner was Herbert Samuel who was a Jew, and his son Edwin married Hadassa Grasovski, Goor. She was once Grasovski, now Goor. So Hadassa Grasovski and Ezerke's mother and two-three others of this type used to go out in Haifa to ride horses. They weren't *moshavah* ladies, and the British set the tone like this. In England people ride horses. I don't know what you watch on television, but if you turn on a British station you always see horses. Always [. . .] in the city there was British influence. In the *moshavah* there was no English influence, in the *moshavah* it was simple since you can't wait, once or twice a day there is a [transportation] connection, and if you need something urgently, then you get on a horse or a good donkey. Because there was Jakhsh—a little donkey—and there is Hmār—a big donkey. You didn't grow up like that. But horses as one of the social things, this came from the British.

"Smell if This is *Khamrā* or *Samrā*"

Like her riding on horses, described as an authentic contrast to the fashionable British riding, Zohar also explains her authenticity by means of her familiarity with the village animals and with the different smells of the soil she grew up with from an early age. She turns to us and asks:

> I was in the *moshavah*, so I knew about chickens. Chickens now begin the season of the eggs, and you eat eggs all year round, right? But what color are the chickens, *nu* [come on], answer me? ["White?" I try, and Zohar smiles in victory] [. . .] It was never white. If you've been in the Arab village and seen the speckled chickens and the handsome rooster with the brown and green and

black tail, then you know the rooster and the hen. After all, this land was not commercial agriculturally. Remember I told you that when we were children the game was "*Nu*, tell me what's this, smell, is it *khamrā* or *samrā?*" We grew up differently. I know that your children will not grow up like that. Your grandchildren won't even know the word "*khamrā*," they won't know that red soil is called *khamrā* and that black soil is called *samrā*, 'cause that's Arabic, and Arabic is disgusting, to know the Arabic language. God forbid. See, even those who study Arabic in high school, they learn literary Arabic. Who needs it?

Recognizing the different smells of the soil is linked in a single continuum to the names of the types of earth in Arabic and to the Arabic language. Even today, she successfully tests her knowledge of Arabic and the use of a specific dialect that indicates she is from the Shomron, or a "Samaritan," as she attests of herself; this is affirmed by an Arab she speaks with at a chance meeting in Jerusalem. Zohar tells:

Look what happened to me a few days ago. I happened to be in some Arab store, I opened my mouth, so then there was a young fellow there, so he says to me: "*anti mish min al-quds*" [you're not from Jerusalem]. I said to him: "Right, I'm not from Jerusalem." Then he says to me: "Where are you from, Netanaya?" I say: "No." He thinks and thinks, then says: "*Min Samarin*." From the Arabic, the Arab has an ear. He could tell from the accent from where. The Jew, talk to him Yiddish as much as you want, but he can't tell from their Yiddish from what country they come. The Arab has an ear. He knows how they talk in each village.

"An Arab Woman Doesn't Sit Like Me"

Heightened senses, which Zohar attributes in her story to local Arabs, are linked for her to a whole world of colonialist hierarchical concepts. Her specializing in textiles, and mainly in local embroidery, gives her a unique position of knowledge and exposes a romantic perception of the Other, as close to nature and embodies "natural" traditionalism, of a time-bound nature:

First of all, an Arab woman doesn't sit like me. She sits on the ground. And then she needs to make a line. Then she threads a needle and stretches and embroiders. They wove the textiles by themselves. I have all the types of textiles. But what they didn't know was proper dyeing. So how to decorate it so

Fig. 6. Zohar in her Jerusalem apartment, 1959.

that the textile won't be one color? You have to also put a few green lines, you
see the Arab women: here a green line, here a white or black or red line.

In Arab culture, as embodied in the women's weaving and embroidery, thoroughness is missing ("she doesn't know proper dyeing"). It is a decorative, colorful culture. In many places in her story, as I will show below, expression is given to hierarchy and relations of dominance and suppression between knowledge and lack of knowledge, between logic and emotion, between masculinity and femininity, a hierarchy that inverts itself intersects at many nodes.

The meeting between the local, "authentic" Arab and Westerners is described by Zohar as destructive, when she tells of the meeting between the Arab women embroiderers and the English women:

The English ruled here for thirty years. That's not a day, that's not two days, thirty years. And then all the self-righteous English women appeared. And they made from this not only propaganda, but also benefited from this because they gave Arab women textiles and threads from England, and already then, the embroidery slowly turned into non-natural embroidery. When all the English women who helped the Arab women showed up, Arab embroidery stopped being Arab embroidery [. . .] because when they bring you the threads from abroad instead of you sitting and making the thread, because when they teach you that there is canvas, instead of you embroidering according to the thread, then all the value of the folk work evaporates.

"Natural" embroidery, and here especially the local Arab embroidery, is set in relation to the precise, fine European work, the kind that Zohar's mother taught. The local embroidery is described as ancient, static, and "natural," while European embroidery ruins it through an encounter based on exploitation.[15] Zohar deals in her narrative, in combination, with two types of meetings between the European and the Oriental: the one, portrayed by the self-righteous English women, by her mother who embroiders the delicate, European embroidery, or even by leaders — including women — is an arrogant and "destructive" encounter, positioned in her narrative opposite another choice: an "integrative" meeting characterized by romantic images of similarity and affinity to the Arab-village culture. Yet, the haughty, destructive meeting, dominated by male images, is precisely the one linked repeatedly in the life story with female figures. Another contrast that Zohar's narrative revolves around is the one between female and male embroidery. The way this contrast is fashioned gives rise to complicated interrelations with the contrast between oriental and occidental embroidery:

If, when you were younger, you would have seen saddles, you would have seen that the Arabs usually embroidered something on the sides. Do you think that women embroidered that? There is a difference between the embroidery by women and by men, since the women's finger is softer. So she embroiders soft items. On leather a woman does not embroider, embroidery on leather is [a type of] work that a woman does not embroider, there is also a difference in the stitches. A woman likes everything to be delicate. I think that a man always takes everything in a rougher way. This means, if [it is] a thicker metal thread — a man will work better; if it is a thicker woolen yarn — a man will work better. A woman, naturally, has delicacy. See, there are decorations made with nails. There are wonderful things decorated this way. A man has to do it. A woman will never work this way with a hammer. Because of her senses, she needs to feel, everything she does she has to feel. Look! This is unpleasant. It's as choppy as from a grater [then Zohar points to embroidery on a leather belt she owns]. When a women wants to embroider, it must be delicate, pleasant.

Fig. 7. Zohar with Megina Shlein's embroidery group at an exhibition of their work at the Jerusalem Theatre in the 1980s.

And more:

> If you've noticed, the men always work in straight lines, a woman makes every-thing curved. That's the way it always comes out for her [. . .] and a flower and everything, when a man embroiders a house the room comes out like this for him [she demonstrates with her hand a triangle with straight lines], when a woman embroiders it comes out like this [again, she demonstrates a curved line].

"You Won't Find a Scent Like This in Any Bottle"

When Zohar talks about body care, she points out the creativity she custom-arily applied to everything related to make-up or perfume.

> Make-up is a wonderful thing. Because as early as the period of the Penta-teuch, the Mishna, and the Talmud, they already knew that it was necessary to anoint with oil, that skin dries, already then they knew that it is necessary to

put in a certain [kind of] flower. If it was make-up, then I always put in what was fitting for hot days, in winter you don't have to, in summer you go out in the sun more. I used to go out on a lot of trips, so I used a lot of all kinds of lotions, and then, finally you get burned, then you need powder, so I had French powder of a certain kind that was supposed to help, but what I really always used was talc for the feet, 'cause if you don't apply it [your] toes stick, and talc is the simplest thing. I didn't deal in this stuff. I had many more things to deal with, I didn't have time for this. What I did do, I would smear my hands with any cream so they would not be dry. Because [when] hands are dry, then later the skin cracks. That's so. ["And perfume"? I added.] Perfume, no! Why? I would also try to take a flower with a scent, now you can take [it], you see the scent it gives? [I say: "The narcissus?"] Did you see? You can go out to see. You won't find a scent like this in any bottle. If you go outside now here, you can smell the narcissus, and see that the Jerusalem narcissus is all scent [and here we go out to the her apartment's balcony to smell the narcissus in a flower pot]. This is the real scent, but in the swamp, the narcissuses are much more beautiful, the petal is thick and white. But they do not have such a scent like these, the scent is very strong, and if you can put it just like it is into a handkerchief.

In the "habitus" she weaves in her life story, traditional femininity — embodied in the daily physical realities of clothing and jewelry, embroidery and cooking — conducts an open dialogue with masculinity generally embodied in building, politics, and "grand history"; this method repeatedly sets up and breaks down contrasts between categories. So, for example, the centrality of handicrafts in the shaping of identity and gender relations stands out in her descriptions of courtship customs common when she was in high school, and from them we learn about the attitude to feminine and masculine hands, and to the handicrafts of "the boys" and "the girls" alike. Zohar relates:

Drying flowers was the main thing. What do you dry? You dry the tiny flower "Forget-Me-Not," to dry flowers you have to know how. There was a sponge. And everybody had a sponge on their desk, there was a blotter. And drying flowers in a sponge is totally different from drying flowers in paper, then the flower still stands out a bit. So you dried the flower in a special way. Then you gave this to the young man who was with you. You tried to arrange them in a pretty shape, writing something, let's say, "forget-me-not," or "remember the trip," "remember the sunrise," "remember the sunset," what do you think, it was so easy? [Zohar laughs.] See, the boys have hands [good for] a pliers, for tongs. How does your name start? "H" and your family name, "S," right? So he would sit down and cut it out for you. So it won't be from silver, it will be from some kind of tin or a piece of copper. He will cut, and work it, and make triangles that you can stick on anything. And so, that is something a girl can't do. She cannot do it! Because to cut out the metal and work the metal she can't do it, a girl. That he does. But a girl can take many beads and embroider his name. Yes. So she can embroider the letters of his name, and make a ribbon bookmark.

"Tehina and Mayonnaise Are Things Women Can Invent"

Again and again Zohar links women and embroidery, embroidery and cooking:

> Look, women love embroidery because the woman deals with minor aesthetics. A man, see, no women ever made a camel saddle. Now take the girls [referring to the women's embroidery group that meets in her house once a week], they were in Transjordan, they brought camel saddles with wonderful woodwork, and there were leather saddles, gorgeous, you've certainly seen [them] in all kinds of museums. No woman made a saddle, it's not for her. But for "Baby Dearest" when she brings him to the circumcision [ceremony], she wants him decorated. When "Baby Dearest" starts to walk — she wants him decorated. So, then she pays attention to the little things, like a chef, the king of chefs, makes very tasty dishes, [so, too] a woman makes a small decoration surrounding the fish. A woman for some cooked dish will make tiny decorations all around it for you. [I asked: "And do you like to make tiny decorations?"] Me, no, but if I do something, then I will take something that will give me the decorations all at once. So then I take thick green pepper and cut it and plunk it down all around, not a tiny piece for each one.[16]

As we continue, I will return to her self-perception, on the seam between the genders, and the seam between the Orient and the Occident, that she exemplifies through embroidery and cooking of "little things," and through "large" cultural and historical characterizations.

The perception of male embroidery as aggressive and "sharp" in contrast to the perception of feminine deeds as emotional and "round" is transferred also to another traditional female field — cooking. It is described by using diminutives — cooking in "small quantities," dealing with decorations:

A woman, as I said before, with her delicacy can only deal with details. Yes. When it is an issue of details, the woman [can do it]. But when [at hand] is quantity, it's the man. He takes the entire calf, takes all the good meat out of the calf, and does everything. She does not have the power to carry this out. The woman is afraid of quantities. The woman is born for fine things [. . .] the chefs who cook quantities are only men. All their inventions always lean toward quantities. They never invented something for four people, they always invent for thirty, fifty people. They are not capable of inventing of four people. I heard that a woman invented mayonnaise. So it seems to me. Anyway, the problem of tehina and mayonnaise are things women can invent. Whether they did invent it or not I don't know.

The miniaturization of feminine endeavor down to limited quantities and tiny, delicate decorations stands out regarding both embroidery and cooking. The idea of sauces fits in with this construction, which presents the man naturally as firm logic, as a base, and the woman as feeling, as a liquid sauce. The relations between basic food and sauce are presented in an asymmetrical manner, through the hierarchical perception of female, emotional thinking and logical male thinking — a concept completely congruent with the declaration by Zohar herself that she "is not a feminist." But Zohar describes herself as someone "who has learned how to go into depth." She brings together feminine embroidery and the other handicrafts, which she deciphers and teaches her students, with male logic that developed within her, as she sees it, owing to her studies in the West — and particularly in the German tradition. Thus, in contrast to other women who "see pictures" (as she stated elsewhere), she herself delves deep, and her proof of that is in taking the picture apart in an attempt to understand the system, the logic, and the order that stands behind it. Zohar explains:

> That I delve deeply is my father's fault, because he claimed that "only in Germany," "in Germany they plow everything with a sharp blade." I had teachers who forced me to go into things seriously. Ask your [female] embroiderers whether the thread twists to the left or to the right, they won't know. The Mishna states that "one thread is spun, two-three woven." Now, if it is woven to the right or to the left makes a tremendous difference! Most of the [female] embroiderers can't tell you!

And in another place: "See, I must always know more details. From where, how, and what. One has to go in depth. No young woman raises questions like these [. . .] The problem is that they see a picture and that's nice. But you have to know the foundation and that's the problem. A man is more thorough. Logical, thorough — whatever you want, while a woman [just] sees mostly pictures."

"To Think With Feeling"

Despite these statements that pay tribute to logical thinking, Zohar also lashes out against thinking that lacks feeling, this time, too, within the feminine context:

> And there are customs! See the custom at a funeral, a woman walking with her head covered, you are one of the funeral party, or you're related to someone — you walk with a head-covering. But when I went down to the street after Rabin's assassination, and an Arab said to me *"mā-bitastahîsh"* — she is not embarrassed? His wife without a headcovering, after all this is not an issue of faith, this is a custom. ["Are you talking about Leah Rabin?" I ask], that's the one. For this is not a matter of belief. Let's assume she does not want to observe commandments, but this is a custom. "From tip to toe," says the Arab — "she is all gold bracelets like they are selling in a store." It is customary during *shiv'a* to not wear jewelry. But this is a custom, no more [than that]. So they say to me, "She certainly didn't know." If she didn't know, more's the pity [. . .] I do not have to hear from an Arab how she is not embarrassed. So a woman must learn the customs of the country she is in, and she has to be a bit sensitive to things that hurt.

The combination of masculine knowledge — perceived as linked to the occidental-European — with feminine knowledge — associated with the Oriental-local-Arab — constitutes the unique Orientalist axis in the authoritative life story of Zohar Wilbush when she stresses the need, prevalent in Eretz Israel, for "thinking with feeling." She repeatedly attests about herself that "they always said about me that I think by palpation." The world of gender distinctions, the one of feeling and emotion in contrast to logical thinking, and the one of the local spatial-cultural versus the foreign, Arab versus European, intersect in various contexts. All along her life story, the "habitus" that Zohar creates links routine experiences (and mainly folk arts, clothing, cooking, fauna and flora) and broad political and historical categories. But serious scrutiny shows that her discourse transforms in many ways, the

"little" experiences — related to actions, to physical surroundings, and to immediate experiences — into universalist, political, and "great" historical categories. We return to the map of the Ottoman Empire hanging proudly over
the desk in the living room, and to the responses given by Zohar when we
asked her about the map:

> Why this map? Because it is a hundred and something years old, and with it I
> know exactly where I am. In my first document [attesting] that I am in this
> world, it clearly states I am Ottoman. It is written in Turkish. Of course, Rabbi
> Kook signed it, but it is written in Turkish. The Turkish provided opportuni-
> ties, until the World War they were very helpful to the Jews, much more than
> the Mandate government. They always tried to develop. They tried to deco-
> rate. Every one of their buildings is ornamented. The Turks, when they built,
> they immediately decorated, too. A Turk, first of all decorates the city where
> he lives.

Her autobiographic narrative is a discourse woven between the individual,
as expressing the "habitus," and the historical process. The "habitus" explains the historical process in which the Ottoman Empire map is a marker
of the starting point to which Zohar wishes to return. Her life story sets up
intersecting axes, and on them the English represent unemotional logic also
connected to masculinity, while the Arabs represent a culture of knowledge
that is not always based on logic. She sees the Ottoman Empire, into which
she herself was born, as a model for the merging of "building with ornamen-
tation," of logic with emotion. One may explain the name change of Zohara
Wilbushewitz as a change along two axes: the one between the feminine and
the masculine, and the other between the Jewish-European and the Orient.
By changing her name from Wilbushewitz to Wilbush (that her father determined) and from Zohara to Zohar, she initiated a shift from the Jewish-
European-feminine pole, to which she had belonged from birth, toward the
masculine and Oriental pole (comprised in this case of two portrayals presented, in other contexts in her narrative, precisely as contrasting), a pole
that is not definitely acquired and which, therefore, cannot be the primary
substitute. About her name change, she relates:

> If you take my documents, the British passport and British identity cards, [you
> will see] it is written: Sarah Zohara, Sarah for my father's mother's name, but
> Mother did not want Sarah. 'Cause she didn't like the sound. 'Cause "s[h]in"
> "resh" she didn't like the sound, so if you see pictures of the first [or] second

class of the Gymnasia, they would go out for a trip wearing kafiyyas and ajals,
Arab clothing. Then it was a kind of oriental poesy. So, then they gave me the
name Zuhura, they made it Zuhura instead of Zohara. Zuhura in Arabic is a
flower, *zuhoor*. ["How did this turn into Zohar?" I asked] How did this turn
into Zohar? When the Russian immigration came. Did you ever hear them
talking with their accent? Every "h" is a "g," isn't it? So then it was *"Zogara"*
or *"hara"* or something like that. Avshalom, may he rest in peace [Avshalom
Feinberg, her uncle], I have letters from him, used to called me Zuhoor. But,
Zuhoor was going too far. It is a bit too much. And so when I came to Jerusalem, I arrived two years before the state, I decided — Zohar.

In a similar way, the romantic attraction to men, who personify in their
body the merging of the East and the West, which she describes at various
points in her narrative, is a fantasy for a different orientalism, that which is
personified by the Armenian men, whom she first meets during a visit to
Alexandria as a teenager:

> I personally do not like the light blond who has no distinctiveness. Nor the
> eyes that are like water and as if they do not see, I much more like dark hair
> and dark eyes. At the time, when I was in Alexandria for the first time, I was
> fifteen when I took a trip there (since my uncle was in Alexandria, so I went
> there), so for the first time I encountered an Armenian orchestra. I said:
> "These are the men I want!" Their skin, too, is not black like the black man,
> but yet not completely white. And their eyes are not brown and not green. So
> I liked the Armenians.

And elsewhere we find:

> But what, in Alexandria I decided that the most handsome men are the Arme-
> nians. From the entire Orient and from all of Europe the most handsome man
> is the Armenian. They are not black and they are not white. They are a kind
> of special *caffe latte*. In Alexandria I decided that the most handsome man is
> the Armenian! The Armenians have maintained their race. I don't know if you
> have met an Armenian orchestra or Armenian athletes, an Armenian is a man
> worthy of the name man!

The aspiration to merge opposites, for joining East with West, feminine
and masculine, is a fantasy of complementary relations. Zohar binds her life
story, her very clear memories that are transmitted with such great sincerity
and candidness and interwoven with detailed descriptions regarding the

many colors of the soil, the scents of the flowers during the different seasons, and with expressions in many languages, to the point of learning lessons based on the fantasy of merging; emotion and logic which complement each other, which are expressed in the melding of the "rounding," "decorating" feminine and the "direct," "sharp," "graceless" masculine. These insights are "recruited" in her life story for the sphere of politics and leadership.

She explains:

> See, it is impossible to be in this country and be an American like Golda Meir or Bibi Netanyahu. Both she and he are Americans. Do they know the country? Give them this [she points to a myrtle branch], will they know what it is? Here sat a girl from Beit Hinukh [school] and asked me, "Who did you vote for, Peres or Bibi?" I said, "Peres is a Pole, Bibi from eight to eighteen was in America, so he looks at the Arabs like the blacks or the Indians." "So for who?" she asks again, so I said "Yigal Alon." "He's dead." So I said, "But he was the only one who understood the country, he was the only one who understood."

And on another occasion she said:

> We miss Yigal Alon more than anyone else, because he knew the country's inhabitants — both Jews and Arabs. He knew the surrounding countries. What I said about Golda Meir, I said that she was an alien plant among her people. Why? Because when the head of Intelligence came to her and said — "The Arab countries want to attack us." Four countries attacked. More than a thousand people were killed. The head of Intelligence came to her and told her they were preparing. So what did she answer? "He's a fantasizer. He's an Oriental Jew [. . .]." For her, all the Oriental Jews were hallucinators. She, the American, she's practical! Why was he the head of Intelligence? Because he knew Arabic, because he understood the mentality. But she held him in contempt, she summed him up as "he's a fantasizer" [. . .] Golda Meir did not know the country, she was not familiar with its customs, she didn't know anything. Bibi, I have nothing for or against him. But Bibi went to America when he was eight, stayed there until he was eighteen. He looks at the Arabs and doesn't understand the mentality, he does not understand what is going on around him. So they said to me "Stop! He's begun to learn Arabic." Thank you!! And if he learned Arabic, so what? You have to know the customs. You want coffee "*ahwe*," so I am ready to make "*ahwe*," but from me you'll get Bedouin "*ahwe*," not from powder and irradiated milk. Yigal Alon knew how to talk to every Arab, and he was familiar with them down to the last detail.

The "Americanization" processes taking place in Israeli society and leadership symbolize for Zohar a uni-directional culture, masculinity without femininity, a separation between the "small," material, local, intimate experience, and the "grand" politique and history; or, in other words, the lack of the cultural "habitus." This lack is symbolized in her statements about the vacuum Yigal Alon left behind him. Yigal Alon's image, which represents for her a combination between knowledge and feeling, between occidental and oriental, between the alien and the local, repeatedly appears in Zohar's life story: and in contrast looms a feminine figure, that of Golda Meir, with the traditional contrast between femininity and masculinity intersecting and turning about in her image, which portrays in Zohar's eyes, precisely in a female body, the keenness of the confrontation.

The construction of autobiographical memory is shaped as an interpretive and didactic process, in which the life story of the individual — especially impressive in this case — allots it place for scrutiny and analysis, linking the individual body and the Other with historical experience.[17] So the "feminine orientalism," which becomes decoded through her life story, constitutes, at one and the same time, the individual voice of the one defining herself — from the very outset of her life story — as an "atypical woman" and as "unique," and a window to the broad cultural perceptions of the "*Yishuv* aristocracy" in Eretz Israel, and especially to the feminine voice that reverberates in it.

Zohar relates the story of her life to Israeli women younger than herself in a way that reveals a complicated, unique orientalistic world view, personified through the fashioning of symbols and meanings taken from the concept of "habitus," in which body and knowledge are interconnected; in it, personal experience becomes a source of generative authority that explains the world. The status of knowledge that the narrator wishes to grant herself exposes a system of relations between pairs of contrasts, the basic one of which is the contrast between the female body and the male body. The rhetoric of the statements and the fashioning of the life story, characterized by authoritative setting up of pairs of contrasts that repeatedly disassemble each other in the course of the narrative, create disharmony between the private life story and the shaping of her life story through a dialog between us, as a didactic story with a vision of acceptance and harmony. Here another, tragic level of connection is revealed: The personal life story creeps into the text against its will, when it is recruited for the didactic, harmonious story.

This multidirectional system of relations between physical, daily experiences that are formulated as traditional femininity or traditional masculinity and broad categories of politics and history are capable of drawing one's attention to theoretical directions that examine the concept of culture and folk epistemology as a process of constructing contrasts and the negating symbolic connection, replete with fantasies, between "small" and private worlds, and between those considered large and universal.

❧ Education, Health, and Politics

❧ *Margalit Shilo*

A Cross-Cultural Message

The Case of Evelina de Rothschild

"In this whole great community [Jerusalem] there is not one single good school for girls, and all the daughters of Zion grow up without any education, without good training, without knowledge of the language of their nation and its history, be it only the smallest part, and therefore their spirits are not raised and they remain in their lowly state."[1] This criticism, published in the newspaper *Hazevi* in the late 1880s, disregarded educational institutions already operating in Jerusalem and complained of the lack of a comprehensive educational network for women and of the inferior spiritual level of the female sector. In contrast to this critique, the system of male education in the Holy City has received copious praise from historian Yosef Salmon: "It is doubtful whether there was any Jewish society in the world which placed such emphasis on the education of its [male] children as Ashkenazi society in the Land of Israel at this time."[2] The Jerusalem community, which had invested heavily in the education of its sons, showed little interest in educating its daughters. Yet, a girls' school was operating in Jerusalem and at the turn of the nineteenth century; it became a well-recognized institution.

The Education of Jewish Girls: The First Seeds (1854, 1855)

The attitude of *halakhah* (Jewish law) to Torah study for women is debated in the Mishnah, in Tractate *Sotah* (3:4): "Ben Azzai [declared]: A man is under the obligation to teach his daughter Torah . . . R. Eliezer says: Whoever teaches his daughter Torah, it is as though he teaches her obscenity."

This article was translated by David Louvish.

The *halakhah* as practiced over the centuries was based on Rabbi Eliezer's approach. Even authorities who permitted women's study limited it to matters within the scope of her activities, or to self-study.[3] Rabbi Eliezer's opinion found its practical expression in the almost universal lack of regular educational institutions for Jewish girls throughout the generations, in all parts of the Diaspora. It was largely responsible for the stigma of ignorance usually attached to women. This was common to all girls almost all over the world.

A real change in all matters connected with women's education took place in Western Europe in the eighteenth century. Schools for girls were established slowly but surely and became very popular. Proponents of women's education did not necessarily advocate identical education for men and women, but did assure basic education for girls.

Until the eighteenth century, the education of Jewish women was not inferior to that of their non-Jewish sisters, whether in the West or in the East; at times, it was even superior. The advent of schools for non-Jewish girls, however, placed Jewish girls in an inferior position. The Jewish Haskalah movement, which arose in the wake of the European Enlightenment, adopted the latter's positive attitude to basic formal education for girls and encouraged girls to close the gap between themselves and their non-Jewish neighbors. Toward the end of the eighteenth and beginning of the nineteenth century, the first Jewish schools for girls were established in Germany, France, and England.[4] By the end of the nineteenth century, innovative educational institutions for girls also appeared in Eastern Europe.[5] Far-reaching innovations with regard to the education of girls occurred in the Mediterranean Basin as well. The revolution also reached the Holy City, where it had a unique facet.

Jerusalem of the nineteenth century had gone through many changes. Newly developing political conditions and modern technologies, coupled with long-standing religious longings and new winds of migration blowing from Europe were all factors that promoted the renewed growth of the Jewish community with a new vigor.[6] Jerusalem had grown at a special pace. By the end of the nineteenth century, the Jewish community in Jerusalem, only about two thousand men and women at the beginning of the century, had increased fifteenfold, and by the outbreak of the World War I, it counted forty-seven thousand.[7] The Jewish immigrants came from a variety of regions, in both Eastern and Western Europe, the Ottoman Empire including Yemen, and even from far-off Persia and Bukhara.

The very bad financial situation of the Jewish community of Jerusalem was a concern for Jews all over the world. The *halukkah,* a unique long-established system, was responsible for money sent to the Holy Land from all the scattered Jewish communities of the Diaspora. Thus, the Jewish community aroused the interest of co-religionists who introduced new initiatives to the Holy City. One of them was — a girls' school.

The first initiatives for the establishment of schools for Jewish girls in the Holy City came from Western Europe, which was a testing-ground for educational innovations in society in general as well as among Jews.[8] The Rothschilds of France and the Montefiores of England saw women's education in the Land of Israel as one of their primary goals. As a matter of fact, the activities of Christian missionaries in Jerusalem, who pioneered the establishment of schools for Jewish girls in Jerusalem, provided the momentum for their activity in this field.

The philanthropist Albert Cohn, who represented the Rothschilds of Paris, founded the first girls' school in Jerusalem in the summer of 1854; Sir Moses Montefiore established a similar institution a year later.[9] In his report on his activities in Jerusalem, Albert Cohn described the girls' school as follows: "A girls' school, where all girls of the Jewish community will be taught women's handicrafts as well as religious and basic general subjects has been established under the auspices of Baroness Nathaniel Rothschild."[10]

Several issues, some procedural and some substantial, stand out in this concise report. Unlike traditional institutions founded by parents or teachers, the initiative for the establishment of new schools came from the outside. Moreover, unlike the then-common community-oriented educational institutions for boys, this school was open to girls of all Jerusalem communities. In its early days, the school's population comprised a few dozen girls, both Ashkenazi (European origin) and Sephardi (Near Eastern origin).[11] Underlying these differences were innovative educational concepts. Vocational training towards the womanly ideal of the housewife was presented as the school's primary goal, and so the most important subject was handicrafts — "sewing and spinning."[12] On the other hand, in the male sector of the Jewish community of Jerusalem, vocational education was customarily intended only for poorer students. Traditional education for boys was exclusively directed towards religious education, whereas modern education directed the pupil to prepare him- or herself for life, to fulfill a role in society.[13] This innovation was applied only in the girls' school. As a consequence of these educational approaches, basic studies for girls, such as, reading and writing skills, were presented as the last educational goal.

Mary Eliza Rogers, an English tourist, visited the Holy Land in the 1850s and her book about daily life in the Holy Land has become a classic. She describes the atmosphere in the Rothschild school at great length. There were about fifty girls, aged seven through fifteen, some of whom were already engaged to be married. The (female) teachers were enthusiastic: "[O]ur guide exhibited to us, with evident pride and pleasure, a considerable stock of wearing apparel, the result of one week's work in that room."[14] The girls, too, "looked busy and bright," and some of them were proficient in reading Hebrew.[15] Competition between the two new schools probably was detrimental to both. The Montefiore school existed only a short time.

The Rothschild school was of considerable importance and pioneering achievements. For the first time, Jewish girls in Jerusalem had become the target of conscientious and systematic educational efforts. The school was the first channel for the transmission of European educational and cultural conceptions and viewpoints, such as the need for formal education for women, for systematic training for domestic tasks, and for a basic religious education. Intended for all Jerusalem girls, it was particularly successful among Sephardi girls who, up to this time, had been excluded systematically from any education whatsoever.[16] Despite its meager achievements, the school blazed a new trail, but its importance was not recognized by all its contemporaries.

Evelina de Rothschild School, 1868–1894: "Bits of Education" or a "Real School"?

The Evelina de Rothschild School was a major point of interest, a veritable "tourist site," for Jewish visitors concerned with change in the Jerusalem community.[17] Evaluations of the institution varied from one extreme to the other, depending on the visitors' expectations. Thus, the closing words of a report published in *Halevanon* in 1869 were as follows: "This institutions will deserve the name of 'school' only if the teachers will be learned women."[18]

In contrast to this critical comment, the school received a more favorable evaluation from the *hakham bashi* (the Sephardi Chief Rabbi of Jerusalem), who at one time publicly examined the girls. He openly declared his positive attitude to the school and to girls' education in general: "I am happy to say that I derived great pleasure from seeing the young girls successfully displaying their achievements, both in the study of our holy tongue and in their knowledge of its sacred commandments."[19] On another occasion, he admitted that "The Jews of Jerusalem have never had such a school for girls in Jerusalem."[20]

For the first thirty-four years of its existence, the school operated as a kind of branch of the Rothschild Hospital, being managed by the wives of the hospital doctors.[21] For reasons of modesty and tradition, most of the teaching staff were women. The number of students increased apace; about fifty in 1868, by 1872 the number of students, aged from four to sixteen, had exceeded two hundred, and it continued to grow.[22]

The school, originally in the Old City, moved to the New City and a new principal, Fortuna Behar, the sister of Nissim Behar (the principal of the Alliance boys' school), was appointed in 1888.[23] This signaled a dramatic change in the institution, arousing considerable hopes both for an improvement in the general level of studies and for the intensification of Hebrew studies.[24] The new building soon proved too small to accommodate would-be students, and hundreds were turned away.

Over the years, the basic curriculum proposed when the school had been founded was expanded. Besides Hebrew reading and writing, the curriculum included sewing, arithmetic, history, geography, and natural science. There was as well a proposal to study "the local language [Arabic] and a European language [French]."[25] There was some criticism of Fortuna Behar for giving priority to French over Hebrew culture.[26]

What was the school's impact on its students? It seems that, whether consciously or unconsciously, the Evelina de Rothschild School for Girls instilled a sense of self-awareness. This was clearly expressed in a speech by one of the students, Bolisa Angel, at a school celebration in 1878. Beginning with an account of the story of Creation, she stressed how woman had been made from a man's rib. She was describing the conventional gender images — the man leaving his home to support his family was "clothed in magnificent garments," while the woman, staying at home to tend his needs, "is subservient." She clearly expressed jealousy of men, pointing to the shortage of girls' schools as an impediment to women bettering their social position.[27] Paradoxically, it was the acquisition of knowledge that opened her eyes and made her recognize her lowly position. As long as she had been denied any education, she did not realize her weakness. Were these thoughts of Bolisa Angel hers alone, or did they occur to her companions as well?

The importance of girls' education for social progress as a whole was pointed out in an article in *Havazelet* in 1886: "We have a hard and fast rule that you cannot be sure of an idea's realization unless it is taken up by women, for it is they who educate their children and also manage their husbands."[28] The Evelina de Rothschild School was a trailblazer in women's education in the East. For all its pioneering role, it seems to have sent out a double message: It had a conservative outlook, on the one hand; but, on the other, it showed faith in women's intellectual talents and their importance in the education and support of their families. Owing to the relatively small number of graduates and the management's desire to insist that "Evelina" was a conservative institution, its public image was that of a small, rather unimportant, school. However, its slow educational efforts in the course of forty years prepared the ground for a real educational revolution.

The Anglo-Jewish Association: Girls' Education as a Path to Western-Style Progress

Philanthropic involvement in girls' education received new impetus in 1894, when the Anglo-Jewish Association (AJA, known in Hebrew as *Aguddat Ahim*, literally: "Association of Brethren") took the Evelina de Rothschild School under its wing. The AJA was founded in 1871 by British Jews who wished to emulate the French Alliance Israélite Universelle and to cooperate with it.[29] Conscious of their improved political position, the Jews of Great Britain were anxious to help Jews of other countries, and particularly those of the Ottoman Empire. The AJA set itself both political and educational goals.[30] Its declared objectives being "to aid in promoting the social, moral, and in- tellectual progress of the Jews," it was particularly concerned with the edu- cation of Jewish boys and girls in Eastern countries.[31] This profound interest in education was shared by all sectors of the Jewish community: Zionists and anti-Zionists, nationalists and assimilationists. The special relationship of the AJA with the Evelina de Rothschild School was established with the full knowledge and assent of the Rothschilds, who continued to provide finan- cial support.[32]

In the nineteenth century, the idea that girls' education was a highly significant tool for social change fueled the activities of many philanthropic organizations, some motivated by colonialist and/or missionary ideals. "If we get the girls, we get the race" was the motto of missionaries working inten- sively among young girls.[33] Or, alternatively, as expressed by AJA officials: "Give me the daughters, and the grandsons will look after themselves."[34] In fact, they considered educating girls to be more important than educating boys, particularly in Eastern countries, given the inferior status of women there.[35] It was generally accepted that "it is the mother who usually makes two-thirds of the man."[36] Women's public activities and girls' education were intimately connected, as witness the establishment of girls' schools all over the world.[37] As put by gender historian Billie Melman, "In the colonial nation state, motherhood was perceived not merely as an expression of femininity, but as women's national social service to the empire."[38] Such perceptions were nourished by a variety of social movements that flourished in the nineteenth century and promoted women's education, women's training as teachers, the founding of kindergartens, and the ideal of domesticity. All these motives found their echo in Jewish girls' schools in England as well, and in the extensive development of a network, founded at the time by Jewish philanthropic organizations, of girls' education throughout the Ottoman Empire.

In contrast to the positive image of the Jewish woman in Western Europe, the Jewish woman in the East was viewed in an unfavorable light even in comparison with her non-Jewish counterpart in that part of the world. An AJA visitor to the Ottoman Empire observed that in cities like Damascus, and perhaps also other Muslim cities, Jewish women seemed to be inferior to both their Muslim and Christian counterparts.[39] The members of the AJA concurred with this evaluation, declaring that "the terrible influence of Islam upon the status and position of women must be checked and counteracted."[40] The official organ of the AJA openly spoke of the need to emancipate Jewish women in the East.[41]

The declarations of the AJA representatives attest to a dual goal: "to give our Jewish boys and girls the virtues of the West without robbing them of the virtues of the East."[42] Britain was the leading country in Europe with regard to involvement in the Holy Land, and British Jews' concern with affairs in the country was in effect a continuation of the extensive interest taken by British Christians in the East as a whole.[43] The AJA saw its work as a national mission.[44]

The Evelina de Rothschild School, 1894–1914: Flagship of the AJA

A first manifestation of the AJA's generous supervision was the move to a spacious new building, which made it possible to admit many more students. In 1895, the Association bought a magnificent house, known as *Bet Mahanayim* (previously the home of a banker named Frutiger), comprising more than forty rooms.[45] The building earned considerable praise; for example, *Hazevi* wrote: "This building is one of the most beautiful in our city, and it has a large garden, beautiful, spacious and with sufficient space for a large school."[46] The girls used to call it "the Queen of Sheba's palace."[47] It was the first step in the AJA's intensive efforts to develop the school.

The number of girls studying in the school rapidly increased. However, even after the student population had doubled, mothers still came to the school's doors begging for their daughters to be admitted and given a chance to study. Adela Goodrich-Freer, an English tourist, described the hubbub at the school gates on the day of registration. The neighborhood was full of people, and fathers eager to have their daughters admitted literally threw them into the school courtyard over the fence.[48] By the beginning of the twentieth century, there were about 200 girls in the kindergarten (which was part of the school), and more than 300 in the school proper. The number peaked in the summer of 1913, with 676 girls in the kindergarten and the school.[49] The school management limited the students' age to fifteen at most, and the increase in school population leveled off, for lack of space.[50] Despite the growth of the institution, AJA officials were well aware that the profound problem of girls' education in Jerusalem had not been solved, and that only some 15 percent of Jewish girls in Jerusalem received formal education.[51] Other philanthropic organizations went into action, beginning in 1905, and established new girls' schools in Jerusalem; but many girls still had not found their place in a suitable educational framework.

Not only were the school's physical accommodations changed; the management was also replaced. In 1900, the veteran headmistress Fortuna Behar was dismissed; she was soon replaced by Miss Annie Landau, brought especially from London.[52] The replacement entailed numerous other administrative changes designed to streamline the running of the school, and a variety of educational measures that sought to change the atmosphere.[53] Miss Landau, as her pupils addressed her, made a decisive imprint on the school and was instrumental in making it an innovative, influential institution. Yehudit Harari, a teacher from Rehovot who joined the staff, described her warmly as an "educated English Jewess, with her energy and good taste; . . . bright, beautiful, gray eyes, childlike laughter and domineering voice."[54] The new headmistress, who was to rule the school with an iron hand for forty-five years, until her death in 1945, was absolutely convinced that she was discharging a mission and moreover that she would be able to influence the character of the Holy City.[55]

An Integrative Educational Institution

The Evelina de Rothschild School sought to reshape Jewish society in the Holy City. The first successfully achieved objective was communal integration. The school provided for girls of all Jewish communities. Together with girls from Yemen, Morocco, Persia, and Georgia, there were Ashkenazi girls of Eastern European families and "real" Sephardi girls from the Balkans.[56] Around the beginning of the twentieth century, about one-half of the students were Ashkenazi, and the other half, Sephardi and Eastern.[57] In the school's early years, girls of different communities were taught in separate classrooms, but by the end of the nineteenth century, the classes were mixed. This constituted a challenge to the traditional separation of communities in Jerusalem. Unlike the Alliance girls' school in Galata, Istanbul, in which the curricula offered to rich and poor girls were different, the Evelina de Rothschild School aimed at complete integration.[58] The school regulations, like those of Alliance institutions, declared that it was open to non-Jews as well.[59] In fact, some Turkish officials sent their daughters to study at the school, a fact that testified to its high educational level and its ability to compete with Christian schools.

Another goal of the school was to raise the average marriage age of girls in Jerusalem. To achieve a good education, a girl had to spend more years in school. In a newspaper interview, Annie Landau told how her attention had been drawn to an earring worn by a Yemenite girl. Inquiries revealed that the girl was engaged. The young bride's mother was astounded at the headmistress's intervention, but Miss Landau saw in postponing the girl's marriage a definite educational goal, which moreover also had a medical aspect.[60] Postponement of marriage would also make it possible to enhance the girl's intellectual and physical maturity.

The school also devoted itself to ramified activities in the field of preventive medicine, thus making an important contribution to the health of Jerusalem's inhabitants. Another expression of the desire to influence Jewish life in Jerusalem was the public celebrations held in honor of the festivals of Hanukkah and Purim.[61] These celebrations were occasions for theater performances directed by the teachers and moreover provided an opportunity to display the girls' achievements in English and Hebrew before residents and visitors to Jerusalem.[62]

As part of its efforts to impart lofty spiritual and social values, the school also aimed to shape its students' character and ethical qualities. Annie Landau believed in encouraging voluntary activities; the girls established a group they called Benot Zion, "Daughters of Zion," whose members undertook to speak only Hebrew.[63] They also established a society for the prevention of cruelty to animals.[64] The desire to influence the girls' way of life in the future as well was the motive for establishing a graduates' association, whose members were encouraged to revisit the school and hold weekly meetings, at which they would discuss Hebrew and English literature, also talking about their lives after leaving school.[65]

The social agents of these innovative ideas were the school's teachers, who had been educated in the pedagogical traditions of Western Europe. Annie Landau was the first harbinger of the trend of young Jewish women to come, mainly from Germany, to teach in the Holy City. They regarded their stay in the country as something of an adventure and a cultural mission at the same time, what one might term today "National Service."[66]

The school management tried to cope with the shortage of appropriate teachers in the country by training some of its graduates as teachers.[67] This also provided a temporary solution for some of the graduates, who wanted to continue their studies or work for a living, whether in the kindergarten or in the school proper.[68] Thus, in 1911–1912, the school introduced a special class for continued studies, essentially a kind of embryonic teachers' college.[69] The school took pride in being the first institution in the Land of Israel to train teachers for kindergartens and schools in the *moshavot*.[70]

Evelina de Rothschild School — Society and Gender

Less than a decade after her arrival, Annie Landau could tell the *Jewish Chronicle* in an interview that the school had brought about a revolution in the girls' values: "I have been accused of making our girls unfit for their surroundings. I admit the impeachment. I was sent to Jerusalem to do that and I hope I may succeed."[71] The girls of "Evelina" underwent a veritable "spiritual metamorphosis," she said on another occasion.[72] "The Evelina School is even more than a school. . . . It is something also of a home."[73] As early as 1911, Miss Landau was able to assert, "By educating the girls of Jerusalem . . . , we are slowly but surely improving conditions in the Holy Land."[74] "Evelina de Rothschild" had become a tool of major significance for the reshaping of Jerusalem society, which was then in the throes of accelerated social transformation.

If one follows the curriculum and the headmistress's declarations, as quoted not infrequently in the Jewish press, one gets the impression that the Evelina de Rothschild School was conveying a rather complex, even paradoxical message, in terms of both national-religious and gender concepts.

The headmistress, who was strictly observant, wrote explicitly of her conviction that "the education of the Jewish girls of Jerusalem must be animated

by a deep and ardent religious spirit in order to produce strong Jewish per-
sonalities."[75] Her school, she declared, was ultra-Orthodox, and it was her intention to respect Eastern culture, not to denigrate it, for "East and West
have still something to learn from and to give to each other."[76] Despite her
religious principles, Miss Landau was in full agreement with Western Jews'
criticism of the *halukkah* and the ideology that it represented. The directors
of the AJA called the *halukkah* a "cancer eating away the vitals of Jerusalem."[77] The school aimed to help solve the problem by educating the girls
to work for a living — not only as a response to a basic economic need but as
an educational value. The girls were taught to love labor and to value economic independence.[78]

In one of her *Jewish Chronicle* interviews, Miss Landau stressed her belief
that "it is every human creature's right to strive to reach the highest rung
in the ladder of life."[79] This simple observation, offered with the utmost cau-
tion, ultimately produced the insight that every woman had the right to
study, not only to achieve her goal as a mother, but also by the mere token
of being human. Girls' education, originally intended to contribute to the
improvement of society by preparing women to educate their sons properly,
became an end in itself. It is worth devoting some attention to the way the
consequences of an innovative educational enterprise sometimes cause the
innovators themselves to revise their concepts.

The teaching of Hebrew, as a language that could facilitate communication and unity among the different communities of the Holy City, redirected
the Anglo-Jewish Association toward an area that it had not aimed for at
all: the development of the new "Hebrew" nationalism. While "Evelina" became known throughout the *Yishuv* as a bastion of the English language, the
paradoxical fact is that it became a valuable source of efforts to promote
the study of Hebrew as a spoken language.

In view of the political dimension of Hebrew speech in pre–World War I
days, the school management distanced itself somewhat from Hebrew and
declared its view that English was more important, whether for the promotion of general culture or as a key for economic success in the future.[80] Some
years after her arrival in the country, Annie Landau explained her complex
attitude toward the revival of the Hebrew language. Denying any connection
with the Zionist movement, she identified with the ultra-Orthodox establishment, declaring: "I am only a Zionist in that I give my life's strength to my
work in Zion."[81]

Yehudit Harari, who taught at the school, writes in her memoirs of her
amazement at the school's official attitude: "How can one be religious, love

the land dearly, and yet oppose Jewish nationalism? [Miss Landau] prays every day for the rebuilding of Jerusalem and the return to Zion, and yet she opposes those returning to Zion!"[82] Many students at the school, rejecting this complex message, identified with the national longing for the revival of Hebrew and saw Hebrew as their mother tongue. Other graduates, however, left the country to work as nursemaids and nurses; the pride expressed by the school in their success in Western Europe and the United States is indicative of its attitude to Jewish settlement in the Holy Land.[83]

The Evelina de Rothschild School prepared its graduates to participate in the Zionist enterprise not only by teaching them Hebrew, but also by shaping the image of a new, rural woman. In 1900, the first Hebrew reader aimed specifically at girls — *Bat Hayil*, subtitled *Torat Em*, — was published by one of the school teachers, Yosef Meyuhas. It throws some light on the other female model that the school was trying to foster. The figure of the young woman most prominent in the various readings that make up the book is one living in the country or a town girl who spends vacations in the country; she is diligent, cheerful, always ready to help in domestic chores. Girls are described milking cows, making cheese, preparing jam from fruit, and so on. At first sight, *Bat Hayil* — the Hebrew phrase, by analogy with the biblical phrase *eshet hayil*, generally translated as "woman of valor" or "capable wife" (Proverbs 31:10), means "capable daughter" — seems to be a conservative figure: "a gracious crown to her husband and a good mother to her children," but at second glance her depiction apparently fits the new *Yishuv* girls in the *moshavah*.[84]

On the tenth anniversary of her assumption of the office of principal, Miss Landau, the "Iron Lady" of Evelina de Rothschild School, summed up the achievements of the school's graduates in the previous three years: About one-half were working in workshops run by "Bezalel," the Jerusalem School of Arts and Crafts, or by the school itself. One-quarter had married and were now housewives. About 10 percent had left the country, some with their parents, others, on their own, seeking a living; a similar number were working in Hebrew kindergartens in various parts of the country; and still others were continuing their studies in new Hebrew schools.[85] Economic independence, home industry, domestic life, Hebrew education, emigration, further study — this picture reflects the influence of the school's complex educational message.

The reform of the East as envisaged by the Evelina de Rothschild School was riddled with contradictions. The new woman shaped within its walls was at one and the same time an observant Jewess, a "real" European woman, and a new Hebrew woman. Her declared mission was to care for her family and work for the good of society and the nation, while at the same time being an independent human being, entitled to self-realization. The ideal girl was perceived first and foremost to be performing her tasks in the family and in the community, and education was considered a primary tool in guaranteeing her success as a wife and a mother.[86] The decision to give priority to the education of girls was a revolutionary element of Jewish educational thought in general, and in particular in Jerusalem.

🌿 *Shifra Shvarts and Zipora Shehory-Rubin*

On Behalf of Mothers and Children in Eretz Israel

The Activity of Hadassah, the Federation of Hebrew Women, and WIZO to Establish Maternal and Infant Welfare Centers — Tipat Halav, 1913–1948

The Activities of Nathan Straus and "Daughters of Zion — Hadassah" on Behalf of Mothers and Children toward the End of the Ottoman Period

In 1908, Henrietta Szold visited Eretz Israel. Henrietta Szold (1860–1945), a native of Baltimore, daughter of a Zionist rabbinical family, one of the founders of the Hadassah organization and its first president, arrived in the country after a trip to Europe. She was shaken by the misery, poverty, and filth in which the people of Jerusalem, Tiberias, and Safed were steeped, and especially by the low state of hygiene that she felt directly affected the public's general state of health. So Szold conceived a comprehensive plan for public health that would bring relief to the women and children. Her plan began to move toward becoming a reality with the founding of Hadassah, the Women's Zionist Organization of America, in 1912. Hadassah set for itself the goal of helping the *Yishuv* in Eretz Israel in the fields of education and health and also strived to work for "a healthy population that would be able to function properly on the personal and public levels, and for the benefit of society that makes possible pleasant motherhood and happy childhood."[1]

Implementation of Szold's plan began in 1913 with the assistance of the Jewish philanthropist Nathan Straus, who already had earned a reputation as experienced in establishing centers in the United States for the distribution of pasteurized milk to needy mothers who could not nurse. Straus visited Eretz Israel with his wife Lina in 1912 on his way to Rome to attend an international conference devoted to the war on tuberculosis. On this visit, Straus set up a soup kitchen and a health center that had three departments: hygiene education, eye diseases, and bacteriology.[2] Upon his return to America, Straus urged Henrietta Szold to begin the immediate application of her plan. So the Hadassah members chose two New York nurses, Rose Kaplan of Mount Sinai Hospital and Rachel Landy, a nurse-supervisor at Harlem Hospital, and sent them to Jerusalem to open a Maternal and Infant Welfare Center on the pattern of the highly successful centers operating in the United States. The two nurses arrived in Eretz Israel in early 1913, accompanied by Straus and his funding; they settled in Meah She'arim in an apartment that he rented for them. The apartment served also as a clinic where they gave guidance to pregnant women and mothers. The center was open to all, regardless of religion or race, and focused on providing the services of midwives, health and hygiene education, home visits to needy mothers, and treatment for schoolchildren suffering trachoma. The nurses worked in cooperation with Dr. Abraham Ticho, an ophthalmologist, and in coordination with the health center. Following Straus's instructions, the nurses patterned their work according to the model developed in New York for the operation of the mother and child welfare centers. So this became the first Maternal and Infant Welfare Center established in Eretz Israel that trained midwives and offered professional guidance by nurses and physicians to mothers and pregnant women in their own homes.

Upon the outbreak of World War I, Rose Kaplan left the country and Rose Landy continued the project with Dr. Helena Kagan, a pioneer in pediatrics, who immigrated to Eretz Israel from Switzerland in 1914.[3] In September 1915, when funding had run out, Landy was forced to return to the United States and the clinic was closed.

Dr. Kagan continued to provide medical assistance in the clinic she opened in her home near the Meah She'arim neighborhood, and even trained Jewish and Arab young women to serve as nurses at the municipal hospital. She trained local nurses to work in the schools and continued to manage the midwifery services that the two Hadassah nurses had founded. In 1916, owing to the economic difficulties in the *Yishuv* during World War I, Dr. Kagan expanded the midwifery services to the city of Jaffa, too, and for that purpose obtained a contribution from the Committee on Palestine Welfare of Chicago.

The American Zionist Medical Unit

A basic change in the condition of the mothers and children in Eretz Israel occurred in August 1918 with the arrival of the delegation for medical assistance on behalf of the Jewish communities of the United States, the American Jewish Joint Distribution Committee — Special Assistance Committee, the American Zionist Federation, and the American Women's Zionist Organization — Hadassah; the group was called the American Zionist Medical Unit and it came to help the medical services of Jewish community in Eretz Israel.

The medical unit included medical personnel, pharmacists, and medical administrators, chief among them Dr. Isaac Rubinow, a physician and social legislation activist in the United States, who directed the unit together with Henrietta Szold.[4] As part of the unit's activities in the field of preventive medicine, the team of physicians and nurses began to formulate a comprehensive plan to aid mothers, infants, and children. Its first act in this direction was the opening of a "consultation center for mothers and pregnant women" in the Old City of Jerusalem, operated in conjunction with the Federation of Hebrew Women. The center quickly expanded its areas of activity and set up, within its quarters, a kitchen for distributing milk, which was called "Tipat Halav" (A Drop of Milk), where milk was pasteurized and then distributed to needy children.

Dr. Rubinow, the medical unit's director, planned to establish a country-wide network of mother and child welfare centers that would be operated by nurses specially trained for that, but a decision taken by the World Zionist Congress (Karlsbad, September 1923) thwarted his plans. The congress determined that the medical unit would change from being a temporary relief organization into a permanent one in Eretz Israel, under the direction of Hadassah and that its name would be the "Hadassah Medical Organization." From then on, Hadassah continued, in cooperation with the Federation of Hebrew Women, with the establishment of centers that the medical unit had begun.

Efforts by the Federation of Hebrew Women and Hadassah in Establishing the Centers for Mother and Child

The Federation of Hebrew Women was founded in Jerusalem in 1920 at the initiation of Bathsheba Kesselman, a Hadassah member in the United

States. When she came to Eretz Israel in 1919, Kesselman encountered harsh reality — unsanitary childbirth conditions and high infant mortality rates. Aware of Hadasshah's power, Kesselman thought of the idea of setting up a local women's group that would cooperate with Hadassah and offer help to mothers and pregnant women.[5] The volunteers set as their goals providing assistance to women during pregnancy and childbirth, teaching them how to take care of the newborn from the day of birth, following up the child's development and growth, taking material care of the mother, training her in a profession according to her capabilities, and even helping find her a job.[6]

The organization of this endeavor was initially local in order to cope with the problems at hand, such as mutual aid and help for new immigrant women who had difficulties with Hebrew, assistance in adjusting to the country's climate and improvement of inadequate nutrition, help for pregnant women and women in distress, and provision of food for infants in danger of dying from malnutrition.

At first the idea of establishing such an organization encountered opposition from various women's organization already operating in the country (such as "Ezer Yoledot" [Aid to Women Giving Birth], Federation of Hebrew Women); they argued that the creation of another group would be redundant and that all forces should be consolidated. To overcome this resistance, Kesselman proposed appointing Henrietta Szold, a well-known personality in the *Yishuv*, as president of the organization. Szold's agreement to take on this role cleared the opposition and prepared the way for turning the Federation of Hebrew Women into an auxiliary body for Hadassah. At the founding assembly, held on 14 July 1920, Szold stressed the overwhelming need for as many volunteers as possible to implement Hadassah's plan to establish mother and child welfare centers throughout the country. So it was decided that the Federation of Hebrew Women would be a popular movement that would encompass women from all levels of society and allow any woman who wanted to join to do so; it was also determined that the organization would focus on giving aid to the pregnant woman and her baby and would educate mothers and children about health, hygiene, and sanitation.[7]

Response was great and many volunteers from all around the country joined the ranks of the organization from the outset. The first branches were established in Haifa (1922), Tiberias (1923), Safed (1923), Tel Aviv (1924), and Rehovot (1924), places with large concentrations of disadvantaged populations, mainly of Oriental Jews, who lived under harsh conditions of poor hygiene, malnutrition, ignorance, and superstition.[8]

Soon, the Federation of Hebrew Women members, under the leadership of Bathsheba Kesselmen, applied themselves vigorously to working among the mothers in Jerusalem. Their volunteer work was conducted in coordination and cooperation with Hadassah: Hadassah provided the medical service and the Federation of Hebrew Women administered the social work and helped in the operation of the mother and child welfare centers. The volunteers began to disseminate information. In the streets of the Old City, they tried to locate pregnant women and convince them to accept medical supervision from Hadassah physicians at the Rothschild-Hadassah Hospital. They persuaded pregnant women to come for examinations during the final months of their pregnancy and to give birth in the hospital. The women who took care to be examined regularly were promised economic and material aid that included medicines, bedding, and underwear for themselves and their newborn. After the birth, volunteers made home visits and provided help for the mother, the newborn, and the entire family, with activities including the buying of groceries and taking care of the other children in the family.[9]

The daily meeting between the mothers and members of the Federation of Hebrew Women proved that it was not enough to deal only with pregnant women and those giving birth and that the provision of information and guidance should be extended also to women who were already mothers. To that end, centers for advising mothers were set up in neighborhoods, on the assumption that with the establishment of the neighborhood center, its services would be available to every mother. The first center was set up in June 1921 in an apartment in the Old City of Jerusalem, and it fulfilled three functions: giving guidance to pregnant women; giving infant-care training and advice to mothers; and pasteurizing milk and distributing it to needy infants. The work at the center was shared by the Hadassah nurses and volunteers from the Federation of Hebrew Women. The nurses carried out the medical tasks that included weighing the new baby, following its development and giving it inoculations, and assisting the volunteer physician, Dr. Helena Kagan. The volunteers did the administrative-social work that included registering the women who had given birth and their infants, producing the "newborn cards," writing monthly reports, recruiting volunteers, and collecting the payment for the pasteurized milk, a fee determined according to a family's social welfare situation.[10] Members of the women's federation even used to register every birth that took place in the Rothschild-Hadassah hospital and personally invite to the center each woman who had just given birth. If a few weeks had passed after the delivery and the woman had not come to the center, a nurse was sent to her house for a home visit, and the nurse convinced her to come to the center.

Initially, there was poor response on the part of the mothers, as they were still influenced by superstitions and archaic customs. They opposed any change and refused to accept the advice of the young, unmarried nurses, arguing that those young women had not yet given birth themselves. They also were against weighing and measuring the infants for fear of the evil eye.[11] The mothers expected to receive real material aid when they came to the center, and they were greatly disappointed when all they got was advice and instruction from the doctor and the nurse!

To encourage the visits and to lessen the women's vehement opposition, it was necessary to promise material assistance. And indeed, the nurses promised the mothers that they would receive, free of charge, all the necessities for the baby (diapers, clothing, bathing needs) as well as pasteurized milk, if they would give birth in the hospital and if, after the birth, they would come regularly to the center with the baby for the continuation of treatment and for advice on childrearing. Only after the nurses had succeeded in gaining the trust of the mothers in their ability and desire to promote their children's health did the visits begin to become regular.[12]

At first, service at the centers was given to Jewish and Arab women no matter what religion or race. Since they gave birth at home, the Arab mothers, Muslim and Christian, came to the center under the influence of their Jewish neighbors or private doctors. Starting in August 1923, an Arabic-speaking nurse was appointed to work with them. As a result of the constantly growing number of Arab mothers, reaching over one hundred, in 1924 a center was opened for them at the Nablus Gate in the Old City.[13]

One of the main problems suffered by a large part of the mothers was their inability to nurse owing to inadequate nutrition and diseases. The pediatrician Dr. Helena Kagan taught the mothers how to get help from a supplement of cows' milk rich in protein, calcium, and thiamine (vitamin B); but the economic situation did not allow most of the mothers to buy cows' milk and to Dr. Kagan's dissatisfaction they bought goats' milk, which was cheaper. To overcome this problem, it was decided to organize the distribution of milk to needy mothers.

The Federation of Hebrew Women assumed responsibility for organizing the distribution of milk through the "Drop of Milk Committee" that it set up among its volunteers. In the Old City counseling center kitchen, a Tipat Halav (A Drop of Milk) station was set up, the necessary amounts of milk were prepared by adding water and sugar for each infant, according to the doctor's instructions. The funding came from Flora Solomon, the wife of Harold Solomon, director of the Commerce and Industry Office in the

Mandate government in Eretz Israel: She financed the equipping of the milk kitchen and the distribution of the milk. Flora Solomon was also the head of the team of volunteers who poured the milk into sterile bottles and gave them out to the needy mothers in return for a token payment. Bathsheba Kesselman's initiative instituting a contribution called "milk collectors" for the benefit of women in Jerusalem helped overcome the project's financial problems.

The first year, milk was also provided to infants living in neighborhoods outside the Old City. Buckets full of ice in which nestled bottles of milk were loaded onto a donkey's back; that way some sixty babies received the daily amounts of milk they needed. In August 1921, a second "Drop of Milk" center was opened in the courtyard of the Rothschild-Hadassah hospital. The center served as a milk distribution point for the New City children and as a place where mothers obtained advice and guidance. In July 1923, the Federation of Hebrew Women initiated the opening of a third center in the New City's Mahaneh Yehuda neighborhood, which served for distributing milk and for providing weekly advice to mothers, including doctors' examinations.[14]

During the first two years of the milk kitchens' operation, the milk was delivered to the mothers' home. But later it was decided to concentrate the distribution of the milk in the counseling centers for mothers. The mothers who came to buy milk received, on the same occasion, guidance from Federation of Hebrew Women volunteers and medical services — from the Hadassah nurses and doctors. This combination contributed to enhancing awareness of the medical services. Gradually, the name Tipat Halav [Drop of Milk] was preferred over the other names ("Counseling Center for Mothers and Pregnant Women" and "Center for the Care of Newborns"), and after the centers were transferred to the administration of Hadassah, it became the official name of the entire service. It is by this name, Tipat Halav, that the system continues to be known today as well.

In managing the milk project, the main problem of the Federation of Hebrew Women came to light: lack of sufficient financial sources. The distribution of the milk greatly increased the number of mothers visiting a center, and a pressing need was created to enlarge the budget to meet the increasing demand and to raise funds from new and additional sources. Bathsheba Kesselman, who visited the United States in 1922, decided on her own initiative to collect money among the women's groups of New York for the establishment of a "Milk Fund" for needy infants in Eretz Israel. Hadassah opposed separate fundraising and considered it an attempt at excessive interference by the Federation of Hebrew Women beyond what had been agreed upon between them. In 1923, with no other option, the Federation turned over the operation of the "milk kitchens" as well as the fundraising for the distribution of milk exclusively to Hadassah.[15] The women's federation continued to work voluntarily alongside Hadassah for the expansion of the entire project until it was transferred, in 1952, to the Israel Ministry of Health.

The Federation of Hebrew Women succeeded in drawing to its ranks many volunteers with welfare and social awareness who wanted to participate in the various activities for the needy. The close cooperation between the Federation of Hebrew Women and Hadassah created a network of mother and child welfare centers throughout the country that provided medical services, and childrearing advice and guidance for mothers.[16] The cooperation between the two women's federations encouraged the volunteering of women from all levels of society for community projects and indicated the need for the creation of an umbrella organization of women's associations in Eretz Israel for improving the status of women, for obtaining the right to vote, and for organizing women's volunteer activity for the benefit of the public. On Purim 5284 (March 1924), the first national convention of the Federation of Hebrew Women took place, and Henrietta Szold, who headed the Federation of Hebrew Women, stressed this need among the organization's aims: "The main goal is to organize the women of the country and to unite the existing federations into a single national federation. Without an umbrella organization it is impossible to carry out any productive work in the country, and it is difficult to make connections with the women from abroad."[17] So it was that during the 1920s, the cooperation between the different women's organization became increasingly close, and in 1933 it was decided to establish the Federation of Zionist Women, a joint organization of national Women's International Zionist Organization (WIZO) and the Federation of Hebrew Women.[18]

The Health Education Work of Hadassah among Mothers and Children

Health services for the mother and her infant were one of most closely defined branches of Hadassah endeavor in Eretz Israel, and this stemmed from awareness that taking care of the health of the mother and child is the foundation for a healthy population and the basis for developed medical work. By implementing its health and education program, Hadassah aspired to train mothers for childrearing and to teach them healthy habits to promote their health and to improve their quality of life. The mother and child welfare centers that Hadassah established with the help of the Federation of Hebrew Women served as the principal, most important means for attaining this goal.

The health education endeavor began with providing care for the pregnant woman from the start of her pregnancy, extended to the newborn, to the child in the "age of transition" (two to four years old), and ended with treatment of children of kindergarten age (four to six). School children became the responsibility of the school's hygiene department.[19]

Hadassah determined goals for its work and took zealous care in implementing them: (1) to teach and inculcate the rules of basic hygiene; (2) to support, aid, and guide the pregnant women during her pregnancy; (3) to teach and instruct mothers about infant nutrition; (4) to encourage natural feeding and to lengthen the period of nursing; (5) to train mothers for the move from natural feeding to artificial nutrition; (6) to insure the provision of pasteurized milk and to teach proper food preparation by the mother in her home; (7) to educate and instruct mothers in raising their children; (8) to teach mothers how to prevent diseases caused by improper nutrition and ignoring the rules of hygiene; (9) to make house calls to become familiar with the needs of the impoverished family and to support it; (10) to promote the health of every child in the family, to discover problems for the purpose of correcting them and dealing with them; (11) to work to improve the mother and child welfare center and to encourage mothers to use its services.

The care for the pregnant woman was not aimed only at conducting a healthy, sound pregnancy, a birth without complications, and care after birth for maintaining the mother's health — but derived from the premise that the contact and connection between the mother and child welfare centers, the doctor, and the nurse, on the one hand, and the pregnant woman, on the other, were laying the foundation for guiding the mother in care of the newborn.

Principles of Hadassah's Effort in the Mother and Child Welfare Centers

From the beginning of its work in Eretz Israel, Hadassah determined basic principles for its health education work and uncompromisingly held to them. Women's organizations that agreed to cooperate with Hadassah had to accept its operational methods and principles unquestioningly:

- *Service at the health centers is provided free of charge and to everyone, with no difference as to religion or race.* In the words of Zelda Goldman, a nurse at the Haifa mother and child welfare center, "We have a rule here: to accept anyone who turns to the center, with no difference as to type, ethnic group, and race," and as stated by the chief nurse, Bertha Landsman: "We do not distinguish between poor and rich . . . The Hadassah Medical Organization does not demand payment for this educational work."[20] Material aid (milk, diapers, clothing) was handed out *only* to needy mothers who came regularly to receive instruction and advice.
- *A uniform system of infant welfare was instituted in all centers in the country.* A uniform system of feeding (natural and artificial), a uniform system of dressing and diapering. The Kupat Holim physicians who cooperated with the center were *obliged* to work according to the system implemented at the centers.
- *Home visits* by the public health nurses were the "cornerstone of the effort."[21] They came under the rubric of the informational work of the centers all over the country and were an integral part of preventive medicine activities. Home visits made it possible to impose a uniform method of operation in the centers throughout the country.
- *The health effort was intended to educate the entire family towards a healthy life and to instill in it a healthy way of life.* Each family constituted an individual unit, and the nurse supervised its health. Through home visits, the nurses learned of the family's material, social, and health situation.
- *The work was aimed at the healthy child.* The centers did not provide medical treatment, they did not accept sick children, and medicines were not distributed, as explained by Bertha Landsman, the chief nurse, "Our motto was care for the healthy child," and in the words of Dr. Baruch Ostrovsky, "I held to a sacred principle, not to give [medical] treatment at Tipat Halav."[22] And indeed, over time the mothers understood that the purpose of the doctor's examination was not therapeutic but rather for giving advice and instruction about the nutrition and general condition of the infants.

WIZO Activity for the Establishment of Mother and Child Welfare Centers and Infant Homes for Working Mothers

WIZO began to operate in Eretz Israel in 1920 following a decision taken at the organization's founding conference in London to establish a central bureau in Eretz Israel. Activity began in Tel Aviv and Jaffa through individual volunteers, since Jerusalem already had an active branch of the Federation of Hebrew Women and in Haifa the first inklings of activity were noticeable. The volunteers were local residents who instructed the mothers, mainly among the new immigrants, in childrearing. Only in 1927 did the volunteers arrange themselves into an organizational framework, calling it "National Federation." The group was subordinate to WIZO in London. The organization in Eretz Israel met opposition from the two other women's bodies: the Federation of Hebrew Women, which saw it as a competitor for financial resources and personnel, and Hadassah, which did not appreciate a women's organization based in Eretz Israel having connections with an organization abroad, particularly in Europe. Despite this, cooperation among the bodies developed over the years, and in 1933, it was decided to establish the Federation of Zionist Women, a joint organization of national WIZO and the Federation of Hebrew Women.[23]

The initial steps of WIZO's volunteer work in Tel Aviv began in 1924 in the area of providing welfare for a woman who had just given birth. In that year, a WIZO emissary from New Zealand opened a center for the welfare of pregnant women in the Neveh Shalom neighborhood. For that purpose, two nurses were sent to England on behalf of WIZO to study a special work method, the "Plunkett system," used in England, New Zealand, and Australia, for treating women giving birth and their infants.[24] On 5 December 1926, WIZO set up an infant welfare center on Nehemiah Street in Kerem ha-Temanim and provided service for infants only up to the age of two. A third center was opened on Ha-Carmel Street. Dr. Theodor Zlocisti directed the centers that WIZO established in Tel Aviv.[25] Later, WIZO's work was extended to Haifa and Jerusalem.

In 1926, working mothers in Jerusalem turned to Hadassah with a request that it find an answer to the problem of children of working mothers. The economic crisis in Eretz Israel from 1924 to 1927 forced many mothers to go out to work to help support the family. So WIZO was asked to compile work procedures that would fit the needs of working mothers and provide an overall solution for childcare outside the family framework. From 1927, WIZO opened day-care centers, first in Tel Aviv and later on throughout the country. The day-care centers were intended for the sole use of working mothers; the centers provided all the educational services for preschoolers, including medical treatment. Supervision and care for nursing children and toddlers were given by nursemaids who had been trained in the WIZO school for nursemaids in Jerusalem. In addition to the ongoing daily care, the caretakers advised the mothers on nutrition, care for the ill child, and the development of the personal connection between the child and the working mother.

The Federation of Hebrew Women, which united with WIZO in 1933, continued with the dissemination of information among the mothers in the poverty-stricken neighborhoods and with convincing them to come to the Tipat Halav centers in the area where they lived. A large contribution by the WIZO women of Australia made it possible to increase the number of centers in Tel Aviv and Haifa. In addition to guidance, medical supervision, and milk, the centers provided food and clothing to the needy in return for a symbolic payment.

Within a decade, WIZO's Tipat Halav centers had become one of the principal bodies helping working mothers all around the country. In 1937, WIZO operated twelve centers, dealt with some 1,370 infants, and made about 7,000 home visits.[26] WIZO also ran two infant homes, in Jerusalem and Tel Aviv, which cared for stray children, orphans, and infants from distressed regions and from new immigrant families, whose nutrition was inadequate. In the Tel Aviv infant home, a section for premature babies was opened and babies were taken to it from the country's hospitals.

In 1952, with the transfer of Hadassah's centers for mother and child to the Israel Ministry of Health, WIZO also transferred its centers to the ministry but continued to operate its day-care centers, children's home, welfare centers, and clubhouses for youth and for women throughout the country.

Afterword

The decision to establish the State of Israel on 15 May 1948 prompted Hadassah and WIZO to discuss the issue of the functioning of the health services as part of the state that was coming into being. It was clear that these services would have to undergo essential changes to fit into the new framework.

In accordance with the decision of the Israel government, led by David Ben-Gurion, it was decided to turn the public health service into a national service. In 1950, Hadassah began to transfer its medical services to the Ministry of Health and retained only hospitalization services in the big cities. The process was completed by 1952, and the Tipat Halav centers and the health services that Hadassah had directed in the schools were handed directly over to the Ministry of Health and became a state service in every respect. Following Hadassah, WIZO transferred the Tipat Halav centers it had run to the Ministry of Health and retained only its children's homes for working mothers.[27] With the transfer of the service to it, the Ministry of Health declared that it intended "to establish an available, accessible service for the entire population of mothers and children, with no discrimination as to religion and race."[28] Although the movement of the Tipat Halav services to the Ministry of Health did not go through a legislative process, the Israeli public accepted it as a "service that had to be provided." Over 90 percent of the country's mothers made use of this service. It continues to function today and is a basic element in the maintenance of children's health in the State of Israel.

☙ *Nira Bartal*

Establishment of a Nursing School in Jerusalem by the American Zionist Medical Unit, 1918

Continuation or Revolution?

Although studies of the development of health services in Eretz Israel during the Mandate period are part of the general investigation of this period, they are in themselves a distinct field for research.[1] Only few studies have focused on the story of nursing in the development of health services;[2] the history of nursing in Israel has not drawn great interest even as part of the discussion on the development of professions, women's organizations, or the incorporation of women in the labor market during the Yishuv period, and not even as part of the historiography of the American Zionist women's project, "Hadassah."[3]

Those dealing with the history of nursing in Eretz Israel should base themselves on the foundations laid by contemporary American scholars, such as B. Melosh, S. Reverby, and P. A. and B. J. Kalisch, on the one hand, and the first Israelis who dealt with this topic, L. Zwanger and R. Adams-Stockler, on the other.[4] Zwanger's study, published over thirty years ago, did not focus solely on the Hadassah School but dealt with the field of nursing education in Eretz Israel in general, and the time period she covered was quite broad: 1918 to 1965. Adams-Stockler discussed one aspect of activity, namely the field of public health nursing in the country, but she does address to a certain extent the training of nurses for field work in this specialty. These researchers did not have available all of the rich material that has been found in recent years in the archives of the Hadassah Medical Organization and the Hadassah Nursing School.[5]

This article is dedicated to Ms. Judith Steiner-Freud, former director of the Nursing School and Deputy Dean of the Faculty of Medicine of Hadassah and the Hebrew University, for her contribution to the advancement of nursing in Israel in general and the study of the history of nursing in Eretz Israel in particular. All rights are retained by the author.

When reconstructing the history of nursing in Eretz Israel during the Mandate period, one must also include aspects deriving from the introduction of Western ideas, such as those relating to the place of women in the *Yishuv*, or the internalization of professional ideology.[6]

This article focuses on the beginning of nurses' training in the country, which was the main component of the struggle to attain professional recognition, in the American spirit, as reflected in the history of the School for Registered Nurses in Jerusalem, established by the Women's Zionist Organization of America, Hadassah. Specifically covered here are the early years of the school, from its founding in 1918 until the end of the term of office of Anna Kaplan, director of the school from 1920 to 1927.[7]

Professional Training of Women at the Beginning of the Twentieth Century

In Eretz Israel at the start of the twentieth century, there were women, with a profession or occupation, whose training had been acquired in the country or elsewhere in three main ways: university studies, usually in Europe (physicians, for instance); training in high school, sometime with an additional period of studies (for example, kindergarten teachers), or by means of traditions handed down from one generation to another, as apprentices (like the local midwives).[8]

We have to differentiate between the training of women who had graduated high school or had a similar education, as was the case with the Hadassah Nursing School, and occupational training intended for young women studying in high schools. Girls with elementary school education were accepted to the Lewinsky Teachers Seminary (founded in 1913) or to the women's agricultural farm at Kinneret.[9]

Within the context of the characteristics of women's education in Eretz Israel, the director of the Hadassah Nursing School from 1934 to 1948, Shulamit Cantor, described the Hadassah project of founding a nursing school:

> As the first professional school for women in Palestine, it aroused sensational interest. Professional education for women was an unheard of thing in that part of the world. For generations Eastern women had lived a sheltered and cloistered life; their area of movement was the home and the courtyard; they did not enter the trades or professions; they took no part whatever in the social, political, and economic life of the community. This condition had been ac-

cepted as natural for women from time immemorial. But the recognition that nurses constitute the backbone of medical service brought an ever-increasing pressure on Hadassah to train nurses.[10]

Training Women for Nursing Work at the Beginning of the Century

At the beginning of the twentieth century, nursing was not recognized as a profession in Eretz Israel. The Ottoman government did not require women working in nursing to obtain a diploma, as was the case for physicians; the title "nurse," "sister of mercy," or "medic" was given to a women who assisted a physician without her ever being asked how she been trained for the job or what made the license she was supposed to receive valid.

In the early years of the twentieth country — until the arrival of delegations from the Red Cross and from the American Zionist Federation and Hadassah in 1918 — the physicians, among them Dr. A. Ticho and Dr. H. Kagan, trained the nurses themselves.[11] But a gap opened between the concept of training local women, from a low social class, and the carrying out of limited, defined activity that was vital for the operation of medical institutions at that time — and perceiving nursing as a profession.

A concept reflecting the professional vision, according to which the Nursing School was fashioned in its first years, was introduced into the country only with the arrival of the nurses belonging to the Hadassah unit. Training in nursing as a profession was intended for educated women, and the educational framework included acquiring knowledge and skills in a wide range of areas. This training was supposed to meet standards recognized by professional or government authorities and to equip the course graduates with a certificate.

This means that the founding of the Hadassah Nursing School in 1918, following the American model, was not the continuation of nurses' training as it had been done until then in Eretz Israel (along the pattern of Dr. Helena Kagan, for example), but rather that this institution reflected a different, broad, revolutionary concept.

The Goals of the Hadassah Nursing School and the Ideas behind It

"The 'Hadassah' federation developed and coalesced into a Zionist-social feminist organization. What the active progressive American women strove for in the city slums was what the 'Hadassah' women aspired to the *Yishuv* in Eretz Israel. They worked to have a healthy population that would be able to function properly on the personal and public level."[12] Progressive ideas stressed faith in the advancement of people and their environment, and science and education served as the main booster for achieving this. In actuality, the progressives called for improving efficiency in the managing of institutions and for strengthening the concept of professionalism.[13]

Ideas in health guidance were influenced, on the one hand, by the educational concepts that developed at that time in New York and, on the other, from movements such as the Antituberculosis League, headed by figures such as C. E. A. Winslow, that disseminated the idea of preventive medicine.[14]

The nurses in the American Zionist Medical Unit saw themselves as emissaries for the dissemination of Western culture in general and the message of nursing in particular. One must keep in mind that in those days there was in the West a comprehensive concept of mission for the advancement of non-developed colonies, and those delegations were part of the idea. This was the context of the ideology of the Hadassah Zionist Women's Organization, which the unit's nurses were intended to implement in Eretz Israel.[15] Alice Seligsberg, one of the leaders of the medical unit until 1921, described the goals behind the establishment of the school as follows:

> The Orient needs professionally trained nurses. . . . Why not train Palestinian girls to take over the work of the American nurses? . . . the inhabitants of this land . . . needed work above all else, and to open a new profession to the intelligent girls of the country, was to render a service thrice blessed. One more reason: to teach Palestinian girls to work and to become economically independent, was a means of elevating the position of women in the Orient.[16]

A pivotal role in the application of these ideas was played by Henrietta Szold.[17]

American Influences on the Development of the Nursing School

In the closing years of the nineteenth century, nursing began a struggle in the United States for the right to be recognized as a profession. Nursing leaders, such as Isabel Hampton-Robb, Isabel M. Stewart, Lavinia L. Dock, and Adelaide M. Nutting strove to turn nursing into a profession as other groups of workers had done in that period. Looking at the history of nursing, one sees that in the United States it was in the middle of a lengthy, complicated transformation when nursing began to cross the borders into Eretz Israel, at the beginning of the twentieth century.

The founding of the Nursing School was one of the first projects of American Jews in Eretz Israel, and an important one. The concept of nursing as understood by the founders of the school in Eretz Israel, such as Henrietta Szold, Alice Seligsberg, and its first directors, was influenced by the American reality.[18] With the establishment of the school, American concepts were brought to the country from the field of medicine and medical administration, and they promoted the process of the shift from the idea of a hospital being a charitable community institution to an institute efficiently operated and guided by economic considerations.

Henrietta Szold, who spoke at the graduation party of the first class of the Nursing School at the end of 1921, called for the cultivating of professional education in Eretz Israel, because "expertise is the mother of mercy."[19]

The school was managed in the American spirit. Just as in America, where a nursing school was directed by a committee composed of professional people above which was a committee of nonprofessional women involved in public works, so too in Eretz Israel it was run by the American nurses Anna Kaplan and Bertha Landsman above whom was a system of women engaged in public works whose base was in New York.[20] This latter body, which was responsible for the economic aspects of the school, constituted a bridge between the Hadassah nurse in Eretz Israel and the leaders, especially Isabel Steward, at the leading nursing center in the United States at that time — Columbia University in New York.

From reviewing source material, we learn that the leaders of the Hadassah women's organization believed that the idea of nursing as a profession comprised a number of components: the need for lengthy training and the acquisition of skills and knowledge for the purpose of efficient activity (and they strove to design these elements according to the best of American standards); selection of the cream of the *Yishuv* women; recognition of the importance of nursing's contribution to society and to the nation; awarding a relatively high status in society to nursing, derived from its close association with medicine and teaching and from the elitist conception of the nursing school as part of the Hadassah institutions; opening the way for achieving economic independence for women in the profession; and stressing the need for special professional language.

The American characterization of the concept of nursing stands out in light of comparison to the European idea. The struggle of the American nurses for recognition of their occupation as a profession preceded that of their European counterparts, and this also stressed the difference between the doctors: In Eretz Israel, there prevailed among the physicians of European origin a conservative notion that considered a nurse as a physician's helper, in contrast to the way their American colleague in the country regarded the essence of nursing.

One of the main topics to which American influence was applied was standardization of the curriculum in nursing education.[21] It also may be that Anna Kaplan brought with her to the school the concept of the curriculum that she had studied at the Lebanon Hospital Nursing School in New York.[22] Training in practical work was carried out by the American registered nurses.

Yet, despite the aspiration to design the school after the American model, the fields of study at the beginning were dictated by the needs of the moment, which were taking care of cleanliness and sanitation, and the typical nurses' duties: distributing medicines and bandaging. The type of lessons taught fit the initial activity of the medical unit, which dealt with treating infectious diseases and epidemics, and only later came the introduction of comprehensive health services.

In 1920, British military rule ended in Eretz Israel and was replaced by a civilian government. At the end of 1921, the Twelfth Zionist Congress, held in Carlsbad, decided to turn the medical unit into "an independent medical organization that will function autonomously in the country and will be directly subordinate to 'Hadassah' which is in America." We may presume that this change in the concept of the unit influenced the school in general and the design of its set curricula in particular.[23]

For 1925, a reform was instituted in the curriculum. Hadassah Schedrovitzky-Sapir, a member of the first graduating class and Kaplan's intended successor, returned from studying at Columbia University in New York and the curriculum of the National League of Nursing Education was implemented.[24]

One of the important elements of change was the incorporation into the curriculum of a course in public health and in midwifery; another aspect of the influence of the spirit of professionalism was the process of academization that gradually had been realized in the United States from the beginning of the century; in Eretz Israel the idea was mentioned as early as the 1920s, but owing to the lack of a university it was held off until 1927, two years after the founding of the Hebrew University.[25] Anna Kaplan then presented a detailed proposal for a four-year curriculum that would be integrated with studies at the Hebrew University. The program was discussed, but postponed to a later date.

An additional expression of Americanization is seen in Anna Kaplan's application to Henrietta Szold and the Hadassah women in New York concerning the need for the translation of manuals, such as the book by A. C. Maxwell and A. E. Pope that dealt with the principles of nursing, or for sending additional nursing books from the United States.[26] The issue of further nurses' training, mainly in the United States but also in Britain, in the fields of administration, teaching, and public health, received great attention from the Hadassah women in New York as well as from directors in Eretz Israel, with the aim of fostering the concept of nursing as a profession.

A concrete expression of the founding of an American school in Eretz Israel was its registration in the 1920s in the State of New York as one of the recognized schools for training nurses.[27] The registration was intended to enable graduates to be examined there so they could obtain a certificate as a registered nurse in New York, which was among the most developed states in the United States in the field of nursing.[28]

The Perception of Nursing as a Profession in the Field of Public Health

The subject of public health was a central component in student training at the Eretz Israel nursing school in light of Hadassah's goals and the local needs. In the United States, the perception of nursing as a profession, in its broadest sense, is expressed mainly in the field of public health.[29] In the 1920s, this field blossomed and attained a status full of potential relative to other nursing fields; because of the remarkable independence of the women working in it, the field served as a model in the struggle for attaining the status of a profession. The leading activity in public health was conducted in New York, at the Henry Street Settlement, founded by the Jewish nurse Lillian Wald in 1891.[30] Evidence of Wald's involvement in Hadassah resides in the fact that at the "Medical Advisory Board," founded in 1916 in New York to "plan and oversee" the emergency campaign for sending the medical unit to Palestine (under the sponsorship of Henrietta Szold) included, among others, Lillian Wald.[31]

The first nurses to arrive in Eretz Israel were American women influenced by the image of the independent woman, unencumbered with family, equipped with a profession and a universalistic, humanistic approach, a woman who conquers areas that had not been treated properly, mainly in the field of public health.[32]

An example of the influence of the professional approach of the Henry Street Settlement was the re-organization of the work of the midwives, led by Bertha Landsman, at the end of 1925.[33]

American Influences in a Context of British Rule

Britain is, to a great extent, the cradle of modern nursing, thanks to the work of Florence Nightingale, who founded the first independent school for training nurses in London. The model of Nightingale's school became well established and was long-lived in England, the United States, and other countries to which its students came.

In England, as early as the end of the nineteenth century, the nurses fought for the registration of nursing and its being anchored in the law.[34]

In 1919, Parliament passed the Nursing Law, and the General Nursing Council for England and Wales was founded to implement the law.[35] In 1948, when the National Health Law was ratified, most of the authorities of the General Nursing Council were transferred to the Health Ministry.

Like American nursing at the beginning of the Mandate period in Eretz Israel, nursing in Britain was deep in the middle of institutionalization. The regulations that the British authority in Eretz Israel imposed were influenced by the arrangements for licensing registered nurses in Britain, which were based on the program of minimal training that was provided at most of the nursing schools in Britain. In this context, the directors of the Hadassah Nursing School took care to institute a maximal curriculum in the spirit of the reform of nursing education in America.

Training of Nurses in Eretz Israel

The British administration, in contrast to its Ottoman predecessor, strove to institute in various areas of life orderly frameworks, laws, and procedures that could be supervised. In the field of health, the British government in 1918, and later in 1922, published the public health regulations, in which there was a section "Licenses for Medical Personnel and Others."[36] In this section, nurses were not included except for midwives, which led to the conclusion that it was permissible to work in nursing even without presenting a certificate, that is, without minimal training. Only on 26 February 1923 were the first government regulations for the training of nurses published, and then anyone who claimed she was a registered nurse was required to present a certificate issued by the British government.[37] From then on, the Nursing School took it upon itself to comply with a number of regulations applicable to the following areas: recognition of the hospital in which school was located as a learning center; registration of students and entrance requirements; a curriculum and a minimal period of study; examinations; and languages of study. These regulations were renewed in 1925, 1942, and 1946, and they became void upon the end of the British Mandate in 1948.[38]

Summary

In the area of the professional education of women in Eretz Israel after World War I, the founding of the first postsecondary occupational school for women stands out, and it is none other than the Hadassah training school for registered nurses in Jerusalem, founded toward the close of 1918.

The concept of the nursing school in its early years was characterized by an America tinge against the background of the needs of the time and place, while maintaining the obligatory supervisory framework of the British authorities; this framework was influenced by the development of nursing in Britain in those days. The Zionist Organization of America and the Hadassah women, and foremost Henrietta Szold, were motivated by an ideology based on concepts of social feminism, Zionism and professionalism, and the colonial idea of the development of backward areas in the spirit of contemporary America. As part of this ideology, nursing was brought to Eretz Israel as a revolution in the area of nurses' training in the nature of the profession. The registered nurse was an educated woman who had been trained, in an educational framework, for a wide range of roles in the field of health services in contrast to the previous period, over whose occupational training there had been no supervision, when she had been trained by doctors to perform simple, limited tasks.

The professional vision lost some of its power toward the end of the 1920s in Eretz Israel, but the struggle to improve it continues to this day.

꙳ *Bat-Sheva Margalit Stern*

"They Have Wings But No Strength to Fly"

The Women Workers' Movement between "Feminine" Control and "Masculine" Dominance

Introduction

This discussion aims at exposing the system of relations and links between the various institutions of the Histadrut ha-Ovedim ha-Kelalit be-Erez Israel (General Federation of Labor in Eretz Israel) and at pointing out the way they coped with the special issues of female workers. Taking this system of relations apart while simultaneously analyzing the plans for action by the Histadrut establishment and its intentions helps separate the concepts of "class" and "gender" and to examine them in the context of women in the Eretz Israel society.[1] The Histadrut's Women Workers' Movement (WWM) was born in protest against discrimination at the founding convention of the Histadrut in 1920.[2]

After an uncompromising battle by the women workers, a special department for women was established in the Histadrut headed by an elected representation that was called "Mo'etzet ha-Po'alot" (Women Workers' Council). Mo'etzet ha-Po'alot was directly subordinate to the Histadrut's Va'ad ha-Po'el (Executive Committee), and it dealt with the issues of the female Histadrut members from one general women workers' convention to the next. The leadership of the women workers' movement included Mo'etzet ha-Po'alot with its various departments, and — from the mid-1920s — the local women workers' committees (eventually departments), which were subordinate to Mo'etzet ha-Po'alot and the municipal Mo'etzet ha-Po'alim (Labor Council).[3]

From the 1930s, the organizational structure of Mo'etzet ha-Po'alot became broader and more ramified, and it included the Municipal Council for Women's Affairs, whose establishment we will discuss below, and the "Irgun

Imahot Ovedot" (Organization of Working Mothers). Initially, this was the organization of Histadrut members' wives and former women workers, which was intended to handle the issues of welfare and of the female members in the women workers' movement in particular and the Histadrut in general.

The leadership of the women workers' movement considered its belonging to the labor camp an unquestioned principle, supported by a ramified network of society and family ties, shared experiences, and a similar historical and cultural heritage. This duplication made it difficult for the leadership of the Women Workers' Movement, whose attachment to the establishment left it split between feminine loyalty — as a unique identifying mark — and loyalty to the Histadrut establishment, which symbolized the general principle.

The interval between the mid-1920s and the close of the 1930s is the background for the happenings discussed below. These years saw changes in the development of the women workers' movement, a derivative of processes that took place in the Histadrut in particular and in the Eretz Israel society in general. The 1920s were rife with crises. The women workers' movement apparatus suffered from operational difficulties and from inadequate work procedures; the organizational structure was weak, as were the definitions of the functions and limits of authority for the women holding those positions. In the 1930s, the historical rivalry between the main labor parties slowly subsided, and the brunt of effort was directed toward creating strong, leading labor power in the *Yishuv*.[4] The Women Workers' Movement, like the Histadrut in general, underwent a clear process of bureaucratization and moderation of the radical forces previously active in it.[5]

Mo'etzet ha-Po'alot, the elected apparatus of the women workers' movement, sought answers to the organizational and fundamental dilemmas it encountered from its outset. Foremost was the issue of isolationism or integration within the General Histadrut with all of its institutions, and the second was the question of partisan politics or nonpartisanship within the women's movement.

One approach strove for expanding the authority of the apparatus and for "feminization" of the movement in the Histadrut. It was represented by Ada Fishman, a member of Ha-Po'el ha-Tza'ir and one of the initiators of the founding of the Histadrut's Women Workers Movement.[6] Ada Fishman persistently worked toward expansion of the authority of Mo'etzet ha-Po'alot and for its glorification as an independent body within the Histadrut. She was consistently and firmly opposed to greater political party involvement in Mo'etzet ha-Po'alot. At the same time, her own attitude was not free of party influence: Fishman's statements were in line with the aspirations of her party, Ha-Po'el ha-Tza'ir, to establish the most decentralized, independent labor federation possible.

The opposite approach, espoused by the women belonging to Ahdut ha-Avodah, the largest among the Histadrut parties and the leading one, called for giving priority to the Histadrut establishment — while subordinating all the other apparatuses including that of the women workers, to its authority. The abolition of the distinctive characteristics of the women workers' apparatus was the obvious result called for by this step.[7]

Two test cases demonstrate the complexity of the issues, namely, the selection of Golda Myerson to serve as the executive secretary of Mo'etzet ha-Po'alot toward the end of the 1920s, and the struggles for the establishment of local women workers' institutions in the 1920s and particularly in the 1930s.

"Never Was Discriminated": Golda Myerson's Appointment to the Mo'etzet ha-Po'alot Executive

Golda Myerson (Meir; 1898–1979) began her public career in Eretz Israel through party activity, with the women workers' movement being one of her channels. In the summer of 1921, she immigrated to the country and about a year later — in September 1922 — she was a delegate in the Second Women Workers' Convention that was held in Haifa. She was chosen to serve on Mo'etzet ha-Po'alot, which operated intermittently and with difficulties until the end of 1925. With the dissolution of the elected council, Golda did not participate in the Central Committee for Women Workers Issues appointed by the Va'ad ha-Po'el — the executive arm of the General Federation of Labor.[8]

Serving on the appointed women workers' committee were other members of her party who already had garnered seniority in movement activity and were involved in what went on it. In contrast to them, Golda Myerson was detached from movement activity in those years; she lived with her family in Jerusalem, under harsh conditions that did not allow her to engage in public activity.[9]

In 1928, she returned to movement participation, after accepting the offer by David Remez, a member of the Va'ad ha-Po'el and eventually General Secretary of the Histadrut (1935–1945), to serve as the secretary of Mo'etzet ha-Po'alot. As she told it, she met Remez accidentally on a rainy day on a street in Tel Aviv; while she was talking with one of her acquaintances on the stairs of the Va'ad ha-Po'el building, Remez turned to her and brought up the idea of "returning to work . . . and to become the secretary of the Histadrut's Mo'etzet ha-Po'alot."[10] On her way back to her family in Jerusalem, Golda Myerson decided to accept the proposal.[11]

The way Golda Meir joined the secretariat of the Mo'etzet ha-Po'alot shows us what the accepted procedures were for filling positions in the Histadrut. In contrast to other women from her party, such as Hannah Chizik, Leah Maron, or Rachel Yanait Ben-Zvi, who had acquired experience in working with the women workers and with personal, unmediated encounter with their working world, Golda Myerson stood out for her meager experience, which did not stem from any special sensitivity toward the subjects of women workers or women in general.[12] Golda's success in joining the secretariat of Mo'etzet ha-Po'alot without having passed through the melting pot from which the other women leaders of the movement had come, teaches us about swooping from above into this central position and not of natural growth to a position of leadership in the movement. But Golda Meir's advantages made up for her junior position in her party and in the women workers' movement. It may even be that her relative anonymity, her partisanship, and her good connections with senior members of the party apparatus — such as with David Remez himself — were her prominent assets. Her connections with Remez, for example, went back to the days when he arranged work for Golda and her husband in Solel Boneh, a major construction company founded and owned by the Histadrut, in Jerusalem, thus helping the family to emerge from its bleak economic situation in Tel Aviv.

David Remez's choice was not by chance. By appointing Golda Meir to the secretariat of Mo'etzet ha-Po'alot, the members of the Histadrut establishment hoped to weaken the opposition inherent in the women workers' movement, as they identified it, namely, Ada Fishman's group and its supporters, members of Ha-Po'el ha-Tza'ir. Ada Fishman, a person holding independent views and one who did not hesitate to challenge the Histadrut leadership, was a nuisance to the Histadrut establishment, and it sought ways to diminish her influence. From their point of view, bringing in Golda Meir from above was a fitting solution. She was an obedient, loyal candidate, dependent upon party institutions, and a person who did not stand out for any prominent feminist tendencies.

Serving on the active secretariat of the Mo'etzet ha-Po'alot was Golda Meir's first practical opportunity to grapple with a real role demanding performance in the Histadrut women's apparatus. Her period as secretary was fragmented and short, lasting for only a year and a half, during which she traveled abroad for extended periods on various missions for her party and the Histadrut.[13] Her appointment to fundraising tasks in America as a representative of the Histadrut, and actually as a representative of her party, caused angry repercussions among women belonging to the movement apparatus.[14]

Women members of Ha-Po'el ha-Tza'ir, and Ada Fishman in the forefront, considered Golda's appointment to go abroad on this mission as a purely political move intended to reinforce Ahdut ha-Avodah by means of connections with the "Pioneer Women's Organization" in America.[15] Ada Fishman argued that if what was involved was a party mission, then it should be balanced — as usual in the Histadrut — by sending two representatives, one from each party. This subject was then raised at different Histadrut forums and roused great controversy — with the decision ultimately reached, as noted, in opposition to Ada Fishman and her supporters, having Golda Myerson traveling alone.[16]

The temporary absence of Golda Myerson from the secretariat did not calm things down. In that period, feelings within the movement apparatus were in a turmoil that did not abate upon Golda's return. The Ha-Po'el ha-Tza'ir women members who supported Ada Fishman were furious over the attempt to displace her and to crown a member of the rival party instead. The rivalry intensified owing to other fundamental issues then on the Mo'etzet ha-Po'alot agenda for which no answer was found that satisfied Ada Fishman's supporters.[17] The tension peaked when members of that group hurtled the threat that they were ready to secede from Mo'etzet ha-Po'alot to establish a rival labor organization![18]

Whether the threats were effective or whether there were other reasons, the battle was won by Ada Fishman and her supporters. In January 1930, after a short, stormy period of service, Golda Myerson turned in her resignation from the Active Secretariat, declaring: "I have the feeling . . . that I am not succeeding and I am not confident that I am doing what is necessary . . . I do not see any possibility for continuing my participation in the work of the secretariat."[19]

These hard feelings resulted from a number of factors, including family obligations and also her poor command of Hebrew.[20] It is even reasonable to assume that Golda Myerson had reached the conclusion that the hopes her mentors had pinned on her could not be fulfilled. She was incapable of turning into a bulwark against the oppositional elements in the Histadrut women's apparatus nor could she drive a wedge between the strong foci of power that operated within the apparatus. In a final, unsuccessful attempt to bring the interparty rivalry in Mo'etzet ha-Po'alot to a conclusion, Golda tried to bring in a substitute from her party, Gusta Strumph.[21]

Of course, Golda Myerson had taken the upper hand in a number of previous confrontations in the movement, but Ada Fishman and members of Ha-Po'el ha-Tza'ir were the victors.[22] Golda Myerson backed down from her demand for a central position in the leadership of the Women Workers' Movement and relinquished her spot, while Ada Fishman remained the leading power in the movement in the coming years. The success of her approach in charting the Histadrut women's movement policy, mainly regarding the economic aspect, which had been controversial until then, now became a fait accompli.[23]

Thus, Golda Myerson's appointment to the Mo'etzet ha-Po'alot Secretariat was a flagrant, never repeated, attempt at tipping the scales of the internal power struggle in the upper level of the Women Workers' Movement. Whether this was a one-time slip or a calculated tactic by the Histadrut establishment, such means were never needed again in the story of the balance of power between the women workers' institutions and the Histadrut. The more radical powers active in the movement in the 1920s became more moderate and gradually were replaced in the apparatus by female party activists much more obedient than their predecessors; their worldview and their methods of operation coincided, or were even coordinated, with the ruling party line in the Histadrut, that is, with Mapai. So more than the changes in Histadrut establishment behavior teach us about the strengthening of Mo'etzet ha-Po'alot, they attest to its submergence within the ruling political culture in the Histadrut and Mapai, its leading party.[24]

The Grip of the Iron Fist: The Battles over the Establishment of Special Institutions for Women Workers

The difficulties involved in deciding whether to establish special institutions for women is not an issue specific to the Women Workers' Movement in the Histadrut.

The existing Histadrut organizational frameworks as well as its public forums seldom referred to women workers' issues, and in any event, the working women rarely expressed themselves.[25] As a result, feelings of isolation and alienation prompted the women to seek a separate, yet affiliated with the Histadrut, gender-based forum that would befit their needs and responding to them.[26] Of course, the creation of separate institutions for the women workers roused great controversy in the Histadrut, crossing gender and party lines.

The controversy, which will be discussed below, revolved around the issue of establishing the Municipal Council for Women Workers, a local organizational body of women workers that was supposed to coordinate the handling of female Histadrut members in each city and large *moshavah*: workers for hire connected to the labor market, and homemakers who were not part of the labor market.

One can identify two main stages in the development of the local organization of the Women Workers' Movement. The first stage began in 1926 with the decision taken at the Third Women Workers' Convention to set up "women workers committees" and its confirmation at the Third Histadrut Convention a year later (1927).[27] A limited number of committees did begin taking initial steps, mainly in the big cities, Haifa, Tel Aviv, and Jerusalem. The second stage began in 1937 with the establishment of the permanent institution: The Urban Council for Women Workers.

Women workers' committees were an integral part of the local Histadrut establishment. Mo'etzet ha-Po'alot, too, strove to dominate these institutions but without particular success. The limits of authority of the women workers' committees and their status were defined by the Mo'etzet ha-Po'alim, which also appointed the members of the women's committees. From their founding in 1926 until they were superseded by new institutions in 1937, the women workers' committees operated only intermittently and limitedly, and regretfully roused a feeling of discomfort among the bodies connected to their operation. Their restricted activity left a scant, insignificant impression among the long-suffering urban women workers.

The long, exhausting discussion about establishing local women workers' institutions began within the apparatus of the Women Workers' Movement as early as the close of 1925. Since no conclusion was reached in internal movement forums, the Va'ad ha-Po'el was called upon to decide, but its efforts were unsuccessful.[28] So the issue was raised at the Third Histadrut Convention in 1927.

Two opposing propositions were raised at this convention. The minority proposal by Ada Fishman and Hayuta Busel, members of Ha-Po'el ha-Tza'ir, supported, of course, the setting up of separate institutions by the women workers. As expected, their proposal was not accepted by the majority of members; the majority's proposal, for which 97 voted in favor and 79 against, determined: "An elected Women Workers' Committee elected by the local [workers] council. Mo'etzet ha-Po'alot, with authority defined by this deci-

sion, elected in each locality in proportional elections by the women workers."[29] The majority, therefore, decided in favor of maintaining its power and
of continuing domination by the Histadrut establishment in the second-
level institutions, this time in those of the women workers.

Yet, under the surface of the proposal accepted at the Third Histadrut
Convention was a minor compromise: Permission was received to elect the
broader body of the women workers, the Urban Council for Women Workers, by the women workers themselves. This body was intended to be an
overarching framework for the local women worker's institutions, the Department (committee) for Women Workers, and the Organization for Working Mothers, which was constituted mostly of wives of Histadrut members,
homemakers, that had begun partial, local operation.

Since implementation of the decision was delayed, the Mo'etzet ha-Po'alot
session, convened in 1928, decided — in opposition to the Third Histadrut
Convention decision — to initiate the establishment of the urban councils
for women workers' issues, so that they could elect the local women workers'
committees. But defying the voice of the Histadrut establishment by part
of the women belonging to the movement apparatus did not work out. This
time, too, the movement apparatus did not manage to come to a decision
that would be acceptable to the majority, and the subject was discussed again
in the Histadrut institutions, this time at the Histadrut Council that met at
the beginning of 1929. But the decision to hold the elections for the urban
women workers' councils along with those for the Mo'etzot ha-Po'alim was
never implemented.[30]

Despite the obstacles, and even in the face of the firm opposition by the
members of the general local workers' councils, the Mo'etzet ha-Po'alot did
not let up on the subject in the following years. Worrisome reports on the
situation of the women workers goaded the women members of the apparatus to try to speed up the activity toward organizing the local institutions.
Their efforts were fruitless and at the Fourth Women Workers' Convention
(1932) the issue held central stage on the agenda.[31] Only near the end of 1934
was a compromise finally achieved between Mo'etzet ha-Po'alot and Mo'etzot
ha-Po'alim. Thus, it was determined that Mo'etzot ha-Po'alim would maintain a permanent urban institution for women workers' issues. A year and a
half passed before the recommendations were presented to the Regulations
Committee for Determining the New Institution, and in 1936, about a
decade after the discussions had begun, it was finally decided to begin organizing the urban councils for women workers' affairs. In 1937, the Urban
Council for Women Workers began to operate in the major cities, Tel Aviv

and Haifa. The establishment of the institutions was a compromise among the different approaches current in both the Histadrut and the Women Workers' Movement. The prolonged discussion attests to the difficulties inherent in resolving the conflicting objectives, and we will discuss that in the next section.

Gender Fear Rises: For and Against the Local Institutions for Women Workers

The stances of the Histadrut's various institutions point out that the heart of the controversy dealt with the source for the authority of the gender-based women's institutions, and in the broader context—the essence of the concept of authority in the Histadrut in general: Whether the whole body of women members of the movement, or at least their institutions elected at the general women workers' convention, should be the source for authority, or should the Histadrut apparatuses, which already had taken command of the women workers and their institutions, continue to do so by carrying on with the appointment of the women members to the various institutions.

In contrast to the Va'ad ha-Po'el, whose members generally supported the establishment of local institutions for women workers, male and female members of the Mo'etzot ha-Po'alim, mainly from Ahdut ha-Avodah, were among the most consistent opponents to the idea. Mo'etzot ha-Po'alim members and the trade unions subordinate to them did not hide their fear that the women workers' institution about to be formed would become a dangerous precedent. They claimed that the power inherent in these institutions was liable to turn them into an oppositionary element in the Histadrut and further entrench the phenomenon of "parallelism" (the establishment of parallel bodies) opposed by the Ahdut ha-Avodah members with all their might.[32]

Their formidable opposition was the main obstacle thwarting the establishment of the institutions. At one of the frequent discussions between the members of the Mo'etzet ha-Po'alot Secretariat and the Mo'etzot ha-Po'alim secretaries, these fears were aired openly: "After that they will demand from us an elected General Employment Office, like the office for the women workers . . . a firm hand is necessary to determine the relations between us and the Mo'etzet ha-Po'alot . . . I am not certain and I have no idea who we will be dealing with."[33]

Yet, even the most aggressive opponents were not able to ignore the plight of the women workers. So it was that Ziama (Zalman) Aranne (Aharonowitz), of the Tel Aviv Labor Council, proposed in mid-1934 relief for the women workers' problems in the form of numerous women workers' assemblies during the year at which the women would be able to speak out on whatever they wished and to pour out their complaints.[34] To put this in other words, therapeutic sessions by all means! But the founding of a special institution to deal with the women workers' organizational, social, and economic problems was deemed totally unacceptable.

The vigorous protests of the women workers and their representatives were in vain. When all the opponents' arguments had been exhausted, Joshua Rabinowitz, another member of the Tel Aviv Labor Council, concluded the discussion of the issue by saying: "No council [of women workers] will be founded by us, because there is no room for it."[35] And he continued: "This is not an issue of [Mo'etzet Po'alot] elected or not elected. For we, too, are in favor of an elected [Mo'etzet ha-Po'alot] — by the Mo'etzot ha-Po'alim[!] [local men workers' council]."

Unfortunately, in the Women Workers' Movement, too, opinions were divided. The dispute between the members involved an issue of principle that had distressed the movement from its inception: isolation or integration into the Histadrut system. Some women activists rejected the idea of setting up separate institutions for women workers. They argued that Mo'etzet ha-Po'alot had to make every effort to integrate into the existing Histadrut institutions and not to invest resources in creating separate institutions.[36] Establishment supporters did not hide their fear of women workers' separatism, saying that the isolationist stance was likely to exacerbate estrangement from the women workers and the unfair treatment their needs received. In 1926, Pesya Gorelick, a member of the Tel Aviv Women Workers' Committee, formulated this feeling explicitly in a letter to Mo'etzet ha-Po'alot: "Our committee for the working woman's affairs discussed the issue and wishes to inform you that it is completely opposed to organizing the committee through special, separate elections for women workers only and to maintaining a separate (women's) committee . . . that is not a general component valid for the entire public of workers in the city . . . we are now presenting to you the committee's opinion, with which we agree and which we support, and ask that you take into consideration when you discuss this issue."[37]

An opposite approach was represented by women belonging to the apparatus who kept foremost in their minds the interests of the women workers. As far as they were concerned, the establishment of special institutions for the women workers was a necessary, justified act owing to the unique group needs of women; one must keep in mind, however, that they, too, began from a position of cooperation with the labor camp and supported joint action effort with the Histadrut establishment: "We do not intend to create a Histadrut of women workers parallel to the General Histadrut, we want to create an institution for women workers' issues — cells for initiative, thought, and sparking the general Histadrut institutions to action."[38] This means that special institutions for women workers was a result of their inferior situation and the institutions were perceived as an efficient means for reinforcing the workers.

The solid cooperation by part of the women's labor movement apparatus with the Histadrut establishment makes one wonder about the issue of commonality of gender consciousness versus movement loyalty. In many instances, one can identify a closeness between men and women at the leadership level that is deeper than the automatic identification of the women among the leadership of the women's apparatus with the general body of the movement women they were supposed to represent.[39] In light of such closeness, it is no wonder that the ills of the Histadrut's organizational culture did not skip over the women workers' institutions: conflicts between camps, party considerations taking precedence over other ones, and so on were no strangers to them at all.[40] What were the position-determining factors among Mo'etzet ha-Po'alot members? A number of factors prompted these split positions. Party affiliation was an important factor but not exclusive. From the members' responses, one may draw the conclusion that total, obligatory congruency did not automatically exist between their political affiliation and their attitudes.[41] To be sure, most of the women supporting direct election to independent women workers' institutions did belong to Ha-Po'el ha-Tza'ir and the leftist Po'alei Zion party, following their parties' positions; but a minority of the supporters came from Ahdut ha-Avodah. Thus, one may say that party affiliation was significant but did not rule out other factors. A much more influential element was the women's position in the party hierarchy; it dictated the attitude of the female members of the apparatus on these issues. Women who held roles at a relatively senior level, who enjoyed status and prestige in their parties, tended more naturally to adopt the approach of their party's institutions. Gender issues remained secondary to national ones as well as to those involving the network of relations and the power struggles between the Histadrut and the parties.[42]

The individual circumstances and personal experience of woman members of the movement apparatus also counted as a determining factor. Those women who had gained actual experience dealing with rank-and-file women laborers knew their needs and difficulties well. They were not able, and probably did not want, to ignore the workers' distress and the strained relations between them and their movement's leadership. Setting up independent institutions for the women workers in which they would be able to exercise influence and express themselves was seen as an effective means for repairing that troubled web of relations and, of course, also for improving the women workers' situation.

The type of profession, level of professional training, and the degree of persistence in the job market are also important components in the creation of the entirety of personal experience of each of the women who were part of the apparatus. The ones who were active among the women workers of the city gained different experience, which molded their viewpoint, than their colleagues who belonged to communal settlements.[43] In contrast to the urban dwellers, the latter lived a relatively protected living style that provided for their basic means of subsistence, mainly shelter, food, and clothing. The communal system of life helped with the burden of daily tasks, such as childcare, housework, laundry, and cooking, freeing the women for activity outside their homes.

Above all those factors was the level of personal commitment of each one of the women to gender principles. A member of the establishment such as Ada Fishman, who although she held a senior position in her party, was foremost a person of vigilant feminist awareness, did not hesitate to admit that there did exist particularly feminine distress. Moreover, she felt duty bound to seek fitting solutions to women's difficulties, even at the price of clashing with the Histadrut establishment.

Therefore, the gender awareness of the women belonging to the apparatus, perhaps even more than the other factors listed, dictated the priority of movement and social importance to which they remained steadfast. The support system unique to the women workers, for which they strove with all their energy, was necessary, so they felt, to help the women workers overcome their inferiority in the labor market, in the Histadrut and party establishment, and in the *Yishuv* society at large.

Assessment of the New Institution

When the new institutions finally were established, none of those involved wanted to relinquish his hold, so the bodies ability to function was impaired. Prevailing among the organization branches was an awkward chain for

reporting whose coordination was impossible.[44] The new organization included the Urban Council for Women Workers that represented, as noted —
according to the Va'ad ha-Po'el's decision — the women workers in the cities,
hired laborers, and homemakers. The Urban Council for Women Workers
was supposed to comprise thirty to fifty members elected by the local women
workers and to serve for a period of a year or two.[45] The Department of
Women Workers, which was the executive body of the local women workers'
institution, operated within it. The Department of Women Workers replaced
the Women Workers' Committee familiar from the 1920s. Similarly, the
Urban Council for Women Workers included the Working Mothers Organization, which in 1934 had become a national body with a secretary affiliated
with Mo'etzet ha-Po'alot.

The Department of Women Workers' secretariat, which had just been established, was obligated to report to three separate bodies: to the Urban
Council for Women's Labor Issues, to Mo'etzet ha-Po'alim, and to Mo'etzet
ha-Po'alot. The Urban Council for Women's Labor Issues, which was supposed to convene monthly, was forced to obtain authorization from Mo'etzet
ha-Po'alot as well as Va'ad ha-Po'el before every gathering. They had to an-
nounce in advance, in writing and in public, the date of the meeting. Obviously, these operational procedures thwarted any chance for real activity.
The need to obtain numerous authorizations within a reasonable period of
time from Histadrut institutions, awkward coordination with different partners, numerous reports to go in different directions, and the watchful eye
of Mo'etzet ha-Po'alim on the one hand and the Mo'etzet ha-Po'alot on
the other — all these turned the new institution into an uncomplimentary
reflection of the convoluted operational procedures then common in the
Histadrut.

So it was that at the end of the year of operation the hopes pinned on the
new institution dissipated. Its members complained that the Histadrut institutions did not take the new institution seriously enough and actually prevented its development. The representatives of the hired women workers,
members of the trade unions, were absent from its meetings and did not
maintain the vital links between the women workers' world of labor and the
level of organization in the Women Workers' Movement. Most injurious of
all was the fact that many of the women among the membership of the new
body did not act as emissaries of the women workers' group or as its representatives, thereby perpetuating its marginality in the movement and the Histadrut system.[46]

In short, these institutions were not able to integrate themselves as an influential, active body within the movement. Since they were not institutions of the women workers but were appointed by the Histadrut establishment and under its auspices, only a few of the women workers' needs were given expression by its activities. Moreover, the appointment of local women workers' institutions by the Histadrut establishment created an imbalanced system of dependence and influence: Mo'etzet ha-Po'alim members kept great power concentrated in their hands, so they influenced — actually, determined — which of the women members would occupy the various functions.[47] In contrast, the women members, who wanted to be appointed to the different positions in the women workers' institutions, needed a lobby that would support them. This situation intensified and underscored their dependence upon their sponsors on the Mo'etzet ha-Po'alim to whom they owed their loyalty.

Summary

The female Histadrut members were caught in the vise of double domination: in the grasp of the Histadrut establishment in the women workers' institutions on the one hand, and the hold of the apparatus of the Histadrut Women Workers' Movement among its body of members, on the other.

The attempts to solve the unique problems of the women workers within the framework of the Histadrut succeeded only in part, as seen in the struggle for the founding of local women's labor institutions. In any sphere where women organizing themselves carried a potential or actual threat to the Histadrut establishment, a process of fading away and retreat took place. So the damage was done by driving a wedge between into the authority of the apparatus at the different levels of organization in the movement, while intensifying the gaps between the movement's leadership and its body of members.

Mo'etzet ha-Po'alot was a partner in these trends. It copied and applied Histadrut centralism to the movement whose members desperately needed other solutions. And, of course, the greater the identification of the women's labor movement with the Histadrut establishment, the more their gender awareness weakened and diminished. In their enthusiasm to become an integral part of the establishment and to receive its blessing, they reproduced the organizational patterns and methods of operation common in the Histadrut and embedded them in the Women Workers' Movement.

In the period under discussion, the Histadrut women's movement leadership saw two main "generations" of leadership and of perception of the organization. In the 1920s, current among part of the movement leadership was a view that combined sensitivity to class and to gender. A portion of the leadership experienced the development of the intimate Women Workers' Movement of the beginning of the twentieth century and the early fruits of its innovative experiments. In contrast, in the 1930s there was a gradual change in Histadrut society, the leadership of the Histadrut women's movement, and the population of women belonging to it; hired workers preferred in many instances not to join the women's labor movement at all. The women workers who remained in the labor market at most joined the Histadrut-wide bodies that were to a great extent impervious to gender issues.

Marching in a safer track as far as the establishment was concerned, and a less controversial one, proved itself worthwhile. From an administrative point of view, the apparatus of the Women Workers' Movement accumulated relative power, while its members turned into "professional" activists similar to their counterparts in the Histadrut establishment. The latter even rewarded its devoted male and female followers by recognizing the importance of their activity and rewarding them accordingly.

Thus, if in its early days the Women Worker's Movement sprouted wings and aspired to try its strength, by the close of the period under discussion it no longer desired to fly by itself.

∞ *Hannah Safran*

International Struggle, Local Victory

Rosa Welt Straus and the Achievement of Suffrage, 1919–1926

"What next will you be introducing from America?" [they asked.] "Strikes, perhaps. We do not want such things in a Jewish Colony in the Holy Land."[1]

Ayear after her arrival in Eretz Israel in 1919, Rosa Welt Straus wrote a letter to Carrie Chapman Catt, president of the International Woman Suffrage Alliance (IWSA); the letter was published in the organization's journal *Jus Suffragii*.[2] In it, Welt Straus tells that on the eve of her departure for Eretz Israel she received a suggestion from Chapman Catt to organize the women in Palestine and to have them join the International Woman Suffrage Alliance. Welt Straus continues that carrying out her task was easy, because upon her arrival she found that women's political associations were already active in the country. Moreover, she learned that the Jewish women had obtained the right to vote the previous year.[3]

But attaining the right to vote for Jewish women in Eretz Israel was not gained as easily as Dr. Welt Straus had thought at first. The struggle for suffrage that the "Association of Hebrew Women for Equal Rights in Eretz Israel" began in 1919 lasted for eight years, ending only in 1926. Three months after coming to Eretz Israel, Welt Straus, who had been active in New York

---

This article is part of my doctorate on "The American Connection: The Influence of American Feminism on the Struggle for Women's Suffrage in the *Yishuv* (1919–1926), and Women's Equality in Israel" (1971–1982), written for the Department of History at the Haifa University, under the guidance of Prof. Michal Sobel and Prof. Deborah Bernstein. I wish to thank both of them for the help, the encouragement, and their support. I would also like to thank Prof. Margalit Shilo for the indefatigable help she provided me in writing the Hebrew version of this article.

on behalf of women's suffrage, became chairperson of the association. She conducted the association's international connections for twenty years.

This article focuses on the Jewish women's fight for suffrage at the time the national institutions of the *Yishuv* in Eretz Israel were established and particularly on the role that American women, such as Welt Straus, played in this struggle as well as in the establishment of women's organizations in Eretz Israel. Their contribution is addressed here for the first time and anchors the discussion of the issue of women in Eretz Israel within feminist activity the world over.[4]

A Forgotten Struggle

For a long time, the struggles for women's suffrage in Eretz Israel and elsewhere, too, were not the object of historical research and exposure. In recent years, these battles for the right to vote have begun to stimulate fresh interest and have become a topic on the historiographic agenda.[5]

In Israel, until recently, women had been missing in the historiography of Zionism and the establishment of the State of Israel, since discussion of women's place had been rooted in the myth of equality. The source of the myth lies in the aspirations and hopes of the labor movement and in the Zionist dream of creating a new society in Eretz Israel, and not in the realities of the life in which the debate and struggle were waged, at times bitterly, on the role of women. The prevailing supposition was that the labor movement, which laid the foundations for the society and the state, was the body that worked for and cared for the rights of woman and that inherent in the creation of the new society were equal rights for women. Challenging the myth of women's equality in Eretz Israel in recent years made possible a reexamination of women's history in the country. Feminist women, who began to be active in the 1970s, found the book by Sarah Azaryahu, which documented the history of the struggle for women's suffrage, and they republished it.[6]

In their studies, Margalit Shilo, Dafna Izraeli, and Deborah Bernstein cast doubt on the myth of the equality of Jewish women in the *Yishuv*. Their research shed light on the centrality of the labor movement that focused on the struggle for the conquest of labor for the women laborers, especially in agriculture.[7] Sylvia Fogiel-Bijaoui and others have pointed out the centrality of the fight for suffrage in the process of building the Jewish society in Eretz Israel.[8] Zohara Bozich-Hertzig inquired into the controversy over the right of women to vote, and Hannah Herzog suggested seeing the reasons for shunting aside the memory of the struggle for suffrage in the link between women's forgotten role in Zionist historiography and the centrality of the labor movement in formulating the past of Israeli society.[9] These studies demonstrated the complexity of Jewish women's place during the Mandate period and enabled a wider discussion of the importance of their struggles.

The struggle for the right of Jewish women in Eretz Israel to vote began with the end of World War I. This battle was waged at the same time that the Zionist movement began to establish national institutions in Eretz Israel with the aim of founding a national home for the Jews. But in contrast to Zionist myth, the Jewish women in the *Yishuv* had to fight for their civil rights.[10] The contribution of women to family, childcare, health, and social welfare was not given a place of pride or value in the new society, thus the role of women in the creation of Jewish society and in public endeavor was forgotten.[11]

The fight for women's suffrage was considered a bourgeois struggle and perceived as a change in the agenda of social struggles of the *Yishuv* in Eretz Israel as well as deriving from Western influence. The women's labor movement, established in the early twentieth century to fight the discrimination suffered by women laborers, concurred with these perceptions. Despite that, Ada Maimon, head of the Women Laborers' Council in the 1920s, considered cooperation among the women's organizations as the right way to attain common goals; obtaining the right to vote for women seemed to her an imperative process that would lead to true achievements for all women.[12]

International Struggle

Since the end of the nineteenth century, international women's organizations have been established that cooperated with each other and supported local struggles in different countries. The active women crossed national borders, and at times also those of class and religion, and created international organizations out of a feeling of solidarity for the status of women the world over and from the need to create additional sources of power. They prepared an international plan of action and perceived international connections and influence as source of power that could change the situation of women everywhere.[13]

Aletta Jacobs and Carrie Chapman Catt set out in 1911 for a journey around the world. On this trip, during which they visited Palestine, they met many women and tried to influence them to establish a women's suffrage organization.[14] In 1921, the chairperson of the IWSA, Millicent Fawcett, was invited to speak by the Association of Hebrew Women for Equal Rights in Eretz Israel, and her visit was publicized around the country.[15]

In many countries, Jewish women took part in the fight for suffrage as members of local organizations, as activists in the founding of international organizations, and as members of Jewish women's organizations. The proportion of Jewish women in international organizations was very much higher than their percentage in the population. In the United States, the participation of Jewish women in feminist activity was great, owing to the influence of the Reform movement in which women had had equality since the nineteenth century.[16] The Jewish women's involvement in these movements led them to demand a change in the attitude of the Jewish community and influenced the initiation of a process of change in the attitude of the Jewish religion toward women.[17] In 1923, the World Council of Jewish Women was established to promote the rights of Jewish women, and women from many countries worked with it.[18]

The Opposite Struggle

In contrast to many countries in which the struggle for women's suffrage dragged on for many years, the Jewish women in Eretz Israel were part of the elected institutions from the time they were founded. The fight for Jewish women's suffrage in Eretz Israel was to a great extent an "opposite" struggle in which the women demanded for themselves the right to vote while they were already part of the elected body. Women attended every gathering that was aimed at establishing a representative body, beginning with the preparatory meeting held in January 1918.[19] Women took part in each of the three preparatory gatherings, in the elections for the First Elected Assembly, as well as for the three sessions of the Elected Assembly.[20] This led Rosa Welt Straus to think that women had already achieved the right to vote. Yet, the presence of the women did not prevent a struggle that lasted for eight years (1918–1926). During this time, women not only participated in the elections, they even founded a women's party that gained representation, and women also were elected as representatives of various parties. In the course of these eight years, the debate changed from a controversy over women's right to vote and be elected to the major issue of how to create a consensus of leadership in the *Yishuv*. Opposition to giving women the right to vote derived

from two factors: the Orthodox/ultra-Orthodox *Yishuv* and the British Mandate authorities. The Legislative Council, the representative of the High
Commissioner in Palestine, did not recognize women's right to vote in the
Palestine Order in Council of September 1922 and not even in that of 1927.[21]
The agreement of the British administration in Palestine was imperative for
obtaining approval of the legal standing of the Elected Assembly. Thus the
situation demanded an external struggle with the British authorities and an
internal one within the Jewish community.[22]

The women were sure that the issue of their right to vote and be elected —
a right they had had in the Zionist movement from its very beginning —
would not be put to question again on the *Yishuv* agenda. But the struggle
for suffrage was more complex than it had seemed to be at first glance. The
presence of women in the representative body did not forestall debate and
opposition to their very being there. The struggle within the Jewish community over the right of women to vote and be elected began with the second
preparatory assembly, with the joining of the Mizrachi and other Orthodox
groups. The ultra-Orthodox and at times the religious groups headed by the
Mizrachi movement conceived the equality of women as undermining the
sexual ethical norms of their society. These groups fought against the attempt to establish a new, secular Jewish society and considered participation
of women in government institutions as a symbol of a society with free relation between the sexes. Religious circles saw in the demand for women's suffrage an expression of the desire "to imitate the culture of the Western nations and its innovations."[23]

The ultra-Orthodox parties managed to postpone the elections to the
founding assembly six times by using various means. The first election was
held finally in April 1920, but in October 1920, the ultra-Orthodox demon-
stratively left the first session of the Elected Assembly. In March 1922, the
ultra-Orthodox as well as the Mizrachi refused to take part in the elections
until the women's right to vote was cancelled. At the third session of the
Elected Assembly, convened in June 1925 — after a difficult period of pressure from the Mizrachi and the ultra-Orthodox — the delegates became
aware of a secret agreement signed between the ultra-Orthodox and the Executive of the Va'ad Le'ummi ("National Council"): It determined that granting the right to vote to women is a religious issue and therefore is not
amenable to political decision and that the issue would be put to the public
in a referendum whose results would determine whether women would join
the Assembly. This agreement aroused fierce opposition.[24]

During the course of the fight to keep the right to vote, Jewish women in

Eretz Israel were helped by their international connections. In response to a proposal to carry out the referendum, the Association of Hebrew Women organized a propaganda day for woman's rights. At the events of the day, Henrietta Szold called upon the *Yishuv* "to preserve at all costs the principles of equality and justice that were laid at the foundation of our national project."[25] The Association of Hebrew Women for Equal Rights mustered the aid of the women's organizations in the world as well as Jewish women's organizations in Europe and America. The Association's many connections, particularly those of Welt Straus, resulted in the broad support of women's organizations the world over.[26] These groups flooded the Va'ad Le'ummi with protests against any attempt to negate women's civil rights. A telegram that Henrietta Szold sent in the name of the Hadassah Women of America states that forty-five thousand members, organized in over one hundred branches, "urgently demand that the Va'ad Le'ummi recognize the right of a woman to vote and to be elected." Protest telegrams came from the Jewish Women's Association in Poland, reading "The women in Eretz Israel are not alone, with them in this battle are all the democratic women of the Diaspora, we protest against any attempt at depriving rights from half of the *Yishuv*." Additional telegrams were received from women's associations in Switzerland, Romania, Austria, and Germany. The Zionists of America convention announced its decision demanding equal rights for the man and the woman in Eretz Israel.[27] The Hebrew press stressed the importance of these telegrams and publicized them.[28] Association members in Eretz Israel presented to the Va'ad Le'ummi the statements from the women abroad and addressed the Va'ad members with a proclamation that said: "Nations the world over have given women the right to vote, while our nation in our national home will deny the rights of the woman that she has already enjoyed for five years? Will Eretz Israel move forward or slide backwards?"[29] These struggles bore fruit, and in January 1926 the right of women to vote was finally ratified.

A women's political party list in the 1920 elections was called "Aguddat Nashim" ("Women's Association"). It ran in the elections in 1925, under the name "Hit'ahdut Nashim Ivriyyot le-Shivvui Zekhuyyot be-Eretz Israel" (Union of Hebrew Women for Equal Rights in Eretz Israel), led the battle to victory in the *Yishuv* in 1926, and to the inclusion of women's suffrage in the Mandate Laws in 1928. In the first elections, held in April 1920, the Aguddah garnered five representatives; in the elections for the second Elected Assembly, thirteen women were elected on behalf of the Union.[30] Together with the women elected for the Labor party, the women had twice as many representatives. Yet, despite the relatively large number of women elected for

Fig. 1. Union of Hebrew Women for Equal Rights in Eretz Israel. Rosa Welt Straus seated in middle. Sarah Azaryahu, Hit'ahdut Nashim Ivriyyot le-Shivvui Zekhuyyot, Perakim le-Toledot Tenu'at ha-Ishah ba-Aretz (Jerusalem, 1949).

two Elected Assemblies, no women were added to the Va'ad Le'ummi Executive until 1931.

Union of Hebrew Women for Equal Rights in Eretz Israel

The need for mutual aid during World War I and the changes that took place in Eretz Israel with the British occupation prompted wide-ranging activity by women. Women began to organize themselves throughout the country, and they established mutual aid societies to provide support for the needy. A portion of the women sought to expand the woman's role in society and to ensure her full participation in the process of creating a new society. Another part considered the establishment of these associations as a way of creating an infrastructure for providing health services and social welfare, particularly to women in need and their children.[31]

The opposition of the ultra-Orthodox and the Mizrachi to giving women the right to vote for the Elected Assembly made clear the need for common effort among the various associations. The women quickly expanded their philanthropic activity into the political sphere, which included the establishment of a women's party. The Union of Hebrew Women for Equal Rights in Eretz Israel, founded toward the end of 1919, was composed of women's associations formed in various settlements.[32]

The first association was organized in Jerusalem, and it offered Hebrew lessons for women, arranged training courses in professions for young women, and held discussions and lectures. Similar women's groups were already operating in six settlements beside Jerusalem, which was the center: Rehovot, Rishon le-Zion, Petah Tikvah, Haifa, Safed, and Tiberias. Five women comprised the Jerusalem committee that coordinated the unification of the groups: Dr. Rosa Welt Straus, Dr. Miriam Nofach, Eshter Yeivin, Hasia Feinsud-Sukenik, and Sarah Azaryahu. Each settlement added one representative to the committee, and with that the activity of the Union began. The Union was apolitical, and women could belong to it as well as to political parties. Most of the members were non-partisan and held democratic, liberal views.[33]

The decision to create a party that would run independently for the elections was exceptional in the politics of women's suffrage in Eretz Israel and elsewhere. Sarah Azaryahu, who was aware of the importance of this decision, called it "a stratagem" and "a very bold step." In her memoirs, Azaryahu, one of the Union leaders, relates with pride the Eretz Israel movement's achievements, which did not diminish the pressing need to join international women's organizations and to obtain international recognition.[34] Worth noting is that the Union was the first Eretz Israel organization accepted into any international association.

The Union did not consider attaining the right to vote as its ultimate goal but rather saw suffrage as a means for achieving equality for women before the law and in every economic level. The women in the organization stressed that the Union's objective was to gain equality for women in human society, and the right to vote was only one of the means to that end. The Union saw the woman as fulfilling traditional roles while at the same time having equal rights. This perception enabled bridging the gap between different concepts of equality and made it possible for different women to share a common, broad basis for engaging in the organization's work. At the same time, the organization remained one of urban, middle-class women, and most of its members were educated professional women. This liberal worldview allowed the women to struggle gradually for their advancement in society and to focus the fight on one defined topic. At the same time, it enabled the expansion of their group of supporters among the public, thereby concealing the potential threat of a struggle such as this to relations between the sexes in society.

The Place of Rosa Welt Straus

The election of Welt Straus as chairperson of the Union of Hebrew Women upon her arrival in Eretz Israel indicated the importance the Union attributed to the international women's movement and its achievements. And indeed, Welt Straus's connections with the International Women's Alliance and with women leading this alliance paved the way for the Union's acceptance, in 1923, as a member of the International Woman Suffrage Alliance.

Rosa Welt Straus was born in 1856 in Czernowitz, Bukovina. She and her three sisters obtained a general education that enabled each of them to continue with higher studies. Welt Straus was among the first women to receive a matriculation certificate from the classic gymnasium, and even one of the first women in Europe to study for and receive a degree in medicine. Immediately upon completing her studies, Rosa left for the United States; she worked in New York as a doctor at an ophthalmologic hospital and at the eye clinic in a women's hospital. She was active in the struggle for women's suffrage in New York and a founder member in the establishment of the International Alliance founded by Chapman-Catt.[35]

Upon her arrival in Eretz Israel in 1919, at the age of sixty-three, to live with her daughter Nellie Straus (later Mossinsohn), Rosa discovered that activity toward maintaining the right to vote for the Elected Assembly was in full force. She was immediately offered the leadership of the Union for Equal Rights that had just been established, and she accepted this role. Welt Straus became the "foreign secretary" of the Union: In July 1920, she traveled to London and participated in the conference that decided to found the Women's International Zionist Organization (WIZO).[36] She represented the Union at the congress of the International Woman Suffrage Alliance (IWSA) held in Geneva in 1920; she took part in all the congresses of the International Alliance for Equal Rights; she was a member, on behalf of the Alliance, on important international committees and was included numerous times in delegations to heads of governments in the countries where the congresses were held. Similarly, she was a member of the Mandates Committee in Geneva and the United Committee of nine international women's organizations that the League of Nations established to seek a solution to the issue of citizenship of women the world over.[37]

Welt Straus brought before the IWSA congress the request of the Union for acceptance as a member of the international alliance, and in 1923 a positive answer was received. This membership was a distinct achievement, since the Union of Hebrew Women for Equal Rights in Eretz Israel represented only the Jewish women, a small part of all the women in the country, while the International Alliance was interested in representing all women. The issue of national or ethnic representation remained ever-present for international women's organizations throughout the years, and in certain cases prevented the acceptance of a country or one or another minority group into international organizations. Undoubtedly Welt Straus's activity and her personal connections with the organization's leaders opened the door to membership for the Union.[38]

Despite her pivotal role in the organization, Rosa seldom made public appearances, because she was not fluent in Hebrew; it was not fitting, so she thought, to speak a foreign language in public. That also explains why she was not chosen as the Union's representative for any public office in the country, but her place among the organization's leadership was not undermined because of this, and she continued to be chairperson of the Union until the day she died. In contrast to the report that Welt Straus gave to Chappman-Catt, the Hadassah women in the United States believed that it was Welt Straus herself who began the struggle in Eretz Israel. Sarah Kussy, a Hadassah leader in New Jersey, made a trip to Eretz Israel in 1923, following which she described the Americans in Eretz Israel as people with organizational experience and a quick, comprehensive eye for locating problems and needs and finding solutions for them. About Welt Straus she wrote: "Dr. Straus has organized the Union of Hebrew Women for Equal Rights, which is highly influential in improving the political status of the women in Palestine. Her work is influential on the creation of a constitution for that country."[39]

As Welt Straus said, she was not alone: Other women, including those who had come from America, such as Henrietta Szold and Bat Sheva Kesselman, worked for the establishment of women's organizations and laid the foundation for health and welfare services. Nellie Mossinsohn, Welt Straus's daughter, was a member of the Hadassah Organization, a personal friend of Henrietta Szold, and the representative of Kehillat Zion in Eretz Israel. She was involved in the establishment of Tel Adashim, Balfouriyya, and Kefar Meir Shfeya, and also was among the founders of the Hebrew Women's Federation.[40]

When Welt Straus came to Eretz Israel, she was part of a community of American women, mostly living in Jerusalem. These women had belonged to women's organizations abroad, Jewish and general, and they brought with them codes of behavior and methods of operation that they had acquired in the course of their previous experience. The feminism of these women was influenced by the ideas of the Progressive movement in America that sought ways to fight poverty and considered the establishment of health services for everyone and caring for the rights of working women and children a socio-political goal.[41]

After the Victory: Mundane Reality

Despite the impressive achievement of gaining the right to vote and be elected, women were a minority in the preparatory assembly and on the Va'ad Le'ummi. They were forced to continue to battle for an equal place in society. With the end of their struggle at the countrywide level, the influence of these women declined. Cooperation among the organizations did not continue, and the women's movement attained no further political achievements. Even so, the Union of Hebrew Women for Equal Rights continued to fight for women's rights. The struggle was centered in various settlements, in each of which was a local need to fight for suffrage for women in the settlement itself. Subjects such as marriage age for minors, polygamy, the right of women to enter the country, and the status of women in the rabbinic courts — all of these continued to occupy the Union. With the growth of the large women's organizations Hadassah, WIZO, and Mo'etzet ha-Po'alot (Womens' Workers Council), and the merging of the Federation of Hebrew Women into WIZO, a large part of the activity shifted to these organizations. The strength of the Union of Hebrew Women during the fight for women's suffrage, expressed in its ability to work toward a single goal, with no other political obligation, turned into a weakness once the goal was attained. The Women's Workers Council, which was part of the Labor movement, became a central factor in the women's movement. The Labor movement grew increasingly stronger, with its main goals being the building of the foundation for the future state and achieving domination within the Jewish community. Promoting the status of women was marginal to the Labor movement agenda, but at the same time it was important for the movement to perceive itself as fighting for equality of women. Apparently inherent in this contrast is the origin for the development of the myth of equality in the *Yishuv* and for the assigning to oblivion the role of the women who did not belong to the Labor movement.

As in other countries, the struggle for women's suffrage in Eretz Israel became a symbol of the women's fight for their right to shape and choose the social and sexual ethics of the new society. The women's ability to organize themselves and to set up the infrastructure for health and welfare services, to mobilize the public in Eretz Israel and abroad, to learn from the activity of other women, and to act together — all of these led to victory in the fight for the right to vote. To be sure, this battle was only part of the fight for the place of women in society, but their achievement made it possible to continue the struggles on different levels.

The struggle for women's suffrage in Eretz Israel during the early years of the Mandate has not been given the attention it deserves in Zionist historiography, and it was almost forgotten in the history of the *Yishuv*. The women waged the battle and led it to victory but they did not get the publicity and fame for it, their names are not known, and the organizations they established merged and disappeared into other women's organizations. The number of women from America among the activists who came to Eretz Israel was not large, but they were among the women who founded, initiated, and led the fight.[42] The struggles toward obtaining suffrage in Eretz Israel were not mute and the quest for that history is not a research into women's silences but into the silencing of the persistent, energetic endeavor to obtain the right to vote.

Creativity in Word and Music

Nehama Puhachewsky

The Alibi of the Arbitrary

Nehama Puhachewsky (1869–1934) played an active role in the public life of the pre-state Jewish community in Palestine (the *Yishuv*), and especially in the life of its women.[1] She contributed to the community's social and intellectual life, not least through her opinions about women's place within the settlement endeavor.[2] Her work (more essays than stories) deals explicitly with the national Zionist project. The female characters in her stories suggest how Puhachewsky experienced female life in the *Yishuv*: On the one hand, women were equal partners in the work, in the very "building of the land"; at the same time, however, they were excluded from real partnership in the community's daily affairs, its intellectual life, and its decision-making processes. In that sense, her stories are unique in placing women and female experience at the center of the narrative, thus creating a space in which they can be active and heard.

Most of the criticism and research devoted to Puhachewsky's stories, however, has focused on their Zionist and settlement-related contexts to appropriate them into the Hebrew literary canon, turning these contexts into the stories' main concern. Such readings, which view the stories' critique of some aspects of the Zionist endeavor, raised through the female protagonists' life, as part of a uniform national Zionist position, subordinates the female subject and female experience to something that is greater than them, but in which they ultimately do not share, and the critique has been read as general, rather than gendered, criticism.

The basic ideological positions of modernist nationalism do not allow the inclusion of women except as representations of something else — "nation," "land," or "the universal." Puhachewsky's stories, then, even when they are recognized as voicing criticism, especially of women's status, remain, within this canonical reading, faithful to the formation of modern national ideals, and hence can be included in the national literary canon. Within these ideals, the national endeavor is perceived from the start as precluding the participation of women, since they do not share in fighting, policymaking, financing, and organizing the modern apparatuses of national governance.

Yet Puhachewsky's stories also can be subjected to a different reading. In order to focus on a female experience capable of striking a path into the modern national-Zionist project, it can be argued, these stories not only voice the canonical critique, but add another, subversive critical trajectory — or, rather, they make possible a subversive reading that uses their own materials to suggest, as a subversive act, an alternative to the construction of a female national subject, one which is not only a symbol of something else.

In his vast and important account of Hebrew literature's evolution, Gershon Shaked catalogues Nehama Puhachewsky's work as realist-actualist fiction, a genre within which she "offers many melodramatic 'victim' stories" intended to "arouse pity and elicit tears."[3] In his brief summary of Puhachewsky's oeuvre, to demonstrate his theory that "Zionist ideology alone is a source of salvation and a source of hope," Shaked quotes from the story *"Bil'adeah"* (Without Her): "The weak institutions of today will grow stronger, and the need to increase the redemption of the land will seep bit by bit into all hearts. And finally the entire people of Israel will throng, rejected from without and attracted from within, to its only source of vitality, where it can still be saved from spiritual and physical annihilation" (p. 85).[4]

But the story *"Bil'adeah"* does not end with the promise of redemption; nor does its conclusion reaffirm and validate the hope and salvation inherent in the Zionist ideology, as Shaked would have it. Rather, the story ends with both husband and wife leaving the country. Yechezkel and Yehudit Weinholz live in a *moshavah* (agricultural settlement) and take care of their farm; they have no children, and Yehudit is seriously ill. Her illness does not keep her from cultivating her garden and performing her other chores. But finally, after a particularly bad night, she realizes that she has no choice. Regardless of her deep desire to remain in the country and on her farm, she must go to Vienna for surgical treatment. Weinholz takes over some of her tasks, writes her letters, and ponders his place in the world. Meanwhile, Yehudit, despite a successful operation, dies suddenly in that foreign land. Weinholz, who by all accounts in the story runs a successful farm and lives in harmonious collaboration with his surroundings, sells his property and leaves the country.

The terrible pain of leaving her land almost kills Yehudit, and perhaps it is indeed what ultimately kills her; Yechezkel, by contrast, leaves even though his farm is successful and he "sits in a fine house enjoying a great abundance" (p. 79). Moreover, *"Bil'adeah"* is not critical of the couple's leaving: the "melodramatic" aspect of the narrative of victimhood — Yehudit falling ill and dying, and the anguished husband who cannot bear life in the country without her — leaves no room for doubt: This is not a story encouraging immigration (*aliyah*) to Eretz Israel. As Nurit Govrin argues, "The futility of living without the beloved is the central motif of the story 'Bil'adeah,' as its name ['without her'] suggests . . . In Yechezkel Weinholz's struggle between his personal problems (his wife's illness and the lack of offspring) and his sense of the homeland (work, the farm and the ideal), the personal side triumphs; as it turns out, redeeming the land, the path of the many, is not enough to outweigh 'the love of a woman and the passion for sons,' the path of the individual."[5]

It is in this depiction of the difficulties and actual crisis encountered while realizing the Zionist dream that Yaffa Berlovitz locates Puhachewsky's protest. The author, she argues, does not share the naiveté of other writers of Zionist literature from the First Aliyah: "Not only did the texts not contain naïve expression, but their distinguishing feature is a harsh and painful awakening from that preliminary naiveté."[6] Defining Puhachewsky's work as a "melancholy" (and not, as Shaked suggests, as "melodrama"), Berlovitz suggests that the sources of the rupture should be sought in "three states of conditioning that might lead to melancholy," the first of which might befit the story *"Bil'adeah"*: "The arbitrariness of human existence. This sense of arbitrariness, of the meaningless nature of human existence, dominates Puhachewsky's stories, especially when the calamities suffered by the protagonists are not a result of the unfolding plot, but rather come raining down out of nowhere."[7]

But what, exactly, does Puhachewsky indicate as an awakening? The arbitrary world does make Yehudit ill and then, after her successful surgery, causes her death, but this arbitrariness does not provide — in the story — a sufficient explanation for Yechezkel Weinholz's decision to abandon the country. At some point, albeit in a different context, Yechezkel even comes to think that "Life without her is not as difficult as he had envisioned." And since the story attests not only to faith in the Zionist enterprise but also to its success (children are born and grow up, hired laborers become land-owning farmers, the collective resolves its problems as a heterogeneous community, Weinholz lives in prosperity), it raises the question: Can the death of a single woman, beloved though she might be, outweigh all that Zionist faith, success, and ardor?

Indeed, it is not only the loss of his wife that pushes Yechezkel to despair: "What does a man leave behind? . . . Creative people — writers and artists leave a name for themselves and a legacy in their works. But what might a man like himself leave behind, a man who will not create new worlds? A simple, earthly man has only one 'immortality of the soul,' and there alone hides the secret of life's continuation: sons, sons! . . . And he — he will walk childless all his days if Yehudit does not return to him safe and sound . . ." (p. 84). After all, "Why and for whom does he toil this way? Who will cherish his efforts? Who will carry on his work? Who will watch over all that he has nurtured when he dies?" (p. 80).

Yechezkel Weinholz, the story's almost sole focalizer, does not blame his beloved wife for leaving and dying overseas. She did not even want to go to Vienna for treatment; instead, she "suffered and worked and said nothing," until he forced her to go "after a great battle" (p. 80). But the causal structure of the story nevertheless identifies Yehudit as the "guilty" party: her illness and death deprive Weinholz of a wife and offspring, the lack of which, in Weinholz's eyes, empties the entire Zionist endeavor of its meaning. The long catalogue of homeland, land, house, garden, field, *moshavah*, work, and ideals does not compensate for the lack of succession. Continuity will not be found in the farming and building shared by the entire Jewish community in Zion; it can only come from private, personal procreation, for which Yechezkel needs a wife. Yehudit's incompatibility with Zionism's agricultural fulfillment is strengthened in the story by an analogy between her and the cows on the farm (whose care is part of Yehudit's chores): just as she wakes Yechezkel in the middle of the night, so he is awakened in the middle of the night by the thought of the "grass for the cows" that will "spoil by tomorrow if he does not feed it to the cows immediately" (p. 88). But whereas Yehudit wakes him terrified of dying, sends him running for the doctor, and later that night finally breaks down and agrees to go to Vienna, from which she will never return, leaving him childless — by contrast "the brown cow's udders are filling up! She will probably calve on Passover Eve! [. . .] And the 'gay one' — how pretty she has grown, eating the grass! And also the 'short one', firstborn daughter of 'stubborn one,' has more milk!" (p. 88).

Accompanying this unpleasant analogy between cow and woman is Weinholz's treatment of his wife as if she were a child. "But this is childishness!" (p. 82) he scolds Yehudit for refusing to go to Vienna; and he is filled with joy when he thinks of the letter that "will bring him happy tidings from his sweet girl" (pp. 86–87), whose eyes are "large, childish, sad" (p. 82) and to whom he is "her old man" (p. 87). Even Yehudit's private thoughts are not safe from the adult's penetrating eye: "Sea breezes whisper between their leaves-needles and tell me the secrets and dreams of my Yehudit . . ." he writes to her (p. 87).

Yehudit's "childishness" fits her incompatibility with the life she so loves. After her departure, Weinholz discovers that "Life without her is not as difficult as he had envisioned. A bit of caretaking in the morning and in the evening was a small matter" (pp. 87–88). Although it is "unpleasant work," he need only "boil the milk" (p. 87), which he later takes to drinking cold (p. 86), and he eats his lunches "in the laborers' kitchen" (p. 79). Eventually, it is no longer clear what exactly was all that hard work that so exhausted Yehudit. Only the garden still awaits her return: "It is forlorn without you, dear! Around the flowers many weeds have sprung up, waiting for your little hoe and your soft, delicate hands!" (p. 87). The little hoe — presumably the same one picked up later, when Yehudit is about to return, by the "little Arab" who "hoes all day long in the vegetable garden and flower patch" (pp. 87–88) — and the soft, delicate hands are apparently unsuitable for the life demanded by this land. The analogy between Yehudit and the garden constructs another analogy, between her and "those simple flowers, which he often longs to replace with others, of the finer species, but cannot, because the good species require water — and there is none" (p. 87). Like the flowers, Yehudit, too, is of a fine species, but this waterless land is not yet ready to welcome anything fine: "'Oh, pipes, pipes!' — groans Weinholz. How happy he would be if this improvement had already come to the moshavah!" (p. 87).[8]

Yehudit's (arbitrary) illness is linked to stereotypical feminine traits (tenderness, childishness), and together these render her unsuitable for life in Eretz Israel. The Zionist ethos, which identifies foreign lands (the Diaspora) with illness and death and experiences this exile as exerting a powerful grip, so that only a revolutionary, even violent act of self-extrication (from one's family, from the past) can release from its clasping power and bring healing and health, is not enough to save Yehudit. Her life in Zion, her tilling of the soil, and her strong conviction that she can only live on her own land — none of these buy her entrance into the narrative, which in this story is "written" by Yechezkel. Her presence in the narrative is limited to two functions: she can serve as a symbol of the disease of diasporic life, and of the poverty of the land (which lacks water for fine flowers) — or she can provide narrative continuity in the form of sons, in the fulfillment of love and desire not only through the national narratological genealogy (the passion for Zion, the love of the land, and the physical merging with it) but through a private, familial, dynastic genealogy. Yehudit's entrance into the narrative of national-Zionist liberation is dependent on her ability to endow the private aspect of Yechezkel's life with meaning. She has no share in the national public sphere or Yechezkel's public life, which the story repeatedly characterizes as successful, fulfilling, perfectly proper: fertile land, a well-appointed home, community involvement and stature, and control of the Arab "other" (the "little" one who works in the garden, Mahmoud leading the horse, and the "two Arab women washing, doing laundry and scrubbing" [p. 87]).

The boundaries of the Zionist space are delineated with precision: from the catalogue cited above, through the Zionist speech (quoted by Shaked), to detailed descriptions of a farmer's life. But Zionist space is demarcated mainly through exclusions: the exclusion of the Arab, who is subordinated to service tasks, some of them feminine (which he performs in Yehudit's absence), others performed on the soil and horse of a Jew; and the exclusion of the two women mentioned in the story, whose occupations are limited to housework, gardening, listening to the men's Zionist speeches, and marrying land-purchasing husbands. The women are not partners of equal ability in the main Zionist effort" — tilling the soil and inhabiting the land. And when there is no exclusion, there is a hierarchical distinction between the "owner of the land" and the "foreigner" who comes to join: "From the south came Yemenites — pitiful people, barefoot, wild-haired, without coats and almost without tunics. Their flesh wrapped in rags, prayer shawls on their shoulders. Their looks are strange and alien, yet they speak Hebrew and praise their brethren and 'Ha-Shem' ['the Lord'] for their salvation and the redemption of their souls, for leaving an impure land and coming to a pure and holy one . . . And the northern ship also disembarked sons returning to their father's table. Young men came — thirty heroes, fresh and vigorous lads. And who can imagine his joy [that of Wienholz visiting Jaffa] at the splendid sight, when north meets south! The same wind gathered them all and brought them here, brought them to build and create . . ." (pp. 83–84). Although north and south are analogous and have gathered to build and create together, the southerners have a "strange and foreign" look, and only the Hebrew they speak makes them acceptable; there are even quotation marks around their belief that "Ha-Shem" helped them to come here. Meanwhile, the new arrivals from the north are called sons returning to their father's homes, as if they were the true sons of this land: heroes, fresh, young and vigorous, so different from those pitiful, barefoot, wild-haired Yemenites, in their patched clothes and prayer shawls, which distance them from the secular-Zionist home that is their salvation — Zionism, not "Ha-Shem."

The acts of exclusion and hierarchical labeling keep the ownership of the Zionist narrative, the "right" to tell this narrative, in the hands of he who has appropriated both the physical space and its space of images — Weinholz. Yehudit, his wife, is thus relegated to the same periphery as all the non-robust, non-fieldworking, non-wealthy (in this story, the bourgeoisie — usually hated by the ruling socialist Zionist narrative — is partially included in the Zionist space by virtue of the capital it invests in the land). Like them, her grasp on the land is partial, temporary, in the service of others. Like them, she is constructed in the story as non-central — as what is not an Ashkenazi Jewish man. The function of Yehudit's story is not to construct an independent and sovereign subject, but to present a foil or image for the central Zionist story. The excluded woman marks the boundary through her positioning as non-central, and is therefore on the boundary's "other side." She characterizes the center by appearing as its negation: the center is everything that Yehudit is not. The text, it seems, opens no channel through which a woman might exist within the national space without either subjecting to the label of "peripheral" or waiving femininity as a gender — that is, waiving the distinction, even the stereotypical one, that grows out of the history of woman's cultural representations, and that would find expression in the exploration of alternative modes of existence, ones that do not presuppose male superiority.

Alongside the option of accepting and embracing an inferior position within the national formation, it is also possible, as Yaffa Berlovitz suggests, to read the text as representing the difficulties of trying to live in the country within the boundaries of the Zionist commitment, and in particular those hardships caused by arbitrary events, for whom no one is responsible. But this specific text itself does not provide a link to Zionism. In this text, Zionism does not contain its own rupture within it, because its boundaries are marked not by physical hardships and limitations, but by exclusions and hierarchies based on race, class, nationality, and gender. However, gender blindness — that is, reading the story as an individual case representing an entire category of "arbitrary" events, whose gender is inconsequential — is, in fact, precisely what allows the text's inclusion within the Zionist cultural repertoire. A reading that retains the critical view of life in Zion (that is, the impossibility of persevering in the Zionist act in the face of random occurrences), but that does not stress the hegemonic position, which accepts the woman's culpability at face value — such a reading relies on the explanation the story itself suggests for the failure of the personal Zionist endeavor of Yechezkel Weinholz. For even if Yehudit has died, and even if he is currently without sons, Weinholz's world might have been filled by the Zionist vision (whose realization, as we learn time and again, is so successful); he himself even tries to console himself with this possibility on several occasions. On top of which there is also the option, painful as it might be, of remarrying and fathering children to carry on the fulfillment of the vision.

But it is precisely at this point that another issue arises. The arbitrariness of Yehudit's illness (the arbitrariness of disaster) does not stand alone, but is intersected with another general issue that troubles Weinholz, a particular failure he experiences: his inability to maintain congruency between fulfillment in his private life and fulfillment on the public level. In "*Bil'adeah*," the demand for this correspondence is articulated not in particular ideological (socialist) or national (Zionist) terms, but rather in universalist terms: Yechezkel's failure to find compensation for his private loss in the fulfillment of the collective vision (that is, compensation for his childlessness in the success of the general Zionist endeavor, to which he contributes) is wrapped in a more comprehensive and universal failure — the failure to privilege human beings above all else. "'What is more important — man or the trees of the field?' — this strange and alien question has been bothering Yechezkel throughout the morning" (p. 79). His answer on this morning is — the tree. He forgoes visiting his ailing former friend, Finkel, preferring instead to tend to his trees, even though he knows that "The trees will not die in a day" (p. 80). The trees vanquish the man; and as the story makes very clear, the triumph of the Zionist endeavor over an interpersonal relationship does not make Weinholz any happier. To the contrary; that night, of all nights, he wonders "why and for whom he was toiling this way" (p. 80). From an ideological perspective that requires a correspondence between fulfillment in public existence and the fulfillment of private, dynastic-familial life, a life that cannot be replaced by the national vision, an ideology that justifies itself by adopting a universalist position, which sees humans as superior to any tree — from that perspective, preferring the tree is a failure so profound that it erases all the successes achieved in growing it (both literally and as a metaphor for fieldwork in the Zionist context).

The shift the text proposes, then, is not from a gender-based debate of national belonging (with which the text is quite preoccupied) to an ideology of the unity of interior and exterior, personal and collective, private-domestic and communal. Since the opposition of interior and exterior, of private and public, is itself gendered (each pole is signified in culture by a different gender: the interior is female, and the exterior, the public, is male), to break away from gender, the text moves to universal values, which transcend nationality (and Zionism) and therefore also transcend ideology. The universal value of human importance joins its concrete realization in a specific life and becomes the national justification; but when the universal value is violated — when Weinholz prefers the tree over the man — then the national system can no longer make up for what is missing in his personal life. The nonfulfillment of the private value is conceived as "punishment" for the distortion of the universal value: Yehudit's illness, which leads to her death and leaves Weinholz lonely and childless, is in fact the concrete realization of this distortion. This is not a case of an arbitrary fate that makes it "difficult" to fulfill the Zionist vision; it is a loss of the correspondence between realization in the private sphere and realization in the public one, a loss born out of the distortion of a universal value. The universal value transcends both ideology and nation, and nationalism is only a concretization of it. It is not the private sphere that moves up the hierarchy of values, rising above the national or the ideological values. It is the universal, as "blind" to nationalism as it is "blind" to gender, that creates the correspondence between public and private, and without which neither one can exist.

The universalist reading is not only made possible, but is, in fact, suggested by the text as the best way of organizing its materials. It is also what allows a story that might be perceived as anti-Zionist to be included in the repertoire of Zionist texts. And the universalist reading of the materials dealing with the causes of Weinholz's failure and departure is what enables a reading from a female positioning to keep the text seemingly "ungendered." Thus, rather than have Yehudit (the woman) represent the failure of Zionist fulfillment, the failure is attributed to the distortion of the universal value and its consequences in private, family life — or, rather, to the absence of such a life. The woman is no longer the destructive witch, but, as is often the case, a symbol of something else, something greater than herself, of which she is only a representation. That "something" is the disruption of the universal order. On the one hand, such a reading rescues the woman from the marginal position of a witch, but at the same time it precludes the construction of a concrete femininity: femininity can only be a symbol for other, more supreme values. Women, then, cannot be full partners in nationalism; only a symbol of the conditions under which nationalism might exist.

Universalism, then, is gender blindness: universalism depends on this blindness (in the sense that it is possible to conceive of a "universal" that is applied to both men and women regardless of their different social positioning and power relations), it ratifies this blindness, and is also the means by which the blindness to gender can be overridden. A stauncher subversive reading of this text would expose in it the claim that because the failure to realize the vision involves a failure in the private sphere, it is actually the consequence of femininity (which exists in the private sphere). In other words, this is not a rendition of a specific, random (arbitrary) case of a certain "Yehudit," but the outcome of imperative feminine aspects that cannot be of service to the Zionist endeavor, but can only destroy it.

In "*Bil'adeah*," this biological-feminine context assumes a particular validity, since Weinholz's despair and departure are caused by a failure of the distinct feminine-biological function: childbearing. The story constructs its entire rationale on the link between female biology and femininity: the woman's softness, tenderness, and childishness are all linked in the narrative to her inability to bear children. The woman is barred from entering nationalism by her (necessary) absence from the loci of Zionist action (the field and the community center), and allowed in only through the symbol (woman symbolizing the private sphere, the domestic, which must find fulfillment in the Zionist discourse, and symbolizing also the universal value of the supremacy of the individual human being) or else through childbirth (the necessary continuation of the private dimension); yet these kinds of inclusion in nationalism rules out physical, flesh-and-blood feminine existence (separate from biological and symbolic motherhood).

The most radical act of subversion made possible by this particular text is the identification within it of two representations of "woman." Yehudit is a woman; yet according to stereotypical female characteristics, combined with characteristics produced by the story, Yechezkel, her husband, is also a "woman." Like her, the "girl," he too is "filled with a youthful joy" (p. 87); like her (and like the Arab digging, as she does, in the garden), "he is but a small man" (who cannot find complete satisfaction in the ideal and needs flesh-and-blood offspring [p. 85]). He takes over Yehudit's household chores (p. 78), is repeatedly shown in the classic female position of passive recumbence (pp. 87, 80 — "lying flat," p. 82 — "falling to the bed," "falling helplessly to the bench"), and like her he leaves the country because he cannot survive in it. Weinholz also indulges in the stereotypical female act of predicting the future (he dreams of Yehudit's death, not once but three times). Even when he acts as a man, his actions go hand in hand with those of a woman: He successfully influences other members of the community, but also gives bad advice to his friend because, like a woman, he does not have a clear view of the situation; like a man, he cares for the trees and waters them, but the text describes in just as much detail how he sews animal skins in the winter, like a woman (p. 85); he races outside to the fields—but at home he returns over and over to the classic female positioning: standing indoors and looking out the window (pp. 82, 84, 85); like a man he stares, but this male pattern crumbles, because his gaze is fixed on the darkness, and also because Yehudit's eyes are fixed on him (p. 82), and the one-eyed woman in his dream surveys him, while Yehudit gives him a reproachful look (p. 84).

These acts and modes of behavior, masculine but also feminine, do not lead to a reading of Weinholz as a "real" woman. They do, however, help undermine a purely biological conception of "femininity" and lend weight to its understanding as a cultural construct based on acquired behavior (Weinholz learns to cook, and apparently also has learned to sew) and cultural conventions (lying as a passive female act, staring as an active male one). Moreover, the "feminization" of Yechezkel allows for a different judgment of abandoning the country: Unlike Yehudit, who leaves against her will and only under the threat of death, Yechezkel, the other "woman," leaves not when his body breaks down, but when his spirit is broken. Yehudit's Zionist struggle, the struggle of her concrete body, tormented by physical pain, remains in Zion and continues to strive for its vision, will not relinquish its function of occupying real, concrete space, which is required for the physical fulfillment of the abstract Zionist dream, emerges as a far deeper commitment than the emotional crisis of the "woman" Yechezkel, who collapses because his family name is cut out.

The claim that "feminine" and "masculine," just like "nationalism" and "Zionism," are cultural constructs whose boundaries are marked by the exclusion of an "Other," are created out of an assigned catalogue of traits, and as such are ideologically biased and organized on the basis of ideological understandings and their interrelations, allows only one body to be signified as concrete. For the woman in this story has a concrete body, a real body, a body that suffers pain, undergoes surgery, and dies. For a body signified as what "lies beyond signification," it responds to the demand for a concrete, physical presence within the marked space of Zionist presence and realization—a demand that the culturally gendered construct "masculinity" does not fulfill in this story. The analogy between Yehudit and Yechezkel, as two subjects with "feminine" signifiers, externalizes the contrast between their identical acts of departure. While both forsake the space and leave it behind, Yehudit, both in leaving and in dying, continues to maintain the necessary concrete body, a real body. Yechezkel, meanwhile, reverts to being what is

the main signifier of exile: the broken spirit, the symbolic illness, the biological and emotional barrenness, the absence signified by life in foreign lands,
which is a kind of death-in-living.

The destabilization of gender does not mean a reversal of gender; rather,
it offers an alternative story of understanding gender and its pertinence to the
national story. The lack of gender stability in the story allows the female gender an alternative positioning, and enables an alternative national relationship based on concretization rather than on abstraction and generalization.
Thus, the construction of a national-Zionist-feminine subject is performed
in the "void," in the empty space left by the Zionist ethos: that of the body.
The space of the concrete, sexual body does not command the center of the
Zionist act, in which the body operates by wielding a pickaxe and by contributing to the community. It remains on the margins, less worthy or a mere
symbol and metaphor for the central Zionist act. But from this position —
stereotypical-peripheral, physical, sexual-feminine — arises the power to rattle
the seeming gender stability and to construct an alternative feminine subject: that of feminine nationalism.

Compared to contemporary women writers (and also to later ones) who
attempted to construct a national feminine subject, Puhachewsky seeks to
constitute agency by means of a uniquely radical act. Unlike other women
authors, she chooses to deconstruct the conceptual system that creates
women's exclusion in the first place. The very concept of gender is critically
deconstructed by her and exposed as an artificial construct, as a cultural pattern. It is revealed as the construction of the center through exclusion, a
construction that delineates itself against a series of constructed identities
that it aspires to present as "biological" and "natural." The concept of femininity is also dissolved into its elements; for Puhachewsky, "femininity" is not
a complete and solid unity, stable and without fractures, but a series of
schemas — childish traits, a structure of disease, exile, motherhood, foreignness, weakness — that do not add up into a single totality that necessarily also
breeds women's public exclusion from partnership in the Zionist enterprise.

Above all, what Puhachewsky deconstructs is the *route* of femininity's
constitution in culture. But here, too, she both makes explicit the mode of
construction and, simultaneously, points to the rupture inherent in this
artificial process. She thus also externalizes how the concrete is annulled
and transformed into a symbol: Yehudit's concrete, ailing, dying, dead body
is replaced by the symbolism of the disease of exile and departure. But at one
and the same time, she exposes the profound rupture within this construction: the arbitrariness of the disease — an arbitrariness that will not submit to

the organization of the illness within an orderly meta-narrative, but that instead repeatedly disorders it — prevents the rigid organization required by cultural construction. It externalizes the randomness of the physical body, which refuses to be forced into artificial structures and mechanisms. This arbitrariness keeps the body as concrete material, despite the constructionist effort to turn it into a symbol: It sickens, weakens, and dies. The female component actually appears here as a body that remains present in Zion, that continues to toil for the Zionist vision and insists on occupying actual, material space. The structure of "masculinity," already presented as fragile and tainted with "femininity," does not, in this story, maintain its requisite physical presence in space, which signifies the Zionist presence and fulfillment.

Almost paradoxically, Puhachewsky uses this series of critical deconstructions of gender, femininity, and their constituting mechanisms to establish femininity as agency. Deconstruction actually presents an option of self-construction, of rectification, through its own critical mode of operation, which materializes in the concretization of the symbolic: Yehudit becomes a factor in Zionism by turning her symbolic value as "illness" into a concrete illness, and her symbolic function as destructive witch into a destructive reality. By intensifying the concretization of the concrete body in a concrete space that is physically and materially abandoned, Puhachewsky performs a critical procedure on the very route through which symbolic femininity is constructed in the Zionist national context.

Puhachewsky's critical act is especially invasive, especially revolutionary, because she creates agency by deconstructing the roots of the cultural practice through which belonging is established. In other words, agency is produced through two mechanisms: on the one hand, the concretization of the symbolic, and on the other hand, the deconstruction and critique of "femininity" and "gender" as cultural terms, and of the cultural mechanisms that construct them. The resulting critical stance exposes the mechanism that constitutes femininity in culture, as well as its fractures and ruptures: The deconstructive act, in other words, also carries a critical power, one that produces agency.

🦚 *Tali Asher*

The Growing Silence of the Poetess Rachel

This is the way — there is no other,
to follow, to go to the end;
and to remember, and sing, and yearn
and to remember, and be silent . . . and be silent.
                              — "My Tiny Joy"

T he way and silence are key concepts in Rachel's poems. Rachel's marching along the path began as progress, with knowledge that the purpose of the journey was to arrive at a target site within a defined period, and turned into treading in space until the end of time. In this article I would like to demonstrate that the emotional and ideological foundation in Rachel's poems is the experience of remaining "afar"; this experience was designed in connection with Moses, the leader of the Jewish people on the *way* from Egypt to Eretz Israel, and is expressed in the poetics discerned in her poems.

The path that Rachel traversed during her life was one of wanderings, of immigration to Eretz Israel, and of exile within its borders. Rachel was born in 1890 in Russia and reached Eretz Israel in 1909 with her sister; in 1911, she made her way to Kinneret following Hannah Maisel-Shohat. In 1913, Rachel went to France to study art and agriculture. Because of World War I, she was forced to go back to Russia, remaining there until her return, ill with tuber-

Behind this article stand those who taught me the meaning of responsibility toward a text that is read and a text that is written — Dr. Ruth Ginsburg, Dr. Ilana Pardes, Tamar Hess, and my teacher Prof. Dan Miron. I thank them for the thought and time they invested in me as a student and for allowing me to feel that I was a teacher, too. In the Hebrew original of this article, all poems were cited as they appear in *Rahel — Shirim, Mikhtavim, Reshimot, Korot Hayyeha* [Rachel — Poems, Letters, Sketches, Biography], ed. U. Milstein (Tel Aviv, 1994) (Hereafter Milstein, *Rahel — Shirim.*)

culosis, to Eretz Israel, to Degania — from which she was asked to leave because of her illness. After five years of wandering between Petah Tikva, Jerusalem, the hospital in Safed, and Tel Aviv, she settled in a small Tel Aviv garret, living there for about five years. In 1931, Rachel spent time in a convalescent home in Gedera and from there she returned to the hospital in Tel Aviv on the day she died, 15 April 1931. She was buried in Kinneret.

This progression, of promise toward the realization of a personal and collective vision by the very act of settlement, and its being shattered on the threshold of realization, is a fundamentally important step towards understanding Rachel's poems. As an individual — with all the facets of her being — Rachel feels she is standing at the threshold, as a *halutzah*, as a woman, as a creative person. In this article, I will focus on the development of the sense of threshold by characterizing the poetics in this light and in the link between Rachel and Moses — on the basis of the shattering that came before realization could be achieved.

Literary Reception

As a poetess, Rachel had to overcome a number of obstacles. The expectations of the masculine establishment in Eretz Israel at the beginning of the twentieth century from the feminine pen were nurtured by phallocentric thought patterns, and they allotted women's poetry limited functionality and minimal access. From the time the feminine voice penetrated cultural discourse, it was identified with the emotional world composed of sensations of love, desire, pregnancy, and motherhood as an imperative thematic foundation, which is not congruent with intellectual-philosophical significance. In his book *Imahot Meyassedot, Ahayot Horgot* (Founding Mothers, Stepsisters), Dan Miron identifies these demands with genre expressions: It was recommended that women's poetry anchor its messages in the realm of the lyrical, become entrenched in the small lyrical poem, and be excluded it from the "higher," more complicated lyrical genres such as the ode and the elegy. Actually, the male cultural establishment was quite amenable to personal, autobiographical, confessional, and sentimental women's poetry, and if despite this, women's poetry did aim for Modernism, it would be best if it would locate itself in its conservative wing.[1]

Rachel did indeed choose the small lyrical poem. With the publication of her first poems in *Davar*, there were signs of the perception of a poem that was likely to deceive many readers; by means of a short, minimalist, lyrical

poem, with clear language and personal-feminine subjects, a poetic framework was fashioned under an innocent guise but with sophisticated content.
This model left an opening for the general step of very reduced appreciation
that dominated the attitude to Rachel's work.

Adjectives such as "small," "innocent," and "simple" characterize the general nature of the lexicon recruited for describing her poems. "Genteel,"
"pleasant," "charming" are frequently used adjectives and despite their positive aura, what is common to all of them is the lack of identifying this
poetry with an aspect of power and strength.[2]

In his article "The Exclusion of Women from Hebrew Literary History,"
Michael Gluzman points out this distortion that was firmly fixed in the description of the development of Modern Hebrew poetry. Defining the 1920s
as the years of Expressionist-Futurist and Neo-Symbolist expressions, while
ignoring an Acmeist such as Rachel and an Impressionist such as Esther
Raab, is only a partial description and therefore askew. Expanding the canon,
by recognizing the stylistic breakthrough inherent in women's poetry, adds
the connecting link between the two waves considered central in Hebrew
poetry — that of Abraham Shlonsky (who came out against the poetics of Bialik) and that of Nathan Zach (who came out against the poetics of Nathan
Alterman). A serious discussion of the poetesses', and including their work in
a review of the development of Hebrew poetry, makes possible a more faithful and complete depiction of Hebrew Modernism, which is characterized
by a "simple style" and rejects rhetorical language.

Rachel made her way into the world of Eretz Israel Hebrew poetry by
sounding the first feminine voice in it. The only way in which Rachel's poetry could have been accepted by this establishment was by being delimited
through formal and thematic conventions, with the idea that they were what
she wanted to implement and that she would continue to exist within their
framework.

The expectations of the target audience for short, simple poems, reinforcing the link between the Jewish people and its land and its historical past on
the social plane and presenting the image of a weak, needy woman on the personal plane, found support in Rachel's poetry. The explanatory process was
halted at a very early stage; the distribution Rachel gained, derived from a one-
dimensional, narrow reading, lead to her evaluation as the spokesperson for
the people, the nation, and the Hebrew language but not as a poetess. And in
the way that "popular" is perceived, according to the romantic critical tradition, as authentic, simple, and naïve, so was her poetry accepted as such.

Most of Rachel's poems offer subversion hegemonically framed. One sees in them the image of a strong and obstinate, independent and rebellious women; the figure of a women that gains for herself exclusive possession of the land by her nature; and a creative woman who makes her way into the masculine cultural and literary discourse.

The Way and the Threshold: The Association between Rachel and Moses

The world of the speaker in Rachel's poem, as developed in the collective consciousness, was painted in the colors of yearning — for a child, for love, and particularly for the Kinneret. The Kinneret was perceived as the region of longings and as a source of inspiration. Actually, the poetess who was identified with the myth of "the longed-for Kinneret" did not write her poems in her Kinneret period. Rachel stayed at Kinneret for only two years and that period did not serve as inspiration for her poetic work; the bulk of her writings came in the last six years of her life.[3] The claim that her work was built out of bricks of yearning for Kinneret indicates a disregard of her symbolic charge and diminishes its reading to a halutzic manifest.

The Kinneret did indeed serve in the construction of the central poetic stance in Rachel's work, but it constituted a symbolic means; Kinneret is the name for defined aspirations, well delineated in the speaker's imagination, embedded in the roots of her consciousness — and impossible to attain:

> There, the mountains of Golan, stretch out your arm and touch them! —
> In sure silence they command: Stop. ("Kinneret")

To see — and not to touch. To live alongside the firm knowledge that the evasive contact will remain just that forever, as an immutable decree.

The basic experience fashioned in the poems is the experience of marching along the way, standing opposite, and remaining on the threshold. Coping with this experience is given expression in three collections of Rachel's poems: *Safi'ah* (Aftergrowth), *Mi-Neged* (From Afar), and *Nebo*. The collections' titles are taken from the biblical context to which the readers are referred even before they meet the poems; at the heart of the biblical context stands Moses. The association that is woven into the poems between the speaking figure and Moses is not exhausted through these references but is interspersed in the speaker's stance, in the shaping of the path as a theme and as poetics that reflect this basic experience and are seen through it.

The way in which Rachel yokes Moses' situation to the definition of her own is a one-time occurrence and is not assimilated as of equal value in the general dialogue that Rachel maintains with other biblical figures. The association between Rachel and Moses organizes around itself the definition of the speaker's identity and accompanies her throughout her changes along the course of the poems

Moses — the infant who was rescued and survived, who was chosen and led, the emissary of God who stumbled and was betrayed — is also the person who was stopped on the threshold and remained standing opposite. At this point, Rachel joins him and stands with him. The speaker in Rachel's poems merges with the figure of Moses; she employs gender reversal when formulating her words and she sees herself as the prodigal son:

> Both of us know: the prodigal son
> will never again see the homeland skies. (*"Kach et Yadi"* [Take My Hand])

The background for the merging of Rachel and Moses, which cuts through generations and genders, is their standing on the threshold and looking directly at the unobtainable goal. In Moses' case, this is the goal that remains an impossible destination; in Rachel's case, this is the place where she lived and blossomed — and wilted and was forever banished. Both of them are dispossessed from the place where they belong — as seen personally and in the eyes of the collective.

Moses is on his way to external exile on Mount Nebo and hears time and again that he will never set foot on the ground of the land to which he is leading the people of Israel. The earth, which at first seems to be a source of life, becomes a region of estrangement, death, and burial. Like the fate of Moses, so too, Rachel is destined to remain beyond the pale:

> If my fate
> is to live far from your borders —
> allow me, Kinneret,
> to rest among your graves.

Even though she is locked in a narrow room in a strange city, Rachel's journey still goes on. The infiniteness of the journey stems from the fact that she will never again live in the space she sought for herself as a home; and from the circular treading that never leads to the finish line, she says

Weary my soul from a journey-without-path
in the vast desert of life. (*"Ki Littuf Ahim"* [For Brothers' Caress])

Marching in the desert, which in the biblical ethos symbolizes the journey
to Eretz Israel, is none other than marching in the desert for Moses. This is
a chronotopical, emotional, verbal tautology.[4] Rachel feels that she, too, is
drowning in a desert of dearth and of absence. The journey she is making
does not succeed in bringing her closer to her destination, which remains
stationary and unobtainable

The heart listens. The ear awaits:
Has he come? Will he come?
In every hope, the sadness of Nebo.

Facing each other — two shores
of one stream.
The stone decree:
distant forever.

Lift up your hands. See over
There — no one comes.
To each person his Nebo
over a wide land. (*"Mi-Neged"* [From Afar])

Inherent in the poem is the link between Rachel and Moses; while she con-
tinually draws further away from Kinneret, Rachel moves closer to Moses.
She has so deeply internalized the sadness of Nebo that for every expectation
engulfing her, she experiences Moses' viewing of and expectation from
Mt. Nebo.

The one who has opened his arms and found himself facing a vacuum
and silence is both Moses and Rachel. The poem creates an illusion as if the
two of them are standing on Mt. Nebo, at different times. The titles of the
collections "From Afar" and "Nebo" are close to each other. Both are bound
up with Moses' punishment and exile from the land he never reached. Yet,
there is a fine distinction between the two: They deal with different stages of
being cut off. Standing "from afar" refers the readers to God's order to Moses
to ascend Mount Nebo where he will die, for the land, as noted, he will see
from a distance (Deut. 32:49–52). Two chapters later, the moment of truth
arrives. Moses, alone, ascends Mount Nebo and climbs to the summit. The

Lord shows him the entire land, and again, as an echo of a great cry, reminds him that he will not cross over to it.

In the title "From Afar," there is an allusion to a picture of two sides, of being located on one of them and looking toward the longed-for goal. In the title "Nebo," one hears despair expressed from being on only one, single side, dispossessed of the hope of reaching the land that stands opposite and even of dreaming about it. "Nebo" is definitely a final stage; of man's burrowing within himself and waiting for death that will gather him once again to the earth.

In the poem *"Eini Kovela"* (I Do Not Complain), taken from her first poetry collection, *"Safi'ah"* (Aftergrowth), Rachel draws a direct comparison between the narrow room in which she is confined and Mount Nebo:

> I do not complain! In a narrow room
> the yearning for space is so very sweet;
> for days of sorrow, the chill autumn has purple and gold.
>
> I do not complain! A song flows
> from a wounded heart in its love,
> and the desert sand — like the green of a meadow
> from the highest peak, from Mount Nebo.

In an article entitled *"Resisim"* (Shards), Lotte Sela writes: "Rachel called her flat rooftop near Haderah 'Mount Nebo,' sitting there and gazing towards the sea and watching everything that was happening below. She was filled with yearnings for life — but she saw this "from afar" and never reached them."[5]

Poetics of Silence

Moses stands between memories of Egypt and dreams of Canaan, the desert is an "intermediate chronotope" in which he is located, as Ilana Pardes defines it.[6] Being situated between, in the middle, is characteristic of the spokesperson in Rachel's poems. She is found between a meeting and a separation from which there is no return, between discovery and renewed searching, between closeness and an ever-increasing distance.

This position, which is neither absolute nothing nor absolute being, is given expression in the poems' structures and in the repeated motif around which they are organized. Rachel's intermediate existence is built on the poetics of silence: She is continuously silent. The speaker's wandering, her steps forward and her retreats all hover around the longed-for goal, an eternal region of yearning. It is the same whether she speaks of a light blue lake or a broad expanse of land; the experience described is one of standing afar and of paralysis that prevents moving closer. This paralysis is mediated by silence. That same space surrounded by clods of the soil from the land is transformed into a vacuum surrounded by words.

Rachel's poems are woven into a network of interactions between speech and silence, with the poetic decision of its creator favoring the expression that is in silence over explicit expression. At times, this is seen through the lexical or graphic design of the text, at others it is realized through an ars poetic declaration within the poems.

In the poem "*Niv*" (Idiom) the speaker declares explicitly:

> I know an infinite number of words —
> So I will be silent.

Out of so much chatter, she chooses the means of silence. Only this channel can transmit the abundance of expression she wishes to deliver. Any other lexical possibility seems too poor and hackneyed; she rejects the use of "flowery phrases" and "decorative rhetoric" because of their restrictedness. The raw material used for her work is that same

> expression that is as innocent as a babe
> and as modest as the dust.

This is the most penetrating possibility that language can afford, other than the option of silence. This is the poetics of the borderline, for we are not speaking of total muteness. The final verse seems even demanding and determined in its aspirations:

> Will your ear take in, even through the silence,
> the phrase as spoken?
> Will you cherish it as a friend, as a brother,
> as a mother in her bosom?

The poetic motto of the speaker is silence, quietude. Yet the speaker herself stresses that under discussion is silence by choice; despite the infinite number of words standing at the ready, she prefers silence over all of them. Now the reason for this poetic choice becomes even clearer: her desire to be received by her listener with full force and internalization, in a way that the addressee will need to absorb the message actively and to fill in the gaps.

The choice in favor of distancing oneself from verbal ornateness and of remaining steadfast to what she calls "the simplicity of expression" is made clear in the poem *"Naftulim"* (Convolutions), written in 1927. The speaker is describing her internal war against her natural attraction —

> To the glory of ruby and emerald,
> to words as beautiful as a gem.

At times she finds herself betraying her stylistic decision:

> I do not know how to distinguish dawn's light,
> I do not listen to that still, small voice.
> Is this me, I swore to be faithful
> to words as simple as a scream?!

The speaker staunchly declares that her artistic path is embedded in what seems to be an oxymoron — simple words and the still voice whose status is like a scream.

In the poem *"Sefer Shirai"* (My Book of Poems) Rachel continues to interweave simplicity and the cry:

> My desperate cries, in pain
> in times of misery and loss,
> have turned into a heartwarming chain of poems,
> into the white book of my poems.

The experiences, likened to screams, turn into a heartwarming chain and a delicate-looking book.[7] The screams go through a transformation and are embodied in the text in the form of silence. Defining the background from which the poems grew as screams reinforces the feeling that the quiet and silence derive their meaning from experiential and expressionistic exhaustion and not from emptiness and non-existence.

The text grants silence an audiovisual standing; silence is presented both as expressional muteness and as a graphic empty space. The genre in which the "scaffolding," in Bakhtin's terms, is particularly prominent and effective is poetry.[8] Those places in the text that are presented as an absence — a dash, a hyphen, an ellipsis — attest to the difficulties inherent in the verbal embodiment of the experience described.[9] The ambiguity of simultaneous utterance and non-utterance fashions two parallel messages: that which derives from what is said and that which arises from the silenced.

There is congruency between the poetics and the basic experience laid in the poems' foundation. The path is the axis bisecting Rachel's poems. The finish line of the progression will not be determined in space but in time; the end of the road will not be determined by reaching a defined goal, but by force of cessation. Even though the end of the path does not symbolize realization — the speaker continues to march toward it, or to hover around it, and with that her experience is one of perpetual absence.

This range of nothing and of being is expressed in the poetics of speechlessness and chatter. Just as the speaker stands at a distance — that is, looking at what exists while remaining within forced confines, prohibited from reaching it — so too is poetry built from written words whose meaning is constructed as a result of the silenced words interspersed with them.

Rachel wanders — and marches in place, writes — and erases. The same way that absence bears no meaning without an axis of presence to which it refers, so also silence is not felt without a voice. Thus Rachel is in the middle: She moves between the ends of hidden and revealed, of stated and muted. The chronotopic lack is translated into the poetics of silence, this is Rachel's "silent space" ("*Helekh Nefesh*").

In 1920, Rachel broke the silence of the women poets. The channel of silence that she established with her poems fashioned "another" voice in relation to the voices that were heard in the cultural discourse of that period. This is her feminine resonance. This is the "from a distance" that she objects to.

In 1927, Rachel published an article entitled "On a Sign of the Times" in which she wrote,

> It is clear to me: the sign of the times in the art of poetry is simplicity of expression. . . . Simplicity of expression is not always matched with ability of expression, though it always makes up for paucity of ability. . . . And even despite ability some will fail in non-simplicity, and this will not be forgiven. Of course, the path of simplicity is difficult. On one side lurks prosaicness, and on the other — floridness. It turns all our usual ideas topsy-turvy.[10]

In this manifesto, Rachel formulates her concept: simplicity as a type of sophistication.

The appearance created by poetics that carries simplicity and quietude on its banner might be understood as diluted and minor, but a different reading of the poems shows that this poetic line held within it great poetic strength and that in the collective consciousness erroneous conclusions took root on the nature of the poems and the poetess. The verbal parsimony, the little poems, the combination of expressing things and silencing them — all of these were not perceived by the critics as strength and power, but as weakness.

The developing Israeli culture did not reject Rachel's silence; quite on the contrary, it was taken warmly into the establishment bosom, since it was perceived as a nonthreatening phenomenon. Rachel's poetry is modest and self-deprecating. It seems that the ideopoetic soil was not mature enough to discern Rachel's syntactic innovations, her linguistic perception, and that all of this was the product of a conscious, mature female pen.

Conclusion — Rachel in the Mirror of Moses

In his book *Moses*, Martin Buber writes,

> Moses, who was sent as the bearer of speech, the intercessor of speech between heaven and earth, is not an orator whose speech flows unabashedly. So he was created and so he was chosen. As such, a divider was set between him and the world of mankind. . . . By serving as the "mouth" of the Lord himself who speaks his word through him, then this is a stammering mouth. . . . The stammering is what brings the voice of the heavens to the earth.[11]

Moses was silent because of his stammering and Rachel silenced her poetry. Both of them delivered statements with a clear, lofty echo, despite their silence. Apparently Rachel plays the role of Aaron; situated on her own Nebo, situating her own idiom — here she is, on the one hand, externalizing another voice that did not succeed in being heard: the voice of Moses, while on the other hand — even though her poetry was etched in the collective consciousness as modest and unpretentious — she is deeply identified with the person who "never again did their arise in Israel a prophet" such as he — with Moses (Deut. 34:10).

In 1927, Rosa R. wrote in *Hedim:* "Months have passed, and you the men have not paid attention to *Safi'ah* (Aftergrowth). What do you care about an aftergrowth when this is a woman?"[12] A women who created in her poetry her own Nebo, who was forced to pay the price of superficiality and miniaturization of her poetic style and her lyrical world in the minds of the addressees — both aesthetically and thematically — in her literary reception. The linguistic simplicity was perceived as obligatory modesty, and the treatment of motherhood, femininity, and the "experiences of the diary writers" was taken as the only area that feminine writing is fit for.[13] The frame that was forced on Rachel's poetry at the time it was read by the critics did not permit readers to move on to that multi-time, general, cosmic register that many people did not even think existed in her poetry.

Rachel maintains a dialog with the biblical text, asking, reworking, and thinking through the verses.[14] The discourse with the Bible stands out for the range of biblical figures starring in her poems and merging with her own figure. The lepers in Samaria, Jonathan, Michal, Job, and Rachel (in two poems) — they are figures introduced into her poems by virtue of the speaker's identification with the various aspects of their relations with God, with fate, and with their close associates.[15]

Many critics have dealt with Rachel's affinity for the Bible, but Rachel's connection to the Bible was limited in the criticism to the matriarch Rachel and to Michal (and resounding here is the expectation of her identification with feminine figures, who also went through experiences of barrenness and unfaithfulness).[16] In light of her perception as a poetess writing little poems about barrenness and disappointed love, about Kinneret and the matriarch Rachel, a poetic stage in which Rachel's self-definition was intertwined with Moses — could not be identified.

The link to Moses is not made specifically, by mentioning his name or weaving in the feeling linking the speaker to the biblical figure; at the same time, the connection with Moses was much deeper. It is based on the deep, common suffering of both — the pain of the threshold, separation from the group, and imprisonment within the borders of one side of the divide:

For you, too, shall go
And I will remain in the vast land alone. ("Hen Yatzanu ba-Sakh")

There are poems in which the dialog with Deuteronomy is specific (by allusion or direct), as in any biblical intertext; but there are poems in which Mount Nebo, the prodigal son, the living desert, and standing opposite are concepts into which Rachel breathed new life; the national narrative turned into a private story. This is an intertext read as text; concepts borrowed from the biblical source appear repeatedly in her poetry and accumulate intertextual and personal meaning.[17]

The chronotopical starting position of Moses served Rachel as a direction by which she tried to answer the conundrum of her life. Gaps of silence are interwoven in her poetry and the enigmatic nature of this poetry demonstrates the intermediate location — not in the home port and not in a safe haven:

> Thus I shall rise . . . thus: for the thousandth time.
> Thus I shall go drained of all strength.
> Thus I shall wander the paths, in heat and in drizzle;
> Thus I will love . . . thus: with no solutions. (*"Ba-Nekhar"*)

※ *Yaffah Berlovitz*

Anda Amir's *Me-Olam, Demuyot mi-Kedem*
A Proposal for a Modern Feminine Bible

Anda Amir's Pantheon of Women

In the summer of 1942 appeared the fourth book of poetry by Anda Pinker-feld (later Amir) titled *Me-Olam* (From Time Immemorial), with the sub-title *Demuyyot mi-Kedem* (Ancient Figures). In the following, I would like to present this book as an attempt at or proposal for a feminine biblical narra-tive. Before that, however, I would like to sketch a few lines from the portrait of Amir, who has remained in our collective cultural memory as a popular poet for children (who still read and sing her poems today), while the other corpus of her poetry, which is not for children, increasingly is neglected, with little attention paid to it even in academic research.[1]

Anda Amir, born in Galicia in 1902, died in 1981. She belonged to Hashomer Hatza'ir and immigrated to Eretz Israel twice: in 1920, as a seven-teen-year-old member of a *hakshara*, and again in 1924, this time as a mar-ried woman. Amir had an academic education (she studied microbiology at the University of Lvov in the early 1920s) but scarcely worked in her field. She wrote her first poetry in Polish (a book of her verse in that language was published in 1921), but from 1928 on she wrote and published only in He-brew. Amir was prominent in public life, pre-state and after the establish-ment of Israel, both as a prolific poet (among the first wave of female Hebrew poets in the country, with Rachel, Esther Raab, Elisheva, and Yokheved Bat-Miriam) and as a communal activist (author of a regular column in *Davar*).[2] After World War II, Amir went to the displaced persons camps to help the survivors, established an archive for the writings of those who died in the War of Independence and immortalized their images in collections and articles of her own, directed the Manya Bialik's Women's Home (1967), and encouraged female writers.[3]

   Me-Olam, Demuyyot Mi-Kedem is actually a corpus of ten poems all of which wend their way toward one topic: biblical figures. As we know, from the very beginning of Modernist Hebrew literature, involvement with the Bible was a kind of political declaration for liberal Judaism: So it was that Enlightenment literature chose biblical language as a weapon in its battle against rabbinic-talmudic Judaism and against the conservatism of the anti-Enlightenment *halakhah,* and so it was with Zionism that placed the national revival in Eretz Israel following the biblical period model of "renew our days as of old," and not the rabbinic period of the Mishna and Talmud. Anda Amir, too, as a Zionist-socialist poet, had sought from the outset of her writing a way to link herself to the Bible and to be imbued with it, whether as poetic masterpiece or as the canon of Hebrew national culture. This is also the case in her books *Yuval* (1932) and *Gitit* (1937), in which she deals, among other things, with biblical figures such as Jubal the ancestor of all who play the lyre and the pipe, Abishag the Shunammite, Yael the wife of Heber the Kenite, and Esau. In contrast, in the volume of poems under discussion, *Me-Olam, Demuyyot mi-Kedem,* the biblical presence is dominant. That is, this is not a random collection of figures from the past, but an intentional poetic arrangement, concerned primarily with the exclusive presence of the biblical woman. Specifically, Amir assembles the three feminine figures whom she had dealt with in her previous books (Ashtoreth, Jael, and Abishag), adds another seven, and inadvertently creates not only a new corpus of creativity but even a new feminist ideological statement. Let's elaborate it.

   Anda Amir sets this pantheon of women in a kind of chronological-genealogical order that relates the development of ancient Israelite history according to a dynasty of women. To the point, she begins with Genesis and concludes with the kingdom of David, with her biblical narrative to be perceived as a matriarchal alternative to the traditional patriarchal story. This feminine historiographical alternative presents the cosmic "genesis" in the figure of Ashtoreth the fertility goddess, the Hebrew-national "genesis" in the image of the founding mothers of the nation (for her they are Hagar and Leah), and the period of the Judges and the first monarchy with a series of women (such as the daughter of Jephthah, Delilah, and, as noted, Abishag). In other words, Amir, in this poetic collection, proposes a different Bible, a feminine Bible, that serves to appropriate these canonic cultural texts and to retell them in her own way. Through this feminine Bible, she turns to defining her identities as a woman, *halutzah*, and poet, while at the same time setting up a representation and "a free approach to the symbolic order" to the rejuvenation of the Eretz Israel spirit.[4] This last idea leads to the question: Why did Amir find such a short feminine history sufficient, and why does she not continue through the kingdoms of Israel and Judah, with their queens, prophetesses, and wise women?

My answer is that this feminine history is actually an analogy for the historical process of the national revival in Eretz Israel, from its genesis: from the first settlers (1882) until Amir's own time, that is, the 1930s and 1940s. These were the formative years of the "State in the making," as a parallel to the formative years of the society of ancient Israel during the period of the judges and the early monarchy (the reign of Saul and the reign of David). So it is no wonder that in this biblical female dynasty, there is no representation of biblical women outside of Eretz Israel, such as, for example, the Jewish women in the Egyptian period, the time of the Exodus, or the sojourn in the desert. Amir's version of the biblical woman is identified solely with the Eretz Israel location, its landscapes, sites, and so on. Another question: Why did Anda Amir choose to populate her Bible with a dynasty composed of these women, and not others; and according to what system of rules, or criteria, was this selection made?

Over time, various types of answers have accumulated in the writings of critics and scholars, such as B. Y. Michali (1942), Shmuel Ridnick (1944), and Nurit Govrin (1972); to these I shall add my interpretation.[5]

A Feminine Morality

The common denominator linking these figures into one feminine historical dynasty is, in my opinion, the fact that all of them appear and operate at junctures of sin, or argue with sin. Obviously, this choice is a demonstrative declaration intended to protest against the biblical text. For, even if the Bible enraptures Amir as a linguistic-cultural canon, as a woman she cannot read it other than as a chauvinistic masculine narrative that defines her as "woman equals sin," that is, Femina which comes from Fe Minus meaning "faithless." In other words, Femina (woman) from its very lexical origin denotes sinning creature, defective creature;[6] and so it is with Amir's chosen dynasty, each of the women is found to be a sinner: whether against God (like Eve in the Garden of Eden or Lot's wife in Sodom), whether against man (Jael kills Sisera, Delilah turns in Samson); whether as a necessary factor that leads to sin (like Leah who collaborates with her father in deceiving Jacob); or whether as a sin offering owing to circumstantial caprices or social norms (such as Jephthah's daughter whose father uses her to fulfill his vow).

As stated, all these women are presented as tragic objects in a criminal-judicial-ethical context; but even though they are embedded in situations so fateful and traumatic, they are not given the opportunity to explain themselves. Moreover, the patriarchal biblical narrator not only silences these women but also interprets them and tells their story from his totally hegemonic position as he sees fit. So the first radical step that Amir takes, as a reader, with the aim of disassembling the biblical text and reloading it with what it lacked, is the subjectification of these women; that is, from a neutral object in silent third person (as they are presented in the biblical narrative), she tells their story anew in first person, with their own "voice" and their own "right to speak." So it is for good reason that these poems are arranged in the formal-poetic structure of a monologue, that of "I speak," while each one of them projects herself in her own way, in her own style, and her own rhythm.

Moreover, the portraiture of these women, in Amir's version, no longer relates to the story of the biblical sin from an apologetic stance of self-defense or self-depreciation, but just the opposite: through their own personal interpretation of the same situation, an interpretation that is product of their worldviews and their understanding, as women of independent, critical minds. In other words, the biblical narrative in Amir's words is the rewriting of the feminine "sin" as historiography of holding one's head high and self-liberation.

The subject of sin is arranged here, as noted above, in feminine monologues that are conducted essentially as polemical ones. Yet, even if these feminine monologues subvert their controversial ideas toward the complete deconstructing of the biblical text, they do not do so "by way of oppositional totality," but rather attempt to construct "a different system of relations with this totality," in the words of R. Radhakrishnan.[7] This system of relations develops, as we have said, as a discourse that argues with the biblical codes of values, ethics, and religiosity; below are a few examples.

Amir opens the series with a dispute with the Book of Genesis and with God's categorical commands against the woman, presenting two women: Eve (the events in the Garden of Eden) and Lot's wife (the events at Sodom and Gomorrah). In her argument with God, Eve absolutely rejects the biblical decree that descended upon on her because of her original sin and, obviously, her original punishment, as it appears in the Bible: "I will make most severe your pangs in childbearing" (Gen. 3:16). According to Eve's arguments, the act of birth is at the same time also the birth of her feminine self, and with the Lord keeping her away from the "Tree of Knowledge," he denied her "the knowledge of birth" and, of course, "the knowledge of her essence"; for what is this immanent feminine essence, if not that inchoate consciousness of the creation of life. Hence Eve's contravening the Divine prohibition was not a case of sin but of illumination and insight: insight into her essence, her body, and the capabilities of her creative power: "And now I shall know / and I shall be heavily weighted also happy." In other words, the God who prohibited "knowledge" to her, sentenced her to degeneration and extinction. Therefore, Eve blesses the feminine human instinct that seduced her to eat from the fruit of the tree, in order to produce her own fruit, or in Amir's language: "Blessed be you snake a whispering in the heart / for the fruit you have brought me / with it I shall be redeemed."[8] The snake in the biblical narrative is a metaphor for Eve's own heart, her feelings and her yearnings for a child; so that in contrast to the masculine biblical stance, it is not a corrupt or cursed representation, but the opposite, a blessed element that redeemed the feminine potential that gives birth from sterility and desolation, and with it, of course, the entire world.

Birth, however, as an act purifying and cleansing from all sin begins for Amir not with Eve but with Ashtoreth (or alternatively, Ishtar, Anat, Asherah). Ashtoreth who is the "Queen of Heaven" (Jer. 7:18), the wife of El in the ancient Semitic cult, namely, the mother-goddess, the goddess of fertility, whose vital dominance drives the continuity of the entire universe. The cult of the goddess Ashtoreth encompassed the entire family (see Jeremiah above), but its focal point in life-cycle rituals, and particularly in birth and fertility rites increased precisely women's involvement (the cakes or cookies baked and dedicated to Ashtoreth were in the shape of the female sex organ). One should take note here that within the feminist writings of the past few decades a discussion has also developed on spiritual feminism that has sought, among other things, to restore the ancient, protective goddesses as a response to the categorical abstract God.[9] Anda Amir followed a similar path when she chose her own feminine divinity, Ashtoreth, who serves her not only as an objective for thanksgiving and adoration, but also as a model for her existence as a woman. For if man were born in the image and likeness of God, then woman, according to Amir, was born in the image and likeness of the feminine divinity Ashtoreth: "For we are your blood and your flesh / every clod of earth / and life hidden in it / are your blood and your flesh." Therefore Amir seeks support and encouragement in this feminine divinity, and as a woman and as a poet even gains strength through her, mainly when she contends with God and with his "J'accuse," aimed at the woman's sins. And indeed, here, as in the poem "Eve," she succeeds by means of the feminine divinity to shake the birth narrative free of any stigma of the eternal curse, and even to turn it from a depressing scene of punishment, sadness, and pain ("in pain you shall bear children," Gen. 3:16), to an occasion of joy, full of excitement, and rhetorical wonder. It is not happenstance that the word "*tzahalah*" ("joy") appears in the poem in combination with the word "*piryon*" ("fertility"), this trio of goddess-joy-fertility is heard more than once as a repeated declaration: "By the persistence of your motherhood [. . .] / the world and all therein shall become green again / in joy [*be-tzahlah*]"; or "the offspring of the flock in bleating will bless you / they will be fruitful and multiply [. . .] in joy"; or "How happy were your eyes / [seeing one] carrying fruit of the womb/and toward every mother / you were joyous toward her."[10]

The feminine divinity stressed by Anda Amir also as a local Eretz Israel divinity leads to the poem "*Eshet Lot*" ("Lot's wife"), and the debate conducted here with God—this time by means of the location (Sodom and Gomorrah). As we remember, Lot's wife violates the Divine prohibition not to look back upon the destruction of Sodom and Gomorrah, and turned into a pillar of salt. Her argumentation, as she phrases it here, is not a writ of defense but a confession. Lot's wife "admits to being guilty" and decides on her death consciously and willingly; for she does not consider this death as punishment but rather as solution by choice. Why did Lot's wife choose to die and not to escape? Amir presents this as decidedly gender behavior, what Carol Gilligan (in her book *In a Different Voice*) describes as the difference between the sexes. As we know, the basic principle according to which Gilligan examines woman's socio-psychological development is the difference in response and behavior of men versus woman in any similar situation examined. These differences apply also to that feminine sample that discerns "the relation between judgment and action in a situation of moral conflict and choice."

In other words, women's way of judging in ethical conflicts also leads to different decisions and methods of action than those of men; for according to Gilligan, male judgment derives from a "formal" and "abstract" type of thinking, maneuvering between legal systems and "competing rights," while the woman's judgment derives from "a mode of thinking that is contextual and narrative" concerned with responsibility and caring for the needs of the other; the man stresses "separation," the woman, "attachment"; the man, "individuation," the woman, "social interacion and personal relationships."[11]

So, here too, feminine-ethical preference is what yields the decision by

Lot's wife to look back and die. For unlike her husband, Lot's wife is inca-pable of cutting herself off or taking leave from the place where she was born and raised, from the spiritual, emotional bonds that link her to the surround-ings, the landscape, the memories. For a moment she even wonders how her husband can just make such a decisive break, separating himself from every-thing as if it had never been: "You, all your past life, from your inward you erased / without a sigh. You dipped yourself in the light of tomorrow." Lot's wife wavers, for an instant she adopts one stance, then for another she changes her mind, and Amir follows after her, registering the seismograph of her swings between following the husband's command, which is the Divine command, or following the command of her own, individual heart.

So at first she goes after her husband, she goes — but she does not run or escape despite the danger. This is the slow pacing of separation, in which she proceeds confused and in shock, continuously pleading to let her take leave of the place at her own rate: "Do not call me / do not urge me, my husband." Conversely, the pain of abandonment, and — worse than that — the pain of betrayal, rend her soul, and she decides to remain faithful to herself and to her feminine ethos, that is, to commit suicide and to be swept away with Sodom. Thus, the death of Lot's wife, according to Amir, is not a derivative of sin (disobedience), but an independent, courageous feminine choice. Be-yond that, Lot's wife does not turn into a pillar of salt prominent on the land-scape (so that all shall see and be afraid), but into an anonymous rock swal-lowed up by the dullness of the local landscape she so loves: "Here I shall cease to be / as a stone of rock I will freeze here [. . .] I will stand like a stone under me / forever I will observe the steps of my yesterdays / I will observe their loss — my loss."[12]

As noted, the polemic between the woman and the Bible in this series of poems is not only religious-divine but primarily moral-human. Anda Amir, as we read in this poem and others, weaves a semiotic-feminine profile that distinguishes the woman as an ethical entity in her own right, that is, the pos-sessor of essential moral codes by her very nature and sex. In "Lot's Wife," this is the steadfastness and loyalty to a place (even if it is one of horrendous crimes as Sodom and Gomorrah); in the poem "Jael" it is love and devotion to one's spouse even to the point of willingness to murder him. For Jael, ac-cording to Amir's interpretation, did not kill Sisera as a gesture of assistance to the Israelites' war, but just the opposite: Sisera is her great love, and he, aware of his desperate situation, escapes to her to share with her their last night of love; but she, the devoted one, precisely owing to her strong feelings for him, decides to kill him in his sleep — to prevent the humiliation, torture, and certain death awaiting him at the hands of his Israelite enemies.[13] Amir examines in this poetic workshop the vista of her expressions of feminine love, while she pulls in unexpected directions and toward surprising messages, among them the striving for equal relations between the sexes.[14]

Obviously, the establishment of this equality requires that it also be applied to the discourse of love in Amir's poetry. To be sure, the poet does not shy from exposing even the difficult and wretched aspects of this discourse, such as with the abandoned Hagar, the conflict-ridden Leah, the suspicious Delilah, or the exploited Avishag; at the same time, each one of these women (wife, concubine, lover, and so on), who is in confrontation with her man, is always in constant rebellion against the practice of "And he shall rule over you," when she remembers fondly those rare moments of caring, emotional mutuality of the type "I am my beloved's and my beloved is mine." So, for example, Hagar, in whose long, tortured confession memory clings to blissful pictures of mutuality; or as it is with Delilah, too, who reconstructs that pleasurable intimacy between her and Samson in which he was not a superman but a human creature the same as she.[15]

"We the Women"

The attempt to reconstruct the semiotic-feminine profile that finds its definition here by means of figures from the past, leads to another discussion that was relevant during the *Yishuv* period and that concerned the anticipated profile of the new woman in Eretz Israel; and in the context of Amir—the new woman as creator and poet.

Lily Ratok, in her article [in Hebrew] "Portrait of the Women as an Israeli Poet," argues that, until the 1960s, women's poetry responded to the masculine cultural message that considered "introversion, modesty, and perhaps even lack of confidence as the characteristics of femininity." That is, the female poet during the *Yishuv* period and the early days of the State took upon herself the dictates that the masculine, hegemonic poetics applied to her and restrained herself from grappling with materials such as "myth," "vision," and "valor," or with the poet's sense of national mission as "prophet" and "watchman for the house of Israel"—which were among the goals of canonic masculine poetry. Thus it turns out, Ratok determines, that the "poetic I" in a large part of Hebrew women's poetry is the inverse of the strong, confident figure that copes with the vistas of history and deep theological questions; but rather, "this is a very private figure, and not at all public in her appearance, who speaks of her innermost feelings, and does not give expression to any metaphysical, religious, or cultural mission."[16]

Yet, if we are dealing with Anda Amir, her definitions and her characterizations cannot be sorted according to these categories of the portrait of the female poet. Of course, while she does not offer poetic images of a female prophet or emissary, she also does not enter the realm of the private, the modest, and the introverted, which come under the rubric of "feminine characteristics" given above (such as "lack of confidence," "fear," and "shame" "of exposure of the internal world"). Just the opposite: Amir reveals issues of her femininity and her sexuality as an individual, the same way she exposes social and national issues in general, when she contends with material — historical or current, philosophical or political — out of national public involvement and concern.[17] *Me-Olam, Demuyyot mi-Kedem*, too, is a poetic work that makes a relevant public statement. So it seems to me that one should read Anda's series of biblical women not only as "metaphors of I," but also as metaphors of us (we the women), as Amir writes in poems such as "*Anahnu ha-Nashim Holkhot ba-Olam ka-Avukot Ahava*" (We the Women Go through Life as Flames of Love), "*Anahnu ha-Galmudot la-ad*" (We Who Are the Lonely Forever"), and so on.[18] In other words, this book of poems is not only a proposal for a feminine biblical narrative but a typological proposal as well of an Eretz Israel cultural feminine model. What does this mean?

As we know, from the outset of the revival of the Eretz Israel national project, the identity of the "New Jew" was set up and fashioned, as if pre-planned, with a repertoire of symbols and characteristics structured as a "system of components" in opposition to those of the Diaspora Jew. It was as if this visionary, ideological foundation did not have the patience to allow the environmental conditions and the fitting rate of development to produce and consolidate a natural Jewish anthropology as a product of the future time and place. It turns out, therefore, that even before the native Eretz-Israel type (the sabra) was created, his "invented" identity populated the journalistic and literary writings of the members of the early Aliyot, as if were solidly based in reality.[19] The situation was not the same regarding the shaping of the woman's identity. A portrait of the Eretz Israeli woman, despite the turnabout from Diaspora to homeland, continues to be delineated here, too, in the canonic *Yishuv* writings, in those same routine, traditional conventions (of the helpmeet or as a romantic object) that nourished most Hebrew writing in the Diaspora.[20] Yet, attempts or tentative tries at consolidating models of Eretz Israel feminine identity ("New Jewess" parallel to "New

Jew"), however, are found only in the works of women. And, indeed, already in the early writings by First Aliyah women discussion of this issue is pivotal, only that in contrast to the oppositional notion in the structuring of the "New Jew," the structuring of the "New Jewess" is not perceived in women's writings in opposition to the Diaspora woman, but in the consolidation of linkage to biblical women. Nehama Puhachewsky, in a militant article written in 1889, demands education and culture for girls, and she uses the models of Miriam and Deborah (the prophetesses); Hannah Trager, in her memoirs from 1886, unfolds the struggle of the young women for the right to vote in Petah Tikva, and she wants to identify them with the biblical model of the daughters of Zelophehad; Hemdah Ben-Yehuda who, in a 1919 article calls for equality of women, pays tribute to fighters such as Jael and Judith who slew leaders of the enemy army.[21]

The identification of the First Aliyah female writers with the portraits of these women indicates that they did not cling to the traditional models of the intimate, domestic periphery (such as the Matriarchs [Sara, Rachel] or the beloved [Shulamith]), but rather that they chose to find renewal according to unique, one-time models of creative women, involved in the overall public arena, such as female fighters, leaders, scholars, and poets.

Anda Amir, too, wishes to become infused with the biblical feminine portrait, but the model of the independent, critical-minded woman facing her is not congruent with that one-time creative, leading woman. Quite the contrary: she picks from among the "ancient figures" those who represent woman whoever she is; women who first of all distinguish themselves in their difference from the man: an essential gender difference expressed in the most elementary manifestations as we saw above (love, parenthood, moral behavior, and so on). In addition, by preferring precisely these biblical women, Amir also stresses the basic element rooted in them that connects them with uncompromising loyalty to place and land (again as different and in contrast to their man); and perhaps this is also the reason for the striking choice of local, Eretz Israel women, not necessarily Jews, such as Jael, Delilah, and Hagar, let alone the goddess Ashtoreth. That is, as Amir sees it, feminine national identity or consciousness is first of all down-to-earth local, alongside all those theoretical, ideological principles. In other words, in the attempt to fill in the lack of a portrait of the "New Jewess" in the Eretz Israel national narrative, Amir proposes an egalitarian typological feminine repertoire based on indicating, approvingly, the difference from the man as well as stressing woman as she is.

In conclusion, let us put it this way: The debate that Amir conducts with the Bible as a masculine hegemonious text is not an argument over the past but about the present. In this controversy, Amir rewrites the Bible as a feminine biblical narrative, while she places at the center of her discourse not only biblical women, but rather the *Yishuv* woman of the twentieth century. And indeed, as in the process of her subversive reading beneath the patriarchal biblical culture, Amir undermines the authority of the androcentric Zionist culture which from the outset banished the woman (the female settler, laborer, pioneer) to the margins of the *Yishuv* discourse, and made dominant an exclusively masculine "renew our days as of old" (the male settler, laborer, pioneer).[22] Amir does not reconcile herself with this, and she springs into action with her own meaning of "renew our days as of old"; that is, not only a portrait of the new woman, but also a foundation for a national feminine alternative culture. So it is that she reads the masculine biblical texts as feminine cultural texts, so it is that she organizes through them new feminine narratives that the *Yishuv* woman was missing (such as feminine history, feminine genealogy, feminine ethos, and of course, a pool of feminine myths), and so it is that she restores forgotten heroines to the collective Zionist memory. In other words, this small book, *Me-Olam, Demuyot mi-Kedem*, is another feminist literary act in the history of pre-state women's literature, in the struggle to extract the woman from her excluded position and to equip her with the proper alternative tools to conduct that problematic dialog with the leading masculine narrative.[23]

☞ *Hannan Hever*

Poems to the Ghetto

The Poetry of Yocheved Bat-Miriam in the 1940s

In 1946 appeared the booklet *1943 — Shirim la-Geto* (1943 — Poems to the Ghetto). This is a cycle of poems that Bat-Miriam wrote immediately after the Holocaust, poems in which she repeatedly evoked the Holocaust period and the ways of coping with its horrors and with its memory. In this book of poetry, her sixth, Bat-Miryam continued the great, rich tradition of the Hebrew symbolist poem of which she was one of the main creators and shapers, when still in Russia in the early 1920s. About a decade later, in the second half of the 1930s, symbolist expression developed into the dominant model in the poetics of Hebrew poetry in Eretz Israel, in the poetry of Abraham Shlonsky, Natan Alterman, Yonathan Ratosh, Lea Goldberg, and others; and this Symbolism then reached significant development and coalescence in the writing of Yocheved Bat-Miriam.

The symbolism in Bat-Miriam's poetry, already described to a fair degree in criticism and research, was characterized mainly by extremely high sensitivity to a varied, rich resonance of the meanings of the poetic word; by ramified figurative continua; by particularly intense attention to the musical suggestivity of the poetic text; by high language from which radiates sublime dimensions of human experience — to the point of mystical sublimation, resulting also in linguistic shifts, too, of representations of time — to language of territory and space.[1] But particularly prominent in the symbolism in her poetry is the presence of narratives that integrate the real, concrete details of external reality within the general narrative. This is a narrative that develops toward harmonious expression that merges the concrete into a metaphysical spiritual meaning, a meaning that graces the diverse details with a function and value in the common collective story. It is no wonder that in the Eretz Israel national culture of the end of the 1930s and of the 1940s, the Symbolist poem served as a central conduit in the establishment of the national narrative.

The movement of such a national narrative is always one of advancement and growing strength toward effecting the "imagined national community," in the terms of Benedict Anderson; this community includes territorial and other components as well as actual people, and thus Symbolist expression is likely and apt to fill the role of establishing it.[2] Symbolist expression does give the concrete components, and particularly the individual people, the common context, general and universal, in which they acquire meaning and value.

This Symbolist universalism was valid and stable until the end of 1942. Until then, other representations of death and bereavement could merge into this sweeping musicality, which granted them power and turned them into a source for collective hope. But toward the end of 1942, when the information reaching Eretz Israel about what was happening in Europe became clearer and more tangible, when the murders, persecutions, suffering, and tortures began to be understood increasingly as genocide, as the Holocaust of the Jewish people,[3] Bat-Miriam's poetry—and like it the entire Symbolist school in Eretz Israel—faced a new cultural reality.

In light of the basic duality in Symbolism, of distance from the real, on one hand, and high sensitivity to it, on the other, it was not surprising that with the outbreak of World War II there was a sudden shuffling of the careful, tense pack of cards that this school had held in Eretz Israel at the end of the 1930s. As early as the outset of the war, in 1939, a severe controversy arose within the Symbolist school on the way poetry should respond to the horrors of the war: leading this debate were Lea Goldberg, Shlonsky, and Alterman. How, they asked, could lyrical, musical expression contain the violent, murderous reality of the world war? But then, at the beginning of the war, despite the argument and confrontation, the members of the Symbolist school remained steadfast to the path they had been following. The Symbolist school perceived poetry as universalist and eternal, and therefore as poetry of hegemonic stature. The poet—argued Eretz Israel Symbolists—owes his loyalty primarily to the world of eternal, human values.

From 1943 on, however, the rift in the school's poetry became progressively deeper. At the center of this fracture was the inability of the literary symbol to contain two trends simultaneously, two narratives that do not accommodate each other. On the one hand—the story of the soaring, the progress, congruent with the modernist narrative of the building of the new Zionist nationality, such as formulated by Bat-Miriam in her poem "Eretz Israel" (1937), or with the sweeping symbolism of Mother Russia that parallels Eretz Israel in "Poems of Russia" (1942); and on the other, a narrative in which devastation and destruction have replaced the narrative of redemption; in which death no longer serves the national endeavor and vision and also does not become sanctified in its name, but just the opposite — it symbolizes non-existence, destruction, and devastation, from which it is no longer possible to produce strength and national hope.

The national significance of the literary symbol was faced with the serious contradiction in the very writing of a symbolist poem, which is simultaneously committed to universalism, musicality and, in particular, the narrative of redemption and hope — and yet, at the same time, has no choice but to represent death, the destruction of the individual devoid of redemption, from a position of despair and surrender. One of the most dramatic steps in this school's poetry was the abrupt, revolutionary, transfer that Natan Alterman implemented — from the redemptive symbolism in the poems *Simhat Aniyyim* ("Joy of the Poor") in 1941 to the allegorical break, devoid of national hope, in *Shirei Makkot Mitzrayim* ("Plagues of Egypt") in 1944.[4]

Bat-Miriam gave incisive expression to this dilemma from the beginning of the collection 1943 — *Shirim la-Geto*, with *"Pesuko shel David"* (David's Verse), the very opening poem in the cycle, which gives the appearance of representing the Holocaust, set as it were within the framework of the narrative of national redemption. The yellow badge first appears in the combination *"tzohav ha-telai"* (the yellowness of the badge), the inverse of the combination *"ha-telai ha-tzahov"* (the yellow badge) — stressing the symbolic value of yellow.[5] Ostensibly, everything is ready for a Symbolist narrative of redemption, in which the speaker is about to tell the story of the ladder "which is set in my heaven of heavens" facing upward and on which [it is] "ascending evermore to vanquish its death / my ghetto with the yellowness of the badge."[6]

But in actuality, the entire story of the approaching redemption and victory is based in the poem on a narrative whose structure is completely opposite, and which instead of indicating the vitality and redemption found in death, demonstrates precisely its finality. "David's Verse," in which the speaker rests the rung of the ladder from which her ladder stretches upward, toward the heavens, is that verse in which King David stopped his mourning for his child by Bathsheba the wife of Uriah, the child who died as a punishment for David's sin (2 Sam. 12:14–23). By relying upon this biblical story, the poem offers a comprehensive symbolic picture that contains, simultaneously, both the hope and continuity of the victory of the yellow badge as well as the bitter recognition of the finality of the destruction, with death that is final and immutable

In this way, Bat-Miriam's symbolic text is a meeting point, actually a clashing point, between the progressive Zionist national narrative, which is formulated in decidedly symbolic language, and the terminal narrative of destruction and despair.

The clearest expression of the primary contradiction prevailing in Hebrew cultural discourse in the 1940s, which is also the most severe contradiction in Symbolist discourse in this paradoxical national situation, stands out in its representation of national-collective time. This time appears here, simultaneously, both as a time of progress — and as static, frozen time; both as a time of advancement — and also as time of a lack of advancement; confronting each other are two incompatible patterns for representations of time, which match the two patterns for representation of time by means of which Walter Benjamin formulated the principle difference between symbol and allegory. On the one side is the symbol, which generalizes without losing the reality and concreteness of the symbolizer; the organic symbol that, therefore, also promises hope and continuity, and on the other side — the mechanical, abstract allegory, which does not include future vitality, and which cannot extend beyond the representation of ideas lacking vitality and continuity.[7] Symbolic time, which promises continuous advancement toward the future, is set in contrast to allegorical time, riven, lifeless, devoid of any clear hope.

In the face of the deep rift and the extremely serious contradiction between the representations of time, the time of national advancement versus the time of static observations of the destruction, Y. Bat-Miriam the Symbolist chose a special kind of representational apparatus. To cope with this contradiction, she elected to fashion Symbolist representation of the collective death, the ghettos, and the extermination camps precisely by means of a shift, a drastic displacement of the representational apparatus, from the contradictory representation of time — to spatial representation. This apparatus, which already had been common in Bat-Miriam's poetry, now became, during the Holocaust, an important instrument for containing this contradictory time.[8] The way to represent the terrible and the horrifying is by means of categories of space.

To be sure, almost every section in the cycle of poems in *Shirim la-Geto* opens from a Symbolist viewpoint, placing the phenomenon represented at the center of the continuity of time of the phenomenon represented. Yet, it quickly becomes apparent that this continuity is only virtual. The section soon develops into the presentation of space as an alternative to the conflict and contradiction of incompatible times, which contains the Symbolist image within it. From this Symbolist credo, which repeatedly merges the ghetto into a verbal continuum that blurs the difference between falsehood and reality; between the one creating the symbol and the symbolized, between the set symbolic formulation and what always extends beyond it as impossible to formulate, as impossible to exhaust in the full — from there Bat-Miriam moves on to the system of reversed, alternative representation that characterizes her poetic expression not as harmony but rather as expression split in space. Thus, she represents "a horrible appearance and flames" that freezes at the look of the generation whose poem she is writing as an entity that exists in spaces, as a persona, the observation of which — that is, the horror — is represented in the poem by means of pointing out its location there, which "as a guest / with us she will sit at the head of the table."[9]

In a similar way, Bat-Miriam splits the poetic voice itself among different locations in space. A striking apparatus in this spatial distribution is the creation of an expression distinct from the voice that it itself makes heard. In place of the merging, blurring Symbolist voice that does away with borders and distinctions, the poem moves to language of fine distinction that splits the voice itself into two: Bat-Miriam distinguishes between the "I" of the speaker and his voice by separating them in space. The "I" is the bearer of the voice of exalted, transcendental, spiritual freedom; but despite that, his voice is also a voice that places physical, external fetters on this freedom: "The freedom in his voice, his voice is also his fetters."[10]

Bat-Miriam garners the harmonic Symbolist expression for the benefit of the double, contradictory representation, and thereby presents the object of the problematic representation, that horrible vision and flames, as a kind of external entity; this entity puts the speaker — who wishes to fill the role of collective speaker — in the position of the intercessor between the representative and the object of the representation: "loved seven-fold more / they will carry our language. And we will not know how to read."[11] In this way, she continues, on the one hand, to use the symbolic language of the collective and preserve the symbol; but on the other hand, she creates, within this symbolic representation, a space of flexibility in the speaker's movement, of distancing oneself and drawing close to the terrifying object of the representation. This is a flexibility whose purpose is to preserve the framework of the national symbol, but at the same time allows it to locate itself within the national framework yet also in a secondary, peripheral setting.

By using this spatial, contradictory symbolic language, Bat-Miriam succeeded in fashioning an alternative space such that the territory appearing within it is not perceived exclusively as national territory. The territory of the ghetto and of the extermination camps, and the territory of "my city," Tel Aviv, is located in the poem within a single, common space that is totally different than the space of the national territory. The national territory includes symbolic space with defined outlines of historical depth and meaning, while in *Poems to the Ghetto* separate spaces are intertwined with different and opposing histories, such as in the lyric voice, cracked into a spatial split between hope and despair and destruction, so that here, too, the shared space includes the national hope of Eretz Israel together with the destruction and eradication of the Golah.

The space that Bat-Miriam depicts in her poems is, therefore, not subjugated to the accepted Zionist-national dichotomy between Eretz Israel and the Golah. That accepted notion held that the *Eretz-Yisraeli* space engulfs and absorbs into it the space of the ghetto, turning it into its extension and continuation; this is exemplified, for example, in presenting the heroism of the ghetto rebels as an Eretz Israel pioneering act, as a national historical continuum between the Warsaw Ghetto uprising and the revolt of the Jews against Rome, as Yitzhak Tabenkin expressed it on May Day 1943.[12]

In contrast to this, the step Bat-Miriam took as a woman, a female poet who introduces a female speaker into her poems, made a dramatic contribution to the establishment of the feminine place, of gender, in the national discourse. The special form she gives to the national space give her attitude toward the dominant national discourse and within it a subversive position, challenging the permanent exclusion that bars the woman from the national discourse. She establishes her feminine location in the national discourse by means of an alternative marking of the territory. The feminine speaker in this space disturbs the fixed order of the dominant masculine national discourse that regularly excludes femininity from it. Until now, the territory had appeared as a national symbol that was always perceived in categories subject to the feminine, national allegory of "Mother Earth," "Mother Russia," and Eretz Israel as grammatically feminine, and on this territory — the land, the platform — was erected the symbolic building of the people; here Bat-Miriam proposes the territory as part a space of junctures and markings that do not submit to the dominant national classification; it is possible to simultaneously mark within it both the ghetto and Tel Aviv, as part of a common space within which the female speaker moves freely, flexibly, not according to the hierarchy and division between Golah and Eretz Israel.

National time, too, like space, splits and moves away from the dominant order, and it, too, presents trends and developments in a way that differs from the accepted national narrative, which binds the territory of Eretz Israel together with the historical advancement toward it within one common national cluster. So these poems depict an image of a split national memory that divides between time and space. By means of spatial figures the poems turn the national memory into a tool for the accumulation of the national time. Representing time as contained and located in spatial proximity within the memory tool enables Bat-Miriam to underscore the gap between time and space: the national memory is a memory "that curves time," while the relation between time and oblivion is described by her as a spatial ratio between two stages of time, the relation between green rust and the copper on which it grows.[13] In that way, Bat-Miriam diverts the focus of observation from existence in time to spatial, territorial existence. This movement does not decide between the representation of the national vision as progressing and developing simultaneously with continuous national time and between its representation as a separate space, a space in which the human presence within it is not congruent with the national time.

This ambivalent, undefined space turns into the only place from which the poetess can lament the fate of her people. In the name of devotion to her people, she glides to the mountains and mourns its fate, and there, appearing side by side with no distinction between them, are a green Eretz Israel orchard and the lands of non-Jews.[14]

But the gender location reaches it climax within the space of national memory in the final section of the cycle, section 14, where the female speaker presents herself as the one who, in contrast to the "daughter of my people" — who will forget the terrors of the Holocaust — she, the speaker, who will carry with her "forever with beating heart, while pacing / Maidanek and Treblinka, the raging Ghetto."[15] Preservation of the memory of the destruction and loss, of Maidanek and Treblinka, is carried out in an different way than the institutionalized national memory, which is ultimately also the memory of a thing that forgets and causes others to forget, and which you, "daughter of my people," are in charge of.

But here, in contrast to the symbolic figure of "daughter of my people," come an unprecedented peak that zigzags, the so-very-energetic dynamism of the feminine location of the female spokesperson; this peak is so extreme that ultimately the poetess undermines her own location and breaks down the gender boundaries. After the gender location had been established, it split in two: one is the location of "daughter of my people," which is the institutionalized national memory that in the end forgets and makes others forget and presents the Holocaust with precise numbers that turn off the imagination and define the horror in real terms, "with sword and wall."[16] And opposite it, in the same position of self-establishment, the female speaker defines her poem as "a sheet of fire in the rock," as something undefined, breaking borders, like the impossible existence of burning rock, that is not stabilized, from which the fire does not flow and in which it cannot gain a foothold nor consume the rock.[17] This is an expression that depicts a breached space, of undefined borders, within whose framework the memory of the history of civilization is represented as dust, as an external covering over stone and rock, on the surface of the memorial stone, the massive, real path and soil, memory of an open space in which a "solitary God observes, viewing the image / extending beyond his borders and his borders in his blue."[18]

The first person voice's being torn between national loyalty and the inability to take hold in the spatial territory is what ultimately brings her to the point of explosion; to the breaking point, to representation of the contradictions in which the large ladder she set up will separate her path into two. That ladder that she erected so that the yellow would mount it and win, the ladder of the scenes and shades and multiple shapes and styles, the ladder on which she tried to present "daughter of my people" as "one you are, and many, of clear style and color / with shores- and border-bound with song and agony," this ladder separates, instead of bridging, divides the path into two and creates a contrasting situation, a kind of oxymoron, in which to be seen, to be reflected in the light, she closes her eyes.[19] The sharp contrast between the light and dark leads to a situation in which "the command in the darkness shines seven-fold / like an oath, wandering I go [Hebrew "*holekh*," masculine, first person, singular] to remember."[20]

This line, however, contains a many more times dramatic, revolutionary turning point: Not only is the space torn in two, not only is the act of memory translated into physical movement in space by the one who declares "wandering I go to remember," and not only does the feminine dynamism and zigzags and swinging from side to side in face of the national symbol accelerate faster—but the rupture is so great that, in the end, it undermines the feminine position itself. Without any advance warning, with astounding suddenness, the spokeswoman switches to speech in the masculine form, using the language of a man, "*holekh ani*" (I am going).

In a mirror image of their passage to Maidanek and Treblinka and the raging Ghetto, a few stanzas earlier, to the language "*aten*" (you; Hebrew, second person, feminine plural)—so now, at the close of the process, the hovering woman, representing the atrocities of the Holocaust while moving through the space of the horror and murder, brings the process of the representation of the terror to such deep extraction—to the point that she relinquishes her feminine location or leaves it empty. She shifts to speaking in a masculine voice, and she concludes her poem with liberation from the national territory and from the dialog with "daughter of my people," for whom "your choice spot . . . [is] a closed cage."[21]

Of course, unity was achieved without the exclusion of the feminine—but not before externalizing the feminine, splitting it in two, returning the masculine; as a strategy against the male hegemony there came at the end the ultimate removal of the gender confrontation, without this clearing away necessarily dragging in its wake a kind of totalization of another component.[22] It is not nationalism that becomes primary in place of gender, nor do the Exile and the ghetto become the founders of the space instead of gender, but the new space is another, different one, and it does not respond to any of these elements, thus ridding itself of any mixture of identity and remains impossible to define, impossible to set permanently, and impossible to identify by name.

Yael Shai and Rachel Kollender

Women and Music in Jewish Society

Woman's Role in the Music Tradition in Israel

The different types of women's singing have always played an important role in the traditional singing of Jewish communities. In the past, singing accompanied women in their daily chores and in life-cycle activities. Today, women continue to play a central role in folk-traditional music works as composers of popular and artistic music as well as performers and researchers.[1]

Woman's status in the ever-evolving society is the focus of the present study.[2] In the past, identifying women with the private sphere and excluding them from the public one was typical of many Jewish communities.[3] While men's roles were mostly community-oriented, women concentrated on the private realm, restricted to child and home care. The woman felt responsible for the continuation of her social, cultural, and religious tradition.[4] In Jewish society, the women provided the various texts for life-cycle events, and in that respect women were given considerable leeway, which was also expressed in their songs, lyrics, and music.

Recent years have witnessed a dramatic change in the perception of women's identity and role.[5] Women's participation in business, public, and political life allows for a better exposure of their talents, aspirations, and adaptability that are not congruent with the common beliefs that formulated woman's image in the past.[6] It seems that Israeli society is currently going through a process of change regarding women's status, yielding an environment that now makes possible the realization of potential beyond the restrictive limitations of the past.

Cultural and social values always have been expressed, through music, among other ways. Understanding musical structures and symbolism as part of culture and addressing historical developments together constitute the first step in understanding culture as a whole.[7] This approach supports the importance of research that combines social concepts with musical analysis.

The cultural heritage of the Jewish communities includes extensive musical data that reflects cultural values and social processes.[8] The present study chose women's singing as a means for understanding the status of the Jewish woman and the changes it has gone through over time.

Woman's singing consists of a wide range of texts expressing a variety of inner emotions and experiences such as love, work, play, longing for the land of Israel, biblical stories, and so on. These texts express women's feelings, longings, and opinions. The singing reflects her involvement in society and her empathy with national-historical events as well as her views, not always concurrent with those of her time.

The songs clearly reflect her standing for her rights and her status vis-à-vis the social conventions of her time. While the singing expresses women's compliance with social conventions—for example, in the wedding song "Listen to My Beautiful Voice," from Haban, in which the young bride is instructed on her future role—there is also the bride's pointed call to her parents, "Oh My Mother, Oh My Father, Why Have You Sold Me," and even her most mutinous longing for different—unacceptable—social norms in "I Went Down the Wadi."[9]

The present article focuses on the woman and her singing in the traditional society of two small Jewish communities: Haban and Yifran. Both communities reflect similar as well as different ways in which women formed their status following the conventions and social processes of their environment. Haban is a small town in southeast Yemen, in the Hadhramaut region, and Yifran is a small village in southwest Libya. Each of these communities, located far apart from one another, zealously kept its social independence and cultural traditions, including its musical repertoire. This repertoire played a significant role in the yearly cycle of events and in life-cycle events, too. The women were well versed not only in the musical repertoire but also in all traditional rituals of their community.

The Haban women were independent and active; they were in charge of many activities, whose range expanded even more after their arrival in Israel, following the rise in their economic status and public awareness. In contrast, the Yifran woman, dependent and subdued, was active mainly in her home, and preserved her way of life in her new country, too.

Both communities immigrated to Israel in the 1950s. They insisted on settling together in villages, each community in a separate place, to preserve their traditions, but both developed relations with other communities in their neighborhoods. By helping to support the family by working outside the home, the women in both communities thus share in the cultural and social changes in their society. The Haban women, for example, joined the village committee, held different public offices, and became influential in the public-communal arena, thereby breaking the boundaries of tradition.[10]

In both communities, musical expression plays an important role in women's as well as men's singing. Observations, interviews, and recordings made of both communities over the past fifty years show a rich and versatile feminine cultural-musical world. Women's music reflects creativity and novelty expressed in their musical productivity and in the adaptation of modern texts to old tunes. We found each gender has a different, independent musical repertoire, with the women's typical lyrics and tunes differing from those of the men's. It might have been assumed that the musical components would differ, too. Yet a thorough investigation reveals that both share similar ones despite the different cultural background of both communities. Of these musical repertoires we have chosen to focus on women's singing and have found the following musical components.[11]

Musical Components

In both communities, women's singing is performed as responsorial singing between two groups (Haban) or between a soloist and a group (Yifran), alternately shifting between the performers. The audiences differed between the two communities. While the Yifran women sang among their own small group, with no men or outsiders present, the Haban women sang in the company of men and for them. Nowadays, the Yifran women continue to sing among themselves, while the Haban women diverted from their old tradition to also sing only among themselves, as the Yifran women do.

In exploring melodic components of women's songs, we discovered a wavy melodic move centered on repetitive tones. This melodic move uses small spaces, a restricted range spanning between a fourth to a sixth with a rare seventh. The melodies usually are composed of a short musical unit including two or three repeated phrases, each consisting of repetitive motifs with the final one usually constant.

Both communities use numerous rhythmic values and constant rhythmic patterns, such as ostinato. These rhythmic patterns usually are performed with percussion instruments accompanied by hand clapping that helps to maintain the performance flow even during pauses in the singing.

Tonal stability in the women's singing has been shown in both communities. The tonal material of the Haban women's singing is constructed around melodic material, while the Yifran songs emphasize the important tones of the major and minor scales. These songs of limited range are somewhat reminiscent of major or minor tetrachords.

Connections between Music and Text

Most of the songs consist of one musical unit, which corresponds to a textual sentence. This musical unit repeats itself time and again throughout the song. Most of the songs in both communities are syllabic, with melismas to mark the end of a sentence. In most of the songs, we find musical sentences composed of meaningless sounds, highlighting the significance of the music over the text.

These typical musical components, like other traditional cultural patterns, have been preserved by the communities until today. Yet, as stated above, the involvement of women in their surroundings has promoted an inevitable process of change in cultural patterns, music among them. Three main factors supported this process: exposure to technological developments; relationships to neighbors and meeting new communities; and the initiative of key figures.

The immigration to Israel, especially at the end of the 1950s, exposed the people of these villages to modern communication technologies, previously unfamiliar in Haban and Yifran. Their use of these new means, initially limited, gradually expanded, particularly from the mid-1970s, enabling different musical styles to exert their influence.

The remarkable openness of the Haban women and their interest in listening to and learning as much as possible from their new surroundings resulted in a change in their behavior patterns, unlike the Yifran women. One such example is the integration of Adenian songs, unfamiliar in Haban, together with the Habanian ones, at traditional events. However, we did not find similar openness in the Yifran women. Although they listen to popular songs in the media, they still stick to their old musical repertoire in their traditional events as it was sung in the past.

We have also witnessed the use of other percussion instruments such as the darbuka in addition to traditional drums in both communities. Moreover, some wood and brass instruments have been replaced by stainless steel and plastic ones.

In both communities, the power of women is significant.[12] They are the ones who usually run the ceremonies and the singing. Yet, during the events, other women, who are not key figures, are allowed to take the initiative and lead a certain song, thus becoming key performers while the others join in. Women also determine the balance between old and new in the choice of text and music, in the entire community repertoire. Of late, a tendency has become evident of decreasing the number of traditional songs while increasing the use of new ones, learned in Israel.

These three factors — technology, contact with the neighborhood, and the initiative of key figures — are more notable among women than in men.[13] These factors brought on the changes in the cultural tradition of the two communities as well as in their musical repertoire. A number of characteristic changes took place in the musical structures, including aspiration for accuracy in pitch of absolute tones, aspiration for accuracy in the rhythmic values and patterns, a tendency to add melismas to different parts of the melodic sentences, gradual escalation toward the songs' endings, incorporating Hebrew texts into the original songs, and cutting down performance duration of songs. All of these changes show the development of two intertwining trends: the absorption of new, different cultural patterns and values on one hand and the wish to preserve tradition on the other. Through their creative effort, expressed in their music, the women of both communities contribute not only to their close-knit societies, but also to the community as a whole. In both places, women are those who zealously keep tradition, and although the traditional role division between women and men has remained unchanged, we currently are witnessing a shift in the perception of women's role and status in traditional societies. The dependent and subdued is replaced by the independent woman, expanding her role beyond her home and contributing to the community through her social involvement.

Music thus takes part in the long process of formulating woman's identity within traditional society in Israel. The women's role has become significant not just in preserving tradition but also in re-drawing the line between tradition and progress. These processes yielded different results in the formation of the woman's image in the community. Thus, these two communities seemingly constitute a sample of two different aspects of one prototype:

- The Yifran women of today represent a pattern of preserving the traditional concept regarding their status. Simultaneously, they are also part of the ongoing process of change that has had only a limited impact on their traditional image and no implications for the various traditional events.

- The Haban women represent a different pattern, one in which preservation and change are intertwined, resulting in a new image of a woman. Beside their zeal to preserve their tradition, they portray considerable openness to their surroundings and become part of the changes their tradition is going through.

The creativity of the Israeli woman undoubtedly reflects the formulation process of her image. The changes in her behavioral patterns and status are at the focus of different anthropological and musical studies on different communities in Israel. We believe this research will shed further light on women's identity and support our thesis of her multifaceted image.

❦ Shaping the Collective Memory

The Legend of Sarah

Gender, Memory, and National Identities
(Eretz Yisrael/Israel, 1917–1990)

Forgetting, I would even go so far as to say historical error, is a crucial factor in the creation of a nation, which is why progress in historical studies often constitutes a danger for [the principle of] nationality. . . . [T]he essence of a nation is that all the individuals have many things in common, and also that they have forgotten many things.

—Ernst Renan[1]

C an there be a surfeit of memory? wonders the historian Charles Maier, referring not only to the collective preoccupation with preserving the past and commemorating certain fragments of it, but also to the burgeoning of the history of memory and commemoration during the last two decades. Students of history and culture, including historians, Maier points out wryly, act as though they were assigned the task of metaphorically dipping their madeleines in the memories of the past.[2] He means, of course, the famous cookies dipped by the narrator in the first volume of Marcel Proust's *Remembrance of Things Past*; their taste, which re-

This article, which was first published in *Zion* 65, no. 3 (2000): 343–78, is dedicated to the memory of George L. Mosse, whose writings on memory, war, and masculinity have brought me to study the associations among gender, memory, and identity and Eretz Yisraeli culture. An English version appeared in the *Journal of Israeli History* 21, nos. 1/2 (Spring/Autumn 2002), special issue; and was reprinted in Hannah Naveh, ed., *Gender and Israeli Society: Women's Time* (London, 2003), part 1, pp. 55–92. I thank Shulamith Shachar and Shulamit Volkov, who read an earlier version of the article. I owe special thanks to Natalie Zemon Davis and Avner Ben-Amos for their contributions to my understanding of the complexity of collective memory. I extend thanks to Deborah Bernstein, Yaffah Berlovitz, Dalia Ofer, and Margalit Shilo for their comments. The staff of the Beit Aaronsohn Archives (BAA) in Zikhron Yaakov helped me find a variety of documents dealing with the commemoration of Sarah Aaronsohn in the 1930s and 1940s. I am also indebted to Devorah Omer, Zohar Shavit, Yael Dar, Rima Shichmenter, and Naama Sheik Eitan.

minds the narrator of the taste of the linden leaf tea that he drank in his child-hood, was enough to carry the weight of "the immense edifice of memory."[3]

This excessive preoccupation with memory, bordering on the obsessive, both within and outside the academe, is also characteristic of Israeli culture.[4] Like the discourse elsewhere, so the Israeli discourse, both in the historiography of *Eretz Yisrael* before and after the establishment of the state and in the broader public debates, is marked by an intense interest in collective memory, in methods of commemoration, and in the preservation of certain narratives of the past and the forgetting of others. This interest is also a reexamination of national identity: of its boundaries and of what it includes and excludes. The "lieux de mémoire" (to use Pierre Nora's term) of Israel and *Eretz Yisrael* have been diligently mapped since the second half of the 1980s. These sites include commemorative sites such as cemeteries and monuments, rites, official and "spontaneous" memorial literature (Emmanuel Sivan's term), the Zionist calendar of Jewish history, as well as old revived or "invented" traditions of sacrifice for the nation such as the tradition of Tel Hai and the story of Masada.[5]

The ongoing fascinating discussion of memory and commemoration is thus, on the one hand, an examination of identity itself and, on the other hand, an elucidation of the question of which groups and which historians own memory and commemoration of the past. To paraphrase Natalie Zemon Davis, this discussion is about "who owns history?"[6] Nevertheless, the debate over memory between so-called "old" and "new" historians, and between them (or some of them) and sociologists of various schools, is somewhat flawed, or deficient. Its deficiency stems from the fact that the concern with the relationship between the memory and myths of "Eretz Yisraeli-ness" and Israeliness, and the formation of national identities is separated from the historical study of male and female gendered identities. With a few exceptions, the "general" discussion of memory has not yet taken into account the ways in which gendered identities formed the boundaries of the collective memory. This lapse can be seen in important studies of identity and commemoration, such as those of Yael Zerubavel, which are gender-blind. The cult of Joseph Trumpeldor and the myth of Tel Hai, which have occupied historians and students of culture more than any other single cult in Israel, are examined without much attention to the fact that Trumpeldor was an exemplar of Zionist masculinity. Similarly, classic studies of *The Yizkor Book* of 1911, the prototype of the new, secular way of commemoration, ignore the fact that the first secular *Eretz Yisraeli* saints were also models of the new man in the nation-in-the-making. Nor does the assemblage of important studies that examine the changes in myth and memory in terms of "the revolutions of Israeli consciousness" consider the possibility of studying the changes from the perspective of gender.[7]

This separation of the history of memory and the study of gender characterizes not only "general" historical study, but also the historiography of women and gender. This historiography has important and impressive accomplishments, but apparently has not yet been integrated into the discussion of collective national memory. As I have pointed out elsewhere, until recently feminist historiography of the period of the *Yishuv* (the pre-state period and pre-state Jewish community in Palestine) has focused on various aspects of women's material experience of the Zionist project. Only very recently has this historiography even begun to show interest in the relationship between the construction of femininity and masculinity, and the formation and representation of the *Eretz Yisraeli* ethoses and identities. The study of a gendered memory as the social dynamic and public action of individuals and collectives that "create, express, and consume" the memory of the past or its commemoration (which Jay Winter and Emanuel Sivan call "public remembrance" or "public recollection") is only just beginning.[8] The scarcity of such historical studies is not manifested simply in the absence of women from the history of memory. Thus, it may not be corrected by simply appending heroines of the past to histories and making a place for them in the national pantheon, although this is important in and of itself. While a more inclusive version, a kind of "herstory" of the history of memory, may serve as a "corrective" to the larger history, it will also perpetuate the distinction between the two areas of study: gender history and the history of memory.

The gendering of the history of collective memory is important because it may help us draw a less homogenous and monolithic map of this memory than the one we have today. Indeed, historians of national memory have been unanimous that this memory is never monolithic, that its very essence, like the essence of a nation, lies precisely in the lack of uniformity, that indeed every nation is characterized by a constant negotiation between its components. At the same time, as Alon Confino has pointed out, one failure of historians of memory is precisely their tendency to homogenize the collective that remembers.[9] These historians still tend to regard the act of remembering (or forgetting) in terms of politics and ideology, and merely as the reflection of the political hegemony of movements, ideologies, or establishments. National memory is still identified with omnipotent entities — the state, the party, the movement, the dominant elite — on whom these historians bestow all-encompassing power as chief agents of culture.

The bias toward the political and toward the apparatus of the state is sometimes accompanied by a reneging on the social and cultural. Such a bias, and with it the homogenization of diverse publics and their perception into a single entity — the *"Yishuv"* — is salient in the discussion of the *Eretz Yisraeli* culture of memory and commemoration. The claim that the collective memory in the period of the *Yishuv* and the first decades of the state was statist and created by "Labor" elites and circles, whose hegemony was fractured and broken only in the second half of the 1970s, still persists. Even historians who locate memory in cells within civil society (and not within the state and its bureaucracy) believe that this memory, at least until the 1950s, was not spontaneous and was governed by the state and officialdom.[10]

Paradoxically, even those who call for including different groups and identities in the Zionist and *Eretz Yisraeli* ethos do not adequately consider the potential that lies in the history of gender, not only in and of itself but also for history in general — namely, the potential to make that history more varied and pluralist.[11] Collective memory, as some of its early students, first and foremost among them Maurice Halbwachs, have taught us, is not formed by general and universal images and practices; rather, this memory is historical and particular. It is made out of the experiences, perceptions, and imaginings of groups. As John Gillis has pointed out, national memory in particular is formed in terms of specific identities, such as those of class, gender, and ethnicity.[12]

This type of memory developed in the *Yishuv* and even more so in Israel after 1948. It may be described in terms taken from from the world of vocal music, borrowing the concept of "polyphony," which Mikhail Bakhtin coined to describe the polyphonic character of "voices in their full value" that are sounded and heard together but maintain their uniqueness. Emanuel Sivan, too, made use of the image of polyphony in relation to memory in Israel. Describing memory as a "chorus," he suggested that alongside the so-called "official," "central," or "establishment" memory, other voices were also heard: of political groups, of social sectors united by specific cultural experiences, and of groups concentrated in a particular locus (for example, as I show later, the memory that crystallized in the urban "Civic Sector" (*hugim ezrahiyyim*) — as opposed to the socialist Labor sector — or in the *moshavot* (agricultural villages).[13] The polyphonic character of national memory was gendered. The one-armed hero of Tel Hai was perceived and represented not only as the new Zionist, but also as a new man. So were the fallen of the 1948 war. Similarly, women who died for the nation were perceived not only as national figures, but also as models of appropriate "national" female be-

havior. Put differently, the chronicles of deaths for country and state also can
be examined in terms of the development of constructions of masculinity
and femininity. Moreover, the gendering of the history of memory makes it
possible not only to render a less homogenous account, but also to re-examine
familiar questions, such as the question of the relationship between elites at
the center and groups at the margins, between the culture of the establishment
and sectorial and local culture, and between these and popular culture.

To focus the discussion and to elucidate the ways in which the polyphonic
chorus of memory evolved in gender terms, I shall examine a single case: the
forgetting (and the suppression) of the memory and commemoration of
Sarah Aaronsohn (1890–1917), one of the leaders of the secret pro-British espionage network, known within British intelligence as the "A. Organization"
and locally as "Nili," which operated under Turkish rule in Syria and Palestine from 1915 to 1917. I shall examine her image from the time of her death,
in October 1917, through the growth of the "legend of Sarah," as Avigdor
Hameiri termed it, in the 1930s and 1940s, up to its annexing, starting in the
late 1960s, into the national pantheon, an annexation that brought on a crucial change in the image.[14] Since the focus of this study is on acts of public
commemoration, I shall deal with the story of Aaronsohn's actual life and
death only insofar as is necessary. As I have shown elsewhere, Aaronsohn regarded her suicide as a conscious and public act, and her death was the first
example in the history of *Eretz Yisrael* of an active female death with secular
and national overtones. I also argued that her death departed radically from
existing models of female heroism, both from the classic Jewish model of female martyrdom that had developed after the waves of violence and persecution raging in Central Europe in 1096 and from the secular, national
model of death which developed in *Eretz Yisrael* at the time of the First
Aliyah and after.[15] Moreover, her death deviated even from the colonial
model of female self-sacrifice for the nation, which evolved in anticolonial
nationalist movements in the Middle East and South Asia, and which has
been studied by Rajeswari Sunder Rajan, Gayatri Spivak, and Beth Baron.[16]

My focus on Sarah Aaronsohn has another motive as well. The changes
in her status as a national hero can be compared to the transformations in
the political and cultural status of the legend of Tel Hai and the myth of
Trumpeldor. This comparison between a central and formative myth and a
memory that was initially peripheral and sectorial, but which subsequently
became an alternative myth, may serve as an example for the comparative
study of memory. Such a study forces us to raise a number of questions. Was
memory homogeneous? Was it controlled by practically omnipotent elites?

How did prevailing perceptions and representations of femininity (or masculinity) shape the narrative of the history of the Jews and of Zionism "written" by various groups? What were the features of a national heroine represented as an historical agent? And, finally, how did memory take form in various periods? Was it homogeneous until the 1970s and perhaps the 1980s, or had its fracturing or splitting (what some term its privatization) already begun in the early *Yishuv*?

To address these questions, I shall focus on two stretches of time that were major junctions in the evolution of "the legend of Sarah": from the beginning of her public commemoration in 1932 to the end of World War II, when the memory of Sarah Aaronsohn was nurtured by various right-wing groups within the Civic Sector (both urban and rural), as well as in popular culture; and after 1967, when local, sectorial, and popular memory was appropriated into the mainstream national memory, which changed and reshaped it, but was also altered by it.

To elucidate the possibilities in gendering memory, I have applied a two-pronged methodology, practicing a dual reading. First, I examine memory, ignoring gender, even though the object of commemoration was a woman. Thus, in the first part of this paper, I survey and attempt to reconstruct the political and social uses of Aaronsohn's memory. This survey is a "herstory": the "hero" of the story is female, but my rendition is deliberately blind to the ways in which different and dynamic perceptions of femininity (and masculinity) shaped the ethos of the national heroine. Only afterward do I pursue a "gender reading" of narratives about Sarah, a reading that is sensitive to the ways in which the various and often competing definitions and notions regarding the role of women in the nation-in-the-making, shaped the collective memory and commemoration.

1917 and 1932–1947: Forgetting and Remembering

In contrast to the battle for Tel Hai (1 March 1920), the death of Sarah Aaronsohn about two and a half years earlier had made no immediate impact on the collective, public memory or upon that of specific groups or sectors in the *Yishuv* such as the *moshavot*. Her violent taking of her own life for her people and country did not immediately become a model of national heroism, and its anniversary was not publicly commemorated. And her death did not stand out as a turning point or a formative event in the history of the *Yishuv*. In fact, in different milieux, both Labor and Civic, Nili's espionage activities were regarded as irresponsible (and by some as mercenary), and not as manifestations of devotion to the national cause. True, Sarah's suicide, which was also interpreted as a conscious choice of self-sacrifice for the nation, sometimes rescued her from the pejorative image that stuck to her colleagues in the leadership of the Nili underground. At least during the first decade after her suicide, her image as a heroine was rather equivocal. There is reference to her heroism in writings of that time (notably in the writings of her contemporaries in the *moshavot*, the socio-economic group in which she grew and among whom, as I show later, her memory as a national heroine was molded), and in the Jewish press in Palestine and elsewhere, but it is scattered and hardly constitutes a tradition of memory.[17] The "invention" of such a tradition, to use Eric Hobsbawm's well-known term, was deferred.[18] In contradistinction to the construction of Trumpeldor as a national icon immediately upon his death, the ethos and myths of Sarah Aaronsohn present a delayed memory, evolving slowly and belatedly.

The appropriation of her heroism into a peripheral and distinctly sectorial remembrance began only fifteen years after her death with the first *"aliyah la-regel"* or pilgrimage to her grave on 10 October 1932. The thirty-five ceremonial pilgrimages that preceded the first official state ceremony in her memory and that of the other dead members of Nili, held in Zikhron Yaakov in 1967, were constructed as a "tradition," as their organizers emphasized from the very beginning. They saw themselves as the agents of a tradition that had the potential to preserve a segment of the national past, create its symbolic patterns, and commemorate it.

A close reading of the detailed descriptions of the pilgrimages allows us to examine not only the dynamics of the construction of public memory, but also to observe, in miniature, the remembering community and the social and political changes that occurred within it. Paraphrasing the anthropologists Clifford Geertz and James Clifford, we may describe the annual ceremony, held around the last day of the holiday of Sukkot in Zikhron Yaakov, as a "synecdoche," that is as a part representing the whole. This is a part, or perhaps a segment, of a culture, or of a cultural activity, that embodies the cultural, social (and political) whole of the observed community.[19] In the case at hand, the community is the Civic Sector of the *Yishuv* during the 1930s and 1940s.

Two thousand women and men of this community took part in the second pilgrimage to Sarah's grave on Tuesday, 10 October 1933, which served as a model for those that took place afterwards. Five hundred of the participants belonged to two leading organizations within the community: Bnei

Binyamin, the Young Farmers' Federation, the best-organized and most dynamic body within the private agricultural sector, and the Revisionist organization, Betar. The other fifteen hundred participants included residents of Zikhron Yaakov and guests from the large cities and other *moshavot*. The "day of the popular procession," as the organizers called it, was described as a mass pilgrimage. The fact that in some of the *moshavot* it was a half-day holiday helped make it successful.

At the head of the parade rode representatives of the First Aliyah and veterans of the *moshavot*, along with members of the "first" native-born "generation": Avram Shapira, his daughters, and the daughters of the Zviatitski family of Petah Tikvah, dressed in riding habits. After them came riders from Brit ha-Rokhvim (Riders' Club) and members of Bnei Binyamin from Zikhron Yaakov, Haderah, Shefeyah, Bat Shlomo, Binyaminah, and elsewhere. Leisurely following them on foot came members of the Bnei Binyamin executive, schoolchildren, members of Betar, and the *"kahal"* (general public).[20] In their procession, the pilgrims retraced parts of the last three journeys that Sarah Aaronsohn had made on the way to her death and burial: from the house of her father, Efrayim Fischel, to the improvised jail where she was interrogated and tortured; from the jail back to the home of her brother, Aharon, where she tried to commit suicide; and from her father's house, where she lay dying for three days, to the cemetery where she was buried. On reaching the important stations in their itinerary, the pilgrims stood to honor the memory of the dead Sarah.

The most prominent cohort of pilgrims, the first native-born generation from the cities, the established *moshavot*, and the new, private capitalist agricultural settlements, had an ambiguous collective status. This ambiguity dated back to the period before World War I and to the time of the war itself, when this generation was socially and economically marginal, yet at the same time occupied a central and even iconic place in the Hebrew *Eretz Yisraeli* discourse, in which they were elevated to a model of a new national experience — masculine and feminine.[21] During the 1930s and 1940s, this relationship between economic marginality and iconic place in the national discourse was reversed. After the economic crisis of the early 1920s, the *moshavot* saw a period of certain expansion, including the founding of new agricultural colonies and urban settlements. During this period, the organizational infrastructure of the agricultural and urban Civic Sector was constructed, and what came to be described as the "Civic culture" developed. Yet *"bnei ha-aretz"* (literally, "sons of the land," a term designating the first generation of native Hebrew speakers) lost their iconic place in the discourse on the nation and were consigned to the periphery.[22] The members of Nili, who represented this generation, especially Sarah Aaronsohn, were seized upon by "the remembering group," that group that sought to commemorate its own cultural heroes, as the site of authentic *Eretz Yisraeli*-ness. In contrast to Trumpeldor, who was an outsider affiliated with the Labor movement, Aaronsohn's conduct and action could become role models, and she was reconstructed and represented by the Civic elites (and particularly by the native-born young elite) as both a sectorial and a national myth. The tension between sectorialism and nationalism is expressed in the first memorial pamphlet published by the Bnei Binyamin executive in 1932:

> Sarah Aaronsohn is a national heroine unrivaled in the annals of the Hebrew revival. . . . Aaronsohn is not only the greatest national heroine in this period of our revival, she is also our own heroine, the heroine of the class of the *Boazim*, people oriented to building the collective through building the individual and through individual responsibility, whose value [others] try to play down at every opportunity, denying them any idealistic tone and any desire and power for national sacrifice; Sarah is not a solitary heroine in our ranks; she was the bearer of a large movement, a wide-ranging organization of Civic farmers, who made sacrifices and invested physical and mental energy in their outstanding devotion to the liberation of the homeland and in extending frequent aid to the *Yishuv* in its most difficult moments.[23]

As the "heroine of the homeland" and a "heroic sacrifice," as "a saint in her life and death" and as a "symbol of national sacrifice and pride," Aaronsohn became a model of national activism.[24] Her tomb became a site "rousing audacity and sacrifice on the altar of liberation and the war to defend the *Yishuv* and the land."[25] The potential inherent in her commemoration was dual. She clearly represented a particular group or "class," and thus was not perceived as a unifying symbol by the peripheral young elite, her own milieu, and certainly not by the dominant "Labor" elite. The story of her heroism was not a part of what Hayden White called a "metanarrative," a metastory organizing the history of the community as a whole and representing homogeneity.[26] Aaronsohn's story was divisive. She was constructed as a heroine of the *Boazim* — an appellation given to the native-born farmers belonging to the land-owning sector within the *moshavot*, named after their prototype, the biblical Boaz — and as an icon of Civic culture, urban and agricultural alike, which saw itself as a "native" culture. The emphasis on "class" in the literature dedicated to Aaronsohn's memory competes with and was an alternative to the Marxist concept of class and to the reality of a strong organized Labor sector and a hegemonic Labor movement. Bnei Binyamin were known for their blunt anti-Labor rhetoric and for their fierce opposition to socialism and collectivism.[27] However, the members of the commemorating group also wished to "speak for" and in the name of the nation as a whole. Thus, Aaronsohn was described as both a "Boazit" heroine and as a national figure embodying the entire *Yishuv*. Her discovery and the promotion of her memory as a "saint" of the Civic Sector reflected the need of groups within it to correct the dominant Labor narrative of the recent Zionist past, from which they felt they had been excluded. Thus the representative of Bnei Binyamin stated on the fourth commemoration of her death (October 1935) that:

> It has always been falsely said of the farmers and their sons, who in fact served as the foundation for the Balfour Declaration and as the first stones for building the Land, that they were concerned only with their own gain. The story of Sarah has removed this accusation. They [the farmers] knew how to sanctify the Hebrew name and Hebrew honor. On this anniversary, and on every day of the year, we teach our youth to remember that, apart from all else, there is national honor and that in case of need, one must withstand the trial and act like Sarah and her friends.[28]

In Sarah Aaronsohn, the commemorating group found their very own saint, who could also be represented as an icon of the nation as a whole. What is more, the organized commemoration transformed the activism of Nili, and especially the active death of Aaronsohn herself, into a model for the youth of the Civic Sector. The emphasis on sacrifice and exemplary death was particularly salient during World War II. In wartime memorial ceremonies, the comparison is repeatedly made between the willingness of the older generation of *Boazim* in World War I to sacrifice themselves for their nation and the hedonism and complacency of the Civic youth in the 1940s. In the ceremony of 1944, Arieh Samsonov of Zikhron Yaakov appealed to the young men of the towns and the *moshavot* and to the "youth of Israel" to volunteer to serve in the British Army in order to prove "that you deserve to be called people of Zikhron, the place where Sarah, the spirit of Nili, was born, raised, and educated!" From this year, the recruits were sworn in on Aaronsohn's grave in a ceremony before a local audience and representatives of the British Army.[29]

The representation of Aaronsohn as a model of *Eretz Yisraeli* nationalism is not unique to the memorial ceremonies organized by the Bnei Binyamin Federation. It recurs in the eulogies for her in the daily Civic press (by writers who were not necessarily identified with Bnei Binyamin), in the children's press of the Civic Sector, such as *Ha-Boker le-Yeladim* (Morning for Children), as well as in stories, plays, and skits written in the 1930s, 1940s, and 1950s.[30] The discussion of her death and its symbolism makes a rich and dense fabric of texts characterized by what Raphael Samuel has called "a density of description and attention to the object of remembrance."[31] This density, along with the multiplicity of various texts, drawing on each other, representing writers of different political orientations, published on different platforms and directed toward different audiences, is what helped construct Sarah Aaronsohn as a cultural icon. The discussion of her life and death, both for those who had taken an active part in them and those who had not, was in fact a debate about the nature of *Eretz Yisraeli*-ness, who owned national history, and who had the right to interpret it.

It was precisely the absence of homogeneity in the collective memory of Sarah Aaronsohn that helped transform her into a "heroine for all," for different groups and at different times. For the older private agricultural sector, represented in the ceremonies by such veterans as Avram Shapira, Aaronsohn was an exemplar of "the farmer's way." For members of her own generation and for Bnei Binyamin youth, who from the beginning presented themselves as the true "natives of the Land," her "national espionage" accorded with the fulfillment of the Zionist project and "building the Land." As Oded Ben-Ami put it in 1932, she was "the one on whose grave we built the great building of the Land." Ben-Ami, like other activists in the Bnei Binyamin Federation, emphasized both Aaronsohn's local connections and her territoriality, the connection to the Land and people of Israel in general, acquired through her unmediated knowledge of nature, the terrain and its flora and fauna. As he presented her, she was a daughter of the Land and a true representative of the authentic native-born generation: "Nor did the *Yishuv* know how to appreciate the value of Sarah and her heroic friends, through malevolence, malice, and envy—because they were children of the Land."[32] Aaronsohn was a "territorial heroine," in accordance with the model that characterized the native Hebrew culture from the beginning, as Itamar Even-Zohar and others have shown.[33]

In contrast to the narrative of Aaronsohn's life and death molded by circles close to Bnei Binyamin, Revisionist as well as maximalist right-wing narratives emphasized blood sacrifice and revolt, which were promulgated as ideals in and of themselves and sometimes divorced from concepts of

territoriality and of settling on the land. From the beginning, the Young
Maccabi movement, Betar, and Betar Youth took an active part in commemorating Sarah Aaronsohn. From the very first memorial ceremony, representatives of Betar attended the annual commemorations officially and in uniform; and their presence became especially conspicuous during World War
II. Moreover, aside from the annual public ritual organized in Zikhron
Yaakov, Nili and Sarah Aaronsohn in particular became models of activism
and revolt among both Revisionists and right-wing maximalists. In the eyes
of the Stern Group and of activists associated with Brit ha-Biryonim, her activities were not only a symbol of heroism and of "deeds" (presented as the
opposite of the passivity and sterile verbosity of the intellectuals), but also
part of a messianic myth. As Joseph Heller has convincingly shown, the
zealot (*kanai*), rebelling against a sovereign ruler, had a central place in the
Stern Group's eclectic messianic ideology. His/her historic role consisted of
self-sacrifice that would bring on "the kingdom of Israel" — not by parlia-
mentary means or through agreement (with colonial and international powers such as Britain), but by violent action. Thus, paradoxically, Nili, with its
definitively pro-British orientation during World War I, became the ideological and operative model for the anti-British Lehi in World War II. The maximalist right appropriated Sarah Aaronsohn and the story of her death and
set her (along with Tomáš Masaryk, Marshal Pilsudski, and Eamon de
Valera) in an eclectic pantheon of national rebels. They even turned her
death into an alternative national narrative of the history of Israel — the
chronicles of the acts of the zealots.[34]

The children's and youth culture of the Civic *Yishuv*, on the other hand,
had no place for the model of the zealot and the saga of apocalyptic violence
invented by the extreme right, or even for the sectorialism and the version of
class identity that characterized the narrative fostered by Bnei Binyamin.
The literature published by the children's newspapers of the Civic Sector
sought to present Sarah Aaronsohn as an exemplary national figure. Like
Trumpeldor, so too Sarah was represented as a hero of the nation as a whole.
Her death had added pedagogical value as an example of a "boundless love
for our people and our homeland" and of "self-sacrifice and devotion, all in
faith and confidence," as pointed out in *Ha-Boker le-Yeladim* of 25 September 1945.

Unlike Trumpeldor, Nili and Sarah Aaronsohn were not included in the
curriculum — neither the curriculum of the general educational system nor
that of schools affiliated with the Labor movement. Her slow appropriation
by the state educational system began only after 1967 (see below). Until then,

and even in the 1950s, Aaronsohn and Nili were absent from school curricula and from the Hebrew school calendar, while the anniversary of Trumpeldor's death, the 11th of Adar, was made a day of ceremonies and the first national secular holiday. Given this absence, Aaronsohn's emergence as a national heroine for youth in the peripheral juvenile culture that emerged in the 1940s is particularly significant.

First occasionally, then more frequently, Sarah Aaronsohn's name and the story of her death appeared in fiction and memorial sections of the Civic children's press. A typical story was published in *Ha-Boker le-Yeladim* on 9 October 1946 (the eve of the traditional pilgrimage in Zikhron Yaakov). In the didactic "frame" story, serving as a setting for the inner narrative, a grandmother explains to her grandchildren why masses of pilgrims throng to the grave of the saint from Zikhron Yaakov every year. As befitting the genre, the story focuses on Sarah Aaronsohn's patriotic childhood and death and, typically, no mention is made of her adolescence or adult years. As the following brief excerpt shows, her death is described in territorial terms and through images of mourning that focus on the landscape and nature ("the heavens wept" "the first hard rain of the year") commonly found in Hebrew children's literature. These clichéd tropes, however, are now inserted into a new narrative of heroism for youth:

> When Sarah was brought to burial in the cemetery of Zikhron Yaakov, the first drops of the first hard rain of the season started to fall. Not only the people cried, the sky too wept for the death of Sarah . . . saintly and pure, who sacrificed herself for the redemption of her people and country. Even the Turkish officers and governors who attended her funeral declared, "She was like a daughter of kings."[35]

The various narratives of Sarah Aaronsohn's life and death reflect the polyphony of collective memory. And this polyphonic quality was in tune with the different and often competing agendas and needs, mainly political but also cultural, of different groups. But despite their differences and plurality of voices, these groups belonged to the same community of memory and may be located in the Civic Sector and the national Civic culture that emerged during the 1930s and 1940s. However, this functional explanation of the polyphony of the remembering community is insufficient. First, there was not always a direct connection between the political affiliation of those who fostered the memory and commemorated the past, and the actual practice of memory. For example, unorganized, popular forms of commemoration, which were not partisan or connected to organizations sprang up (see below). Moreover, an explanation that reduces memory to a simple relationship between needs (mainly political) and organized social activities (such as public mourning and commemoration ceremonies) errs in ignoring the complexities of the object of the memory, its images, and the reconstruction of this object by individuals and groups. This kind of functional explanation also ignores the relationships among gender, memory, and identity.

How, then, was the discourse on Sarah Aaronsohn made into a gendered memory? Was she invented as a national *hero* of Eretz Yisrael who *happened to be a woman*, or, put differently, was her "femaleness" relevant to the myth of *Eretz Yisraeli*-ness that she represented? I shall argue that the memory of Sarah Aaronsohn cannot be understood outside of gender, since her construction as a model of *Eretz Yisraeli*-ness by the groups examined above, as well as by other groups, was related to the identification between nationalism and the active sacrifice and historical action of women. To examine the associations among gender, identity, and memory, I shall consider, from the perspective of gender, the same narratives that were examined above in a functional and neutral way. In addition, I shall discuss other sources: plays, high and popular literature, and the practices of memory in daily life, such as the custom of giving girls and boys "national" names associated with the history of Nili.

1917–1967: Memory and Gender

The most salient feature of the formation of the memory of Sarah Aaronsohn's life and death is the identification of nationalism with activism and femininity. This identification is manifest, first and foremost, in Sarah's very centrality in the many varied narratives of the history of Nili, its rise, deeds, and fall. The typical plot of the 1930s and 1940s did feature the central male figures in the anti-Ottoman underground: her older brother, Aaron Aaronsohn, and Avshalom Feinberg, presenting both of them as models of *Eretz Yisraeli* masculinity (Feinberg was described as "the first Sabra").[36] But Sarah Aaronsohn, the only woman in the Nili leadership (though not the only female member of the organization), who coordinated and from late 1916 practically ran the organization and the wider network that supported it, was the only activist to be elevated to a paragon of sacrifice and a model of national conduct. The relative marginality of the underground men within the memory undoubtedly had technical reasons, to do with the local-territorial aspect of every presence of the past in private and collective memory. Sarah Aaronsohn had a *site* of memory and even "sacred" relics, which the pilgrims to her grave visited in their ritual processions. Aaron Aaronsohn and Avshalom Feinberg had no place of burial or relics. Their death was not final because their bodies disappeared and this disappearance was shrouded in uncertainty: The plane in which Aaronsohn flew to the Versailles Conference vanished over the English Channel, and Feinberg disappeared on his unfortunate journey to Egypt in 1917, and the remains of his body were recovered by chance only in 1967.

As historians of memory such as Pierre Nora, Raphael Samuel, and Frances Yates have noted, the act of remembering the past, whether to preserve an individual past or to reconstruct a public myth, is related to the practices and techniques of recall as a spatial art — remembering, preserving, and memorizing places or individuals in a space. The technique of recall is based on memorizing the exact location and arrangement of the disparate items that the rememberers "saw" at a particular site. This also characterizes the building of sites of commemoration. Without place, Frances Yates has pointed out, there is no practice of memory.[37]

Sarah Aaronsohn has had a definite place of memory: the site of her death and her burial place. The presence of her remains in the local space of Zikhron Yaakov aided in the "arrangement" and formation of the narrative of her activities and its incorporation into the history of the heroism of the nation, both by those who perpetuated her memory and by the groups who made pilgrimages to Zikhron Yaakov on the anniversary of her death. Her memory was preserved in the series of sacred places and relics: the room where she was tortured, the place where she committed suicide (the bathroom of Aaron Aaronsohn's house in the Aaronsohn family's back yard), the "instrument" of death (the gun), the blood-stained suicide letter, the white dress in which she committed suicide, and her grave. Every year from the 1940s, a *sukkah* was erected in the Aaronsohn yard, which the local schoolchildren and the general public were encouraged to visit throughout the festival of Sukkot and on Shmini Atzeret, the eighth and last day, when Jews in Israel no longer sit in the *sukkah*. At the center of the *sukkah*, on a table decorated with branches and flowers, stood Sarah Aaronsohn's photograph. In this iconic presentation of the dead "saint" in a public *sukkah*, the local ritual of the pilgrimage to Sarah's grave was combined with the tradition of the three pilgrimages to the Temple in Jerusalem at Passover, Shavuot, and Sukkot.

Aaronsohn's centrality in the narrative of Nili, and of *Eretz Yisraeli* heroism as a whole, however, is rooted in her complex gender identity. Sarah Aaronsohn's femininity was defined and interpreted in various ways, according to available models of gender — particularly the model of the "new" *Eretz Yisraeli* woman — that already had emerged before World War I and were refined during the interwar years. Both the definition and the memory contained an unresolved (and insoluble) tension between two perceptions of femininity and between two practices of *Eretz Yisraeli* female public behavior, which cohabited in the national discourse and in particular in the culture of the Civic Sector.

One perception may be termed "maternalist." This was based on the assumption that women were mothers of the nation, in two senses of the word: Literally, by virtue of their reproductive capacity, they were responsible for reproducing the nation, and in the sense that they were the conduit for the transmission of the national culture through teaching their children the Hebrew language. This twofold contribution to the nation was seen not merely as a "natural" (biological) role but also as a social and cultural activity.[38] The other perception, which cohabited with the maternalist definition, blurred gender differences and detached national female identity from motherhood. This perception was conspicuous, as I have demonstrated elsewhere, among women of the first native Hebrew-speaking generation and especially among Nili members and their female supporters. Sarah Aaronsohn's own conduct was an eloquent manifestation of this perception.[39] I shall now discuss each of these components in the gendered memory.

National-Maternalist Perception and Memory

As is well known, Zionist gender ideology in the first decades of the twentieth century was no different from Western nationalist ideology in general. Like nationalism in the West, so too Zionism "invited" women into the budding community of the nation and bestowed upon them historical agency by virtue of their essence as mothers. The vast body of studies on maternalism, most notably the writings of Gisela Bock, Patricia Thane, Sonia Michel, and Seth Koven on Western Europe and of Beth Baron and Fatma Müge Göçek on the Ottoman Empire, clearly shows how maternalism enabled the recruitment of women to nationalist movements. Yet, this selfsame image of femininity, which served to include women in the nation, at the same time led to their exclusion from what was perceived as the apotheosis of national liberation: blood-sacrifice for the nation and participation as combatants on the battlefield.[40] "Translated" into *Eretz Yisraeli* terms, the maternalist model prevented women from acquiring (and in Hebrew *kniyah*, literally "buying") the land with their blood. Until Sarah Aaronsohn's death, this possibility was restricted to men, for example, the martyrs of Ha-Shomer. Although women also died in the battle for Tel Hai, blood sacrifice "for the Land" was identified with a new Hebrew hero, Trumpeldor, and with masculine characteristics.[41] Of course, the maternalist perception of the *Eretz Yisraeli* woman, as the embodiment of motherhood and of the family of the nation, did leave a certain space for women to act as agents of the national revival. Indeed, this space is one of the components of the memory of Sarah Aaronsohn. Various versions of the story of her heroism emphasized characteristics that were considered feminine, among them her devotion to her family, her willingness to sacrifice herself, and, lastly, her capacity for emotional identification with human suffering, as clearly manifest in her attitude toward the genocide of the Armenians (this last, considered as a major factor in her joining a political movement). These feminine traits turned her story into a part of a repertoire of alternative, feminine versions of the story of Jewish heroism.

In one such version, Aaronsohn's act of nationalism was described as a part of a domestic, family drama. This displacement of heroism from the public realm to the home and its presentation as part of a feminine biography is quite conspicuous in the hagiographies of Aaronsohn that were written under the aegis of the Aaronsohn family, especially of her brother Alexander. A typical example may be found in the volume dedicated to Sarah in Yaari-Polskin's work on Nili, which relates in detail the story of the growth and *bildung* of an *Eretz Yisraeli* heroine. This story of pioneering, represented as a source of heroism and sacrifice, is distinctly gendered:

> The pioneers had to create and develop everything. Isolated among their Arab neighbors, whose language and customs they did not know, they were forced to learn the work . . . to adapt to everything. And how difficult the life of these women pioneers was! They had to do everything with their own hands. They took care of their children by themselves, because there was no "daycare" yet. And every mother cooked, baked, washed, and sewed for her household; for in those days the pioneers had not yet come to believe that they could give up their personal lives and families. . . . Sarah grew up in a life of work, heroism, and sacrifice. From childhood, she worked, like all the daughters of the pioneers. Hand in hand, shoulder to shoulder with her mother, she washed floors, scrubbed tables and chairs . . .

After specifying the various household chores, he continues:

> And Sarah also inhaled spiritual heroism daily in her life with her mother. . . . From her she learned to suffer in silence, to dry her tears quickly, and to present a laughing face . . . to do her daily chores despite the ache in her body, in her heart. From her mother she learned that there was no obstacle, no hindrance, no power on earth that could keep the soul from rising and exalting above all and soaring, soaring to the heavens![42]

From her father, Yaari-Polskin points out, Sarah Aaronsohn learned a more earthly and territorial love: love for the land, a land identified with the space outside the home and the female sphere.

The relationship between memory and group or class, emphasized in the first part of this study and given social and political interpretations, is a gendered relationship. The "class" of farmers is endowed with qualities or a history that, in the view of Yaari-Polskin and other members of his group, had been expropriated from them: namely, a history of pioneering. Just like the people of the Labor movement, so too the Aaronsohns and the farmers of Zikhron Yaakov are "pioneers," insists Yaari-Polskin. And, most relevant here, this pioneering is gendered. Women's pioneering is domestic and spiritual. This spirituality is embodied in the Aaronsohns' mother, Malkah, and in her daughter Sarah, and does not characterize the men of the family, who represent the material connection to the land.

In another version of the maternalist narrative, Sarah Aaronsohn's life is detached from the domestic and familial framework and integrated, as an epic and a public story, into a clearly feminine narrative of the history of heroism. In this version, Sarah is described as a link in the chain of mothers of the nation, which includes the biblical Sarah, Deborah, and Yael, and sometimes even mothers from the Jewish apocrypha. In the necrologue, "Sarah Aaronsohn" by Avigdor Hameiri, which was first published in the newspaper *Doar ha-Yom* (Today's Mail) in 1923, Sarah is presented as a "Judith," a "great and gigantic" mythical heroine. Her mythological status and power are conveyed through images of femininity, seduction, and sexuality, which remain only symbolic: "And Judith bestows Greek compliments on Holophernes . . . and her eyes [Sarah's] were light, her face always smiling, and her lips full and somewhat obdurate."[43] Judith the tyrant-slayer is a founding mother of the nation. The fact that Sarah Aaronsohn, like Judith, was never a mother and, strictly speaking, did not fulfill wifely duties, since she abandoned her husband and home, has little or no significance. For maternalism identified all women as mothers, regardless of their biological or family status.

The Blurred Boundaries of Gender

Alongside this genealogy of national mothers and daughters, there evolved another memory of Aaronsohn's heroism and death, in which her role as an agent, in Jewish history and that of the *Yishuv*, was severed from the maternalist notion of action. This memory, in which the boundaries of femininity are blurred, took shape between the early 1920s and the end of the 1950s. Yet, at the same time, this non-maternalist (sometimes even anti-maternalist) image draws on the images of femininity and on social behaviors of the women of the native-born elite before and during World War I.

The blurring of gender boundaries and a pointed criticism of the identification of national femininity with motherhood were salient features of Aaronsohn's own writings and public conduct. Aaronsohn occasionally wore men's clothing and used the masculine form when writing about herself. She also criticized the way in which her male colleagues in the underground perceived femininity and represented women as mothers, saints, or asexual creatures. And she herself was a very sensual woman. Her challenge to notions of femininity and its boundaries culminated in the way in which she designed her death, in the last letter, and in her behavior until the moment of suicide.[44]

After her death, and especially after the early 1930s, right-wing movements and youth organizations within the private agricultural sector adopted the non-maternalist and open-ended definition of *Eretz Yisraeli* femininity formulated by Aaronsohn herself and other women of her generation. This model was not entirely political, however, for it also penetrated into popular culture, especially into popular women's culture. In this alternative narrative, memory operated as a sieve that sifted features identified as feminine and domestic out of Sarah Aaronsohn's biography, retaining details that were not perceived as purely feminine or that could be deemed "masculine." For example, a great many descriptions emphasized her physical prowess, her freedom of movement outside her home, her horsemanship, her mastery of various weapons, as well as qualities such as her unperturbability, unemotionality, contempt for pathos, and the desire to "do" rather than talk. Some of the traditional maternalist biographies also included these characteristics. Yaari-Polskin, for example, gives Sarah's love of riding a central place:

[She loved] horse riding and life in nature. . . . She bore a sword and galloped in the mountains. . . . How beautiful she was . . . as she rode her noble and gleaming horse, rejoicing in gatherings and competitions with our Arab neighbors. Sarah was perhaps one of the first Hebrew women in the land [to participate] in heroism and horse racing and even in raids on a caravan of camels in the dark of the night.[45]

This portrayal of Aaronsohn as a horseman, a *man* of nature and the land, is very similar to descriptions of her by the historian Joseph Klausner. The portrayal is intriguing precisely because of the analogy between the Sabra woman and the Bedouin man, involving a broad notion of gender and elements of orientalism, an approach that idealizes the oriental man while blurring his gender.[46] Such comparison of the first Sabra women to Bedouin men and heroes was most common from the turn of the twentieth century, as was the custom of *Eretz Yisraeli* women to dress up as Arab men. Moreover, the compound of masculine traits, activities, and appearance attributed to the female "hero" would be applied to the Sabra male. It was precisely at this time that the masculinist ethos of the native-born male, a man of deeds, lacking pathos, was promulgated.[47]

The authenticity of Aaronsohn as a daughter of the Land, her love of nature, her contempt for verbiage and her admiration for action were contrasted to the behavior of the men around her. Thus, this narrative of her heroism was based not only on the blurring of gender (as in the analogy to the Bedouin man), but also on the reversal of gender behaviors. Aaronsohn's behavior is presented as diametrically opposed to the feminine conduct of the men in Nili. Such a reversal is salient in the writings of Moshe Smilansky, who deserves attention as an exception among the activists in the farmers' and nationalist bloc. Although Smilansky served as the president of the Hebrew Farmers' Association and as editor of its newspaper, *Bustana'i* (Orchardist) till the early 1920s, he detached himself from the ideology of the organization and from Bnei Binyamin. And it was at the time that the memory and the commemoration of Nili and of Sarah Aaronsohn were being shaped that he began to formulate his own special views about Hebrew labor and about the relationship between Jews and Arabs.

What is unique about Smilansky is that his rendition of the myth of Sarah Aaronsohn was neither political nor strictly partisan. In the play *Rohele*, which he wrote in 1933, underground leader Rohele — Sarah Aaronsohn — prefers an active political life to family and the love of a man, while her male colleagues (who are portrayed as feminine) long for home, family, and the love of a woman. The heroine reproaches them: "Go without asking, with-out enquiring, with eyes shut, through fire and water, in blood and in death, always forward. Death with honor in an instant is better than a life of shame of the vanquished."[48] For "life of shame" read a comfortable domestic life. Rohele/Sarah's death is depicted as an especially "active" death. In the last scene of the play, Smilansky describes a duel between equals — between the heroine and Hassan Beck (the Ottoman interrogator). Rohele stabs Hassan Beck, and only then kills herself and dies on the spot.[49] Such reversal of gen-der roles and the relegation of the men in the underground to the margins of the narrative reach their peak in the article on Sarah that Smilansky wrote in 1935. The article ends with the sentence: "If there is truth in the statement that there is a next world, and that in the next world there are two parts, one for Paradise and one for Hell, and her male friends chance to go to Paradise, may her place be in Hell, and may she not meet them there."[50]

The blurring of the boundaries of femininity and the reversal of gender images characterize not only the statements of a "rebel" like Smilansky, but also the memory and acts of commemoration of Bnei Binyamin and the Revisionist and maximalist organizations of the right. Indeed, Aaronsohn's biography was integrated not only into the genealogy of the rebels and zealots discussed above, but also into an alternative history of Western fe-male heroism.

From the early 1930s, Aaronsohn was commonly compared to non-Jewish female warriors or heroines whose myths were marked by gender ambiguity. These myths commemorated "masculine" traits such as courage on the battlefield and soldiering, on the one hand, and idealized female qualities such as sexual purity and sometimes even virginity, on the other hand. The two most common analogies in the memorial literature dedicated to Aaron-sohn in the interwar years were to Joan of Arc, the Maid of Orleans, born in 1412, captured by the Burgundians and burnt by the English in 1431, and can-onized in 1920, and to Edith Cavell, the British nurse who was executed in Belgium for anti-German espionage during World War I. Cavell, executed in 1915, promptly became a national saint in Britain and a propaganda asset for the Allied forces.[51] Her blood sacrifice was associated with the sacrifice of occupied Belgium, which was routinely feminized and described as a woman in the propaganda. It is noteworthy that no comparison was made between Sarah and the best-known spy of World War I, Mata Hari. The rea-sons are clear. Hari spied, apparently, for personal gain and not for any na-tion. Moreover, by the first decade of the twentieth century she was already a sex symbol and an orientalist icon of sensuality and exotic Eastern femininity. Saint Joan and the nurse Cavell, in contrast, were symbols of a national femininity, distinctly nonsexual, and asexual. The military nurse and the virgin-warrior crossed the gender lines without endangering the prototype and ideal of the female saint. A similar tendency to desexualize the heroine and distance her from an ascribed gender role also characterizes the memory of Sarah Aaronsohn and bears little relation to her "real" life.

The comparisons to Christian myths and images of womanhood are especially important because they manifest not only the tension, enhanced by the blurring of the borderlines of gender, between definitions of femininity and nationalism, but also the syncretism of the national symbols of the center and right-wing circles in Eretz Israel. Some of the images of femininity taken on by these circles were not Jewish but Catholic or Protestant Evangelical. The use of the myth of Joan of Arc in relation to Sarah Aaronsohn is an examplar of such syncretism. Joan was a virgin, and her virginity endowed her with exceptional power in contrast to other women, though her special power also derived from her assumption of the role of a soldier and cross-dressing as a man. As a man-woman who transgressed the boundaries of gender, Joan became a symbol of national movements as well as of many political and social movements: Catholic and Protestant, right-wing royalist movements, and radical movements on the right and left in France, anti-feminist movements and militant feminists such as the WSPU (Women's Social and Political Union, the British suffragette organization).[52]

The analogy between Sarah Aaronsohn, the woman farmer and native of the land, and Joan of Arc, the French peasant of Lorraine, was quite prevalent in the political rhetoric of Bnei Binyamin and various right-wing circles. The heroism of Aaronsohn, who "invited" the British to her land, was compared to Joan of Arc's anti-Burgundian and anti-English patriotism. Moreover, both women were depicted as soldiers and at times referred to in the masculine gender. Already in the second pilgrimage to Aaronsohn's grave, in 1933, Bnei Binyamin activist Ze'ev Neiderman, also a native of Zikhron Yaakov, compared Aaronsohn's acts to the "nobility and heroism of this daughter of Orleans, 'Joanna of Arc'": In the pilgrimage "to the holy grave of Sarah of Zikhron, we today went up to this holy place to stand at attention before the same exalted soul and to remind future generations of this heroine of Zikhron Yaakov, like the heroine of Orleans."[53] In the pilgrimage of 1941, Aaronsohn was called a heroine "greater than Joan of Arc," and, speaking at her grave in October 1946, Betar member Baruch Weinstein called her "the Hebrew Joan of Arc . . . Commander of Nili."[54] But here the resemblance ends:

between Joan of Arc, the Frenchwoman, and Sarah, the Hebrew. They made their appearance in different national frameworks, in different periods, and under different conditions. Joan of Arc — among her own people, sitting on their own land, healthy in body and soul . . . who saw her, the heroine, as their emissary — their leader — of their own flesh. Joan of Arc made her appearance in an atmosphere of sympathy and admiration. The French people understood the value of her mission, gave her their assistance and backing for her actions. And our Sarah? She [appeared] under conditions of a cruel foreign government [and in a society] that had not reached a stage of complete national development. . . . Under these conditions, Sarah the Commander appeared.

Weinstein's typical speech is marked by his alternating use of the masculine and feminine gender, especially in his description of Joan-Sarah as a military commander. Joan of Arc, as noted, donned a uniform, and was depicted in uniform in the religious and secular iconography of both the right and left in the early twentieth century, as well as in feminist iconography. However, another source of her power was her virginity. Virginity was perceived as a source of female power and, more important, of authority, in Western Christian culture.[55] Beginning in the early 1930s, Aaronsohn was described as a (female) commander or as a (male) soldier and officer. The militarizing of her image and concomitant blurring of her sexuality (and femininity) culminate during World War II. Already in 1935, a Betar boat and naval unit were named after her, and from 1941, representatives of the British Army attended her memorial.[56] From 1942, her graveside eulogies became army recruitment speeches, and a number of recruits swore allegiance to Sarah Aaronsohn and committed themselves to avenging her sacrifice by freeing Eretz Yisrael and world Jewry from the National-Socialist threat. These recruits included not only members of Betar, but also members of *moshavot* whose political affiliation may not be determined with certainty.[57]

With the end of World War II, there was no longer a need to militarize Sarah Aaronsohn or to imagine her as a soldier. However, her blurred sexuality and sexual identity remained a part of her image as the alternative national saint of the Revisionist right. Thus, in 1958, the historian Joseph Klausner found it necessary to point out:

Another people would have bestowed a laurel wreath on her. I do not know what the world view of the French was, but the French people as a whole fall on their knees before Joan of Arc, who, in actuality, did not bring about victory and permitted the desecration of her body. And how do we treat Sarah? And this after the State has already been established. . . . How many books have been written about Sarah? To what extent are her history and heroic act taught in schools?[58]

Klausner in fact urged women to constitute an alternative memory of the "heroine": "Women should have established something special in her memory." Women and girls indeed took an active part in the pilgrimages to the grave, both as members of the organizations involved in the commemoration, such as Young Maccabi and Betar, and as members of women's organizations, such as the Federation of National Women affiliated with the New Zionist Federation. Women's participation, however, like the blurring of gender in the political memory of Sarah Aaronsohn, may not be taken as proof of an egalitarian outlook on gender relations within the Civic Sector or in its dominant political movements. As several historians of gender have shown, integral nationalist movements identified with the right, whether the radical or the traditional right, tended (more than liberal or left-wing movements), to foster non-maternalist images of femininity. In some of the former, women succeeded in carving out major roles for themselves.[59] However, the process by which access to the nation and the right to act on its behalf were extended to women did not involve an egalitarian politics, nor a liberal universalist notion of rights. Thus, in the *Yishuv's* right-wing circles and in the various farmers' organizations, the radical view of femininity that characterized the myth of Aaronsohn did not manifest itself in practice. Bnei Binyamin, for example, did not accept women as members. Moreover, its rhetoric (except for Aaronsohn's memorial rituals) celebrated male brotherhood, as one of the organization's publications noted.[60] Thus, Bnei Binyamin carried on the pre–World War I tradition of the "Gidonim" (after the biblical Gideon, the semi-military, all-male organization of the native-born from which Nili eventually emerged) and, unlike other youth movements, excluded women. Mixed organizations as well as nationalist women's organizations that criticized the militarism and militaristic rituals of the exclusively male organizations were established before, during, and after the war. Nili itself was a mixed organization, in which the borderlines of the definition of femininity and nation were stretched in an unprecedented manner, especially in Sarah Aaronsohn's activities.[61] However, as Mary Louise Roberts and Rajeswari Sunder Rajan have shown, a gender model that blurs the difference between what is considered "feminine" and what is accepted as "masculine" may develop, and is actually to be more likely to develop, within hierarchical communities with a patriarchal tradition lacking gender equality. It is precisely in such communities that images of exceptional and extraordinary women, embodying ideal qualities that are not necessarily "essentially" feminine, can develop.[62] What needs stressing in the anti-maternalist narrative reviewed here is not the disparity between this narrative and the actual position of women in the Civic Sector in the *Yishuv*, but women's conspicuous presence in the nationalist discourse and the ways in which this presence shaped the collective memory.

This narrative should not be seen as a political "invention" manufactured by bodies with clear programs and political affiliations. Obviously, the narrative was political. However, it seeped into popular memory and created that fabric of representations and practices that Raphael termed "the density of memory." These practices testify to the extent to which Sarah Aaronsohn — as a symbol of active female heroism that challenged the definitions of femininity — was identified with Nili. A clear case of this permeation of the myth into collective memory was the practice of naming girls "Nili." Choosing a name is a way of bestowing identity, both on those who choose it and on the person for whom it is chosen. Nili was a national and native name, an acronym that stood for the biblical phrase *"Netzah Yisrael lo yeshaker"* (the Glory of Israel does not deceive [1 Sam. 15:29]).

Prior to the second half of the 1930s, the name Nili was chosen rarely and sporadically. Yet, as the data on Hebrew names gathered by Sasha Weitman shows, it appeared on the population register regularly from 1936 onwards. Between 1936 and 1979, 2,889 girls were named Nili. In contrast, only 1,300 boys were given the name Avshalom, which was both biblical and native, and was not exclusively identified with the underground figure Avshalom Feinberg. The name Nili was most popular in the early 1940s: It was given to 75 girls in 1940, to 106 in 1942, to 150 in 1943, and to 141 in 1944. In the early 1950s, its popularity declined, rising again at the end of the decade, with an increase from 46 in 1955 to 59 in 1958. A further increase occurred in 1967, when 71 baby girls were named Nili.[63] The value of these figures is rather limited since there is no way of breaking them down and analyzing them by ethnic origin, economic and social status, or political affiliation of the families that named their daughters Nili. The clear national character of this name, however, and the fact that it was most popular during periods of national emergency (like World War II and the Six-Day War) and security crises (during the 1950s) point to the feminization of the memory of heroism. Oral testimonies indicate that the choice of the name Nili was not limited to right-wing circles.[64]

The domestication of memory and its appropriation to the daily life of women and girls are also manifest in Sarah Aaronsohn's legitimization in the women's press, where her biography began to appear in the second half of the 1940s. In one commemorative article published on the thirtieth anniversary of her death (1947) in the weekly magazine *La-Ishah* (literally, For the Woman) — which would become a prototype for writing about her in this press — Sarah's story served as a way of inverting a conventional gender fairy tale: the story of the rescued princess. This biographical article, entitled "Captain without Stars," completely reverses the customary image of the princess. Sarah is not rescued or saved by any of the men around her, but rather frees herself of them. She chooses to liberate herself from an unsatisfying marriage and the burden of home and family and becomes the "captain of her fate" as well as the captain of the underground.

As captain, she rejects the suggestion of her older brother, Aaron Aaronsohn, to escape in the British warship *Managem*, which had been sent to retrieve the activists in the espionage network. And as "captain" of her ship, she commits suicide.[65] It is precisely on a platform like the weekly women's magazine, which perpetuated cults of femininity and domesticity, that Aaronsohn's military behavior is portrayed not as a contradiction of feminine ideals but rather as a possibility for a correct gendered nationalist behavior. This kind of diffusion (and internalization) of the story of Nili raises doubts about the assumption, still widely accepted in the debate on memory, that centers and elites mold the national ethos by means of cultural hegemony and have an omnipotent power over collective memory. Memory became part of the everyday, here the everyday of women and girls. It developed in the arena outside the core of hegemony — outside the ceremonial and the distinctly political space of official rites of commemoration and in "sites" outside unifying systems with repressive powers. This very process serves as proof of the tenacity and durability of a gendered memory that is both marginal and peripheral.

1967: Into "the National Pantheon"?

In the debate on memory and identity in Israeli society, the year 1967 has the special status of an *annus mirabilis* (or, depending on the interlocutor's politics and ideology, an *annus horribilis*). It is generally described as heralding a profound change and as the beginning of an ongoing process of the disintegration of collective ethoses and of a uniform, hegemonic, and cohesive culture of memory. Above all, the period beginning in 1967 is associated with the process of the "privatization of memory" and its expropriation from the nation and from national needs to groups and individuals within the nation.[66] However, an examination of the evolution of the memory of Sarah Aaronsohn as a gendered process may change our perspective on the broader changes in Israeli culture and society as well as on the relationship between periphery and "center" within the national community.

The year 1967 indeed represents a surfeit of memory and commemoration; but, in contrast to the practices of the 1930s and 1940s, the commemorations of the fiftieth anniversary of the death of Sarah Aaronsohn were marked by her appropriation into the mainstream ethos and consensus and her consolidation as a popular figure. Along with these developments, there also occurred a perceptible change in her status as a heroine. These changes were related, of course, to the political and cultural changes of the times. The Six-Day War, with the arrogance that followed in its wake, happened to occur in the fiftieth anniversary year of the eradication of Nili. It was in this year that Sarah Aaronsohn first received official state recognition by the representatives of the hegemonic and ruling Labor movement culture. In 1967, the men and women members of the Nili underground who had been killed were recognized as soldiers in uniform who had died in action, and those who had survived were decorated with the "Nili Medal." That same year, the bones of Avshalom Feinberg were discovered by chance and brought to burial in a full military ceremony. In tandem with these events, the first official state ceremony was held at the grave of Sarah Aaronsohn in Zikhron Yaakov.

In the memorial ceremonies conducted between 1967 and the death in 1981 of Rivkah Aaronsohn, Sarah's younger sister and the force behind her local commemoration, the local Zikhron Yaakov tradition and the state tradition intermingled in the annual pilgrimage to Sarah's grave. The revised syncretic ceremony had a clear feminine element: Members of the Bnot Brit Organization of Zikhron Yaakov gathered together with women from the adjacent *moshavot*, many of whom had been active in the Bnot Binyamin Federation, the women's equivalent of Bnei Binyamin.[67] They gathered in the Aaronsohn family home before the public ceremony and marched to Sarah's grave, led by Rivkah Aaronsohn.

Such signs that the peripheral memory was penetrating the central and official tradition were not restricted to the ceremonies. The peripheral memory was legitimized in the gender discourse within the Labor movement itself. Already in November 1967, after the jubilee ceremony, Rachel Katzenelson, editor of *Dvar ha-Po'elet* (Word of the Woman Worker), the flagship magazine of women's activity in the movement, published a lead article on Sarah Aaronsohn in which she described Aaronsohn as the first *Tzabarit* (female Sabra) and a national heroine. More important, she also settled accounts with the leadership of the *Yishuv* during World War I and with the pre-state and Israeli Labor leadership on the suppression of the story of the Nili heroine. Katzenelson even called for reburying Aaronsohn — metaphorically, of course — in the state pantheon:

> From now own, she shall belong not only to the national pantheon of the re-newed Eretz Israel[!]. She shall also be incorporated into the innermost soul of the nation. . . . So, now, after some fifty years of silencing, they win the recognized title of admired heroes of the nation, a model for coming generations. Indeed, Sarah's home in Zikhron Yaakov still remains something of a "private national museum," a family heirloom, administered as a national asset and serving as a sanctified site for mass pilgrimages, by the young and old of all kinds.[68]

Katznelson's sermon undoubtedly was inspired by political motives. As one of the founders of the Livneh group, the first adherents of the idea of Greater Israel in the Labor movement, Katznelson may have been attracted to the territorialism and political activism of the heroes of the "native" culture in general and of Sarah Aaronsohn in particular. But a narrow biographical-political explanation does not suffice here, as Aaronsohn and Nili were rehabilitated within the Labor movement as a whole, and not only in its Greater Israel circles. Even before Katznelson's article, *Davar*, the Labor daily and the most authoritative platform of official discourse, had devoted some columns to the debate on Sarah Aaronsohn and her actions. In October through December 1967, the newspaper published a series of articles, by writers of both the Revisionist right and the Labor movement, on the Nili affair, the attitude toward the underground, and the association between this attitude and the formation of the collective memory. Yehuda Slutsky claimed that the "Nili group" was "from a social and historical perspective . . . the first sign of independent political activity on the part of the 'Sabra'." He saw Nili as a reflection of the native-born hero Yoash, "the new Jew of Eretz Yisrael" in the story by this name by Joseph Luidor (1912). Slutsky, who evidently was not a member of the Labor movement, portrayed Aaronsohn as a moral authority and as "the first link in the chain of the fallen for the establishment of the State of Israel."[69] However, the fact that his voice was heard from a platform such as *Davar* is evidence of the change in Labor's attitude toward this chapter in the history of the *Yishuv*. Nonetheless, one of the responses to the article leveled criticism at the attempt—attributed to the right, but also to voices identified with the Labor movement—to "falsify our history" and to include in it persons, like Nili members, who harmed the security of the *Yishuv.*[70]

The debate on the death and memory of Aaronsohn thus became, at one and the same time, a negotiation over her inclusion in the official national ideology and a discourse on the development of the nationalist memory of Labor itself—her exclusion in the past from this discourse, on the one hand, and the integration of different kinds of heroic ethos into the discourse, on the other. Katzenelson, for example, found it necessary to compare Sarah Aaronsohn to "the female workers" and female socialist settlers of the Second Aliyah, Manya Shochat and Dvorah Dayan. Dayan, who was perceived as one of the female saints of pioneer Labor settlement, was the mother of a national Sabra icon, Moshe Dayan.[71]

The rehabilitation of the memory of Sarah Aaronsohn, and the efforts to bring her memory to bear on the history and ethos of Hebrew labor and settlement did not impair her appeal as a popular, and not necessarily political, heroine. In contrast to the memory of Trumpeldor and the myth of Tel Hai, the memory of Aaronsohn and Nili survived outside clearly political and official sites of memory. In fact, the single most important feature of the narratives of her heroism fashioned after 1967 was the depoliticization of her national activity. Depoliticization was accompanied by another crucial change: Aaronsohn's feminization—an emphasis on the feminine and domestic essence of her activities, on the one hand, and the sexualization of these activities, or her representation as a product of the relations between the sexes and sometimes as a product of female identity and sexuality, on the other hand. Whereas before 1967, and especially before 1948, there had been a concerted effort to blur Aaronsohn's sexuality and the gender boundaries of her activities, after 1967, she was pushed to the margins of the story of Nili, while efforts were made to include her in the national pantheon. Her involvement in national affairs was interpreted as the outcome of her position in her family and in the extended "family" of the Nili underground.

These two changes, occurring simultaneously, are especially striking in the shaping of Aaronsohn's image as a "historical" and didactic heroine for juveniles. Nili gradually made its way into the curriculum of the mainstream state school system as well as into the special curricula of the kibbutz movement. From the second half of the 1960s, the moralizing position regarding Nili's activities was almost totally abandoned, and discussion of Nili was no longer political. At the same time, Sarah Aaronsohn's role in the underground was rarely mentioned, while the deeds of the men were discussed in great detail. She was rendered mostly in terms of her familial and gender affiliations: as the younger sister of Aaron, "father" of the underground, and as a loyal daughter. This feminization of her image is striking, for example, in the second edition of *The History of the People of Israel in Our Generation* by Shimshon Leib Kirshenbaum (1965), in the nine editions of his book *The History of Israel in Recent Generations* published between 1968 and 1973 as well as in *A Brief History of Israel in Recent Times*, by Shlomo Horowitz, which was used by teachers and pupils of the Reali High School in Haifa (1973).[72]

Sarah's marginality is also manifest in the guidelines for teachers put out by the Curricula Division of Ha-Kibbutz ha-Artzi, the kibbutz movement of the left-wing Ha-Shomer ha-Tza'ir. These guidelines stipulated that the Nili affair was to be taught in the movement's schools by means of reenactment games with the triple aim of first, "encouraging the consideration of and thinking about Nili as a social-historical group"; second, rousing debate "on the moral image of Ha-Shomer" and of the Labor movement in general, given the history of Nili and their treatment of this organization; and third, "expressing feelings and opinions about concepts such as 'the politically persecuted'." In the detailed quiz that accompanied the program, Sarah was mentioned only marginally and characterized by the gendered trait of "nobility" (described as a feminine quality), rather than by her actions or ideas.[73]

It is difficult to assess the influence of these schoolbooks on different juvenile readerships. It is easier to appraise the distribution and impact of texts such as *Sarah giborat Nili* (Sarah, Heroine of Nili) by Devorah Omer, which contributed more than any other book to spreading the memory and myth of Aaronsohn as a heroine for young people and as a model of *Eretz Yisraeli*-ness. Between 1967, when it was published, and 1990, the book went through twenty-five printings, and between 1970 and 2000 it sold 88,009 copies. It was a "steady seller," its sales never falling beneath 1,500 copies or rising above 3,300 copies a year.[74] In the wake of its success, Omer wrote a play with the same title, which ran for fifteen consecutive years at the Theater for Children and Youth. The book deserves special note since it was the first monograph written for children on Sarah Aaronsohn and Nili, a subject that until then, as already noted, had been treated only in the children's and juvenile press of the periphery. Moreover, the book is a clear example of the penetration of spontaneous and apolitical popular memory into the hegemonic mythology of *Eretz Yisraeli* heroism, and also of the complex relationship between dominant, official myths and those evolving in the periphery. A test case of this set of relationships between the center and periphery in Israeli culture, the success of *Sarah giborat Nili* raises questions about the power of establishments or of so-called "central agents of culture." Moreover, the book also encapsulates the changes, noted above, in the relationship between gender and identity: that is, the feminization of the female national "hero," on the one hand, and the integration of this "hero" into an epic national narrative, on the other hand.

The book, like *Ha-No'azim* (The Audacious) series of which it was a part, was the brain-child of the educator, editor, and writer Uriel Ofek, who suggested it to Omer as an "educational story."[75] The very view of Sarah Aaronsohn as a model "educational figure" was totally new, since, until then, the activities of Nili and Aaronsohn had not been deemed "educating" or even as properly nationalist, outside Civic circles.

For Omer, who had been raised in a kibbutz and was identified, like Ofek, with the Labor movement and with the mainstream culture, Sarah Aaronsohn was a political and sexual adventuress. Omer and Ofek felt a need to provide young people with literature that would rescue "stories of *Eretz Yisraeli* heroism" from oblivion.[76] Thus the *Ha-Noazim* series, which included canonical figures such as Hannah Senesh and Manya Shochat, also made room for peripheral figures like Sarah Aaronsohn, the pugilist and spiritualist Raphael Halperin, and Etzel terrorist/freedom fighter Dov Gruner. Not only was the book not published on the initiative of the establishment; it was not supported by it either. It was brought out by the small, politically unaffiliated Sherberk publishing house.[77] Yet it received no funding from the "local" commemorative apparatus based in Zikhron Yaakov, under the direction of Rivkah Aaronsohn, who helped finance a number of hagiographies of Sarah Aaronsohn and other Nili figures that were published from the 1930s. Rivkah Aaronsohn cooperated with Omer only after the book had proven a success, and even tried (with little success) to interfere in how her sister's image would be shaped, attempting to remove details that undermined Sarah's asexual image, such as the descriptions of her in the company of Turkish and German officers.[78]

The book's indisputable success led to its adoption both by the educational establishment and by the local memorial center. From the early 1970s onward, the Ministry of Education ordered numerous copies of the book through projects such as "A Book for Every Home" and "The Literature Fund for the Children of Israel." From 1970, about ten thousand copies of *Sarah giborat Nili* (5,009 of them in 1970 alone) were produced for the Ministry of Education.[79] At the same time, the book's success also transformed the Beit Aaronsohn Museum into a flourishing center, especially for schoolchildren. As early as 1970, it was visited by pupils from the very sectors that in the past had excluded Sarah Aaronsohn and Nili from the collective memory and youth culture: namely, the kibbutzim and the Labor-affiliated agricultural settlements.[80]

It may seem that the Sarah Aaronsohn in the 1967 version is the focus of Omer's novel and of the newly defined memory of Nili's heroic deeds. She bestows her name on the novel; indeed, the novel itself is the first *Bildungsroman* about a young *Eretz Yisraeli* girl. Without doubt, Omer had intended to tell the historical story from a female perspective. She preferred to narrate the epic of Sabra-ness through the figure of Sarah Aaronsohn and not through that of Avshalom Feinberg precisely "because she was a woman, and I could identify with her better" and because women were absent from [Israel's] history and youth culture.[81]

In addition, Omer's version of Sarah's life is in no way domestic. It is a story of adventures and heroism, a "thriller," in the words of the boy listening to the narrator in the "outer" story that frames the inner plot of World War I heroism. Sarah is apparently a "hero." She possesses the traits of the non-essentialist woman, who is not a mother: physical prowess and the skills of a scout and warrior and horsemanship.[82] She and her younger sister Rivkah are even included in the quasi-military activities of the Gidonim (in fact, the Gidonim had excluded women and girls).[83]

However, this narrative of national political activity is undermined and even canceled out by a separate, albeit parallel, narrative. This is the story of one woman's personal drama, in which the personal engenders the political act in an almost deterministic way over which Sarah has no control. Sarah is driven to her activities for Eretz Yisrael through and by the men around her. "Girls don't fight, but you must know how to defend yourselves," her brother Alexander tells her. "It's good I was born a girl," Sarah declares. "I'm terrified of blood and afraid of every pain, even the tiniest."[84] And, elsewhere: "Only if she becomes a heroine will he [Avshalom] value her."[85] Sarah's death scene at the end of the book merges the feminine, essentialist narrative with memory itself: "I'm coming, Avshalom . . . Remember me, don't forget. . . ."[86]

From the Periphery to the National Pantheon

That the "legend of Sarah" took such a circuitous road from the periphery to the national pantheon of heroism clearly has a political reason and explanation. This chapter discussed the suppression of Sarah's death, and of the Nili affair itself, as well as the delayed evolution and peripheral nature of her memory. All these were undoubtedly outcomes of her political, social, and cultural affiliation with a group that was excluded from the hegemonic memory, and not the result of her gender. However, as the first part of the chapter argues, this political explanation is inadequate. For when the memory did evolve, it was distinctively gendered. It was shaped by different, and sometimes competing, perceptions of the national female-social identity. The survey offered here of these perceptions, of their dynamics, and of their representation in the dense fabric of memory may teach us some lessons that could prove useful for students of the history of memory, for those who map Israeli identity, and for historians of women and gender.

The first lesson concerns the dynamic and frequently changing presence of group — or collective — memory in culture and society. The memory of a voluntary death for the nation was shaped by the Labor movement establishment, as historians of the legend of Tel Hai and the story of Trumpeldor have shown. However, this memory was not homogenous, and not even hegemonic. Alongside this central and unifying myth, other memories also emerged in "cells" or sectors of civil society, in what is generally viewed as the cultural and political periphery. Moreover, these memories had begun to crystallize before the disintegration of the Labor hegemony and a long time before the processes that are conventionally described as the segmentation and disintegration of the Israeli national ethos. The alternative memory of Sarah Aaronsohn, which started off as a marginal and sectorial compound of rites and practices of remembrance memory and evolved into a popular memory, was crystallized precisely during that same period that is seen as the zenith of Labor hegemony and cultural domination. However, the Labor establishment did not have unchallenged control over the narrative of the past or the contents of memory; these were subjects of a continuous negotiation, in which individuals and groups outside the center (whether or not they were identified with specific political groups) took part. It is thus quite clear that "center" and "margins" or periphery are relative and complementary, rather than binary entities.

The second lesson, which is closely related to the first, concerns not only the periodization of the history of the particular memory studied here — or of Israeli memory more broadly — but also the periodization of *Eretz Yisraeli* and Israeli culture as a uniform and cohesive entity. In the historiography and study of Israeli culture in general, the collapse of cohesiveness is still associated with the emergence of the critique of the Zionist project voiced in the 1980s and 1990s as well as with the profound changes in Israel's social fabric after the 1960s. However, the example of Aaronsohn indicates that the sharp distinction between an "official" and central monolithic memory during the *Yishuv* era and the early years of the State, and the splitting and pluralization afterward, has little or no validity. Pluralism and the "polyphonic" chorus of memory characterized the discourse on Sarah Aaronsohn from the very beginning.

The third and most important lesson concerns the use of gender in the study of memory. This is considerably more than the mere "addition" of a forgotten historical female subject to a historical pantheon. It is an indispensable tool for analyzing nationalism and nationalist myths. It is also a valuable methodology, which provides us with additional — and perhaps new — understanding of the manner in which images and constructs of female identities formed the ways in which the past was remembered, represented, and commemorated.

Precisely the fact that Aaronsohn was commemorated as a figure embodying competing, and sometimes conflicting, images of femininity, whose interrelationships changed over time, reinforces her enduring image as a national heroine. Aaronsohn embodied the maternalist ideal of female patriotism but at the same time crossed the boundaries of femininity. She represented essentialized female features and secular Zionist ideals of femininity, but also Western Christian perceptions that had undergone processes of secularization and syncretization. Once again, the lack of compatibilities in gendered memory are apparent, the very contradictions within the national images of femininity and women, which cannot and need not be resolved. These "insoluble paradoxes" (Joan Wallach Scott's term) are saliencies of constructs of gender and of the definition of femininity in the modern nationalist age.[87] The paradoxes do not detract from the power of the myth, but strengthen it, as illustrated above. Significantly, the paradox of the maternal woman and the sexless soldier, which cohabit in the discourse on Sarah Aaronsohn, was especially pronounced in times of crises and transitions, for example in the 1930s and 1940s. Moreover, at such times, the female image also served as a metaphor, a tool, and as the locus of a discussion of the broader issues concerning individuals' and groups' relationship to Eretz Yisrael and *Eretz Yisraeli* identity.

Yet Aaronsohn's survival as a female icon of the nation well into the so-called post-Zionist era, also involved her transformation into a more conventional figure. From the late 1960s, with the rehabilitation of her memory, Aaronsohn's image became wholly essentialist. Paradoxically, the narrative of her heroism and death seeped into the narrative of sacrifice for the nation at the very same time as the story of her heroism was detached from the political and public sphere. As my analysis of the novel *Sarah giborat Nili* shows, the hierarchy between the political and the personal that character- ized the 1930s and 1940s was reversed in the depiction of the character of the *Eretz Yisraeli* heroine. The story is made by the personal drama of the *Eretz Yisraeli* woman; and the public and political are explained in terms of the personal and intimate.

This reversal is even more striking in the 1993 television drama *Sarah*, whose creators enjoyed liberties that Omer, as the writer of a book for chil- dren and adolescents, never had. The depoliticization of the myth and the sexualization of Sarah are reinforced in various ways: the script of the tele- drama, the contents of the introduction to the story, which is spoken in a male voice, visual images, props, dress and body language, and sentimental- romantic music. The new hierarchy is established in the polarities within the opening statement: "Sarah came to politics from love, and to love from politics." It is consistently reinforced through Sarah's appearances on screen, where camera shots of her face create a claustrophobic, domestic ambiance: in her tiny bedroom; in the kitchen, where she performs female chores like cooking and sewing; and on the balcony of the experimental agriculture sta- tion at Atlit, where she hangs out colored washing (to signal the British ship *Managem*), a shot that relays political and domestic meanings at one and the same time. Only for 2.39 minutes out of over 50 minutes of film is Aaronsohn seen in outdoor shots, in which she plays a secondary or passive role. In the opening and final scenes, which frame the story, the camera travels from her scarred and bloody legs to her unkempt hair, as she walks along the main street of Zikhron Yaakov. The historical Aaronsohn took care to tie up her hair, and various sources describe her walk from the interrogation room to her brother's house as proud and dignified. In the teledrama, neighbors re- gale her with shouts of "whore, whore. . . ."[88] There may be no sharper con- trast than that between this comparison of Aaronsohn to a prostitute in the early 1990s and the analogies to the Maid of Orléans in the 1940s.

We must be wary, however, of a simplistic and linear view of the gendered memory studied here that would describe it as a move from the periphery to the center, or from the right to the center, hence to the left. We must also be careful not to idealize the peripheral memory, for this will lead us to chart a decline in or a deviation from an original powerful image to one represent- ing powerlessness, thus delineating a process in which a memory that fea- tures an activity that crosses the boundaries of gender turns into an essential- ist and sexual memory. Such a reduction to a movement from Joan of Arc to the sexual Sarah ignores the complexity of the images during the two periods studied here, the "insoluble paradoxes" that characterize them. It may of course be argued that endowing Sarah Aaronsohn with masculine qualities and the rituals commemorating her as a "soldier" and as "Sarah, the [male] commander" actually reinforced inequality. For these images were shaped by political and military organizations that were highly patriarchal and excluded women from their activities. Yet it would be mistaken to reduce the blurring of gender boundaries to a manifestation of total repression or the silencing of women's voices. The emphasis on the absence of female sexuality, the erasure of the image of the "mother of the nation," and the blurring of gender — all these characterized native *Eretz Yisraeli* women's discourse until 1920. As I have shown in great detail elsewhere, the crossing of the borderlines of gender was particularly salient in the activities of Nili and those close to this group, and characterized the activities, writings and self-image of Sarah Aaronsohn herself.[89] In other words, the martial images that were so central to the commemorative rituals prior to the 1950s were not created by a "male elite." They were drawn from a reservoir of images and representations that were available to the men and women of the time, and especially to the men and women of the remembering group.

The appropriation of Aaronsohn's memory and her commemoration in the national pantheon, from the end of the 1960s, are closely related to an essentialist perception of women and femininity within the state. Nonetheless, this essentialism is not peculiar to the hegemonic culture or the so-called formal "agents" of this culture, but rather is conspicuous in feminist and postmodern interpretations of the female Zionist story, for example in Ben-Dor's and Landau's teledrama. The three lessons related here may tell us that gender and memory are closely intertwined and are quite inseparable — whether as subjects for research or as possibilities for analyzing national culture. If we acknowledge this, we shall perhaps be able to write a history that will allow a different and more complex interpretation of Israeliness, of national memory and of national amnesia than is available to us at the present.

☙   *Judith Baumel-Schwartz*

"We Were There Too"

Women's Commemoration in Israeli War Memorials

Introduction

This article deals with the tension between myth and reality, as reflected in the gender narrative arising from Israeli war memorials. This issue alludes to a wider one that will be touched upon only briefly here (in the hope of dealing with it more fully elsewhere): the connections among nationalism, space, militarism, and gender stereotypes, in developing countries in general and in Israel in particular.[1]

One of the places in which the national narrative is reflected in general, and its gender components in particular, is in the area of commemoration. Plastic commemoration is one of the accepted methods for granting an image or myth eternal life and passing it on to future generations. One of the prevalent myths commemorated plastically — in long-established countries as well as in new societies — is that of the "the brave soldier," tall, sturdy, and handsome, who expresses nationalist aspirations but does not always match the physical reality of the fighters. This is the case with the large statues erected to commemorate freedom fighters in Italy, or the famous statue by Nathan Rapaport in memory of the Warsaw Ghetto fighters, a copy of which is in Yad Vashem. To adapt the fighters both to the Zionist ideal and the ideal of the European fighter, Rapaport turned the thin, hungry Ghetto people into robust, muscular fighters. The aim of "beautifying" reality and adapting it to myth is more pronounced for everything connected to death: In plastic commemoration soldiers die a sterile death, without wounds, without drip-

This article was written as part of a research study sponsored by the Littauer Foundation and I wish to thank the foundation for the support it gave me.

ping in blood, without even a bullet's entry point. They are handsome, robust, admirable — the asthetics of death at its best.

Does the statement that the memorial is intended to perpetuate the myth and not necessarily reality also apply to the images of women that appear in the commemoration of men and women who died while on active military service for the State of Israel? And if so, what are the myths — or ethoses — that this commemoration wishes to nurture in relation to Israeli women? How does the gender image, literal and figurative, ascertained through commemoration of the fallen, mesh with the role intended for women in the developing Israeli society? In what way does the woman's image in the area of commemoration contribute to gender construction in Israel? To answer these questions, I will first present the state of plastic commemoration in Israel and I will propose a typology of repeated feminine motifs. Then I will discuss the cultural roots of these motifs and I will treat the question of their generational development. All of this will be done while comparing the military and civilian roles of women, in different periods in the *Yishuv* and the State, with their gender and biological reflection in memorials and monuments erected in memory of Israeli military dead. Finally, I will ask in which ways the gender commemoration of fallen men and women reflects the status of women in changing Israeli society in general and in Israel military society in particular, and to what extent this contributes to a new delineation of this status.

Memorials Commemorating Fallen Soldiers in the State of Israel

Modern research considers memorials an array of symbols through which one may examine the culture and ideological system of a society.[2] Like any "text," one must read plastic commemoration within the "context" in which it is located, which is the interrelationship between the body commissioning the work, the body executing the work, and the viewers. Similarly, the range of plastic commemoration teaches us a great deal about the essence of a society. The State of Israel constitutes a special field of study for this matter, owing to the large number of memorials, of all types, scattered throughout the country.[3]

For this study I reviewed over nine hundred memorials that had been erected up to 1998 and that appear on the listing of the Defense Ministry's Unit for Soldier Commemoration. Of them, twenty-seven are connected in some way to women: Some of them commemorate only women, others commemorate both men and women, and a third group commemorates men but has a female figure appearing in it. Most of them memorialize male and female soldiers; a few were put up in the name of civilian victims of war or terrorist attacks. Sixteen of those with women figures, or 60 percent, are figurative, while figurative commemoration is used only in 13 percent of all Israeli military memorials. One possible explanation is the fact that most of the memorials with women were erected up to the 1970s, a period in which the figurative trend was at its height. Another explanation derives from the distinctiveness of the feminine image in the masculine sector, a distinctiveness that requires, as it were, prominent literal or figurative expression. It is difficult to connect this fact with the sex of the artist, since only four of the twenty-seven memorials under discussion were planned by women.

Although female figures are found in memorials commemorating men who fell within military frameworks in Israel — and not only in those commemorating female soldiers or mixed groups — the percentage of military memorials erected to memorialize women, that mention women in their text, or that portray female images mirrors the percent of women soldiers who lost their lives while on active duty. Defense ministry figures from 31 January 1998 show that out of a total of 20,298 soldiers who lost their lives since the early days of pre-State Israel, 704 (or 3.5 percent) were women. Twenty-seven of the 900 memorials (3 percent) mention women or portray a female image, while 2 percent of all military memorials were dedicated to the memory of women who fell in battle, were murdered in terrorist attacks or hostile acts, or were killed in accidents. There are also a few memorials in which there is a mention of women in textual but not in figurative expression. Chronologically, the largest number of memorials that refer to women or in which the figure of a woman appears are in memory of victims of the War of Independence; this was the only war in which women fought in the front lines and the one that claimed the largest number of female casualties in any Israeli war. Yet, the percentage of female soldiers who have been killed among all military victims has been rising gradually since the First Lebanon War in 1982, and especially since the outbreak of the first intifada (1987), as most were victims of terrorist attacks and accidents, which for the most part are not gender-related. These statistics, which change frequently as a result of the deaths of additional male and female soldiers — caused by combat, hostile acts, accidents, and illnesses — are not absolute and are intended to provide the reader with a general idea of the reference to women in memorials and monuments to Israel soldiers.[4]

Women in the Defense Force and the Israel Defense Force (IDF)

Israel is the only country in the world that conscripts women for mandatory military service. Since the War of Independence the socialist ideology of sexual equality and the pre-State tradition in which men and women shared all military tasks gave birth to the image of the fighting woman soldier who takes her place alongside the armed men. Studies that have appeared in recent years show that in actuality, even in the days of ostensible "equality," that is, in the time of the Haganah and the Palmah, the status of women in the defense force was very complex. Since the establishment of Bar Giora, in the early days of Sejera (1907), women have taken part in guard duty, but this did not become the norm and remained limited to the very few.[5] In the Haganah, groups of women trained for duty as officers and even a Gedud ha-Banot ha-Lohamot (Legion of Fighting Girls) was founded under the command of Shoshana Gestetner-Wilensky and Hana Sternfeld. Yet, most of the women were not trained for combat but rather were integrated into the military support system of nursing and communication.[6]

The creation of the Palmah in May 1941 triggered a series of debates over whether women should be trained for battle or auxiliary tasks. A turning point occurred in 1944, when the *haksharot* joined the Palmah, raising the percentage of women from 10 percent to 30 percent among all those mobilized. The high point of women participating in combat roles at that time was during the campaign to send paratroopers to Europe in the spring of 1944, when three Palmah women participated. Two of them — Hannah Szenes and Havivah Reik — lost their lives after being captured by the enemy.[7]

Most of the local women who enlisted in the British army during World War II did so within the more common frameworks. In addition to the above mentioned Palmah women, volunteers from the *Yishuv* served in the British women's auxiliary forces (A.T.S.) and nearly six hundred more in the British air force (R.A.F.). Women soldiers served as wireless operators, clerical staff, radar operators, photographers, parachute inspectors, truck and ambulance drivers, mechanics, nurses, and medical orderlies. Aside from a few exceptions, women did not take part in combat.

At the end of World War II, the Palmah was the largest military framework in which *Yishuv* women could participate. Between the end of the Second World War and the beginning of the War of Independence, a period in which the Palmah changed from being a British military framework into an underground organization, women in the Palmah engaged in four types of roles: *operational* — duties such as manning battle stations, engaging in open warfare, and accompanying convoys; *professional* activity — in the fields of communication, nursing, medicine, and quartermastering; *administrative* tasks — working as regimental adjutancy clerks and division secretaries; and *instructional* — training for field maneuvers, sport, and weaponry. These roles were supposed to train women to take their place within the military framework that would be set up upon the establishment of an independent Jewish entity in Eretz Israel. Three female Haganah members even completed a flight course and served as pilots, but in the War of Independence, it was decided that they would not participate actively in combat for fear they would fall into captivity.[8]

The War of Independence was the last war in which women actively participated in combat, in line with the tradition already set in the Palmah days. After a woman soldier's body was mutilated near kibbutz Gevulot early in the war, the Israeli High Command decided to remove women soldiers from the front lines and forbid them from participating in future battles. The compulsory nature of the IDF draft as opposed to the voluntary nature of the Haganah and the Palmah also prevented the integration of women in combat roles. Finally, the first women officers in the IDF had received their training in the British army where women were not permitted in battle, strengthening the reversal of gender policy. Even tasks that had been open to women in the British army, such as driving heavy vehicles, were forbidden to them in the IDF — so they would not be placed in the front lines during war. Consequently, by the mid-1970s, only 150 military classifications were open to women in the IDF, as opposed to 571 which were available to women serving at that time in the American army. Today, some 500 military classifications are accessible to women serving in the IDF, of which 100 are reserved for officers.[9]

The ways in which women were integrated into military frameworks prior to the establishment of the state and the motives for doing so are reminiscent of a common pattern that characterizes many developing societies in the throes of an intense or ongoing national struggle. In many Third World countries, even among those that had not had any egalitarian, socialist tradition, many women joined the national struggle as a way to free themselves from the double bonds of servitude from their standing as women and their colonialist status.[10] Even in Western countries, such as Ireland during the days of national struggle, the differentiation between the public and the private sphere became blurred, similar to the situation in Palestine in the 1940s during the struggle against the British. This process enabled women to join the gender-related discourse of the war, which simultaneously reinforced their traditional role while upsetting the social equilibrium and ruining the stability of these functions.[11] The dissonance between the two elements provides a partial explanation for the change that occurred in the role of women in Israel, in the national discourse in general and in the military framework in particular, after the establishment of the state. As a continuation to Nira Yuval-Davis's determination of the five ways in which women participate in ethnic and national processes in civilian society, it seems that removing women from combat roles in the IDF, and transferring them to solely auxiliary jobs, was a stage in turning them into "mothers of the nation," "the biological production house of the members of the ethnic collective," as she says. By means of ensuring the masculine nature of most of the activist military functions, it was possible to reinforce the role of the woman as biological childbearer, as the cultural reinforcer, as the arbiter of the limits of national groups, and as a symbol in the ideological discourse in the construction of ethnic groups. Only after the woman has taken her place in these four areas, states Yuval-Davis, can she integrate into her fifth role in developing countries: taking part in the national, economic, political, and especially — in the military struggle of the new state.[12]

Typology of Images

Although most of the women in the IDF served as auxiliaries, for several decades the collective public memory retained the original image of the fighting woman soldier. This image, particularly with regard to the War of Independence was reinforced in fiction and autobiography, such as in the books by Netiva Ben-Yehudah and Tamar Avidar.[13] How were the public image of women in the IDF and the reality behind it translated into military memorials? We can identify six types of women that recur in figurative memorials:

1. **Combat soldiers and frontliners.** The principle of sexual equality and the pre-State policy of allowing women into combat moulded an image of women combatants in the collective public memory. One would therefore expect a plethora of the fighters in Israeli plastic commemoration, particularly in that appearing in the wake of the War of Independence. Yet, only two combat women appear in Israeli iconography: One is in the statue by Batya Lishansky in Kefar Yehoshua (from the years 1949–1953), and the other is in a relief by Aharon Priver at kibbutz Tel Yosef (1955). Contrary to Levinger's

determination that only Lishansky gave the woman a role equal to that of the man, it turns out that the initiator of the memorial in Kefar Yehoshua and the person who proposed the model was precisely a man, Menahem Zaharoni, the teacher of local residents who fell in 1948. No Kefar Yehoshua girls were killed, but they did go to fight together with the boys, so it was obvious that they would appear on the memorial. Two young women from Tel Yosef were killed in 1948, and they are commemorated in Priver's memorial.[14]

The image of the female fighter no longer appears in memorials erected after 1953. So it appears that descriptions of female fighting found only a minor echo in plastic commemoration, even in those memorials erected not long after the war ended. As women's combat activities during the War of Independence were limited to specific sectors and were not a widespread phenomenon, their plastic commemoration appears to have been more faithful to reality than the literary image or myth of women's military equality, which never really achieved large-scale practical expression.

2. The auxiliary. A second group of figures assist the fighters by providing support in the field of medical care and communication. The female auxiliary appears in three memorials erected in the memory of soldiers who lost their lives in the War of Independence and does not recur in later ones. In Nitzanim and Tel Yosef, where female fighters fell, the figure is a young woman kneeling next to a wounded soldier and proffering assistance. The third auxiliary is part of Nathan Rapoport's monumental tableau at kibbutz Negba (1953) portraying an armed soldier flanked by male and female figures. Initially the muscular woman appears to be a combat soldier (in an article that appeared in Kol Negbah in October 1953, she is called "a fighting comrade"), but in truth she is a medic carrying a first-aid kit. Even though the auxiliary and nursing roles of women reached the IDF from the British army, these memorials are not at all reminiscent of the British memorials erected in memory of the nurses and auxiliary staff who lost their lives during the First and Second World Wars. Those images usually take the form of a nurse or suffice with a textual mention—a list of names that appears beneath the memorial cross.[15]

As most female soldiers both during the War of Independence and throughout the history of the IDF served as auxiliaries, one might assume that this would be the most prominent figure to appear in Israeli military memorials. The fact that only three female auxiliaries appear in over nine hundred such memorials teaches us how little impact this image had on the collective Israeli public memory of women in military settings, even though it reflects the most prevalent historical reality of the roles women played within military frameworks in Israel, even during the War of Independence. The combat and auxiliary images are the only ones in plastic commemoration that reflect women soldiers in any military role. In contradistinction to the male soldier, who also appears as a single figure in a memorial, the combat and auxiliary female soldier always appears in a group. In this, Israel differs from Britain and the United States, where a female image appearing in the role of auxiliary force occurs as a single figure, such as in the memorial to the U.S. soldiers who fell in World War II in the Pacific region, in which one finds the figure of the nurse looking off to the distance. The explanation for that may be cultural, ideological, or even practical: Perhaps the difference between the Israeli pattern to that seen elsewhere derives from the strong collective awareness of Israeli society, from the feeling common in Israel that a woman has no right to independent existence within a military framework, or from the fact that since the Palmah period the IDF has not created any units of fighting women or any an active auxiliary force consisting only of women.[16]

It seems that the toning down (and even the disappearance) of the female soldier from the dominant Israeli culture seems to be connected with a two-dimensional, or even machoistic conception that dominated Israeli society for decades regarding the essence and purpose of the Israeli army (as exemplified in the slogan "the best men [should belong] to the air force and the best women [should belong] to the pilots." In a culture that equated the term "army" solely with a fighting corps, female soldiers, barred from combat status since the War of Independence, carried little weight. Hence, they were also excluded from figurative military commemoration, and barely any place in textual commemoration, as their deaths almost always occurred in non-combat situations, such as accidents. This dichotomy also had given semantic expression. Although the military inscriptions on tombstones were determined by the way the male or female soldier had lost their lives, regardless of their sex, a different tradition became entrenched in practice. In contrast to the male soldier, about whom it was customary to say that "he fell in the line of duty" — even if he had been killed in circumstances other than combat — people usually said about a female soldier that "she was killed during her military service." In recent years, this concept has changed, in light of the transformations in Israeli society regarding the army and because of the large number of male and female soldiers murdered in terrorist attacks. Still, this change is not yet expressed figuratively in commemoration of those in uniform, perhaps because of religious radicalization; it has prevented Israeli society from again adopting the figurative genre, which of late has returned to popularity in the Western world, particularly in Europe. An exception in this respect is Maya Lin's Vietnam War memorial, designed as a wall of remembrance. Elsewhere, especially in France, one can again see the erection of monuments bearing the figure of man as part of the process of his artistic return in many fields.

3. **Young mothers.** This is the most common figurative image of women appearing in plastic commemoration. At times it represents a real mother, such as in Hannah Orloff's 1952 statue at Ein Gev of a mother holding a baby in the air, erected in memory of Hannah Touchman-Adlerstein, a kibbutz mother who lost her life during the 1948 war. In other instances, such as David Paulus's 1949 statue at Ramat Rahel of a woman holding a torch and protecting two small children, she symbolizes the motherland. Even in the original cast of the Negba statue, which had six figures rather than three, one of them was a young mother embracing an infant.[17] During the War of Independence, the image of the fallen mother was more fitting to civilian reality than military: Only two of the war's female military casualties (1.5 percent of all women who died in the war) were mothers while 170 of the female civilian victims (about 47 percent) were mothers.[18] The motif of the young mother appears in later memorials, too, such as the one from 1965 by Matanya Abramson in *moshavah* Kineret and that by sculptor Rivka Keren, "United Family," in Kefar Yovel in memory of a terrorist act that occurred in 1975. The most unusual image of a young mother is a woman in early pregnancy who is also the mother of a soldier that appears in the Givatayim memorial to the fallen (erected 1978), and we shall return to this subject later.

4. **Older mothers.** The older mother who sends her son to war, a common image figure in European iconography, appears in only two Israeli memorials. One is in that by Nathan Rapoport in Be'er Tuviah (from 1975), and the other, from the early 1970s, is by Mordecai Kafri at Balfouriyyah.[19] It is not surprising that this motif is missing in memorials erected soon after the 1948 war. Despite the fact that one of the hit plays of those days was Nathan Shaham's, *Hem yaggi'u mahar* (They Will Arrive Tomorrow), about a mother who sends her son to his death, and one of the best-selling books of the time was Moshe Shamir's *Hu halakh ba-sadot* (He Walked in the Fields) that describes the system of relations between a mother in the kibbutz and her son the soldier, a large number of soldiers had immigrated from Europe without parents, while others were Holocaust survivors (40 percent of those killed in 1948 were survivors as opposed to 20 percent in the general population) who

were war orphans. Consequently, the image of a mother sending her son off to war was irrelevant to many of those participating in the War of Independence.[20] Moreover, in the days when "the entire country is the front," mothers were often part of the defense system, so it was difficult to speak of a mother sending her son to battle as if she was not involved at all in what was happening. Only after the generational metamorphosis occurring between the Sinai Campaign and the Six-Day War, and the sociocultural changes that occurred in their wake, could one totally separate combatants from the civilians and depict a mother sending her son off to war like the mythological mother in Sparta — who tells her son to return with his shield or on his shield, meaning, be victorious or die in battle. The contrast between the diminutive elderly mother in a long gown and the young, bare-chested son the soldier embracing her with one hand and holding his weapon in the other, is clearly expressed in Rapoport's statue.

   5. **Weeping women.** Weeping women, or more precisely mothers mourning their sons, constitute another common motif in memorials in European iconography. In Israel, this motif appears three times: in the 1954 statue by Aaron Ashkenazi at kibbutz Revadim in honor of the Gush Etzion victims; in the Faigin memorial in Haifa, executed in 1974, in which a mother is kneeling at the feet of her fallen son; and in the 1979 marble plaque at moshav Kefar Yehoshua designed by Batya Lishansky after the Yom Kippur War. The same artist, Lishansky, had been identified, thirty years earlier, in collective public memory with the images of women fighters. Since military monuments are intended to serve as a kind of gravestone for the bereaved families, the motif of the weeping mother seems at first glance quite natural; but apparently the contrast between the figure of the weeping mother, who symbolizes giving in to tragedy, and the Zionist ethos of parents standing firm in the face of bereavement, prevented most of the early designers of memorials from utilizing this image.
   The appearance of older and particularly weeping mothers in Israeli iconography from the 1950s on has a sociocultural significance beyond the expression of personal bereavement. The inclusion of these images in military commemoration indicates the perpetual existence of a popular immigrant culture that allowed mothers (and at times fathers) publicly and vocally to mourn the death of their children. Simultaneously it was a first indication of the psychological transformation that was about to occur in all of Israeli society from the 1970s onward, when the first cracks in the heroic national and personal façade regarding the treatment of bereavement began to show.

6. The virgin. The virgin, and particularly the fighting virgin based on the pagan tradition of Artemis and later Christian tradition of Joan of Arc, frequently appears in European Christian iconography. In Israel, the image of the innocent maiden is found only once, in a commemorative relief created in 1970 by Gershon Kinspel at the Kefar Gallim agricultural school depicting a teenage boy and girl carrying sheaves of wheat and flowers. The interweaving of the motif of innocence and pastorality suits both the time — an agricultural school and the years between the Six-Day War and the Yom Kippur War when many Israelis lived in hope that active combat had become an issue of the past.

Several gender motifs are striking in their absence. The first is a pietà-like image of a mother holding her dead son, common in both Western and Eastern European military iconography. It is difficult to know if the abstention from presenting an image similar to the Christian *Pietà* stems from Judeo-traditional or psychological reasons. Equally absent is the wounded female soldier, even though the figure of the wounded male soldier does appear in many memorials. This applies to European memorials: One of the few places in which a wounded woman appears is among the sculpted figures by Fritz Kremer and Willy Lammert at the Ravensbrück concentration camp in Germany. Perhaps it comes from the cultural aversion to confronting the reality of female war casualties, even though this phenomenon did, of course, actually occur, mainly in the War of Independence.[21]

Factors Influencing Israeli Military Commemoration

To understand the typology presented here, one must analyze it against the background of the specific factors influencing commemoration in Israel. In contrast to most countries in which the iconographic system refers to time-bound events or to a number of wars separated by decades or more, it seems that Israeli memorialization is a dense, continuous, ongoing process that began prior to the establishment of the state and has gone on to the present. From Melnikoff's "Roaring Lion" in memory of the defenders of Tel Hai (1934) — the first Israeli memorial to list women casualties and whose original cast was a female form — to the memorial at the Ashkelon junction in memory of the female soldier, Hofit Ayyash, who was murdered in a terrorist attack in 1996, Israeli iconography consists of an ongoing, developing system of images that reflects the changing attitude toward an interaction between the variables of gender and the military. No similar developing continuum of memorial imagery appears elsewhere, as plastic commemoration in most countries reflects a static-retrospective view of women and/or female combatants through a prism of a specific war.

Religious dictates are a second factor influencing Israeli commemorative iconography. From the medieval period onward, Jewish religious prohibitions stemming from a broad interpretation of the commandment "You shall not make for yourself a sculptured image, or any likeness" (Exodus 20:4) eradicated any traces of figurative iconography in the cultural sphere.[22] Consequently it is not surprising that close to 90 percent of the figurative memorials in which women appear are found in secular *moshavim* or kibbutzim, which did not feel themselves curtailed by religious cultural prohibitions of this sort. It is also clear why these memorials — erected in settlements where only a pure Israeli identity could be considered suitable to commemorate military casualties — bear no religious imagery. An exception to this rule is the military memorial in Givatayim, which has both religious and gender elements: a mother in her first pregnancy, a grandfather in *tallit* (prayer shawl) and *tefillin* (phylacteries), a grandson who is looking forward toward the horizon and going off to battle (and to his death), and a wall with letters in Rashi script.[23]

The dynamics surrounding the design of a memorial and the dialog between artist and viewer bring me to a final point: the historical sources of Israeli military commemoration. "Memory is not created in a vacuum," writes James Young, in his book *The Texture of Memory*, and its plastic expression is rooted in various iconographic traditions.[24] One must not forget the Judeo-cultural context of the images I mentioned — Rachel lamenting her children, Deborah the valiant prophet, Hannah and her seven sons, and so on — but the lack of any regular tradition of figurative iconography in both Judaism and the *Yishuv*, except for the few exception noted (Melnikoff, Lishansky) point us toward another cultural context: the European.

Most of the motifs I have cited are well rooted in some European cultural tradition: religious, ideological, artistic, or historical. When searching for the roots of Israeli iconography, one must, therefore, keep in mind European iconography, in both Western and, especially, Eastern Europe.

Conclusion

"Landscapes are culture before they are nature," claims Simon Schama in *Landscape and Memory*; "constructs of the imagination projected onto wood and water and rock."[25] An observer of the Israeli commemorative landscape will find it defies it to recover a single collective memory of either female military casualties or gender images that is embodied in Israeli commemorative culture. Instead one finds a developing continuum of images that reflects the emotional and physical maturation process of the young state and even sheds light on the construction and transformation of Israeli gender identity over the course of fifty years. From the image of the female combatant, the only type in evidence before 1948, which disappeared in the Israeli reality after the establishment of the state, there was a shift in the early 1950s to the image of the auxiliary and the young mother; this symbolizes not only the dozens of mothers who were killed in the War of Independence, both soldiers and civilians, but also the homeland and the hope of continuity. As one progresses chronologically from the period in which women played an active role in military and civil defense, the auxiliaries and young mothers fade away and are replaced by images that represent the passive role relegated to most Israeli women from the Sinai Campaign onward: older, weeping mothers, sacrificing their children for the motherland. The same image was chosen to commemorate male and female soldiers alike, the woman who supplies fighters for the nation from the imperative of her biological function and who mourns their death—for only a mother can mourn in public—by gendered privilege. From this point onward the elderly mother image remains dominant in Israeli commemorative iconography until figurative images disappear at the end of the 1980s.

Beyond reflecting the military and civilian process of the disappearance of female combatants, the dwarfing of the position of the auxiliaries, and the transition to the mothers, the transformation of the female image in plastic commemoration alludes to three wide-ranging processes that have left their mark on Israeli society from the establishment of the state until the present. The first is a process of genderization and retreat from the egalitarian-socialist ethos, conveyed in the figurative commemoration of female military casualties and particularly in the transition from the image of the female combatant and auxiliary to that of the mother. In removing women soldiers from combat roles—and thus also from Israeli commemorative iconography—the military was turned into a completely masculine sector, one of the expressions of genderization of Israel society in recent years. Other areas evidencing this same process are labor relations, allotment of public resources, and the definition of obligations in the public and private sector, all of which contradicted the egalitarian ethos that the *halutzim* adopted as their credo. The struggle for equality in these areas began in the days of the

Yishuv and has remained one of the focal points of political, economic, and social tension throughout the history of the state.[26]

The transition to the image of the mother in the plastic military commemoration alludes to an additional process of genderization that characterizes the gender construction in developing countries: turning women into "the mother of the nation," a birth machine ensuring the existence of the nation, while at the same time maintaining the ethnocultural uniqueness of the new state.[27] This situation was common also in developing countries outside the Third World, as one can see from the Australian model of the 1930s. In the song competition held on the "white continent" in 1938, songs of praise were sung to women who were outstanding in perpetual fertility and people encouraged this situation as preserving the cultured nation:

> Ye girls of British race, Famous for your beauty,
> reed Fast in all your grace, For this is your duty.
> As Anzac gave in war, So daughters at your call,
> will quick respond the more. To replace those that fall.[28]

In Israel, this process meshed with one of the central issues that troubled David Ben-Gurion in the early years of the state: the demographic question. His belief that the state's existence could only be guaranteed by swift demographic growth was expressed in his plan for mass immigration that recruited the economic resources of the new state, but also in the encouragement of "internal immigration." Expressions of the latter were birth grants, cash allotments for children, prizes to mother's of large families, and the creation of the ethos that determined a special place for the Hebrew women as a mother and particularly as the mother of soldiers. As early as his first speeches during War of Independence, Ben-Gurion awarded particular honor to mothers of the fallen and spoke of the special connection between them and their sons and daughters, who had given their lives for the state.[29] How deeply etched in the public consciousness was the image of the mother as an instrument for the nation's continuity can be seen in the way midwives in the 1950s and 1960s informed mothers of the newborn's sex (*mazzal tov*, you have a soldier boy; *mazzal tov*, you have a soldier girl). The iconographic transfer of bereavement from the female soldier to the mother — young or mature — is indicative of the changes in the Israeli ethos about the way in which a Hebrew woman is to bear the burden of the nation: no longer as a one defending it with her body but as one providing the future defenders, by means of her body. The genderization process in Israeli society — both in the ethos and in action—reflects, therefore, a change in the image of the woman in figurative commemoration in the State of Israel.

The transformations in the image of the mother allude to another process that shaped the national discourse in Israel from the 1960s: the trend toward decollectivization. The first images of young mothers that appeared in plastic commemoration, such as the one in Ramat Rahel (1949), were very similar to their European counterparts in that they represented the homeland more than the image of the individual mother. The beauty and purity, the bravery and vision that the young mother embodied were intended to reflect the collective characteristics of the people of that homeland and to serve as a model. Yet, the iconographic feminization of the motherland, a model well known from Europe (Marianne in France and *Winged Victory* in Britain) that left its marked in the East as well (such the monumental statue in memory of the Stalingrad fighters in the form of a women holding a sword), barely registered in a country that was called *eretz hemdat avot* ("the lovely country of the Partriarchs"). The problematics in equating the motherland with a mother image resulted in the situation whereby the mothers that appeared in Israeli commemorative iconography from the end of the 1950s already had ceased to represent the collective ethos and became flesh-and-blood mothers. An expression of this is the shift from the image of the pretty, young, striking mother to that of the mature, minor key mother representing only herself. The decollectivization of the mother image in Israeli iconography, therefore, *predates* the general trend of diminishing the collective ethos in Israeli society, which left its mark in the areas of society, culture, and the state almost a decade later.[30]

A third process that characterized the discourse within Israeli society and expressed itself in the iconographic sphere is the transition to multiculturalism. Despite the broad cultural spectrum that the immigrants brought with them — prior to the establishment of the state and afterward as well — the official culture, reflecting the definitive Israeli ethos for over two decades, was both dominant and all-encompassing. Nevertheless, the richness and diversity of immigrant sub-cultures continued to express themselves in certain fields, particularly during major transitional events such as births, marriage, and death. In the commemorative sphere, tension between the official, dominant culture and the influence of the immigrant cultures — both from Europe as well as Eastern countries — is expressed by the image of the older, weeping mothers. "Who can describe a mother's pain; who can assuage the pain of her mourning and who can heal her mortal wound, even if she hides it with innocent humility and courage from the eyes of strangers?"

writes Ben-Gurion in spring 1950.[31] Even before the national ethos of concealing bereavement began to soften, a process that reached its climax in recent years with soldiers crying over the graves of their comrades in arms, Israeli iconography recognized the right of the bereaved family to mourn publicly — a central component of some of the immigrant subcultures, even those from Europe. As noted, an example of that is the 1974 memorial by Faigin in Haifa of a mother kneeling weeping over her fallen son. Apparently, in this area, too, plastic commemoration in Israel that contains images of women preceded the general trend in Israeli society.

These last two processes — the decollectivization and the move to multiculturalism — were supposed to yield new patterns of military commemoration, reflecting the cluster of military and civilian roles that women filled over the course of years. Thereby, commemoration was not only to reflect the complete picture of women's activity within the military framework but even to contribute to the process of refashioning the national discourse over the place of women in this framework. Yet, unfortunately, we are witnessing an almost totally opposite process: In the commemorative memorial for the Women's Corps ("Memorial to the Fighting Hebrew Woman") that was erected during the state's jubilee year near the Shikmim field school in the old kibbutz Nitzanim, it was decided to present a number of groups of women in the form of semi-abstract figures. Among the groups, one may discern a woman supporting her friend and even a mother protecting her small children, but there is no hint of female combat soldiers, not even one in an auxiliary role. Toward the close of the twentieth century, too, when more opportunities were available to the young women joining the army than ever before, the image of the woman in plastic commemoration and accompanying text is somewhat passive, and in its form and motifs it is reminiscent more of the works of Kremer and Lammert in the women's concentration camp Ravensbruck than the "fighting Hebrew woman" who does everything, it seems, except fight. In Israeli society at the beginning of the twenty-first century, one is not supposed to create a figurative connection between the woman and militarism, even though she stood at the center of the public discourse concerned with sexism, racism, violence in general, and especially violence in the family, not as an abstract figure but as a real victim.[32] It also does not seem that the presentation of women in plastic military commemoration will change in the near future. For even at a time, when young women are accepted to military pilot training or other elite units, in a society in which political discourse is conducted mainly by former members of the General Staff's commando unit and the social discourse is shaped in the offices of the representatives of the clerical-patriarchal parties, it is hard to believe that women in active combat roles will receive expression in the area of commemoration.[33]

And now for the final question: myth versus reality. Plastic commemoration of men — even in Israel — tends to reinforce the myth, while the iconography related to the country's women focuses unequivocally on the universal reality of the mother figure, she who stands outside the circle of combat. Is adherence to the image of the mother, young and old alike, the image prevalent in Israeli military iconography and Holocaust memorials, nothing more than an expression of yearning for normalization and family continuity, in a country forced to grapple almost daily with additions to the "family of bereavement"?[34]

To sum up, when discussing a memorial continuum that reflects a tragic, lengthy, and ongoing process, the universality of motherhood — "the source of all life" in the words of Mordecai Kafri, and the focal point of human consolation — effaces any competing image. The female combatants and auxiliaries belong to the past, and who knows, perhaps also to the future. But the mother links the past to the present and future alike, and traditionally the utterance "mama" is considered the child's first cry and the final whisper of the dying. There are myths that are stronger than reality, but there is, apparently, also a reality that is stronger than myth.

Aftermath

A decade after an international conference that took place on Mount Scopus in Jerusalem and culminated in the publication in Hebrew of this volume, the new English version is now available. Our original aim was for the book to serve as a stimulus for more research in the field. Substantial interest has been generated. Demand for the first edition was high, and it went out of print almost immediately. Research in gender and women in the fields of history, literature, anthropology, sociology, art, and more has entered the mainstream of the Israeli academic sphere. All the major research universities in Israel have special Gender Studies programs, and the number of papers and books appearing on this topic grows steadily. Our hope is that the English edition is similarly catalytic abroad.

The concept inspiring our book, namely, the idea that the Jewish community in the Land of Israel since the emergence of the Zionist immigration gave rise to new gender identities, is now commonly accepted. The vibrant heterogeneous society that constituted the new State of Israel produced, and is still producing, diverse newly shaped identities.

Studies following our original volume, and inspired in part by it, have engaged in many new topics. These arenas include women of the religious sector, both national religious women and ultra-orthodox women; Mizrahi women; Arab Palestinian women; women in different professions, such as the military, medicine, high technology, and the arts; and women in various phases of their lives, including girls, mature women, widows, and bereaved mothers. At the same time, the historical research of Jewish women's life and creativity in ancient and medieval times has proliferated and deepened, enriching the understanding of early modern, modern, and contemporary conceptions.

Interest in gender research and especially research on women has un-earthed forgotten materials, including old diaries, abandoned letters, and ne-glected autobiographies. Women's writings, a field that a few years ago seemed deserted, have suddenly surfaced. For example, an English author, Hannah Trager, who was brought to Ottoman Palestine as a baby and later moved back to London, wrote about women's experiences while building Petah Tikvah in 1878.[1] Yehudit Harari, who also came as a baby to one of the first colonies nearly a decade after Trager, wrote her life story, depicting her love affair with her future husband and casting new light on intimate rela-tionships between the sexes.[2] In a republished book, a young Zionist girl, Henya Pekelman, who immigrated to Mandatory Palestine, where she worked as a builder and suffered hunger and rape, told her life story including sex-ual abuse before she committed suicide.[3] Such forgotten yet evocative voices have now received the attention of new audiences.

Study of the history of women and gender also has opened new spheres of interest: the history of motherhood, the history of childhood, and espe-cially the history of young girls. Gaining an understanding of the past of the Jewish people and particularly of the new Jewish society in the State of Israel is impossible without an acquaintance with the various histories of the Jew-ish people and Jewish culture. Such work enriches worldwide research on these topics and opens doors to new understandings of our society, its origins, and its connections with other societies.

The uniqueness of gender studies lies in their twofold nature: theoretical as well as empirical. Academics who have taught gender studies sometimes sense a hidden vibration in the class whenever students feel that the theories they encounter enable them to view their own lives in a new way. We hope this volume similarly touches the lives of its readers.

It is difficult to assess the influence of a single book. We do not pretend that the new understandings prevailing in Israeli society in the last decade concerning women's roles in society were influenced by this book or any other book. Yet, the Hebrew volume and the burst of research activity follow-ing in its wake are a clear and resonant voice documenting the transforma-tion of Israeli society as it experiences its gender revolution. The roots of this revolution are here depicted and brought to life for the English-speaking audience.

Notes

Introduction (pages 1–4)

1. H. Herzog, *"Irgunei Nashim ba-Hugim ha-Ezrahiyyim — Perek Nishkakh be-Historiyyografiyya shel ha-Yishuv"* [Women's Organizations in Civilian Circles — A Forgotten Chapter in the Historiography of the Yishuv], *Cathedra*, 70 (January 1994): 111–13, and also articles by Deborah Bernstein and Yossi Ben-Artzi in this collection.

2. From the article by Hannan Hever in the Hebrew edition of this volume, p. 393.

3. Y. Atzmon, ed. and intro., *Eshnav le-Hayyehen shel Nashim be-Hevrot Yehudiyyot* [A View into the Lives of Women in Jewish Societies], (Jerusalem, 1995), pp. 21–23.

4. See the article by Einat Ramon in this volume.

5. Amia Lieblich, *"Zipporah Az ve-Akhshav"* [Zipporah Then and Now], in ed. Ruth Ravitsky, *Kor'ot mi-Bereishit: Nashim Yisra'eliyyot Kotevot al Neshot Seter Bereishit* [(Women) Reading from Genesis: Israeli Women Writing about the Women in Genesis] (Tel Aviv, 1999), p. 406.

6. B. Melman, *"Min ha-shulayim el ha-historiyah shel ha-Yishuv: Migdar ve-eretz yisre'eliyut (1890–1920)"* [From the Periphery to the Center of *Yishuv* History: Gender and Nationalism in Eretz Israel (1890–1920)], *Zion* 62, no. 3 (1997): 246.

7. Ibid., 243–78.

The Study of Women in Israeli Historiography (pages 7–17)

1. D. Kandiyoti, "Contemporary Feminist Scholarship and Middle East Studies," in *Gendering the Middle East*, ed. D. Kandiyoti (London, 1996), p. 9.

2. See, for example, Sh. Rowbotham, *Hidden from History* (London, 1977); G. Lerner, *The Majority Finds Its Past: Placing Women in History* (New York, 1979); and many others. J. Wallach Scott, "Women's History and the Rewriting of History," in *The Impact of Feminist Research in the Academy*, ed. Ch. Farnham, pp. 34–50 (Bloomington, Ind., 1987) (hereafter cited as Scott, "Women's"); D. Kandiyoti, ed., *Gendering the Middle East* (London, 1996), p. 9.

3. D. Boyarin, *"Neshef ha-Masekhot ha-Koloni'ali: Ziyyonut, Migdar, Hikkui"* [The Colonial Masqued Ball: Zionism, Gender, Imitation], *Theory and Criticism* 11 (1997): 123–44 (hereafter cited as Boyarin, "Colonial"); M. Gluzman, *"Ha-Kemihah le-heteroseksu'aliyyut: Ziyyonut u-Miniyyut be-Altnoyland"* [The Yearning for Heterosexuality: Zionism and Sexuality in *Altneuland*], *Theory and Criticism* 11 (1997): 145–62; D. Biale, *Eros and the Jews* (New York, 1992), chapter 8; Sh. H. Katz, "Adam and Adama, Ird and Ard: En-gendering Political Conflict and identity in Early Jewish and Palestinian Nationalism," in *Gendering the Middle East*, ed. D. Kandiyoti (London, 1996) (hereafter cited as Katz, "Adam"); T. Mayer, ed., *Women and the Israeli Occupation* (London & New York, 1994), mainly in relation to the period of the Israeli occupation since 1967; J. M. Peteet, "Authenticity and Gender, The Presentation of Culture," in *Arab Women, Old Boundaries, New Frontiers*, ed. J. E. Tucker, pp. 49–62 (Bloomington, Ind., 1993).

4. Scott, "Woman's," p. 37.

5. Ibid., p. 38.

6. J. W. Scott, *Gender and the Politics of History* (New York, 1988), p. 27.

7. J. Bennett, "Feminism and History," *Gender and History* 1, no. 3 (1989): 58.

8. B. Melman, *"Min ha-Shulayyim el ha-Historiyyah shel ha-Yishuv: Migdar ve-Eretz Yisra'eliyyut (1890–1920)"* [From the Margins to the History of the *Yishuv*: Gender and Eretz-Israeliness (1890–1920)], *Zion* 62, no. 3 (1997): 245.

9. Boyarin, "Colonial," p. 125.

10. N. Yuval-Davis, "Gender and Nation," *Ethnic and Racial Studies* 16, no. 4 (1993): 621–32.

11. Katz, "Adam."

12. For example, Y. Azmon, ed., *Eshnav le-Hayyehen shel Nashim ve-Hevrot Yehudioyyot* [A View into the Lives of Women in Jewish Societies], pp. 325–26 (Jerusalem, 1995); Y. Azmon, ed., *Ha-Tishma Koli? Yitzugim shel Nashim be-Tarbut ha-Yisra'elit* [Will You Listen to My Voice? Representations of Women in Israeli Culture] (Tel Aviv, 2001); T. Elor & T. Rapport, eds., *Women Studies International Forum* (Special issue) 20, nos. 5/6 (1997); Special issues of *Israel Social Science Research on Feminist Theory and Research: Israeli Institutions and Society* 12, nos. 1, 2 (1997).

Have Gender Studies Changed Our Attitude toward the Historiography
of the Aliyah *and Settlement Process? (pages 18–32)*

1. We note here the collective publication projects of Yad Yitzhak Ben-Zvi
and the Israel Academy for Sciences and Humanities: M. Eliav, ed., *Sefer
ha-Aliyah ha-Rishonah* [The First Aliyah book] (Jerusalem, 1981); Y. Bartal,
Z. Tzahor, and Y. Kani'el, eds., *Sefer ha-Aliyah ha-Sheniyyah* [The Second
Aliyah book] (Jerusalem, 1997); also, I. Kollat et al., eds., *Toledot ha-Yishuv
ha-Yehudi be-Eretz Yisra'el me'az ha-Aliyah ha-Rishonah — ha-Tekufah ha-
Othmanit* [History of the Jewish settlement in Eretz Israel since the First
Aliyah — the Ottoman period], pt. 1 (Jerusalem, 1990); they contain dozens of
articles relating to the study of *aliyah*, settlement, and the formation of *Yishuv*
society in Eretz Israel. Also see Y. Ben-Artzi, *Ha-Moshavah ha-Ivrit be-Nof
Eretz Yisra'el 1882–1914* [The Hebrew moshavah in Eretz Israel landscape
1882–1914] (Jerusalem, 1988) (hereafter cited as Ben-Artzi, *Ha-Moshavah*);
M. Shilo, *Nisyonot be-Hityashevut — ha-Misrad ha-Eretzyisraeli 1908–1914* [At-
tempts at Settlement — the Palestine Office 1908–1914] (Jerusalem, 1988); Y. Katz,
Ha-Yozma ha-Peratit be-Binyan Eretz Israel bi-Tekufat ha-Aliyah ha-Sheniyyah
[Private Initiative in the Building of Eretz Israel during the Period of the Second Aliyah] (Jerusalem, 1989) (hereafter cited as Katz, *Ha-Yozma*); R. Aaronsohn, *Ha-Baron ve-ha-Moshavot* [The Baron and the Moshavot] (Jerusalem,
1990) (hereafter cited as Aaronsohn, *Ha-Baron*); Z. Shiloni, *Ha-Keren ha-
Kayemet le-Yisra'el ve-ha-Hityashevut 1903–1914* [The Jewish National Fund
and Settlement 1903–1914] (Jerusalem, 1990).

2. Compare the position of the moshavah in the "classic" literature such as
A. Bein, *Toldot ha-Hitayashevut ha-Tziyonit me-Herzl ve-ad Yameinu* [History
of Zionist Settlement from Herzl until Today] (Tel Aviv, 1954) or H. Gvati, *100
Shenot Hityashevut* [100 Years of Settlement] (Tel Aviv, 1981), to its position in
Aaronsohn, *Ha-Baron* and Ben-Artzi, *Ha-Moshavah*.

3. Aaronsohn, *Ha-Baron*; S. Schama, *Bet Rotshild ve-Eretz Yisra'el* [The
Rothschild Family and Eretz Israel] (Jerusalem, 1980); M. Naor & D. Giladi,
Rotshild "Avi ha-Yishuv" u-mif'alo be-Eretz Israel [Rothschild "the Father of
the *Yishuv*" and His Endeavors in Eretz Israel] (Jerusalem, 1982).

4. For example, Katz, *Ha-Yozma*; R. Kark, *Yazamim Sefardim be-Eretz Israel* [Sefardi Entrepreneurs in Eretz Israel] (Jerusalem, 1993).

5. M. Shilo, "*Havvat ha-po'alot be-Kinneret 1911–1917, ke-fitaron le-va'ayat
ha-po'alot ba-aliyyah ha-sheniyyah*" [The Women's Agricultural Training
Farm at Kinneret, 1911–1917, as a Solution to the Women's Labor Problem in
the Second Aliyah], *Cathedra* 14 (1980): 81–112; D. Bernstein, *Isha be-Eretz
Yisra'el-ha-She'ifah le-Shivyon bi-Tekufat ha-Yishuv* [A Woman in Eretz
Israel — the Aspiration for Equality in the *Yishuv* Period] (Tel Aviv, 1987);
D. Izraeli, "*Tenuat ha-Po'alot be-Eretz Israel me-Reishitah ad 1927*" [The

Women's Labor Movement in Eretz Israel from its Beginnings until 1927],
Cathedra 32 (1984): 109–40.

6. A. Bar-Adon, "*Ha-Imahot ha-meyassedot u-menat helkan be-tehiyyat ha-ivrit ve-hithavvutah (1882–1913)*" [The Founding Mothers and Their Role in the Revival of Hebrew and its Formation (1882–1914)], *Lashon ve-Ivrit* 3 (1990): 5–26.

7. Note 5 above; see also D. Bernstein, "*Po'alot ve-Halutzot ba-Aliyah ha-Sheniyyah—Tikvot ve-Akhzavot*" [Female Workers and Pioneers in the Second Aliyah—Hopes and Disappointments], *Idan* 8 (1985): 145–63.

8. R. Aaronsohn, "*Nashim ve-Hayyei ha-Yom-yom be-Reishit ha-hityashevut ha-yehudit be-eretz yisra'el*" [Women in Daily Life at the Beginning of Jewish Settlement in Eretz Israel], in *Proceedings of the World Congress for Jewish Studies*, 10, B (Jerusalem 1989), pp. 305–11; Y. Ben-Artzi, "*Ha-Ishah be-Reishit ha-Hityashevut be-Eretz Israel (1882–1914)*" [The Woman at the Beginning of Settlement in Eretz Israel (1882–1914)], in *Eshnav le-Hayyehen shel Nashim be-Hevrot Yehudiyyot* [A View into the Lives of Women in Jewish Societies: A Collection of Interdisciplinary Studies], ed. Y. Azmon, pp. 309–24 (Jerusalem, 1995).

9. M. Shilo, "*Ha-Ishah—'Ovedet' o 'Haverah' be-Mifal ha-Tehiyyah? Al Mekomah shel ha-Ishah ba-Aliyah ha-Rishonah (1882–1903)*" [The Woman—"Laborer" or "Member" in the Revival Project? On the Place of the Woman in the First Aliyah (1882–1903)], *Yahadut Zemanenu* 10 (1995): 121–47; see also M. Nevo, "*Ha-Ishah ba-Aliyah ha-Rishonah*" [The Woman in the First Aliyah], M.A. thesis (Haifa University, 1994).

10. Y. Berlovitz, *Sippurei Nashim Benot ha-Aliyah ha-Rishonah* [Stories of Women of the First Aliyah] (Tel Aviv, 1984); idem, *Lehamtzi Eretz Lehamtzi Am—Tashtiyyot Sifrut ve-Tarbut bi-Yetzirah shel ha-Aliyah ha-Rishonah* [Inventing a Land, Inventing a People: Cultural and Literary Patterns in the Writings of the First Aliyah] (Tel Aviv, 1996).

11. R. Elboim-Dror, *Ha-Hinukh ha-Ivri be-Eretz Yisra'el* [Hebrew Education in Eretz Israel] (Jerusalem, 1986).

12. Y. Katz and S. Neuman, "Women's Quest for Occupational Equality: The Case of Jewish Female Agriculture Workers in Pre-State Israel," *Rural History* 7 (1996): 33–52.

13. A. Shapira, *Herev ha-Yonah, ha-Tziyonut ve-ha-Ko'ah 1881–1948* [Land and Power, the Zionist Resort to Force, 1881–1948] (Tel Aviv, 1992), p. 94 ff.

14. M. Smilansky, *Mishpahat ha-Adamah* [Family of the Soil] 2, 1942, pp. 132–41; R. Kark and I. Amit, *Yehoshu'a Hankin—Shtei Ahavot* [Yehoshua Hankin—two loves] (Tel Aviv, 1996).

15. Note 8 above.

16. Ben-Artzi, *Ha-Moshavah*.

17. Y. Klausner, *Am ve-Aretz Kamim li-Tehiyyah* [A Nation and a Land Come to Life] (Tel Aviv, 1949), p. 14.

18. N. Druyan, *Be-Ein Marvad Kesamim* [Without a Magic Carpet] (Tel Aviv, 1984); Y. Nini, *He-Hayita o Halamti Halom* [Were You [there] or Did I Dream a Dream] (Tel Aviv, 1996); see also A. Savorai and M. Kaspi-Masuri, *Nahliel* (Hadera, 1998).

19. A study on the topic has been initiated using primary material in the Rehovot Municipality Historical Archive.

20. Fanya Nahumovsky to Va'ad Yishuv ha-Aretz, 3 Av 5635 (1904), CZA A24/61.

21. Ben-Artzi, *Ha-Moshavah*, p. 313.

22. Y. Kollat, *"Ide'ologiyyah u-Metzi'ut bi-Tenu'at ha-Avodah ha-Artziyis-ra'elit"* [Ideology and Reality in the Eretz Israel Labor Movement] (Ph.D. diss., Hebrew University of Jerusalem, 1994), served as the basis for understanding the transformation in the ideas of the members of the Second Aliyah in the shift to settlement; on the establishment of *moshavei ha-po'alim* (workers' villages): Y. Ben-Artzi, *"Moshav ha-Po'alim u-Mekomo be-Toledot ha-Hityashevut"* [The Worker's Village and Its Place in the History of Settlement], *Ha-Tziyyonut* 20 (1996): 103–34; on the formation of the kevutzah, see the debate by R. Frankel, *"Ha-Meni'im ha-Ide'ologiyyim be-Hithavutah shel ha-Kevutzah bi-Ymei ha-Aliyah ha-Sheniyyah"* [Ideological Motivation in the Formation of the Kevutzah during the Second Aliyah], *Cathedra* 18 (1981): 111–17; B. Ben-Avram, *"Tzemihata shel ha-Kevutzah mitokh Ma'aveihem shel Benei ha-Aliyah ha-Sheniyyah la-Avodah Atzmit* [The Growth of the *Kevutzah* Out of the Yearnings of the Members of the Second Aliyah for Self-Labor], ibid., pp. 118–23; H. Near, *"Ide'ologiyyah ve-Anti Ide'ologiyyah"* [Ideology and Anti-Ideology], ibid., pp. 124–29. None of them presents women as any kind of factor in the formation of the *kevutzah*.

23. S. Malkin, *Darki ba-Aretz* [My Way in the Country], in *Sefer ha-Aliyah ha-Sheniyyah* [The Second Aliyah book], ed. Bracha Habas, pp. 488–89 (Tel Aviv, 1947); see also A. Schidlowski, "Hevlei Kelitah" [Absorption Tribulations], in ibid., pp. 554–58; E. Bekker, *"Mi-Hayyei Mishpahat Shomer"* [Of the Life of a Shomer's Family], in ibid., pp. 512–13.

24. A. Maimon, *Hamishim Shenot Tenu'at ha-Po'a lot* [Fifty Years of the Women's Labor Movement] (Tel Aviv, 1957), pp. 7–26; a different view is given by R. Thon, *Ha-Ma'avak li-Zekhuyyot ha-Ishah, Sippur Hayyeha shel Sarah Thon* [The Struggle for Women's Rights, the Story of the Life of Sarah Thon] (Private publication: Israel, 1996).

25. Y. Ben-Artzi, "Changes in the Agricultural Sector of the Moshavot 1882–1914," in *Ottoman Palestine 1800–1914*, ed. G. Gilbar, pp. 131–58 (Leiden, 1990).

26. N. Talman, *"Ofyo ve-Hitpathuto shel ha-Meshek ha-Hakla'i ba-Moshavot ha-Germaniyyot ha-Templariyyot be-Eretz Yisra'el"* [The Character and Development of the Agricultural Farm in the German Templar Villages in the Land of Israel] (Ph.D. diss., Hebrew University of Jerusalem, 1991).

27. Y. Wilkansky, *"Siddur ha-Moshavim"* [Arrangement of the Moshavim], *Ba-Derekh* 6 (Jaffa, 1918): 244–45.

28. A. Ruppin, *Ha-Hityashevut ha-Hakla'it shel ha-Histadrut ha-Tziyyonit be-Eretz Yisra'el* [Agricultural Settlement by the Zionist Federation in Eretz Israel] (Tel Aviv, 1925), p. 45.

29. Y. Shavit and D. Giladi, *"Ha-Refet ve-ha-Meshek ha-Artziyisra'eli bi-Tekufat ha-Mandat"* [The Role of the Dairy Farm in the Development of Jewish Settlement during the Mandate Period], *Cathedra* 18 (1981): 178–92.

30. B. Melman, *"Min ha-Shulayyim el ha-Historiyyah shel ha-Yishuv: Migdar ve-Artziyisra'elityyut (1890–1920)"* [From the Margins to the History of the *Yishuv*: Gender and *Ertzi-Yisra'eliyyut*] (1890–1920), *Zion* 62, no. 3 (1997): 248; see also an attempt in this direction in R. Aaronsohn, "Through the Eyes of a Settler's Wife: Letters from the Moshava," in *Pioneers and Homemakers,* ed. D. Bernstein, pp. 29–47 (Albany, 1992).

Mizrahi Women (pages 33–47)

1. S. Okin, *Women in Western Political Thought* (Princeton, 1979).

2. Ibid., p. 273.

3. S. Harding, *Whose Science? Whose Knowledge? Thinking from Women's Lives* (Ithaca, 1991) (hereafter cited as Harding, *Whose*); see also Donna Haraway, "Situated Knowledge: The Science Question in Feminism as a Site of Discourse on the Privilege of Partial Perspective," *Feminist Studies* 14, no. 3 (1988): 575–99 (hereafter cited as Haraway, "Situated").

4. Harding, *Whose*, 143; Haraway, "Situated," 577.

5. G. Ch. Spivak, *The Post-Colonial Critic* (New York, 1990).

6. Most of the women's organizations are situated in the Israeli political center and left, and they are based on activity of members of the middle class, mostly veteran Israelis or women of Anglo-Saxon origin.

7. In S. L. Kirshenbaum, *Toledot Yisra'el ba-Zeman he-Hadash* [History of Israel in Modern Times] (Tel Aviv, 1969), the Mizrahi merit nine pages out of four hundred.

8. The history of women in Israel is also absent in social research, and of late a number of sources have been found that became the subject of studies on the topic that were carried out recently: books by women such as Ada Maimon, Sarah Azaryahu, and sources from *Davar ha-Po'elet*. These works and

those that will follow deal with women in Israel without any internal distinction, so that they appear to represent the history of women in Israel, the same way that the narrative of the patriarchal history seems to narrate also women's story at the same time it is unfolding male Israeli history.

9. E. Shohat, *Ha-Kolno'a ha-Yisra'eli: Historiyyah ve-Ide'ologiyyah* [Israeli Cinema History and Ideology] (Tel Aviv, 1989) (herafter cited as Shohat, *Ha-Kolno'a*); V. Shiran, "Feminist Identity vs. Mizrahi Identity," in *Calling the Equality Bluff*, ed. B. Swirski and M. Safir, pp. 303–11 (New York, 1991) (hereafter cited as Shiran, "Feminist"); D. Bernstein, "Mizrahi and Ashkenazi Jewish Women in the Labor Market," in ibid., pp. 192–200.

10. Y. Shenhav and Y. Haberfeld, "*Megamot be-Aflayah bi-Sekhar shel Nashim ve-shel Benei Edot ha-Mizrah ba-Universita'ot, be-Ma'abadot, M[ehkar] u-P[itu'ah], u-be-Batei Holim be-Shanim* 1972–1983" [Trends in Salary Discrimination of Women and Mizrahi Jews in Universities, R & D Laboratories, and Hospitals 1972–1983], *Megamot* 33 (1990): 77–99.

11. See E. Meir-Glitzenstein, "Ethnic and Gender Identity of Iraqi Women Immigrants in the Kibbutz in the 1940s" in this volume.

12. Harding, *Whose*; Haraway, "Situated"; L. H. Nelson, *Who Knows — From Quine to a Feminist Empiricism* (Philadelphia, 1990).

13. This political development is doubly misleading, since it not only creates an illusion of taking care of the problem of the representation of Palestinian women who are citizens of Israel but also lays the foundation for the idea that there is representation and even a chance for representation of other weak sectors in Israel.

14. Bracha Seri, *Shiv'im Shirei Shotetut* [Seventy Poems of Wandering], (self-published by Bracha Seri, Jerusalem, 1983) (hereafter cited as Seri, *Shiv'im*); Atalyia, *Migrashim Harusim* [Destroyed Lots] (Tel Aviv, 1993); Tikva Levy, "At the Bus Station," in *After Jews and Arabs*, ed. Ammiel Alcalay, pp. 267–72 (Minneapolis, 1993).

15. Yael Azmon and Dafna Izraeli, eds., *Women in Israel* (New Brunswick, 1993); Doron Gideon and Daniella Shenkar, *Mehakot le-Yitzug* [Waiting for Representation] (Tel Aviv, 1998).

16. Judith Butler, *Gender Trouble* (New York, 1990) (hereafter cited as Butler, *Gender*); Sh. Benhabib, *Situating the Self* (New York, 1992) (hereafter cited as Benhabib, *Situating*); Since Hegel was not an outstanding feminist, the dialectic approach is blind to the gender perspective, says Susan Okin in her work on women in Western political thought. What was needed was to genderize Hegel. Yet, even concentrating on the history of women in Israel as a gender category leaves the Mizrahi women invisible and misses out on their rich, unique experience as Israelis nurtured from Arab sources and from countries of Muslim culture.

17. Butler, *Gender*, pp. 149, 213–18; Benhabib, *Situating*, p. 16.

18. G. M. Breakwell, "Women: Group and Identity?" *Women's Studies International Quarterly* 2 (1979): 9–10.

19. A. Weir, *Sacrificial Logics: Feminist Theory and the Critique of Identity* (New York, 1996), pp. 1–13.

20. I propose interpreting the search for the existence of a sense of self, in the feminist context, as the search for sources of the self.

21. Butler, *Gender*, p. 149.

22. I. Gur-Zev, *Hinukh be-Idan ha-Si'ah ha-Postmodernisti* [Education in the Era of Postmodernist discourse] (Jerusalem, 1999); U. Ram, "*Hevrah u-Mada ha-Hevrah*" [Society and Sociology], in *Ha-Hevrah ha-Yisra'elit: Hebbetim Bikortiyyim* [Israeli Society: Critical Aspects], ed. U. Ram (Tel Aviv, 1993) (hereafter Ram, "*Hevrah*"); E. Said, *Orientalism* (New York, 1979).

23. Seri, *Shiv'im*; Atalya, *Migrashim*; and Levy, "At the Bus Station."

24. Ram, "*Hevrah*"; Karl Fuerstein and M. Richel, *The Children of the Melah — The Cultural Retardation among Moroccan Children and Its Meaning in Education*, (published by the Henrietta Szold Institute and the Jewish Agency, Jerusalem, 1953), p. 17 [Hebrew]; Karl Frankenstein, "On Ethnic Differences," *Megamot* B3 (1951), pp. 261–76 [Hebrew]; Karl Frankenstein, "On the Concept of Primitivity," *Megamot* B4 (1951), p. 342, 344, 347 [Hebrew]; Shmuel Noah Eisenstadt, *Israel, A Society in the Making* (Jerusalem, 1967) [Hebrew]; Shmuel Noah Eisenstadt, "Leadership Problems among the 'Olim,'" *Megamot* 32 (1953) 182–91 [Hebrew]; Rivka Bar Yossef, The Moroccans: "The Background of the Problem, 1960–1961," MOLAD, pp. 249–59.

25. *Hila News Bulletins*, 6 (in Hebrew); for further elaboration on the topic see Henriette Dahan-Kalev, "Tensions in Israeli Feminism: The Mizrahi Ashkenazi Rift," in *Women's Studies International Forum* 24 (2001): 1–16. Z. Zameret, *Melting Pot in Israel: The Commission of Inquiry on Education in the Immigrant Camp during the Early Years of the State* (State University of New York Press, 2002); Lotte Salzberger et al., *Patterns of Contraceptive Behavior among Jerusalem Women Seeking Pregnancy Counseling 1980–1989* (Jerusalem: Hebrew University School of Social Work, 1991).

26. Said, *Orientalism*, pp. 1–3, 11–12.

27. See note 8.

28. Rivka Bar-Yosef, "*Ha-Maroka'im — Reka ha-Be'ayah*" [Moroccans: The Roots of the Problem], (Molad, 1960–1961), 249–59; S. N. Eisenstadt, ed., *Social Stratification in Israel* (Jerusalem, 1968).

29. I. Troen, "Europe and America in the Education of Israelis," in *Judaism and Education: Essays in Honor of W. I. Ackerman*, ed. H. Marantz, pp. 181–206 (Beersheba, 1998).

30. D. Noy, series of three collections entitled *Shiv'im Sippurim ve-Sippur mi-Pi Yehudei Tunisiyya, Luv, Maroko* [Seventy and One Tales from Jews of Tunisia, Lybia, Morocco] (Jerusalem, 1967–1968).

31. Seri, *Shiv'im*; Shiran, "Feminist"; Shohat, *Ha-Kolno'a*.

32. See note 25.

33. Frantz Fanon, *Black Skin White Masks* (New York, 1967); Toni Morrison, *Playing in the Dark* (New York, 1992), p. 222.

34. The rifts and conflicts among the different groups in Israel deter research into these topics. The tendency is to refrain from "poking about" in what is perceived as deepening the rifts and disintegrating the ethos of national unity.

Women's Aliyah *(pages 51–62)*

1. In addition to this volume, see for example, Deborah S. Bernstein, ed., *Pioneers and Homemakers: Jewish Women in Pre-State Israel* (Albany, 1992) (hereafter cited as Bernstein, *Pioneers*) as well as numerous articles since published in various journals and collections.

2. Groundbreaking work on these non-pioneering women has been done by Margalit Shilo, *Princess or Prisoner? Jewish Women in Jerusalem, 1840–1914* (Hanover, N.H., 2005). In the area of religious education for girls at the beginning of the twentieth century, see also Deborah Weissman, "Chana Spitzer—An Educational Leader," in *A Woman in Jerusalem: Gender, Society and Religion* [in Hebrew], eds. T. Cohen and J. Schwartz, pp. 79–89 (Ramat-Gan, 2002).

3. One short diary, written by a Moroccan Jew, describes his pilgrimage visit to Eretz Israel in 1903, see Henry Toledano, "The Diary of R. Isaac Nissim Toledano's Journey to Eretz Israel" [in Hebrew] (1903), in *East and Maghreb, Researches in the History of the Jews in the Orient and North Africa* 3, ed. S. Schwarzfuchs, pp. 141–58 (Jerusalem, 1981) (hereafter cited as Toledano, "Diary"). See also short references in letters published in Ya'akov Moshe Toledano, *Otzar Genazim* (Jerusalem, 1960) (hereafter cited as Toledano, *Otzar*).

4. See, for example, R. Yosef Messas, *Collections of Letters* [in Hebrew] (Jerusalem, 1968), 1:16 (hereafter cited as Messas, *Collections*).

5. For a discussion of these censuses, see Michal Ben Ya'akov, "The Montefiore Census: The First Modern Census of Jews in Eretz Israel," in *Papers in Jewish Demography, 1997*, ed. S. DellaPergola and J. Even, pp. 79–87 (Jerusalem, 2001); idem, "The Montefiore Census as a Source for the History of North African Jews in the Nineteenth Century" [in Hebrew], *Pe'amim, Studies in Oriental Jewry* 107 (2006): 117–149. The original census lists are found in the Montefiore Collection, London School of Jewish Studies (formerly Jews College) Library, ms 528–557 (hereafter cited as Montefiore Collection), and on microfilm in the Institute of Microfilmed Jewish manuscripts, Jewish National and University Library, Jerusalem, reels 35115, 6151–6179.

6. For Eretz Israel, see Uziel O. Schmelz, "Some Demographic Peculiarities of the Jews of Jerusalem in the Nineteenth Century," in *Studies on Palestine During the Ottoman Period*, ed. M. Ma'oz, pp. 126–30 (Jerusalem, 1975) (hereafter cited as Schmelz, "Some Demographic"); for Morocco, see Doris Bensimon-Donath, *Evolution du Judaisme Marocaine sous le Protectorate Français, 1912–1956* (Paris, 1968), p. 99.

7. Norman Stillman, *The Jews of Arab Lands in Modern Times* (Philadelphia, 1991), p. 201; idem, "The Sefrou Remnant," *Jewish Social Studies* 35, nos. 3–4 (1973): 263.

8. Kertzer claims, "the overwhelming predominance of women at older ages in the West today is certainly a recent phenomenon." However, he does add, "the sex ratio disparities at older ages is still not well known." David I. Kertzer, "Toward a Historical Demography of Aging," in *Aging in the Past: Demography, Society and Old Age*, eds. D. I. Kertzer and P. Laslett, p. 374 (Berkeley, 1995) (hereafter cited as Kertzer and Laslett, *Aging*). My statistical analysis of nineteenth-century censuses points to continuity, and not change, in the significant majority of older women. See also Schmelz, "Some Demographic," pp. 131–32.

9. On the economic activities of Jewish males in Morocco, see Shlomo Deshen, *The Mellah Society: Jewish Community Life in Sherifian Nineteenth-Century Morocco* (Chicago, 1989), pp. 30–45 (hereafter cited as Deshen, *Mellah*). For a discussion of occupations in nineteenth-century Palestine, see Svi Karagila, *The Jewish Community in Palestine ("Yishuv") during the Egyptian Rule* (1831–1840) [in Hebrew] (Tel Aviv, 1990), pp. 133–40. On women's economic activities in Palestine, see ibid., p. 140; on their activities in the Maghreb, see Eliezer Bashan, "The Role of the Jewish Woman in the Economic Life of North African Jewry" [in Hebrew], *Miqqedem Umiyyam: Studies in the Jewry of Islamic Countries* 1 (1981): 67–84.

10. Among some two thousand North African immigrant men enumerated as heads of households in the nineteenth-century censuses in the Holy Land, less than 3 percent were divorced or widowed at the time of the census. Although polygamy did exist, its occurrence was relatively uncommon in the nineteenth century, both in North Africa and in Eretz Israel. Less than ten examples of polygamy were noted in the cases studied. On the low incidence of polygamy in Morocco, see Deshen, *Mellah*, p. 30.

11. Michal Ben Ya'akov, "The Immigration and Settlement of North African Jews in Nineteenth-Century Jerusalem," [in Hebrew] including English abstract (Ph.D. diss., The Hebrew University of Jerusalem, 2001), pp. 307–12 (hereafter cited as Ben Ya'akov, "Immigration").

12. Sergio DellaPergola, "*Aliyah* and Other Jewish Migrations: Toward an Integrated Perspective," in *Studies in the Population of Israel in Honor of Roberto Bachi* (*Scripta Hierosolymitana*, 30), ed. U. O. Schmelz and G. Nathan,

pp. 172–209 (Jerusalem, 1986) (hereafter cited as DellaPergola, *"Aliyah"*); Reginald G. Golledge, "A Behavioral View of Mobility and Migration Research," *Professional Geographer* 32, no. 1 (1980): 14–21.

13. Mirjana Morokvašic, "Birds of Passage are also Women . . . ," *International Migration Review* 18, no. 4 (1984): 886–907 (hereafter cited as Morokvašic, "Birds"); Lin Lean Lim, "Effects of Women's Position on Their Migration," in *Women's Position and Demographic Change*, ed. N. Federici, K. Oppenheim Mason, and S. Sogner, pp. 225–42 (Oxford, 1993). For a discussion of Jewish women migrating within an historical context, see Paula Hyman, "Culture and Gender: Women in the Immigrant Jewish Community," in *The Legacy of Jewish Migration*, ed. D. Berger, pp. 157–68 (New York, 1983).

14. Everett S. Lee, "A Theory of Migration," *Demography* 3, no. 1 (1966): 51.

15. For a discussion of these qualities within the context of North African *aliyah*, see Michal Ben Ya'akov, "Aliyah from North Africa to Eretz Israel in the Nineteenth Century: Myth and Reality" [in Hebrew], in *Zion and Zionism among Sephardi and Oriental Jews*, ed. W. Z. Harvey et al., pp. 297–303 (Jerusalem, 2002); Tobi and Hasan-Rokem, in Harvey, ibid.

16. For a broader discussion, see Zvi Zohar, "The Meaning of Life in the Holy Land in the Writings of Sephardic Rabbis, 1777–1849" [in Hebrew], in *Eretz Yisrael be-Hagut ha-Yehudit ba-Et ha-Hadashah* [The Land of Israel in Modern Jewish Thought], ed. A. Ravitsky, pp. 326–58 (Jerusalem, 1998).

17. Compare with the case of Yemenite women who arrived in Eretz Israel in the same period: Nitza Druyan, "Yemenite Jewish Women — Between Tradition and Change," in Bernstein, *Pioneers*, p. 79.

18. Issachar Ben-Ami, "Folk-Veneration of Saints among the Moroccan Jews," in *Studies in Judaism and Islam, Presented to Shelomo Dov Goitein*, ed. S. Morag, I. Ben-Ami, and N. A. Stillman, pp. 282–344 (Jerusalem, 1981).

19. Deshen, *Mellah*, p. 83, 134 n. 15; Harvey Goldberg, "The Zohar in Southern Morocco: A Study in the Ethnography of Texts," *History of Religions* 29, no. 3 (1990): 233–58. See also the pioneering work of Chava Weissler on Ashkenazi women in Europe in the seventeenth and eighteenth centuries, as in "The Religion of Traditional Ashkenazic Women: Some Methodological Issues," *AJS Review* 12, no. 1 (1987): 73–94.

20. Ben-Ami, "Folk-Veneration," p. 344.

21. Messas, *Collections*, p. 11; Toledano, "Diary," pp. 145, 156–57; idem, "Moroccan Jewry and the Settlement of Eretz Israel: A History of the Various Aliyot of Moroccan Jews from the Sixteenth Century until the Beginning of the Twentieth Century" [in Hebrew], in *Hagut Ivrit be-Artzot ha-Islam*, ed. M. Zohari et al., pp. 228–52 (Jerusalem, 1982).

22. In her discussion of medieval and early modern Jewish women in

Spain, for example, Melammed notes, "[R]eligious devotion . . . most certainly provided an opportunity for self-expression in a society that rarely allowed female voices to be heard." Renée Levine Melammed, "Sephardi Women in Medieval and Early Modern Periods," in *Jewish Women in Historical Perspective*, ed. J. R. Baskin, p. 127 (Detroit, 1991) (hereafter cited as Melammed, "Sephardi"). See also various works by Chava Weissler (above, note 19, and others).

23. This characteristic is not particular to Jewish migration to Eretz Israel, but to Jewish migrations in general. See DellaPergola, "*Aliyah*," pp. 172–209.

24. *The Jewish Expositor* 14 (1829): 111.

25. Ben Ya'akov, "Immigration," pp. 65–66.

26. On the functions of an extended family, especially in regard to migration, see Kevin Schurer, "The Role of the Family in the Process of Migration," in *Migrants, Emigrants and Immigrants, a Social History of Migration*, ed. C. G. Pooley and I. D. Whyte, pp. 106–42 (London, 1991); and Frederick W. Boal, "Ethical Residential Segregation," in *Social Areas in Cities, Processes, Patterns and Problems*, ed. D. T. Herbert and R. J. Johnston, pp. 61–72 (Chichester, 1978).

27. Messas, *Otzar*, p. 14.

28. Edmondo de Amicis, *Morocco: Its People and Places* (transl. from Italian by C. Rollin-Tilton), p. 264 (London, 1882); Charles de Foucauld, *Reconnaissance au Maroc, 1883–1884*, p. 394 (Paris, 1939 [1888]); Joseph Thomson, *Travels in the Atlas and Southern Morocco, a Narrative of Exploration*, p. 252 (London, 1889).

29. Heinrich von Maltzan, *Drei Jahre im Nordwesten von Afrika, Reisen in Algerien und Marokko*, p. 198 (Leipzig, 1863). See also William Shaler, *Sketches of Algers*, p. 68 (Boston, 1826) (hereafter cited as Shaler, *Sketches*); and Ferdinand C. Ewald, "Tunis, Journal of the Rev. F. C. Ewald," *Monthly Intelligence* (April 1834), p. 63 (hereafter cited as Ewald, "Tunis").

30. J. E. Budgett Meakin, "The Jews of Morocco," *Jewish Quarterly Review* 4 (1892): 381.

31. Raphael Moshe Elbaz, *Halakhah le-Moshe, Even ha-Ezer* [Law unto Moses, Even ha-Ezer] section 7, p. 12b; section 8, p. 13a (Jerusalem, 1911). For a brief discussion, see Eliezer Bashan, "On the Attitudes of Moroccan Sages in the Eighteenth and Nineteenth Centuries towards the Obligation of *Aliyah* to Eretz Israel" [in Hebrew], in *Vatikin*, ed. H. Z. Hirschberg and Y. Kaniel, pp. 37–41 (Ramat Gan, 1975) (hereafter cited as Bashan, "On Attitudes").

32. Haim Zafrani, *Pédagogie Juive en Terre d'Islam*, p. 114 (Paris, 1969). See also Bashan, "On Attitudes," pp. 40–41.

33. Shaler, *Sketches*, p. 68. See also Ewald, "Tunis," p. 63.

34. Montefiore Collection, ms 531/microfilm 6153.

35. Messas, *Collections*, p. 14.

36. Montefiore Collection, ms 532/microfilm 6154. The same census list enumerates only five married men arriving from Jerba during this period.

37. Compare with David Kertzer and Nancy Karweit, "The Impact of Widowhood in Nineteenth-Century Italy," in Kertzer and Laslett, *Aging,* pp. 244–46.

38. For further examples, see ibid., pp. 137–38; Rachel Simon, "Mores and Chores as Determinants of the Status of Jewish Women in Libya," in *From Iberia to Diaspora*, ed. Y. K. Stillman and N. A. Stillman, pp. 114–20 (Leiden, 1999), and also works noted above, note 13.

39. Morokvašic, "Birds," pp. 896–98. On positive and negative selection, see Harley L. Browning and Waltraut Feindt, "Selectivity of Migrants to a Metropolis in a Developing Country: A Mexican Case Study," *Demography* 6, no. 4 (1969): 347–57.

40. On the status of widowed matriarchs in Jewish families, see Ruth Lamdan, *A Separate People: Jewish Women in Palestine, Syria and Egypt in the Sixteenth Century* (Leiden, 2000), pp. 196–201 (hereafter cited as Lamdan, *A Separate People*); Deshen, *Mellah*, p. 115.

41. Michal Ben Ya'akov, "*Aliyah* in the Lives of North African Widows: The Realization of a Dream or a Solution to a Problem?" *Nashim* 8 (2004): 5–24; Susan Sered, *Women as Ritual Experts* (New York, 1992), pp. 106–14; Lamdan, *A Separate People*, pp. 196–201; Melammed, "Sephardi," pp. 122–26. On the status of widows in nineteenth-century Morocco, see Shlomo Deshen, "Women in the Jewish Family in Pre-Colonial Morocco," *Anthropological Quarterly* 56, no. 3 (1983): 138–40.

American Jewish Women and Palestine (pages 63–82)

1. For an expanded discussion, see Joseph B. Glass, *From New Zion to Old Zion: American Jewish Immigration and Settlement in Palestine* (Detroit, 2002).

2. Caroline B. Brettell and Rita James Simon, "Immigrant Women: An Introduction," in *International Migration: The Female Experience*, ed. Rita James Simon and Caroline B. Brettell, pp. 4–6 (Totowa, N.J., 1986).

3. Mark Wischnitzer, *To Dwell in Safety: The Story of Jewish Migration since 1800* (Philadelphia, 1948), pp. 141–223.

4. William A. Scott and Ruth Scott, *Adaptation of Immigrants: Individual Differences and Determinants* (Oxford, 1989), p. 4.

5. *Shabbosdige Post* (St. Paul), 1, no. 5 (21 October 1921): 242 (in Yiddish); Mordechai Naor, ed., *Sefer Rishonei Herzliya 1924–1934* [The Pioneers of Herzliya, the Story of the First Settlers, 1924–1934], vol. 2 (Herzlia, 1990).

6. Dorothy Ruth Kahn, *Spring Up, O Well* (London, 1936), pp. 83–84

(hereafter cited as Kahn, *Spring Up*). Born in Philadelphia in 1907, she migrated to Palestine in 1933.

7. Shabtei Teveth, *Ben-Gurion: The Burning Ground, 1886–1948* (Boston, 1987), pp. 119–28.

8. Ze'ev Safrai, "*Ha-Talmud ha-Bavli ke-Tashtit Ra'yonot le-Aliyah la-Aretz*" [The Influence of the Babylonian Talmud on the Attitude to *Aliyah*," in *Kibbutz Galuyot, Aliyah le-Eretz Yisrael — Mitos u-Metzi'ut* [Ingathering of Exiles, *Aliyah* to the Land of Israel, Myth and Reality], ed. Dvora Hacohen, p. 38 (Jerusalem, 1998).

9. Simcha Fishbane, "The Founding of Kollel America Tifereth Yerushelayim," *American Jewish Historical Quarterly* 64, no. 2 (December–June 1974): 129–35.

10. *Agunah* is a halakhic term for a Jewish woman who is chained to her marriage because her husband's whereabouts are unknown. The term is also used for a woman whose husband refuses or is unable to grant her a *get* (official bill of divorce).

11. Interview with Abraham Zelig, Tel Aviv, 16 September 1998.

12. Palestine Service and Information Bureau, "Statistical Report on Applicants and Registrants for Immigration to Palestine from America," 31 May 1920, Central Zionist Archives, Jerusalem (hereafter cited as CZA), F25/33.

13. Marie Syrkin, ed., *Golda Meir Speaks Out* (London, 1973), p. 31.

14. Herztel Fishman, "A Zionist Childhood in St. Albans, VT," *Kfari* (February 1989): 5; interview with Hertzel Fishman, Jerusalem, 13 February 1994.

15. Kahn, *Spring Up*, p. 82.

16. Government of Palestine, Immigration Ordinances 1925–1926 and Regulations, Orders, etc., Made Thereunder (Jerusalem, April 1926); David Gurevich, Aaron Gretz, and Roberto Bachi, *Ha-Aliyah, ha-Yishuv ve-ha-Tenu'ah ha-Tiv'it shel ha-Ukhlusiyyah be-Eretz Yisrael* [The Jewish Population of Palestine, Immigration, Demographic Structure and Natural Growth] (Jerusalem, 1944), Table 12.

17. Bertha Schoolman, "Three American Pioneers in Israel," *Hadassah Newsletter* 36, no. 5 (January 1956): 15 (hereafter cited as Schoolman, "Three American").

18. Nili Fox, "Balfouriya: An American Zionist Failure or Secret Success?" *American Jewish History* 78, no. 4 (June 1989): 501; Joseph B. Glass, "Balfouria: An American Zionist Colony," *Studies in Zionism* 14, no. 1 (Spring 1993): 53–72.

19. Mordechai Seletsky letters, CZA J33/95; Solomon J. Weinstein, New York, to Avraham Silverstein, Haifa, 18 March 1924, CZA L65/386.

20. Aaron David Gordon, *Selected Essays* (New York, 1938), pp. 138–39.

21. Mimeographed letter from Tziporah Greenspan, Highstown, New Jersey, 1 February 1944, Givat Haviva Archives, RG Taf-Vav, box 19, file 11.

22. Circular from 13 January 1941, GHA RG Taf-1, box 7, file 1.

23. Irving Howe, *World of Our Fathers: the Journey of the Eastern European Jews to America and the Life They Found and Made* (New York, 1976), pp. 266–67.

24. Rachel Katznelson Shazar, ed., *The Plough Woman: Memoirs of the Pioneer Women of Palestine*, trans. Maurice Samuel (New York, 1975), p. vii.

25. Marlin Levin, *Balm in Gilead: The Story of Hadassah* (New York, 1971), pp. 81–84; Sylvia M. Gelber, *No Balm in Gilead: A Personal Retrospective of Mandate Days in Palestine* (Ottawa, 1989), pp. 104–105.

26. Jessie Sampter, Jerusalem, to Lotta Levensohn, New York, 28 December 1920, CAHJP, P3/851.

27. Schoolman, "Three American," 15.

28. Lotta Levensohn, New York, to Hannah Meisel-Schochat, Nahalal, 5 April 1925, Archives of the Women's Agricultural Training School, Nahalal, file 1.90.06. Graciously furnished by Esther Hakim-Rokem.

29. Shulamith Schwartz, "Americans in Palestine," *Jewish Frontier Anthology, 1934–1944* (New York, 1945), pp. 44–45.

30. Jessie Sampter, Jerusalem, to Sister, n.p., 1 June 1920, CZA A219/2/1.

31. Irma L. Lindheim to Stephan S. Wise, n.p., 21 May 1929, AJHSA, P-134 Wise Papers, 113:3; Irma L. Lindheim, *Parallel Quest: A Search of a Person and a People* (New York, 1962), pp. ix–x, 356–72, 381–84.

32. Arthur A. Goren, ed., *Dissenter in Zion: From the Writings of Judah L. Magnes* (Cambridge, Mass., 1982), diary entry for 6 August 1923, p. 218. See also pp. 207, 214–18.

33. Interview with Ben-Ami Fish, Tel Aviv, 6 September 1998.

34. Myriam Harry, *A Springtide in Palestine* (London, 1924), p. 51.

35. Ben Halpern, *The American Jew: A Zionist Analysis* (New York, 1983), p. 16.

36. P. E. Lapide, *Century of U.S. Aliya* (Jerusalem, 1961), p. 127, arrived at 31–32 per hundred by piecing together unspecified sources; Ralph G. Martin, *Golda: A Biography* (New York, 1988), p. 118, mentions one in three.

37. Addison E. Southard, American Consul in Charge, Jerusalem, to Secretary of State, Washington, D.C., 18 October 1921, United States National Archives, Washington, D.C. RG 84 353/86, p. 64.

38. Jessie Sampter, Jerusalem, to Elvie, Edgars and little Jessie, n.p., 3 January 1921, CZA A219/21.

39. Ibid.

40. Menachem Mendel Freidman, "Memoirs," Tel Aviv University Archives T-11/263, p. 124.

41. Kahn, *Spring Up*, p. 192. See pp. 191–202 for a full account.

42. For details of the settlement of American Jewish women in Palestine, see Joseph B. Glass, "Settling the Old-New Homeland: The Decisions of

American Jewish Women during the Interwar Years," in *American Jewish Women and the Zionist Enterprise*, ed. Shulamit Reinharz and Mark A. Raider, pp. 192–215 (Waltham, Mass., 2005).

Ethnic and Gender Identity of Iraqi Women Immigrants in the Kibbutz in the 1940s (pages 83–99)

1. On Iraqi immigrants in the cooperative settlement movement, see S. Sehayik, *Be-Netivei ha-Hagshamah: No'ar Tziyyoni Halutzi me-Iraq ba-Yishuv ha-Yehudi* [On the Path of Fulfillment, Integration of Iraqi Zionist Pioneering Youth into Eretz Yisrael Settlement] (Or Yehuda, 1997), p. 102 (hereafter cited as Sehayik, *Be-Netivei*).

2. D. Hacohen, *Olim be-Sa'arah: Ha-Aliyyah ha-Gedolah u-Kelitatah be-Yisra'el, 1948–1953* [Immigrants in the Tempest: The Mass Immigration and Its Absorption in Israel, 1948–1953] (Jerusalem, 1994), pp. 138–39.

3. About the Zionist movement members, see Esther Meir-Glitzenstein, *Zionism in an Arab Country: Jews in Iraq in the 1940s* (London, 2004), esp. chapters 3–4.

4. On the undermining of their status and security, see E. Meir, "*Ha-Sikhsukh al Eretz Yisra'el ve-Yahasei Yehudim-Muslemim be-Iraq*" [The Palestinian Dispute and Jewish-Muslim Relations in Iraq in the 1940s], *Pe'amim* 62 (1995): 111–31; N. Kazaz, *Ha-Yehudim be-Iraq ba-Me'ah ha-Esrim* [The Jews in Iraq in the Twentieth Century] (Jerusalem, 1991), pp. 189–209.

5. For an extensive discussion of this topic, see E. Meir, "*Sinderellot Yehudiyyot be-Bagdad — Ma'avakan shel Ne'arot Tziyyoniyyot be-Iraq al Shiv-yon Zekhuyyot ve-al Aliyya le-Eretz Yisr'el*" [Jewish Cinderellas in Baghdad — The Struggle for Women's Liberation among Zionists in Iraq in the 1940s] (hereafter cited as Meir, "*Sindarellot*"), in *Ha-Tishma Koli, Yitzugam shel Nashim be-Tarbut ha-Yisra'elit* [Will you Listen to my Voice?], ed. Y. Azmon, pp. 365–90 (Tel Aviv, 2001).

6. S. Sehayik, "*Temurot be-Ma'amad ha-Yehudiyyot ha-Ironiyyot be-Bavel mi-Sof ha-Me'ah ha-19*" [Changes in the Status of Urban Jewish Women in Iraq since the End of the Nineteenth Century], *Pe'amim* 36 (1988): 64–88.

7. A. Rodrigue, *Hinukh, Hevrah ve-Historiyyah, 'Kol Yisra'el Haverim' vi-Yhudei Agan ha-Yam ha-Tikhon, 1860–1929* [Education, Society, and History, "Alliance Israelite Universelle" and the Jews of the Mediterranean Basin, 1860–1929] (Jerusalem, 1991), pp. 87–88.

8. H. Cohen, *Ha-Yehudim be-Artzot ha-Mizrah ha-Tikhon be-Yameinu* [The Jews in the Middle Eastern Countries] (Tel Aviv, 1993), pp. 115, 121 (hereafter cited as Cohen, *Ha-Yehudim*).

9. Lower-class women could work at service jobs, as maids, laundresses,

seamstresses, or embroiderers, on the one hand, or — with a world of difference between them — in prostitution. The middle-class women customarily did not go out to work even if they had a profession — as teachers, nurses, and office workers — while those that had to work stopped doing so once they married. At the same time, in the 1940s there were women who worked by choice, mainly in education. Among the 35,000 female immigrants above the age of fifteen who arrived in Israel in the period 1949 to 1951, 2,300 (6.5 percent) had worked, and of them, 60 percent in sewing and 20 percent in office work, teaching, and medicine. See Cohen, *Ha-Yehudim*, p. 166.

10. On the women's activity in the Zionist movement, see Meir, "*Sindarellot.*"

11. See Sehayik, *Be-Netivei*. This article is based mainly on sources written by the *olot* during their stay in the kibbutz: essays that appeared in *hakhsharah* newsletters, personal letters, and diaries. Added to these were memoirs, among them the book by Shoshana Arbelli Almoslino, *Me-ha-Mahteret be-Bavel le-Memshelet Yisra'el* [From the Bavli Underground to the Government of Israel] (Tel Aviv, 1999); and interviews and conversations with former *haverot*, including Aliza Biron, Ruth Karagila, Shulamit Ginnosar, Arella Balbul, and Tikva Shohat. Methodologically, the newsletters, a main component of the source material, are problematic; all articles are "colored" by Zionist ideology, because of the nature of the framework as well as, apparently, the guiding hand of the *madrikhim*. This means that the newsletters must be given a careful, critical reading, while cross-checking them with material from other sources and taking into consideration interviews that shed light on the atmosphere of that period and help with the critical examination.

12. Hadassah Hamina, *Alon mi-Garin 4 mi-Babel* [Newsletter of Gar'in 4 from Bavel], Giv'at ha-Sheloshah, 10 December 1948, pp. 2–3.

13. For example, the essay by Aryeh Ezra (Mu'allem) in the newsletter Bi-Netiv ha-Hagshamah [On the path to realization], Ashdot Ya'akov, Heshvan 5708 (1948).

14. A. Shapira, *Yehudim Hadashim Yehudim Yeshanim* (New Jews Old Jews) (Tel Aviv, 1997), pp. 167–71.

15. From Shoshana to Amnon, 4 July 1947, personal file of Shoshana Mu'allem, Archives of Babylonian Jewry Heritage Center (hereafter cited as BJHC).

16. Ruth Iliya, *Bi-Netiv ha-Hagshamah*, Ashdot Ya'akov, Heshvan 5708 (1948), p. 11.

17. Avner Sha'ashu'a, *Bi-Netiv ha-Hagshamah*, Heshvan 5708 (1948).

18. Yoel Shohat, *Alon Ashdot Ya'akov* [Ashdot Ya'akov Newsletter], No. 1058, 23 April 1948.

19. See above, n. 16.

20. "*Im Bo'einu li-Sdeh Nahum*" [Upon our arrival at Sdeh Nahum], drafts of essays written by members of the Bavli *gar'in* (settlement nucleus) (BJHC).

21. Sylvia Fogel-Bijaoui, "*Immahot u-Mahapeikha, ha-Mikreh shel Nashim ba-Kibbutz, 1910–1948*" [Mothers and Revolution, the Case of Women in the Kibbutz, 1910–1948], *Shorashim* 6 (1991): 49 (hereafter cited as Fogel-Bijaoui, "*Immahot*").

22. *Alon Hevrat ha-No'ar ha-Oleh* 1 [The Immigrant Youth Group Newsletter 1], Oranim 4, Yad Tabenkin Archives.

23. "It was difficult to change from a life of leisure to one of labor, especially for a girl who had been pampered in her parents home," writes Tamar R. in the newsletter prepared for the end of the Bavli *gar'in hakhsharah* at Ma'oz Haim, 19 October 1950, Yad Tabenkin Archives, Section 2 foreign, container 3 file 4.

24. The group's newsletter in Bet ha-Shitah.

25. Ibid.

26. Shlomo Artzi, "*Divrei Bikkoret* [Some Criticism], *Alonenu* [Our Newsletter] No. 2, the Bavli *gar'in* in Afikim, 16 June 1950, Yad Tabenkin Archives.

27. One of the girls, Rina T., expressed her inner struggles writing: "I am a young woman who happily breathed city air for years, she never saw a village, she never tasted the life of labor and creativity, in this I was no different than thousands of women and young ladies in the east who never had to worry about supporting themselves. The father, brothers, or husband were charged with this duty. What captured my heart and what power brought me this far?" ("*Im Bo'einu li-Sdeh Nahum*"], drafts, see n. 20 above.

28. On women's work in the kibbutz during the 1930s and 1940s, see Fogel-Bijaoui, "*Immahot*," pp. 154–60.

29. Yehoshua, "*Ha-Olim mi-Bavel Mevate'im et Atzmam*" [The Bavli Immigrants Express Themselves], from *Alon ha-Giv'ah* [Giv'at ha-Sheloshah], no. 1105. Emphasis mine, E. M-G.

30. Report by Tzviyah, *madrikhah* at Kvutzat Keisariyyah, "*Im No'ar Oleh mi-Babel*" [With the Immigrant Youth from Iraq], *Devar ha-Po'elet*, Sivan 5710 (1950), issue 5, p. 142.

31. Ruth Yosef, "*Ba-Ma'avak*" [In the Battle], newsletter of the Bavli *gar'in* at Yagur, 6 December 1950, Yad Tabenkin Archives, Section 2 foreign, container 3, file 4.

32. Naomi Kashi, *Me-Irak le'Yisrael, Pirkei Yoman ve-Zihronot* [From Iraq to Israel, Diary Selections and Memoirs], personal diary (unpublished), p. 25 (hereafter cited as Kashi, *Me-Irak*).

33. "The style of dress, too, is a problem. It was mainly the young women who suffered the most from this. All the clothes they had brought with from Iraq were out of place here. The clothing made in the kibbutz was not enough, so there were complications in the clothing storehouse and lots of problems," writes Pesya, who assisted in absorbing the Bavli *gar'in* at Giv'at ha-Sheloshah, Newsletter of Gar'in 4 from Babylonia [in Hebrew], Giv'at ha-Sheloshah, 10 December 1948, Yad Tabenkin Archives.

34. Kashi, *Me-Irak*, p. 40.

35. A letter to her brother in Basra, 4 July 1944, Shoshana Mu'allem file, CHIJ.

36. Letter from Yoel in Ashdot to Gideon [Golani] in Be'eri, 20 June 1947, Shoshana Mu'allem File, BJHC Archives.

37. Report by Shimshon ben Yehuda, at the fourth convention of the Bavli *aliyah* held at Nahbir [Be'eri], 25 July 1947, *Tzeror Yedi'ot* [A Bundle of News], No. 4, Hehalutz Movement Archives.

38. Rozka, Ein ha-Horesh, *"Ha-Gar'inim ha-Bavli'im be-Kibbutzeinu"* [The Bavli *gar'inim* in Our Kibbutz], *Devar ha-Po'elet*, Pamphlets 1–2, 5711 [1951], p. 21.

39. Protocol of a meeting of the members of the El Al *hakhsharah*, 2 September 1948, Hehalutz Movement in Bavel Archives, BJHC. Not all *gar'in* members had come through the pioneering underground.

40. Shimshon S., "Upon Our Arrival," p. 15 (see n. 20 above).

41. Letter from Aryeh Mu'allem to Shoshan Murad [Mu'allem], Ashdot Ya'akov, 13 November 1947, Shoshana Mu'allem File, CHIJ Archives. Shulamit Ginossar, who was a member of kibbutz Palmahim, related in a conversation that took place on 12 March 1999 that among the members there were even couples who had intimate relations, or in her language "they did not refrain." She explained it by the revolutionary nature of Zionism.

42. From Aryeh Mu'allem to Shoshana, 13 November 1947, Shoshana Mu'allam File, BJHC Archives.

43. See Cohen, *Ha-Yehudim*, pp. 153–54. On secularization processes in Eretz Israel, see T. Benski et al., *Yehudei Iraq be-Yisra'el ba-Hevrah u-va-Kalkalah* [Iraqi Jews in Israel in Society and Economics] (Tel Aviv, 1991), pp. 218–35.

44. From Aryeh to Shoshana, 9 December 1947, Shoshana Mu'allem File, BJHC Archives; from Shoshana to her brother Nadji [Amnon], 4 August 1947, translated by Dr. Saul Sehayik, ibid. On the complexity of the attitude to religion in the labor movement, see Shapira, *"Ha-Motiviyyim ha-Datiyyim shel Tenu'at ha-Avodah"* [The Religious Motifs of the Labor Movement], in Shapira, *New Jews*. On intentional contempt for the mourning on Tisha b'Av, see Shapira, *New Jews*, pp. 269–70. We must point out that the Bavli members could not have been aware of the complexity of the attitude toward religion since they were strangers and new to the kibbutz, and they related only to the practical aspects of this issue.

45. Decisions of the Labor Committee, 12 January 1948, Hehalutz Movement Archives, CHIJ Archives.

46. Naomi, n. 32 above, p. 36. At the second meeting of the National Center of the Zionist Movement in Iraq, 8–9 September 1945, it was reported that kibbutz Ma'oz Haim had forced members to light a fire on the Sabbath. The spokesperson warned that reports on antireligious education were liable to de-

stroy the movement. Section 2 foreign, Container 2 File 5, Yad Tabenkin Archives.

47. Tzivyah Nahum, *Oranim B*, the newsletter of the immigrant youth group at Bet Oren (Bavlim and Syrians), Yad Tabenkin Archives.

48. See n. 26.

49. An exception is Naomi Kashi's memoirs.

50. Sehayik, *Be-Netivei*, p. 102. From the protocol of the Kibbutz ha-Me'uhad Secretariat, Section 2 Container 8 Book 35, p. 96, Yad Tabenkin Archives. At the second meeting of the National Center of the Zionist Movement in Baghdad, it was reported: "There is a suspicion of exploitation after they have taken away the day for studies. The *haverim* have begun to despair. They have begun to evade work. The determination of the work schedule opposed the day for studies," 8–9 September 1945, Section 2 foreign, Container 2 File 5, Yad Tabenkin Archives.

51. H. Jablonka, *Ahim Zarim: Nitzolei ha-Sho'ah bi-Medinat Yisra'el, 1948–1952* [Foreign Brothers: Holocaust Survivors in the State of Israel, 1948–1952] (Jerusalem, 1994), pp. 159–64, 207–208, 223–24.

52. Sehayik, *Be-Netivei*, pp. 100, 114.

53. Emanuel, Protocol of the Seventh Convention of Bavli Immigration in Kibbutz ha-Me'uhad, 21 May 1950, He-Halutz Movement Archives, CHIJ; Sehayik, *Be-Netivei*, p. 100.

54. Naomi, n. 32 above, p. 30.

55. See Arbelli Almoslino, *Me-ha-Mahteret*, n. 11 above.

Social Networks of Immigrant Women in the Early 1950s in Israel (pages 100–108)

1. Several studies dealt with women as part of the overall population investigated, but they did not focus on their role or their unique contribution to the absorption process. See D. Weintraub, "*Hashpa'at ha-Herkev ha-Demografi shel Mishpahot Olim al Histaglut la-Moshav*" [The Influence of the Demographic Composition of Immigrant Families on Adaptation to the Moshav], *Megamot* 10, no. 4 (March 1960); idem, "*Defusei Shinnui Hevrati shel Kevutzot Adatiyyot be-Moshavei Olim*" [Patterns of Social Change of Ethnic Groups in Immigrant Settlements], *Shenaton ha-Histadrut* 2 (1966); H. Weil, "*Be'ayot Kehilatiyyot be-Yishuv Olim*" [Community Problems in Immigrant Settlements], *Mehkarim be-Sotziologiyyah* 2 (1957); A. Winograd, "*Yahadut Maroko be-Ma'avar*" [Moroccan Jewry in Transition], *Megamot* 10, no. 3 (January 1960); S. Deshen and M. Shoked, eds., "*Dor ha-Temurah*" [The Generation of Transformation], (Jerusalem 1977). The countries from which they immigrated were Iraq, Yemen, Aden, Morocco, Algeria, Tunis, Bulgaria, Turkey,

Libya, Iran, Romania, Poland, Czechoslovakia, Hungary, Germany, Austria, Egypt, the USSR, and Yugoslavia; M. Sicron, *"Ha-Aliyah ha-Hamonit — Memadeha, Me'afyeneha, ve-Hashpa'ata al Mivneh Ukhlusiyyat Yisra'el"* ['Mass Immigration' — Its Dimensions, Characteristics, and Influence on the Population Structure of Israel], in *Olim u-Ma'abarot 1948–1952*, ed. M. Naor, p. 34 (Jerusalem, 1986) (hereafter cited as Sicron, *"Ha-Aliyah"*).

2. S. N. Eisenstadt, *Kelitat Aliyah: Mehkar Sotziologi* [Absorption of Immigration: A Sociological Study], (Jerusalem, 1952).

3. Data from 1948 to 1954 indicate that among women who immigrated from Asian-African countries, 57.8 percent never attended school versus 6.3 percent from European countries; 26.2 percent of women from Asian-African countries did not complete elementary school versus 31.9 percent from European countries; Sicron, *"Ha-Aliyah,"* p. 40.

4. J. L. Moreno, *Who Shall Survive?* (Washington, 1934); J. L. Barnes, "Class and Committees in a Norwegian Island Parish," *Human Relations* 7 (1954): 39–58; E. Bott, *Family and Social Network: Roles, Norms, and External Relationships in Ordinary Urban Families* (London, 1957); D. Crane, *Invisible Colleges* (Chicago, 1972); L. C. Freeman, *Bibliography on Social Networks* (Monticello, Ill., 1976); K. Wendt, "Electronic Mail and Scientific Communication: A Study of the SOAR Extended Research Group," *Knowledge* 12 (1991): 406–40.

5. The teacher Rina Shapiro and her pupils in the Talpiot *ma'abara*: a symposium of the "ma'abara children" thirty years later, *Olim u-Ma'abarot* (n. 2 above), p. 161.

A "Woman-Human" *(pages 111–121)*

1. I have dealt with various aspects of this issue in my doctoral thesis: E. Ramon, "God, the Mother: A Critique of Domination in the Religious Zionist Thought of A. D. Gordon (1856–1922)," Ph.D. diss., Stanford University, 1999. I wish to thank all the foundations and bodies that assisted while I wrote the dissertation: Memorial Foundation for Jewish Culture, American Association for University Women, and The Shalom Hartman Institute.

2. A. D. Gordon, *Mivhar Ketavim* [Selected Writings] (Jerusalem, 1983), p. 306 (hereafter cited as Gordon, *Mivhar*).

3. A. Fishman, *"Li-She'elat ha-Ovedet"* [Concerning the Question of the Woman Laborer], *Ha-Po'el ha-Tza'ir* 15, nos. 1–2 (1921): 14.

4. *Kitvei A. D. Gordon* [Writings of A. D. Gordon], ed. Y. Aharonowitz, 2:28 (Tel Aviv, 1925–1929) (hereafter cited as *Kitvei*).

5. Ibid., p. 28.

6. Y. Aharonowitz, *"Reshimot le-Toledot Hayyav shel A. D. Gordon"* [Biographical Notes on the Life of A. D. Gordon], *Kitvei*, 1, p. vi.

7. Labor and He-Halutz Archives–Lavon Institute, file 104–13; see also *"Resisei Zikhronot al A. D. Gordon she-He'elta Bitto Yael"* [Bits of Memory on A. D. Gordon Presented by his Daughter Yael], in *Ro'enu Morenu* (Our Leader, Our Teacher) (Deganya Alef, 1962), p. 11.

8. Y. Midrashi, *Yosef Ahronovich* [in Hebrew] (Tel Aviv, 1965), pp. 220–22.

9. B. Schochetman, *"Yedi'ot Bi'ografiyyot Nosafot al A. D. Gordon"* [Additional Biographical Information on A. D. Gordon], *Ha-Po'el ha-Tza'ir* 33, nos. 16–17 (1940), pp. 12–13.

10. Memoirs that Yael wrote at the behest of Y. Palmoni, January–April 1947, Gordon Archives, Gordon's Corner, Deganya Alef, pp. 23–24.

11. E. Schweid, *Ha-Yahid: Olamo shel A. D. Gordon* [The Only One: The World of A. D. Gordon] (Tel Aviv, 1970), p. 35.

12. H. Rutenberg, *"Aharon David Gordon u-bitto Yael"* [Aharon David Gordon and His Daughter Yael], *Be-Givatayim* 9–10 (Tishri 5727 [1966]: 35.

13. Letter written Kislev 1925, located in Pinat Gordon, Bet Gordon, Deganya Alef.

14. Y. Gordon, *"Ha-Ve'idah ha-Rishonah le-Po'alot"* [The First Women Laborers' Convention], ed. E. Shohat and H. Sorer, *Pirkei Ha-Poel ha-Tza'ir* 3 (Tel Aviv, 1935): 215–16.

15. Gordon, *Mivhar*, p. 392.

16. M. Tzur, *"At Einekh Bodedah — Mikhtavim me-A. D. Gordon ve-Elav"* [You Are Not Alone — Letters to and from A. D. Gordon] (Tel Aviv, 1998), p. 59.

17. *"Mitokh Keri'ah"* [While Reading], in *Kitvei*, pp. 232–33.

18. Ibid., p. 234.

19. *"Pitaron Ratziyyonali"* [Rational Solution], in *Kitvei*, 1, p. 13.

20. Fourth letter to *Der Jude*, published in 1917, in *Kitvei*, 2, p. 277.

21. *"Universitah Ivrit"* [Hebrew University], in *Kitvei*, 1, p. 117; *"Me'at Hitbonenut"* [A Little Observation] (1911), in ibid., 1, p. 86.

22. H. Chizik, *"Im A. D. Gordon"* [With A. D. Gordon], *Davar ha-Po'elet* 13, nos. 2/3 (1947): 50.

23. Ibid.

24. *"Mah Hayah Gordon"* [What Was Gordon?], *Davar ha-Po'elet* 22, no. 6 (1957): 170.

25. B. Israeli, *Ketavim u-Devarim* [Writings and Notions] (Tel Aviv and Kevutzat Kinneret, 1957), pp. 75–76.

26. A. Shapira, *Berl* [in Hebrew] (Tel Aviv, 1980), 1:105.

27. R. Katznelson-Shazar, *Masot u-Reshimot* [Essays and Articles] (Tel Aviv, 1946), p. 247.

28. A. Maimon (Fishman), *Hamishim Shenot Tenu'at ha-Po'alot, 1904–54* [Fifty Years of the Women Laborers' Movement] (Tel Aviv and Ayanot, 1955), p. 50.

29. A. Maimon, *Le-Orekh ha-Derekh* [Along the Way], collected and edited by Yehuda Erez (Tel Aviv, 1972), p. 45.

30. Ibid.

31. Ibid., pp. 42–43.

What Troubled Them? *(pages 122–130)*

1. Meir Ya'ari, *"Ba-Derekh le-Shivyon"* [On the Way to Equality], *Hedim* (April 1936): p. 2.

2. L. Bassevitz, *"Ha-Haverah ba-Kibbutz"* [The Woman in the Kibbutz], *Mibifnim* 11, no. 3 (January 1946): 351, 357 (hereafter Bassevitz, *"Ha-Haverah"*).

3. Ibid., p. 351.

4. For instance, see L. Bassevitz, *"Ha-Haverah ba-Meshek ha-Kibbutzi"* [The Woman in the Kibbutz Economy], *Mibifnim* 52 (23 November 1931): 656, 657; S. Frankel, *"Le-Tikkun ha-Me'uvvat"* [To Correct the Injustice], *Hedim* (April 1947): 63–64.

5. On agricultural work, see Bassevitz, *"Ha-Haverah,"* p. 348; on the "rule of the third," see Lilia [Bassevitz], *"Hishtattefut ha-Haverah ba-Hayyim ba-Kibbutz"* [Women's Participation in the Public Life of the Kibbutz], *Mibifnim* 52 (23 November 1931): 665–68; on women on guard duty, see Y. Bat-Rachel and others, series of articles in *Mi-Bifnim*, June 1936.

6. Niv Hakvutza (Iyar–Sivan 1947), 48–49.

7. M. Poznansky and M. Shehori, eds.; material collected by L. Bassevitz and Y. Bat-Rachel, *Haverot ba-Kibbutz* [Women in the Kibbutz] (Ein Harod, 1944; repr. 1947, 1949).

8. For instance, the famous speech by Sojourner Truth ("I plow and plant and reap and bring to the barn . . . And ain't I a woman" — Seneca Falls, 1851), quoted by S. Rowbotham, *Women, Resistance and Revolution* (London, 1972), p. 100.

9. *Mi-Bifnim* 11, no. 3 (January 1946): 344–63.

10. Bassevitz, *"Ha-Haverah,"* p. 345.

11. Ibid., pp. 356–57.

12. S. Goldman, *"He'arot li-She'elat ha-Haverah ba-Kibbutz"* [Comments on the Question of the Woman in the Kibbutz)], *Hedim* (September 1947): 85.

13. Letter from Hania Shulami, who was killed in 1939. *Sikkumim* (Kfar Yehoshu'a, 1939).

14. T. Lieberson, *Pirkei Hayyim* [Chapters in a Life] (Tel-Aviv, 1970).

15. A. Maimon, *Hamishim Shenot Ten'uat ha-Po'alot* [Fifty Years of the Women Workers' Movement] (Tel-Aviv, 1955), pp. 158–59.

16. S. Kaplan, *"Ha-Haverah ba-Moshav"* [The Woman in the *Moshav*], *T'lamim* (Adar–Nissan 1942): 14–17; A. Assaf, *"Ha-Moshav u-Ba'ayotav"* [The *Moshav* and its Problems], *T'lamim* (Tishrei–Kislev 1948): 4–5.

17. Quoted in M. Tsur, T. Zevulun, and H. Porat, eds., *Kan al pnei ha-Adamah* [The Beginning of the Kibbutz] (Tel-Aviv, 1981), p. 90.

Forging the Image of Pioneering Women (pages 131–140)

1. See D. Biale, *Eros and the Jews* (Berkeley, 1997); M. Gluzman, "*Ha-Kemihah le-Heteroseksu'aliyyut: Tziyyonut u-Miniyyut be-Altneuland*" [The Yearning for Heterosexuality: Zionism and Sexuality in Altneuland], *Theory and Criticism* 11 (Winter 1997): 145–62; D. Boyarin, *Unheroic Conduct* (Berkeley, 1997).

2. D. Miron, *Immahot Meyassedot, Ahayot Horgot, al Shetei Hathalot be-Shirah ha-Erziyisra'elit* [Founding Mothers, Stepsisters, the Emergence of the First Hebrew Poetesses and Other Essays] (Tel Aviv, 1991), p. 137.

3. D. Miron, *Mul ha-Ah ha-Shotek: Iyyunim be-Shirat Milhemet ha-Atzma'ut* [Facing the Silent Brother: Studies in the Poetry of the War of Independence] (Tel Aviv, 1992), p. 48.

4. G. Shaked, *Ha-Sipporet ha-Ivrit 1880–1980* [Hebrew Fiction 1880–1980], vol. 4, *Be-Havlei ha-Zeman* [In the Throes of Time] (Tel Aviv, 1993), p. 15 (hereafter cited as Shaked, *Ha-Sipporet*).

5. N. Shaham, *Kirot Ets Dakim* (Tel Aviv, 1977), pp. 81–149. The book appeared in English translated by Leonard Gold, *The Other Side of the Wall* (Philadelphia, 1983) (hereafter cited as Shaham, *Kirot*).

6. Of course, *My Michael* by Amos Oz was published in 1968, but it is difficult to see Hannah Gonen as a powerful feminine figure, who goes beyond the stereotypes of "femininity." She fits in rather well with the masculine stereotypes of women (weak, hysterical, and unpractical: a princess estranged and isolated in her ivory tower, prey to her imaginings and dreams).

7. O. Almog, *Ha-Tzabar: Deyukan* [The Sabra: A Portrait] (Tel Aviv, 1997).

8. As to Nathan Shaham's socio-cultural status and cultural affiliation, see the chapter devoted to him in G. Shaked, *Ha-Sipporet*, "*Tamid Anahnu Guf Rishon Rabbim?*" [Are We Always First-Person Plural?] (Tel Aviv, 1993), pp. 317–47.

9. S. Lapid, *Gei Oni* (Hebrew; Jerusalem, 1982). I shall discuss this novel later on in this article.

10. Shaham, *Kirot*, p. 87 (Gold translation, p. 109).

11. Ibid., p. 98 (Gold translation, p. 125).

12. Ibid., p. 90 (Gold translation, p. 113).

13. Ibid., p. 118 (Gold translation, p. 151).

14. Ibid., p. 117 (Gold translation, p. 149).

15. Ibid., p. 119 (Gold translation, p. 152).

16. Ibid. (Gold translation, p. 160, emphasis mine — S.S.)

17. Quoted in M. Rozner, *Temurot bi-Tefisah al Shivyon ha-Ishah ba-Kibbutz* [Changes in the Perception of the Equality of the Woman in the Kibbutz] (Givat Havivah, 1969), p. 3.

18. Ibid.

19. Ibid., pp. 147–48 (Gold translation, p. 189).

20. Shaked, *Ha-Sipporet*, p. 317.

21. On the exclusion of women from the hegemonic center in the *Yishuv* in Eretz Israel, see, for example, Y. Berlovits, *Lehamtzi Eretz Lehamtzi Am* [Inventing a Land, Inventing a People] (Tel Aviv, 1996); D. Bernstein, *Ishah be-Eretz Yisra'el* [A Woman in Eretz Israel] (Tel Aviv, 1987); B. Melman, "*Historiyyah shel Nashim, Historiyyah u-Politikah*" [History of Women, History and Politics 1880–1993], *Zemanim* 46–47 (1993): 19–33. Bernstein explains, "The inequality was expressed in the re-creation of traditional, patriarchal elements . . . the majority of [the women] did not have a chance at productive physical labor, which was considered the liberating work, which creates the new human being" (Bernstein, p. 11), and this "despite the aspiration of many women toward equal relations, despite the commitment of the laborers' movement to social equality, including equality between women and men" (ibid., p. 140).

22. I would like to mention here Yael Feldman's pioneering work on this novel and this subject. See Y. Feldman, "*Roman Histori o Autobiografia be-Masecha*" [A Historical Novel or a Masked Autobiography], *Siman Kri'a* 19 (1986): 208–213; see also idem, *No Room of Their Own* (New York, 1999).

23. Lapid, *Gei Oni*, p. 68.

24. Ibid., p. 104.

25. Ibid., p. 236 (emphasis mine—S.S.).

26. Ibid., p. 251.

27. Ibid., p. 266. One could, of course, argue that the inability of a single woman burdened with four children to support herself in Rosh Pina at the beginning of the twentieth century is a "realistic" fact, but if this woman can conduct business by herself in the Galilee teeming with robbers, it should have been possible to let her somehow support herself, even without being saved by a new man.

28. Ibid., p. 144.

29. Ibid., p. 175.

30. Ibid., p. 104.

31. Within the limited framework of this article, I will not try to present a general analysis of Shaham's work, but perhaps it is worth mentioning his novel *The Rosendorf Quartet*, which convincingly and impressively presents a-Zionist or even anti-Zionist positions: N. Shaham, *The Rosendorf Quartet* (Tel Aviv, 1987).

A Woman's Life Story as a Foundation Legend
of Local Identity (pages 141–163)

1. In a previous study we focused on the women's embroidery group. See H. Salamon and G. Hasan-Rokem, *"Rokemot et Atzman: Rikmah ve-Nashiyyut bi-Kevutzah Yerushalmit"* [Embroidering Themselves: Embroidery and Femininity in a Jerusalem Group], *Theory and Criticism* 10 (1997): 55–68.

2. The life story of Zohar Wilbush was told to this article's writer and to another listener, Sharon Agur, who assisted in the field work.

3. On the colonial characteristics of the Oriental, see E. W. Said, "Zionism from the Standpoint of Its Victims," in *Anatomy of Racism*, ed. D. T. Goldberg, pp. 210–46 (Minneapolis, 1990).

4. See particularly P. Bourdieu, *Outline of a Theory of Practice* (Cambridge, 1977); idem, *The Logic of Practice* (Stanford, 1990) (hereafter cited as Bourdieu, *Logic*).

5. On Geertz's interpretation of culture as an exegetical system, see C. Geertz, *The Interpretation of Culture* (New York, 1973) (Hebrew edition: *Parshanut shel Tarbut* [Jerusalem, 1990], pp. 15–39). For the development of the idea of the habitus, see Bourdieu, *Logic*, pp. 52–65.

6. Bourdieu, *Logic*, pp. 66–79.

7. E. W. Said, *Orientalism* (Harmondsworth, 1978).

8. On the connection between ethnography, Orientalism, and power, see, for example, J. Clifford, "On Orientalism," in *The Predicament of Culture: Twentieth-Century Ethnography, Literature and Art* (Cambridge, Mass., 1988); on power, resistance, colonialism, and women, see, for example, J. Comaroff, *Body of Power, Spirits of Resistance: The Culture and History of a South-African People* (Chicago, 1985).

9. On mutuality, see, for example, H. K. Bhabha, *"She'elat ha-Aher: Hevdel, Aflayah ve-Si'ah Post-Kolonyali"* [The Question of the Other: Difference, Discrimination, and Post-Colonial Discourse], *Theory and Criticism* 5 (1994), 145–57; G. Ch. Spivak, "Three Women's Texts and a Critique of Imperialism," in *'Race', Writing, and Difference*, ed. H. L. Gates (Chicago, 1986) (hereafter cited as Spivak, "Three Women's"); J. C. Scott, *Domination and the Arts of Resistance: Hidden Transcripts* (New Haven, 1990). On deconstruction, see J. Derrida, "Deconstruction and the Other: An Interview with Richard Kearney," in *Dialogues with Contemporary Continental Thinkers: The Phenomenological Heritage*, ed. R. Kearney (Manchester, 1984); G. Ch. Spivak, "Displacement and the Discourse of Woman," in *Displacement: Derrida and After*, ed. M. Krupnick, pp. 169–95 (Bloomington, Ind., 1987); Spivak, "Three Women's"; R. Young, *Colonial Desire: Hybridity in Theory, Culture and Race* (London & New York, 1995). On Lacanian thinking, see J. Butler, *Bodies That Matter: On the Discursive Limits of "Sex"* (New York, 1993) (hereafter cited as Butler, *Bodies*).

10. E. W. Said, "Orientalism Reconsidered," *Cultural Critique* 1 (1985); R. Radhakrishnan, "Nationalism, Gender, and the Narrative of Identity," in *Nationalism and Sexualities*, ed. Andrew Parker et al. (New York, 1992); Butler, *Bodies*; M. Yeğenoğlu, *Colonial Fantasies: Towards a Feminist Reading of Orientalism* (Cambridge, 1998) (hereafter cited as Yeğenoğlu, *Colonial*). See also R. Kabbani, *Europe's Myths of Orient* (Bloomington, 1986).

11. In this context, Young's discussion is of interest (*Colonial Desire*, pp. 173–75), which addresses in a new manner the concept of hybridity in the colonialist context in Bhabha, "*She'elat ha-Aher*"; and also in Yeğenoğlu, *Colonial*, p. 35.

12. On the political aspect of Palestinian representation by means of embroidery and other feminine crafts, see, for example, G. Frank, "Crafts Production and Resistance to Domination in the Late 20th Century," *Journal of Occupational Science* 3, no. 2 (1996): 56–64. For a fresh perspective on the connection between personal biography and objects, see J. Hoskins, *Biographical Objects: How Things Tell the Stories of People's Lives* (New York & London, 1998).

13. In this context, Yoram Bilu writes: "There are many ways, all of them partial, to analyze and understand life histories. The portrait of the Other crystallizes only through the process of its construction, during the course of the interaction between the researcher and the object of the study. The design of the portrait is guided, inter alia, by the researcher's prior knowledge (such as of social conventions, cultural traditions, theoretical paradigms, and so on). This system is likely to be such a useful framework for sorting through, organizing, and processing the raw data that in some cases it might be possible to accept the blunt claim that ethnography and biography, more than they create a 'narrative' are created by it." Y. Bilu, "*Historyat Hayyim ke-Tekst*" [Life History as Text], *Megamot: Behavioral Sciences Quarterly* 29, no. 4 (1985/1986): 350. On the rhetoric of biography and the importance of the literary aspects through which the narrative is fashioned, see also A. Lieblich, T. Zilber, and R. Tuvel-Mashiach, "*Mehappesim u-Motze'im: Hakhlalah ve-Avhanah be-Sippurei Hayyim*" [Seeking and Finding: Generalization and Distinction in Life Stories], *Psychology* 5 (1995): 84–95. For another discussion of these aspects, see, for example, V. Crapanzano, *Hermes' Dilemma and Hamlet's Desire* (Cambridge, Mass., 1992).

14. This text is characterized by the repeated use of Arabic terms, undoubtedly intended to reinforce the local impression that Zohar wants to present. To each term a "translation" is usually appended. I wish to thank Ruth Kark who drew my attention to the Arabic name Buzaburah used by Zohar, which is Mikhmoret today.

15. For a discussion of the construction of Otherness and the concept of a different kind of temporality, see J. Fabian, *Time and the Other: How Anthropology Makes Its Objects* (New York, 1983).

16. On the women's embroidery group, see Salamon and Hasan-Rokem, "*Rokemot et Atzman*," n. 1 above.

17. For an important discussion of memory and its narrative, see J. Bahloul, *The Architecture of Memory* (Cambridge, 1996), particularly chapter five. Ethnographic and theoretical material that deals with life stories and their narrative design is a broad, expanding field in the research of culture that treats it only by allusion.

A Cross-Cultural Message (pages 167–179)

1. *Hazevi*, no. 7, 29 Tevet [5]648 [= 13 January 1888]. For a wider discussion of this topic, see Margalit Shilo, *Princess or Prisoner? Jewish Women in Jerusalem, 1840–1914* (Hanover, N.H., 2005), chapter 5.

2. Yosef Salmon, "Ha-Hinukh ha-Ashkenazi be-Eretz Yisra'el bein 'Yashan' le-'Hadash'" [Ashkenazi Education in Eretz Israel between the "Old" and the "New" (1840–1906)], *Shalem* 6 (1992): 281–301.

3. Eliakim Ellinson, *Ha-Ishah ve-ha-Mitzvot; Mekorot Hilkhatiyyim Mevo'arim* [The Woman and the Commandments: A Collection of Teachings of Our Sages and Halakhic Decisions] (Jerusalem, 1974), pp. 160–71; Deborah Weissman, "Hinnukh Banot bi-Yrushalayim bi-Tekufat ha-Shilton ha-Beriti" [Girls' Education in Jerusalem during the Mandate Period] (Ph.D. diss., Hebrew University of Jerusalem, 1994), p. 113; Iris Parush, *Nashim Kor'ot* [Women Reading] (Tel Aviv, 2001), pp. 14–17.

4. Mordechai Eliav, *Ha-Hinnukh ha-Yehudi be-Germanya bi-Ymei ha-Haskalah ve-ha-Imantzipatziyyah* [Jewish Education in Germany in the Period of the Haskalah and Emancipation] (Jerusalem, 1961), pp. 271–79; Thomas Woody, *A History of Women's Education in the U.S.*, vols. 1–2 (New York, 1966 [1929]); Zosa Szajkowski, *Jewish Education in France 1789–1938* (Jewish Social Sciences Monograph Series 2; New York, 1980), pp. 4–9; James C. Albisetti, "The Feminization of Teaching: A Comparative Perspective," *History of Education* 22, nos. 1–4 (1993): 253–63.

5. Sh. P. Zolty, "And All Your Children Shall Be Learned," *Woman and the Study of Tora in Jewish Law and History* (New Jersey, 1992), pp. 238–41.

6. In the years 1831 to 1840, Palestine was ruled by Mohamed Ali, the Egyptian ruler, who introduced modernity into the country. His innovations were followed by the Ottoman rulers who recaptured the country.

7. Mordechai Eliav, *Eretz Yisra'el ve-Yishuvah ba-Me'ah ha-Tesha Esreh, 1777–1914* [The Land of Israel and Its Settlement in the Nineteenth Century, 1777–1914] (Jerusalem, 1978), p. 498; Yehoshua ben-Arieh, *Jerusalem in the 19th Century: Emergence of the New City* (Jerusalem, 1986), p. 466.

8. Josephine Kamm, *Hope Deferred: Girls' Education in English History* (London, 1965), pp. 152–65; Jane Martin, *Women and the Politics of Schooling in Victorian and Edwardian England* (London, 1998), pp. 75–84.

9. The school was sponsored by the French Rothschilds until 1868, when it came under the protection of the English branch of the family. On the Montefiore school, see A. M. Luncz, *Yerushalayim* 2 (1887): 121–22.

10. M. Eliav, *Be-Hasut Mamlekhet Ostriyah* [Under Imperial Austrian Protection] (Jerusalem, 1985), p. 98 (hereafter cited as Eliav, *Be-Hasut*). The reference is to Charlotte, daughter of James (Jacob) Rothschild of Paris and wife of Nathaniel Rothschild of the London branch.

11. Daniel Carpi and Moshe Rinot, *"Yoman Mas'oteha shel Morah Yehudiyyah mi-Triest li-Yrushalayim"* [Diary of the Journey of a [Female] Jewish Teacher from Trieste to Jerusalem], in *Kevatzim le-heker toledot ha-hinnukh ha-yehudi be-Yisra'el u-va-tefuzot* [Anthologies for Research on the History of Jewish Education in Israel and the Dispersion], 1982, p. 126; Eliezer Mannenberg, "Modernization and Educational Change: A Case Study in the Transition of a Jewish Community Antedating the Israeli Society," *Jewish Social Studies* 40 (1978): 293–302.

12. Letter from Albert Cohn to the Austrian Emperor, 28 July 1854; Eliav, *Be-Hasut*, p. 298; Rachel Elboim-Dror, *Hahinnukh ha-Ivri be-Eretz Israel* [Jewish Education in the Land of Israel], 1 (Jerusalem, 1986), pp. 80–82, 86–89.

13. Hagai Erlich, *No'ar u-Politikah* [Youth and Politics] (Tel Aviv, 1998), p. 25.

14. Mary Eliza Rogers, *Domestic Life in Palestine* (London, 1862), p. 336.

15. Rogers, *Domestic Life*.

16. *Havazelet*, no. 39, 27 Tamuz [5]635 [= 30 July 1875].

17. In 1868, the school was named after Evelina, the youngest daughter of Lionel Rothschild, who died while giving birth. Tehiya Sapir, *"Ma'arekhet Simanim ve-Heksheram ha-Tarbuti be-Khartisei Hazmanah la-Hatunah be-Erez Yisra'el mi-Tehilat ha-Me'ah ve-ad Yameinu"* [System of Symbols and Their Cultural Acceptance in Wedding Invitations in Eretz Israel from the Beginning of the Century until Today] (M.A. thesis, Hebrew University of Jerusalem, 1997), pp. 169–172.

18. *Halevanon*, no. 20, 14 Sivan [5]629 [= 23 May 1969].

19. *Havazelet*, no. 42, 28 Elul [5]641 [= 22 September 1881].

20. Supplement to *Hazevi*, no. 17, 1890; see also *Anglo-Jewish Association (AJA) 13th Annual Report*, 1883–1884, p. 28.

21. *AJA 14th Annual Report*, 1884–1885, Appendix e, p. 74.

22. Yaakov Kellner, *Le-Ma'an Tziyyon* [For Zion's Sake] (Jerusalem, 1977), pp. 179, 208; *Havazelet*, no. 27, 21 Iyar [5]641 [= 20 May 1881].

23. David Tidhar, *Enziklopediyah le-Halutsei ha-Yishuv u-Vonav* [Encyclopedia of Pioneers of the *Yishuv* and Personages], 1 (Tel Aviv, 1947), pp. 75a–76, s.v. "Nissim Behar" (entirely ignoring Fortuna's achievements!) (hereafter Tidhar, *Enziklopediyah*).

24. Supplement to *Hazevi*, no. 17, 26 Adar II [5]6499 [= 29 March 1889]; *Hazevi*, no. 29, 19 Av [5]648 [= 27 July 1888].

25. *Havazelet*, no. 2, 30 Tishri [5]636 [= 29 October 1875].

26. *Hazevi*, no 38, 9 Tamuz [5]653 [=23 June 1893].

27. *Havazelet*, no. 21, 2 Nisan [5]638 [= 5 April 1878].

28. *Havazelet*, no. 43, 26 Av [5]646 [= 27 August 1886].

29. The school came under AJA management on 1 July 1894; see *AJA, 24th Annual Report*, 1894–1895, p. 24; see also Sapir, "*Gishatah ve-'Ofi Terumatah . . .*" [Her Approach and the Nature of Her Contribution . . .], pp. 182–186; *AJA, 23rd Annual Report*, 1893–1894, p. 32.

30. *AJA, 35th Annual Report*, 1905–1906, p. 50

31. *AJA, 1st Annual Report*, 1871–1872, Appendix a, p. 21.

32. Southampton Archives, AJ95/ADD/2.

33. Carol Devens, "'If We Get the Girls, We Get the Race': Missionary Education of Native American Girls," *Journal of World History* 3, no. 2 (1992): 218.

34. *AJA, 43rd Annual Report*, 1913–1914, p. 47.

35. *AJA, 30th Annual Report*, 1900–1901, p. 47

36. *AJA, 31st Annual Report*, 1902–1903 , p. 51.

37. M. A. Scherer, "A Cross Cultural Conflict Reexamined: Annette Akroyd and Keshub Chunder Sen," *Journal of World History* 7, no. 2 (1996): 231–57.

38. Billie Melman, "*Re'alot Shekufot: Kolonializm ve-Dzender—Likrat Diyyun Histori Mehudash*" [Transparent Veils: Colonialism and Gender—Towards a Renewed Historical Discussion], *Zemanim* 62 (1998): 96; see also Nancy B. Sinkoff, "Educating for 'Proper' Jewish Womanhood: A Case Study in Domesticity and Vocational Training, 1987–1926," *American Jewish History* 77 (1987): 572–99.

39. *AJA, 23rd Annual Report*, 1893–1894, pp. 49–51.

40. *AJA, 30th Annual Report*, 1900–1901, p. 47.

41. *AJA, 25th Annual Report*, 1895–1896, p. 34.

42. *AJA, 30th Annual Report*, 1900–1901, p. 47.

43. Barbara Tuchman, *Bible and Sword: England and Palestine from the Bronze Age to Balfour* (New York, 1956).

44. *AJA, 3rd Annual Report*, 1873–1874, p. 21.

45. D. Yellin, *Ketavim* [Collected Writings], 1: 6–7; Alex Carmel, "*Le-Toldotav shel Johannes Frutiger, bankai biYrushalaym*" [On the History of Johannes Frutiger, a Banker in Jerusalem], *Cathedra* 48 (1988): 49–72.

46. *Hazevi*, no. 35, 1 Tamuz [5]656 [= 12 June 1896].

47. *Jewish Chronicle*, 11 October 1912, pp. 20–21.

48. Adela Goodrich-Freer, *Inner Jerusalem* (London, 1904), p. viii; Nathan Schur, *Sefer ha-Nose'im le-Eretz Yisra'el be-Me'ah ha-19* [Book of Travelers to the Land of Israel in the Nineteenth Century] (Jerusalem, 1988), pp. 216–17.

49. Figures for the total number of students in the school, as supplied by the annual *AJA Reports* for 1900–1914, are as follows: 1900: 292 in the school,

225 in the kindergarten; total: 517; 1902: total 606; 1903: total 600; 1905: total 620; 1912: total 530; 1913: 426 in the school, 250 in the kindergarten: total 676.

50. Resolutions of the AJA Committee, Southampton Archives, 13 March 1900, AJ95/ADD/3.

51. AJA, 33rd Annual Report, 1903–1904, p. 59.

52. Resolution of the London Women's Committee, 3 December 1899, Southampton Archives AJ95/ADD/3 (decision to dismiss Behar). Annie Landau first came to Palestine in March 1898; see Albert M. Hyamson, The British Consulate in Jerusalem in Relation to the Jews of Palestine 1838–1914 (London, 1941), 2:548.

53. Southampton Archives, February 1900, AJ95/ADD/3; Yellin, Ketavim, 4:150.

54. Yehudit Harari, Bein ha-Keramim [Between the Vineyards] (Tel Aviv, 1947), 1:83–84 (hereafter Harari, Bein ha-Keramim).

55. Yehudit Harari, Ishah va-Em be-Yisra'el: Mi-Tekufat ha-Tanakh ad Shenat he-Asor li-Mdinat Yisra'el [Woman and Mother among the Jewish People from Biblical Times to the First Decade of the State of Israel] (Tel Aviv, 1959), pp. 271–72; Tidhar, Enziklopediyah, 1:802–803; AJA, 44th Annual Report, 1914–1915, p. 16.

56. AJA, 34th Annual Report, 1904–1905, p. 28.

57. Jewish Chronicle, 28 June 1911, p. 20

58. Esther Benbassa, "Education for Jewish Girls in the East: A Portrait of the Galata School in Istanbul, 1879–1912," Studies in Contemporary Jewry 9 (1993): 163–73.

59. School Regulations, para. 5, Gaster Papers, 14/274.

60. Jewish Chronicle, 21 April 1911, p. 10.

61. AJA, 31st Annual Report, 1901–1902, p. 29; Hazevi, no. 10, 6 Tevet [5]661 [= 28 December 1900]; AJA, 34th Annual Report, 1904–1905, p. 28.

62. Hashkafah, no. 55, 21 Adar II [5]665 [= 28 March 1905]; Hashkafah, no. 38, 5 Adar [5]666 [= 2 March 1906].

63. Havazelet, 10 Heshvan [5]658 [= 5 November 1897]; Hannah Yellin, letter to the Russian-Jewish children's weekly Olam Katan 2 (1902): 36; Harari, Bein ha-Keramim, 1:107.

64. AJA, 41st Annual Report, 1911–1912, p. 29.

65. Jewish Chronicle, 16 June 1911, p. 17.

66. Jewish Chronicle, 11 November 1910, pp. 1–2.

67. AJA, 30th Annual Report, 1900–1901, p. 34.

68. Jewish Chronicle, 28 June 1901, p. 8.

69. AJA, 42nd Annual Report, 1912–1913, p. 26.

70. AJA, 32nd Annual Report, 1902–1903, p. 36.

71. Jewish Chronicle, 7 June 1907, p. 21.

72. *Jewish Chronicle*, 30 March 1903, p. 21. See also *Jewish Chronicle*, 30 October 1903.

73. AJA, *42nd Annual Report*, 1912–1913, p. 41.

74. *Jewish Chronicle*, 16 June 1911, p. 18.

75. *Jewish Chronicle*, 16 June 1911, p. 17.

76. AJA, *37th Annual Report*, 1907–1908, p. 48; *Jewish Chronicle*, 19 May 1911, p. 20.

77. *Jewish Chronicle*, 19 May 1911, p. 20.

78. AJA, *37th Annual Report*, 1907–1908, p. 54.

79. *Jewish Chronicle*, 7 June 1907, p. 21.

80. *Jewish Chronicle*, 12 May 1911, p. 18.

81. *Jewish Chronicle*, 7 June 1907, p. 21.

82. Harari, *Bein ha-Keramim*, 1:84.

83. *Jewish Chronicle*, 8 November 1907, p. 17.

84. Joseph Meyuhas, *Bat Hayil o Torat Em, Sefer Mikra li-Venot Yisrael* [Daughter of Valor or Mother's Teachings, a Reader of Jewish Young Women], vol. 1 (Warsaw, 1902), p. 2.

85. *Jewish Chronicle*, 16 June 1911, p. 18

86. AJA, *33rd Annual Report*, 1903–1904, p. 49.

On Behalf of Mothers and Children in Eretz Israel (pages 180–192)

1. Constitution of Hadassah, Central Zionist Archives (CZA), J113/1661; A. Gal, *"Medinat Yisra'el ha-Ide'alit be-Einei 'Hadassah,' 1945–1955"* [The Ideal State of Israel in the Eyes of "Hadassah," 1945–1955], *Yahadut Zemanenu* 4 (1988): 157.

2. Z. Shilony, *"Ha-Sherut ha-Refu'i u-Batei Holim bi-Tkufat ha-Milhamah"* [Medical Services and Hospitals in Jerusalem during the War], in *Be-Matzor u-be-Matzok* [Siege and Distress], ed. M. Eliav (Jerusalem, 1991), pp. 62, 75–76.

3. Turkestan-born Dr. Helena Kagan (1889–1978), completed her medical studies in Geneva and immigrated to Eretz Israel in 1914. She was the first pediatrician in the country; in 1916, she established a clinic for women and children alongside the Straus Health Center in Jerusalem. From 1933, she worked as a pediatrician in Jerusalem's Bikkur Cholim Hospital. In 1975, she was award the Israel Prize. See Z. Shehory-Rubin, "Dr. Helena Kagan — The Doctor Who became a Legend," *Cathedra* 118 (January 2006): 89–114.

4. Dr. Isaac Max Rubinow, a Russian-born physician, studied medicine in New York and worked as a doctor in the slums there. From 1915 to 1917, he was active within the American Association for Labor Legislation (AALL) in calling for the legislation of a compulsory health insurance law in the United States. After the British conquest of Palestine, Henrietta Szold asked Rubinow

to head the medical unit that was sent there, and he served as its general direc-tor until 1923. Upon completing this task, Rubinow returned to the United States and for many years was active there in B'nai B'rith. J. L. Kreader, "Isaac Max Rubinow: Pioneering Specialist in Social Insurance," *Social Service Review* 9 (1976): 405–11. Henrietta Szold was the chairman of the board and was in charge of the unit's outside connections and of fundraising in the United States, while Dr. Rubinow served as the unit's general director and was responsible for its medical work. See S. Shvarts, *"Mi Yetappel be-Anshei Eretz Yisra'el? Pe'ilutah shel ha-Yehidah ha-Tziyyonit Refu'it Amerika'it le-Hakamatah shel Ma'arekhet Beri'ut Tzibburit be-Reishit Tekufat ha-Mandat 1918–1921"* [Who Will Treat the People of Eretz Israel? The Activity of the American Zionist Medical Unit toward the Establishment of the Public Health System in the Early Mandate Period, 1918–1921], *Iyunim* 8 (1998).

5. O. Greenberg and H. Herzog, *Terumatah shel Vitzo be-Hevrah Mithav-vah* [WIZO's Contribution to a Society in the Making] (Tel Aviv, 1978), p. 14 (hereafter cited as Greenberg and Herzog, *Terumatah*).

6. By-laws of the Federation of Hebrew Women, Jerusalem, 1920.

7. Founding assembly of the Federation of Hebrew Women, 14 July 1920, CZA, J35/7.

8. Greenberg and Herzog, *Terumatah*, p. 14.

9. Dr. Rubinow to Henrietta Szold, Federation of Hebrew Women, 12 May 1921, CZA, J113/1346; L. Kleinman, *"Gevulot ha-Avodah shel ha-Ahot ha-Tzibburit ve-ha-Ovedet ha-Sotzi'alit* [Limits of the Work of Public Health Nurses and So-cial Workers], *Ha-Ahot* 4 (Tevet-Iyyar 5703 [1943]): 63.

10. Bertha Landsman, chief nurse in the mother and child welfare centers in the country to the Federation of Hebrew Women on the subject of recruit-ing volunteers to help in the centers, 26 May 1923, CZA, J113/1346.

11. B. Greenfield, *"Emunot Shav u-Minhagim Tefeilim be-Tippul be-Yonkim be-Gil ha-Yaldut"* [Fallacies and Superstitious Customs in Caring for Infants in Early Childhood], *Ha-Ishah* 3 (1928): 23–26; A. Stahl, *"Hitpatehut Minhag Hittul ha-Tinokot be-Edot Shonot u-vi-meyuhad etzel Yehudim: Sekirat Mekorot"* [The Development of the Custom of Swaddling Infants among Eth-nic Groups and Especially among the Jews: A Review of Sources], *Korot*, nos. 7–8 (Elul 5743 [1983]): 247–51.

12. A review of Infant Welfare and Prenatal Work in Palestine, 1921–1926, Hadassah Archive, New York, RG/72/1.

13. Bertha Landsman, Infant Welfare Work done by Hadassah Medical Or-ganization in Jerusalem, July 1923, for H.M.O. Report to XIII Congress, Carls-bad, August 1923, Hadassah Archive, New York, RG/72/1.

14. Infant Welfare and Milk Distribution Work in Palestine, Hadassah Archive, New York, RG/72/1; "The Milk Problem before the League," *Pales-tine Weekly*, 30 October 1925.

15. Greenberg and Herzog, *Terumatah*, p. 22.

16. *"Ha-Avodah ha-Meshutefet shel Hadasah ve-Histadrut ha-Nashim ha-Ivriyyot ba-Aretz"* [The Joint Effort by Hadassah and the Federation of Hebrew Women in Eretz Israel], *Ha-Ishah* 2 [second year] (1927): 29.

17. The First National Convention of the Federation of Hebrew Women, 24 March 1923–24, CZA, J35/7.

18. Greenberg and Herzog, *Terumatah*, p. 27; *"Ha-Massa u-Mattan bein Histadrut Nashim Ivriyyot u-vein Histadrut Olamit le-Nashim Tziyyoniyyot"* [The Negotiations between the Federation of Hebrew Women and WIZO], *Ha-Ishah* 8 (1927): 32–33 (hereafter *"Ha-Massa"*).

19. On the activity of the school hygiene department, see for details Z. She-hory-Rubin, "Hadassah's Educational Enterprises and Health Activities during Mandatory Times" (Ph.D. diss., Ben-Gurion University of the Negev, 1998).

20. Zelda Goldman, Minutes of the Public Health Nurses Meeting in Haifa, 21 March 1930, CZA, J113/1402; Bertha Landsman to Dr. Isaac Glicker, Kupat Holim Haifa, 15.4.1928, CZA, J113/1401.

21. H. Yassky, "Al Be'ayot Ahdut shel ha-Refu'ah ha-Mona'at [On Some Problems in Preventive Medicine], *Yedi'ot al ha-Avodah ha-Sozialit be-Erez Yisra'el* 3–4 [third year] (Tevet-Shevat 5698/1938): 85.

22. Bertha Landsman to Zelda Goldman, nurse supervisor, Hadassah Haifa, 20 March 1931, CZA, J113/1402; B. Ostrovsky, *"Toledot Mahleket ha-Yeladim shel Beit ha-Holim "Rotshild" be-Haifa, 1929–1957"* [The History of the Children's Department of the Rothschild Hospital in Haifa, 1929–1957], *Korot* 10 (5753–5754 [1993–1994]): 22.

23. Greenberg and Herzog, *Terumatah*, pp. 18–27; H. Thon, *"Likrat Ve'idat Vitzo ha-Ba'a"* [Towards the Coming WIZO Convention], *Ha-Ishah* 2 [second year] (5687 [1927]): 6–8; *"Ha-Massa."*

24. The "Plunkett System" espoused three principles: (1) propaganda for breastfeeding of infants; (2) enriching infants' nutrition with dairy cream; (3) massaging the breasts to obtain a richer milk supply. The Hadassah doctors opposed this system, claiming that it did not fit the climate and nature of the country. According to the Hadassah, most of the mothers in Eretz Israel nursed their babies and did not need "propaganda for nursing," and in the long summer months, infants should not be given food rich in fat. The Hadassah physicians also considered massaging the breasts important, whenever it was necessary, but they vehemently protested against this treatment being carried out by the nurses, arguing that this was an invasion into the area of medical treatment. Dr. Benno Gruenfelder, chief physician for childrens diseases for Hadassah in Eretz Israel, to the Hadassah Medical Organization for Dr. Yassky, 27 April 1930, CZA, J113/1405.

25. German-born Dr. Theodor Zlocisti studied medicine in Berlin. He

headed the German Red Cross delegation to Turkey during World War I. In 1921, he immigrated to Eretz Israel and directed the Tipat Halav centers and the WIZO's children's home. In addition to his medical activity, he wrote volumes of poetry.

26. Greenberg and Herzog, *Terumatah*, p. 35.

27. T. Ladizinsky [Chairman of the Department of Child Welfare in 1946–1951], *Yediot Vizo be-Yisra'el* [Bulletin of WIZO in Israel] 37 (August 1951): 28.

28. H. Palti, *"Hashlakhot al Sheirutei Beri'ut Meni'atiyyim la-Em ve-la-Yeled — 'Hok Bittu'ah Beri'ut Mamlakhti'"* [The National Health Insurance Law — Ramifications for the Preventive Health Services for Mother and Child'), *Bitahon Sozi'ali* 47 (1997): 81.

Establishment of a Nursing School in Jerusalem by the American Zionist Medical Unit, 1918 (pages 193–201)

1. E. Rubinstein, *"Ha-Yishuv ke-Ma'arekhet Otonomit: Hinukh Beri'ut u-Mishpat"* [The Yishuv as an Autonomous System: Education, Health, and Law], in *Ha-Yishuv bi-Ymei ha-Bayit ha-Le'ummi* [The Yishuv during the Period of the National Home], ed. B. Eliav (Jerusalem, 1976), pp. 223–26; J. Reuveny, *Mimshal ha-Mandat be-Eretz Israel 1920–1948* [The Administration of Palestine under the British Mandate, 1920–1948] (Ramat Gan, 1993), pp. 178–91; D. Niederland, *"Hashpa'at ha-Rofe'im ha-Olim mi-Germanyah al hitpatehut ha-Refu'ah be-Eretz Yisrael, 1933–1948"* [Influence of German-Jewish Immigrant Doctors on Medicine in Eretz-Izrael, 1933–1948], *Cathedra* 30 (1983): 111–60; S. Shvarts, *Kuppat ha-Holim ha-Kellalit 1911–1937* [Kupat Holim Haclalit, The General Health Fund, 1911–1937] (Beersheba, 1997) (hereafter cited as Shvarts, *Kuppat*); B. Hurwich, *"Kol ha-Am Hazit": Ha-Sherut ha-Refu'i ha-Tzeva'i be-Eretz Yisrael, 1911–1947* ["We Are All on the Front Line": Military Medicine in Israel, 1911–1947] (Tel Aviv, 1997); N. Levy, *Perakim be-Toledot ha-Refu'ah be-Eretz Yisra'el 1799–1948* [The History of Medicine in the Holy Land: 1799–1948] (Haifa, 1998).

2. L. Zwanger, "Preparation of Graduate Nurses in Israel, 1918–1965" (Ph.D. diss., Columbia University, 1968) (hereafter cited as Zwanger, "Preparation"); R. Adams-Stockler, "Development of Public Health Nursing Practice as Related to the Health Needs of the Jewish Population in Palestine, 1913–1948" (Ph.D. diss., Columbia University, 1975) (hereafter cited as Adams-Stockler, "Development"); D. Weiss, *"Ha-Sie'ud ke-Helek mi-Sherutei ha-Beri'ut ha-Yehudiyyim bi-Keravot Yeurshalayim bi-Tekufat Milhemet ha-Atzma'ut"* [Nursing as Part of Jewish Health Services around Jerusalem during the War of Independence 1947–1949] (Master's thesis, Tel Aviv University, 1993); D. Weiss, "Nursing's Role in Jewish Health Services in the Mauritius, Aden, Cyprus and

Atlit Refugee Camps, 1940–1948" (Ph.D. diss., Tel Aviv University, 2002); R. Adams-Stockler and R. Sharon, eds. *Tziyyunel Derekh be-Si'ud: Kovetz Mehkarim Historiyyim be-Se'ud she-Nikhtevu be-Yisrael* [Landmarks in Nursing: Historical Research Studies in Nursing Written in Israel] (Tel Aviv, 1996).

3. For example, J. Ben-David, *"Ha-Mivneh ha-Hevrati shel ha-Miktzo'ot ha-Hofshiyyim be-Yisra'el"* [The Social Structure of the Free Professions in Israel] (Ph.D. diss., Hebrew University of Jerusalem, 1956); D. H. Miller, "A History of Hadassah 1912–1935" (Ph.D. diss., New York University, 1968); M. Levin, *Balm in Gilead: The Story of Hadassah* (New York, 1974); A. Gal, *"Medinat Yisra'el ha-Ide'alit be-Einei 'Hadassah'"* [The Ideal Israel in the Eyes of "Hadassah," 1945–1955], *Yahadut Zemanenu* 4 (1988): 157–70 (hereafter cited as Gal, "Ideal"); M. Katzburg-Yungman, *"'Hadassah'—Asiyyah ve-Ide'ologyah, 1948–1956"* ["Hadassah"—Action and Ideology, 1948–1956] (Ph.D. diss., Hebrew University of Jerusalem, 1997) (hereafter cited as Katzburg-Yungman, "Hadassah"); J. Dash, *Summoned to Jerusalem: The Life of Henrietta Szold* (New York, 1979).

4. B. Melosh, *The Physician's Hand: Work Culture and Conflict in American Nursing* (Philadelphia, 1982); M. Reverby, *Ordered to Care: The Dilemma of American Nursing, 1850–1945* (Cambridge, Mass., 1989); P. A. Kalisch and B. J. Kalisch, *The Advance of American Nursing* (Philadelphia, 1995); See Zwanger, "Preparation," and Adams-Stockler, "Development."

5. Archives of the Hadassah Medical Organization J113, Central Zionist Archives (CZA), Jerusalem. The school archives, now located in the CZA as section number J117 (hereafter Archives of the Nursing School of Hadassah), has been catalogued and is currently accessible to researchers; when the current study was written, however, the material had not yet been handed over to the CZA for cataloguing, so this article does not contain precise references to its documents.

6. B. Melman, *"Min ha-Shulayyim el ha-Historiyyah shel ha-Yishuv: Migdar ve-Eretz Yisra'eliyyut* [From the Periphery to the Center of History: Gender and National Identity in the Yishuv (1890–1920)], *Zion* 62, no. 3 (1997): 243–78. The profession is defined by means of criteria, as for example by E. Freidson, *Professionalism Reborn: Theory, Prophecy, and Policy* (Chicago, 1994).

7. The nursing school was founded by the American Zionist Medical Unit organized by the Women's Zionist Organization of America as part of its health services' project, beginning in 1918. The name of the unit was changed in 1921 to "Hadassah Medical Organization." For the sake of brevity, the nursing school and the activity of the "Unit" are referred to in this article by the name "Hadassah" also for the years 1918 to 1921.

8. Y. Ben-Artzi, *"Bein ha-Ikkarim la-Po'alim: Ha-Ishah be-Reishit ha-Hityashvut be-Erez Yisra'el (1882–1912)"* [Between Farmers and Laborers: The Woman at the Beginning of Settlement in Eretz Israel (1882–1912)], in *Eshnav*

le-Hayyehen shel Nashim be-Hevrot Yehuddiyot: Kovez Mehkarim Bein-Tehumi [A View into the Lives of Women in Jewish Societies: A Collection of Interdisciplinary Studies], ed. Y. Azmon, pp. 309–24 (Jerusalem, 1996).

9. B. C. Kutscher, "The Early Years of Hadassah, 1912–1921" (Ph.D. diss., Brandeis University, 1976), pp. 41–42; E. W. Slaff, "Palestine Nurses' School, Marks Twentieth Anniversary, 1938," pp. 1–5, in the Archives of Hadassah New York, Hadassah Medical Organization section, Series 2, box 45, file 2; M. M. Shilo, "*Havvat ha-Po'alot be-Kinneret, 1911–1917, ke-Pitron le-Be'ayat ha-Po'alot ba-Aliyyah ha-Sheniyyah*" [The Women's Agricultural Training Farm at Kinneret, 1911–1917], *Cathedra* 14 (January 1980): 81–112, esp. p. 92; R. Elboim-Dror, *Ha-Hinukh ha-Ivri be-Erez Yisra'el, 1914–1920* [Hebrew Education in Eretz Israel, 1914–1920], vol. 2, pp. 61–84 (Jerusalem, 1990); S. Sitton, "*Bein Feminizm la-Ziyyonut: Ma'avakan shel ha-Gannanot ha-Ivriyot le-Hakkara Mikzo'it*" [Between Feminism and Zionism: The Hebrew-Language Kindergarten Teachers' Struggle for Professional Recognition], *Zemanim* 61 (1997/8): 26–37, esp. p. 34.

10. S. L. Cantor, "A Nursing School in Palestine," *American Journal of Nursing* 40, no. 8 (1940): 880–84; the extract is from page 882.

11. H. Kagan, *Reishit Darki bi-Yrushalayim* [My First Steps in Jerusalem] (Tel Yitzhak, 1983), p. 53.

12. Gal, "The Ideal," p. 159.

13. M. Waserman, "Henrietta Szold: American Progressivism, Zionism, and Modern Public Health," in *Health and Disease in the Holy Land*, ed. M. Waserman and S. S. Kottek (Lewiston, 1996), pp. 263–99, esp. 267–73 (hereafter cited as Waserman, "Henrietta"); M. Brown, *The Israeli-American Connection: Its Roots in the Yishuv 1914–45* (Detroit, 1996), esp. p. 134.

14. Waserman, "Henrietta," p. 272.

15. Katzburg-Yungman, "Hadassah," pp. 57–61.

16. A. Seligsberg, "A Modern Training School for Nurses in Jerusalem," *American Journal of Nursing* 21 (July 1921): 721–23; the extract is from page 722.

17. Waserman, "Henrietta," p. 293.

18. The English term "profession" was translated at the beginning of the twentieth century by the Hebrew term "profesia" even though this translation was likely to change the meaning of the concept to some extent.

19. "*Ne'um ha-Geveret Sold*" [Miss Szold's Speech], *Do'ar ha-Yom*, 9 December 1921, Archives of the Nursing School of Hadassah.

20. Bertha Landsman was one of the founders of the field of community nursing in the early 1920s in Eretz Israel.

21. A. Kaplan, "The First Nine Years . . . ," *Hadassah News Letter*, April 1938, pp. 127–29, 138.

22. The school committee, 24 December 1920, Archives of the Nursing School of Hadassah.

23. Shvarts, *Kuppat*, p. 117.

24. Hadassah Schedrovitzky-Sapir, "Hadassah Nursing School, Its Founding and Years 1918–1932," documents I received from Ms. Judith Steiner-Freud.

25. One must keep in mind that in its early years, the Hebrew University was a research institute and not an instructional institution, a situation that constituted another delaying factor in the process of academization of nursing.

26. Correspondence between Kaplan and Szold and the Hadassah women in New York at the beginning of the 1920s, Archives of the Nursing School of Hadassah; A. C. Maxwell and A. E. Pope, *Practical Points in Nursing* (New York-London; the date of the edition is not indicated but the reference was apparently to the third edition, 1914).

27. Letter from Bertha Landsman to Dr. J. E. Robbons, American Women's Hospital in Athens, 2 December 1928, Archives of the Nursing School of Hadassah.

28. Slaff, "Palestine Nurses' School."

29. K. Buhler-Wilkerson, "False Dawn: The Rise and Decline of Public Health Nursing, 1900–1930" (Ph.D. diss., University of Pennsylvania, 1984), p. 111.

30. K. Buhler-Wilkerson, "The Call to the Nurse, 1893–1943," in *Healing at Home: Visiting Nurses Service of New York 1893–1933*, ed. E. P. Denker, pp. 8–15 (New York, 1993); Adams-Stockler, "Development," pp. 34–35, on "Henry Street Settlement."

31. M. Waserman, "For Mother and Child: Hadassah in the Holy Land, 1913 through 1993," *Bulletin of the New York Academy of Medicine* (Winter 1993): 251–74, esp. 255–56; E. R. Benson, "Public Health Nursing and the Jewish Contribution," *Public Health Nursing* 10, no. 1 (1993): 55–57, esp. 56.

32. C. A. Estabrooks, "Lavinia Lloyd Dock, The Henry Street Years," *Nursing History Review* 3 (1995): 143–72.

33. Letter from Bertha Landsman to Dr. A. Salkind, acting director of Hadassah Hospital in Jerusalem, 16 September 1925, Archives of the Nursing School of Hadassah.

34. P. D. Nuttall, "Nursing in England and Wales," *The Canadian Nurse* 62, no. 4 (April 1966): 32–36; S. Murphy, "The United Kingdom," in *Nursing — The European Dimension*, ed. D. S. Quinn and S. Russel (Middlesex, England, 1994), pp. 211–33, esp. p. 231.

35. P. D. Nuttall, "Nursing Education in Britain Today," *International Nursing Review* 12, no. 6 (November/December, 1965): 6–12.

36. A. W. Money (Major General Chief Administrator), Occupied Enemy Territory, *Public Notice, Public Health Regulation*, 16 May 1918, reprinted 12 January 1922, Archives of the Nursing School of Hadassah.

37. Department of Health, Government of Palestine, *Regulations Govern-*

ing the Training of Nurses in Palestine, 26 February 1923, Jerusalem, Circular No. 127, Archives of the Nursing School of Hadassah.

    38. Zwanger, "Preparation," pp. 56–64.

"They Have Wings But No Strength to Fly" (pages 202–216)

    1. Class is defined by men as they experience their history, and ultimately this is its only definition, claimed Thompson, a researcher of the English working class, while completely ignoring the issue of gender. E. P. Thompson, *The Making of the English Working Class* (New York, 1966), p. 11. The cry to grant women a separate research category was heard more than a decade ago in historiography devoted to study of the labor movements. Take, for example, Joan Wallach Scott, *Gender and the Politics of History* (New York, 1988), pp. 53–67.

    2. Ada Fishman carried the banner of protest when she objected to the meager representation of women at the founding conference. Even those women attending were guests at the convention and not delegates on behalf of women workers. She demanded that women should have direct representation, threatening an "election war" if her request was not met. *"'Milhemet Behirot' Im Mevukashah lo Yinaten"* ["War of the Elections" — If She Doesn't Get What She Wants] (Events at the founding convention of the Histadrut), *Asufot* 1, no. 14 (December 1974): 60–61.

    3. Mo'etzet ha-Po'alot was elected at the general women workers' convention, officially held every four years. In reality, the council served for much longer periods. Mo'etzet ha-Po'alot elected the secretariat, the executive arm of the movement apparatus; the number of secretariat members changed over the years. In the 1920s, the women elected representatives from the two large parties in the Histadrut, Ahdut ha-Avodah and Ha-Po'el ha-Tza'ir, according to a method called "the pairing system." After the Third Women Workers' Convention (1926), it was decided to set up another limited body that was called the "Active Secretariat" on which served two members, one from each party. The Active Secretariat was the most important executive body of the women workers' movement apparatus. For further information, see Bat-Sheva Margalit-Stern, *"Tenu'at ha-Po'alot be-Eretz Yisra'el: Mo'etzet ha-Po'alot 1921–1939"* [The Women Workers' Movement in Eretz Israel: Mo'etzet ha-Po'alot 1921–1939] (Ph.D. diss., University of Haifa, 1997), pp. 45–60 (hereafter cited as Margalit-Stern, *"Tenu'at ha-Po'alot"*).

    4. On the establishment of Mapai and its becoming the leading power in the *Yishuv*, see Y. Goldstein, *Be-Derekh le-Hegemoniyyah — Mapai, Hitgabeshut Mediniyyutah* [On the Way to Hegemony — Mapai, the Crystallization of its Policy (1930–1936)] (Tel Aviv, 1980), p. 18; idem, *Mifleget Po'alei*

Eretz Yisra'el — Ha-Gormim le-Hakamatah [Mifleget Po'alei Eretz Yisra'el — The Factors Behind Its Establishment] (Tel Aviv, 1975), chapters 1–2; A. Shapira, *Halikhah al Kav ha-Ofek* (Walking on the Horizon) (Tel Aviv, 1989), pp. 355–72.

5. These changes occurred in various labor movement institutions and organizations and were not specific to the working women. Thus, Gedud ha-Avodah was abolished, the communists were expelled from the Histadrut, and so on. Of course, one should not automatically apply these trends to the changes of the women workers' institutions that we will consider in the continuation of this article. See, for example, Elkanah Margalit, *Anatomiyyah shel Semol: Po'ale Tziyyon Semol be-Eretz Yisra'el 1919–1946* [Anatomy of the Left: Po'alei Zion Left in Eretz Israel 1919–1946] (Jerusalem, 1976), pp. 95–119; Shemuel Dotan, *"Reishito shel Komunizm Le'ummi Yehudi be-Eretz Yisra'el"* [The Beginning of National Jewish Communism in Eretz Israel], *Hazionut* 2 (1971): 208–36.

6. She later changed her surname to Maimon, together with her brother Rabbi Maimon. A member of the Second Aliyah, Maimon was one of the forceful figures in the women workers' movement. She held a number of pivotal functions at the top of the Histadrut. In 1921, she became a member of the Aliyah Center, from which she resigned over internal conflicts in 1925. In 1930, she was elected to serve on the Histadrut's Va'ad ha-Po'el (executive council); she resigned three years later, claiming that she would not relinquish freedom of thought. Toward the end of the 1930s, she was a member of the Histadrut Council, belonged to the Va'ad ha-Po'el's Guarding Committee, and held other positions. She was one of the initiators of connections between Mo'etzet ha-Po'alot and WIZO and succeeded in implementing them in the early 1930s. In 1931, she was even elected to WIZO's Executive. With the formation of Mapai, she also became active in the party. In 1934, she took over management of the women workers' farm at Ayanot, the last large women workers' farm to be established. At the same time, she continued to serve in central positions in the women workers' movement apparatus. Upon the establishment of the state, she became a Knesset member representing Mapai. Her book, *Hamishim Shenot Tenu'at ha-Po'alot* [Fifty Years of the Women Workers' Movement], which first appeared in the 1930s, was the first of its kind devoted to the topic and stirred controversy in the movement apparatus.

7. On the attitudes of the various parties in the Histadrut, see J. Gorni, *Ahdut ha-Avodah 1919–1930: Ha-Yesodot ha-Ra'ayoniyyim ve-ha-Shitah ha-Medinit* [Ahdut ha-Avodah 1919–1930: The Ideological Foundations and the Political System] (Tel Aviv, 1973), pp. 209–61; Z. Tzahor, *"'Ahdut ha-Avodah' and 'Ha-Po'el ha-Tza'ir' — Dinamika shel Kera* ['Ahdut ha-Avodah' and 'Ha-Po'el ha-Tza'ir' — Dynamics of Rift], in *Me'asef le-Heker Tenu'at ha-Avodah ha-Tziyyonit ve-ha-Sotzi'alizm* 10 (1978): 81–96; idem, *Ba-Derekh le-Hanhagat*

ha-Yishuv — Ha-Histadrut be-Reishitah [On the Way to Leadership of the *Yishuv* — The Early Histadrut] (Jerusalem, 1982), p. 78. On the women workers' movement, see D. Izraeli, *"Tenu'at ha-Po'alot be-Eretz Yisra'el ad 1927"* [The Women Workers' Movement in Eretz Israel until 1927], *Cathedra* 32 (Tammuz 5744 [1984]): 109–40 (hereafter cited as Izraeli, *"Tenu'at"*).

8. The dissolution of the Mo'etzet ha-Po'alot came from repeated squabbles in the executive between member of Ha-Po'el ha-Tza'ir and members of Ahdut ha-Avodah over the members' representation in delegations to Zionist organizations abroad. Ada Fishman, as noted, represented Mo'etzet ha-Po'alot in its WIZO links, while Rahel Yanait Ben-Zvi made the connection with the "Women's League for the Halutza in Eretz Israel." The "Women's League," founded by the Po'alei Zion Party in America, was affiliated with Ahdut ha-Avoda. As a result of the resignation, the Va'ad ha-Poel appointed a temporary Women Workers' Committee on its behalf that functioned until the Third General Women Workers' Convention held about a year and a half later, in April 1926. Margalit-Stern, *"Tenu'at ha-Po'alot."*

9. There is evidence of this from other sources; for example, Berl Katznelson in his letter to Lily Tzedek in the book by A. Shapira, *Berl* (Tel Aviv, 1980), 2: 705–706 n (in Hebrew); also the testimony of Golda Meir in the article by M. Gilboa, *"Prolog: Tze'adim Rishonim"* [Prologue: First Steps, in *Golda — Tzemihatah shel Manhigah* [Golda — The Growth of a Leader (1921–1956)], ed. M. Avizohar et al. (Tel Aviv, 1994), p. 32. In her autobiography, too, Golda Meir did not make any mention of her activity on Mo'etzet ha-Po'alot in this period. *Golda Meir, My Life* (Tel Aviv, 1975), pp. 70–71.

10. Meir, *My Life,* p. 87. David Remez's diaries from this period, full of all kinds of slips of paper with notes on them, do not have the slightest mention of this; Labor Archive, IV 104-13-14, IV-20-113-104, and others. Even in the minutes of the meetings of the Va'ad ha-Po'el Secretariat in the period under discussion, this subject is not noted.

11. Golda Myerson was paired with Elisheva Kaplan (later Eshkol) from Ha-Po'el ha-Tza'ir; they served together on the Secretariat of Mo'etzet ha-Po'alot.

12. Chana Chizik, a member of Ahdut ha-Avodah and of Mapai from its founding, directed the women laborers' farm in north Tel Aviv and was active in different institutions of the women workers' movement, such as the Working Mothers Organization in Tel Aviv, and in the Histadrut. Leah Maron immigrated to Eretz Israel in 1909 after training herself as a seamstress; she moved to Galilee and worked on the Migdal farm on the Kinneret shore, at Sejera, and at Kinneret. She was active in the women workers' movement from its outset. In 1919, she joined Berl Katznelson in Jaffa and she stayed there on and off from 1919 to 1921. After she left Kinneret, she moved for a time to Ein Harod. In 1922, she took part in the establishment of the women workers' farm in the

Borochov neighborhood, and from that time on she lived in Tel Aviv. In the 1930s, she drew away from activity in the main institutions of the women workers' movement, apparently owing to family circumstances. Rachel Yanait Ben-Zvi (1886–1979) immigrated to Eretz Israel in 1908 and was one of the first women in the women workers' movement. In the 1920s, she was a central active figure in the movement institutions while at the same time directing the women workers' plant nursery in Jerusalem. In addition to her functions in the women workers' movement, she held central positions in the Histadrut, she was party to the establishment of the Haganah, was sent on many missions abroad, on which she helped found the Women's League in America, and more.

13. Golda Myerson actually served from January 1928 to January 1929; then the Mo'etzet ha-Po'alot's expanded secretariat elected Chana Chizik of Ahdut ha-Avodah and Zipporah Bat Ami from Ha-Po'el ha-Tza'ir to the Active Secretariat. In September 1929, upon her return from America, Golda was elected to serve on the Active Secretariat until her resignation, a total of five months. Golda Myerson went on to serve from time to time on the expanded secretariat of the Mo'etzet ha-Po'alot, on Mo'etzet ha-Po'alot, and even in the Working Mothers Organization; see evidence of that from various official letters, for example, Mo'etzet ha-Po'alot to the Jewish Agency, 10 February 1938, Labor Archive, IV-230-6-38b.

14. Between 1928 and 1930, the subject came up for discussion at six meetings of the Va'ad ha-Po'el Secretariat and once at the Histadrut Council — a uncommonly high concentration for discussion of issues related to women in the Histadrut (on the dates 10 September 1928; 20 September 1928; 3 June 1929; 11 October 1929; 18 November 1929; 16 December 1929). Labor Archive, Minutes Books of meetings of the Va'ad ha-Po'el Secretariat.

15. The Pioneer Women's Organization was established in 1926 by women of Po'alei Zion in America, the mother party of Ahdut ha-Avodah. The organization's aim was to assist *halutzot* in Eretz Israel, mainly through financial support of the Histadrut and the Mo'etzet ha-Po'alot.

16. Ada Fishman declared her opposition at meetings of the Va'ad ha-Po'el Secretariat on 18 June 1928 and 20 September 1928, Labor Archives, Minutes Book, 1928. At the meeting of the Va'ad ha-Po'el Secretariat in September 1928, it was decided in favor of Golda Myerson making the trip by herself.

17. The ongoing conflict was nurtured by the undecided battle between members of Ha-Po'el ha-Tza'ir (Ada Fishman and her supporters) and members of Ahdut ha-Avodah (mainly Golda Myerson). Intervention by the Va'ad ha-Po'el, dominated by Ahdut ha-Avodah, exacerbated the situation. There were many manifestations of this main issue; among the most prominent were the appointment of Golda Myerson to the Mo'etzet ha-Po'alot Secretariat; her going abroad to reinforce the connection between her party and Pioneer

Women, and the dispute over the links between Mo'etzet ha-Po'alot and WIZO. See Margalit-Stern, *"Tenu'at ha-Po'alot,"* pp. 95–98.

18. The tense relations in the Mo'etzet ha-Po'alot Secretariat were clear and obvious to the Va'ad ha-Po'el. Elisheva Kaplan, a member of the Mo'etzet ha-Po'alot Secretariat, brought a short version of the chain of events to the Va'ad ha-Po'el Secretariat. Ben-Gurion was furious over the threat of a "putsch" by Ada Fishman's supporters and called it: "a criminal act in the Histadrut." Ada Fishman was not fazed and audaciously answered: "No one should think me less Histadrut-oriented than you, and I will do it if the Va'ad ha-Po'el does not come to a decision"; statements at the Va'ad ha-Po'el Secretariat meeting, 16 December 1929, Labor Archive, Minutes Book of the Va'ad ha-Po'el secretariat meetings, 1929.

19. Meeting of the Mo'etzet ha-Po'alot Secretariat, 9 January 1930, Labor Archive, IV-230-5-17.

20. In that period, Golda already was separated from her husband and the responsibility for childrearing fell on her. See statements to this effect: Ben-Gurion, March 1930, Labor Archive, IV-208-1-174.

21. *Ben-Gurion Diary,* 25 March (no year given), Labor Archive, IV-208-1-174.

22. As was mentioned above, one of these challenges had been the picking of the people for the delegation to America in 1928. Ada Fishman and her supporters were against this mission, which they considered political and not a general Histadrut mission, since Pioneer Women in America was under the auspices of Po'alei Zion, the mother party of Ahdut ha-Avodah. Ada Fishman argued that just as they had added Golda Myerson to her trip to the WIZO convention a few months earlier, the Va'ad ha-Po'el should apply the same standard to Golda's trip to America and have a member of Ha-Po'el ha-Tza'ir accompany Golda. The Va'ad ha-Po'el rejected the suggestion, claiming that the strained relations of Mo'etzet ha-Po'alot might adversely affect the Pioneer Women in America. So Golda went by herself on the mission, which would yield nice economic rewards for her party in the Histadrut; see the record of the meetings of the Va'ad ha-Po'el Secretariat, 20 September 1928 and 5 November 1928. Labor Archive, the Minutes Book of the Va'ad ha-Po'el Secretariat meetings.

23. Among these steps, one may list the establishment of the last large women's farm at Ayanot in 1932, and the signing of the contract with WIZO in summer 1931. Setting up the contract with WIZO was especially important, since it paved the way for a central element outside the labor movement to fashion the aims and directions of work within it.

24. Beba Idelson is an outstanding example of this. She began her career with local activity in Petah Tikva and afterwards, in the early 1930s, on the Women's Workers Committee in Tel Aviv. In 1933, she was elected to the

Mo'etzet ha-Po'alot Secretariat and served for many years with no turnover. See Izraeli, *"Tenu'at."*

25. On the meager reference to women workers' issues at the beginning of pioneering settlement, see S. Shmueli, *"Mamashi"* ("Real"), I, no. 4 (1911); B-S. Stern, *"Hinukh Nashim bi-Tenu'at ha-Po'a lot ha-Eretz Yisra'elit: Bein Masoret le-Kidmah"* [Women's Education in the Eretz Israel Women's Labor Movement: Between Tradition and Progress], in *Hinukh ve-Historia: Heksherim Tarbutiyyim u-Politiyyim*, ed. E. Etkes and R. Feldhay, pp. 391–404 (Jerusalem, 1999).

26. For a similar debate, also see C. A. Hyman, "Labor Organizing and Female Institution-Building: The Chicago Women's Trade Union League, 1904–24," in *Women, Work and Protest*, ed. R. Milkman, pp. 22–41 (London 1985); P. Graves, "An Experiment in Women-Centered Socialism, Labour Women in Britain," in *Women and Socialism, Socialism and Women*, ed. P. Garuber and P. Graves, pp. 180–214 (New York, 1998); Sh. Lewenhak, *Women and Trade Unions: An Outline History of Women in the British Trade Union Movement* (New York, 1977), pp. 221–43; R. M. Jacoby, *The British and American Women's Trade Union Leagues, 1890–1925: A Case-Study of Feminism and Class* (New York, 1994), pp. 1–18.

27. For the elections of the Women Workers' Committees in the cities and *moshavot*, two proposals were made. One recommended that the committees would be elected by the Mo'etzot ha-Po'alim. An imperative condition for the establishment of fitting Women Workers' Committees was incorporating the women workers into the Labor Councils by a number that matched their number in every location. The other suggestion determined that the committees would be chosen by general assemblies of the women workers in a given location. The committees' functions included participating in the distribution of work through the Employment Office, organizing the women members into trade unions, and finding new jobs for the women. Since the issue of the committees' composition had not been fully clarified, it was decided to hand the issue over for decision to the Histadrut's Va'ad ha-Po'el, in conjunction with Mo'etzet ha-Po'alot; see Report of the Third Convention of the General Labor Federation, Va'ad ha-Po'el of the Histadrut, p. 224; minutes of the Third Women Workers' Convention (1926), Labor Archive IV-230-2-3.

28. At the Mo'etzet ha-Po'alot session in 1925, the Third Women Workers' Convention in April 1926, the meeting of the Va'ad ha-Po'el Secretariat on 28 November 1926, and the Histadrut Council session in February 1927. At the meeting of the Mo'etzet ha-Po'alot Secretariat on 1 January 1927, Fishman again pushed for dealing with this issue.

29. Decisions of the Third Histadrut Convention 1927, Va'ad ha-Po'el of the Histadrut, p. 260.

30. Decisions of the Fourth Session of the Mo'etzet ha-Po'alot, Labor Archive, IV-230-5-16b.

31. The debate over the issues of the woman worker in the city and the *moshavah*, Fourth Women Workers' Convention, Labor Archive, 230–5–9d-IV, as well as statements made around the time of the convention: Ada Fishman, "On the Fourth Women Workers' Convention," *Davar*, 2 October 1932, p. 9.

32. Statements at the National Council of Ahdut ha-Avodah, 1 July 1926, Labor Archive, IV-404-1-11.

33. Minutes of the meeting of the Mo'etzet ha-Po'alot Secretariat and the Mo'etzot ha-Po'alim secretaries, 20 August 1934, Labor Archive, IV-404-1-11.

34. Ziama (Zalman) Aharonowitz (Aranne), later secretary of Mapai and Minister of Education in the government of Israel. A member of the Third Aliyah and one of the leading members of the Histadrut apparatus, in the 1920s he was one of the leading opponents to Yosef Kitzis' control over the Tel Aviv Labor Council. See below, n. 38.

35. Minutes of a meeting of the Mo'etzet ha-Po'alot Secretariat and Mo'etzot ha-Po'alim secretaries, 20 August 1934, Labor Archive, IV-230-5-24b.

36. The controversies broke out at the Third Women Workers' Convention (1926) and continued at the Fourth Convention (1932) in Tel Aviv, and at the fifteenth session of Mo'etzet ha-Po'alot (December 1932). See, for example, Judith Mazan from Nes Ziona, Labor Archive, IV-230-5-24b.

37. Labor Archive, IV-250-72-1-1980. Pesya Gorelick, from kibbutz Givat ha-Sheloshah, was a member of Ahdut ha-Avodah and demonstrated excessive loyalty to her party's positions. She took part in Mo'etzet ha-Po'alot activity beginning in 1926, and she was a member of the Women Workers' Committee in Tel Aviv. She consistently negated the institutional reservation of positions for women workers in the kibbutzim, too, even though there she held a minority opinion.

38. Lilia Bassewitz (one of the activists on Mo'etzet ha-Po'alot), statements at the Third Women Workers' Convention, Labor Archive, IV-230-2-3. Tzippora Laskov or Penina Sternfeld supported the establishment of separate institutions. See also the 15th session of the Mo'etzet ha-Po'alot, above n. 36.

39. So it was that Pesya Gorelick, mentioned previously, omitted the fact that Yosef Kitzis from her own party initiated publication of the letter negating the establishment of local women workers' institutions. Gorelick was certainly aware of Kitzis' motives. These were closely connected to the power struggles within the Mo'etzet ha-Po'alim (the local general workers' council) and to his weak status on the council, and not necessarily from caring for the special interests of the women workers. In that same period, there popped up in the Tel Aviv Labor Council the first opposition to what was called "Kitzis' autocratic rule." This was the backdrop to the development of his fear of the founding of a possibly competitive institution that was liable to chip away at his authority. On Kitzis' standing on the Tel Aviv Workers' Council, see Z. Sternhell, *Binyan*

Ummah o Tikkun Hevrah [Building a Nation or Correcting a Society] (Tel Aviv 1995), p. 347 (hereafter cited as Sternhell, *Binyan*).

40. Manya Starkman of the Women Workers Committee in Tel Aviv, Minutes of the Women Workers' Committee meeting, 5 June 1928. Tzipora Baran, also from Tel Aviv, complained about the decrease in the Women Workers' Committee's freedom of action owing to party motives, and see Meeting of the Women Workers' Committee in Tel Aviv, 2 July 1928, Labor Archive, IV-2367-1-72-250b. Women from other parts of the country aired the same kind of opinions.

41. Bat-Sheva Chaikin of Ahdut ha-Avodah pointed out the lack of consensus among the women members of her party; see Bat-Sheva Chaikin at the Fifth Ahdut ha-Avodah Convention, Tel Aviv (Heshvan 5687/1927), p. 162. Also in the rival party, Ha-Po'el ha-Tza'ir, opinions were not uniform; see, for example, the statements by Tova Yaffe at the meeting of the Ha-Po'el ha-Tza'ir Secretariat, 24 October 1926, Labor Archive, IV-402-1-24.

42. A clear example of that is Golda Meir's statement in which she expressed her doubts about "feminism . . . that leads to bra burning," and pointed out that she had never encountered any special difficulty on the basis of her sex; see Meir, *My Life*, p. 84. This quotation is used in the title on p. 5 of her book.

43. Statements at the Fourth Women Workers' Convention (1932), such as by Clara Madar, Tzipora Baran, and others, Labor Archive, IV-230-5-9d.

44. According to the data from Tel Aviv, meetings were not held at their appointed times nor as they should be; see, for example, Hanna Lamdan, 18 October 1937, Labor Archive, IV-250-72-1-401; and idem, meeting of the Women Workers' Department in Tel Aviv, 21 May 1938, Labor Archive, IV-250-72-1-2367a.

45. The number of members on the Urban Council for Women Workers was supposed to change according to the size of the group of women in each location. In Tel Aviv, for example, the number of members was supposed to be about one hundred. The principles of operation indicated above were determined in the course of work and changed from time to time. See Beba Idelson in the discussion in Mo'etzet ha-Po'alot about the structure of the council, September 1937, Labor Archive, IV-250-77; idem, "*Al ha-Perek—She'elot Irgun*" [On the Agenda of the Women's Labor Movement—Questions of Organization], *Davar ha-Po'elet* 5, nos. 7–8 (25 October 1938): 161–63.

46. Complaints of this nature were aired by members of Mo'etzet ha-Po'alim in Tel Aviv. Even the women members did not refrain from criticizing the low level of activity by the female representatives—see statements from a meeting of the Department of Women Workers' in Tel Aviv, 19 November 1938, Labor Archive, IV-230-6-65.

47. A. Dickenstein, a member of the Tel Aviv Mo'etzet ha-Po'alim, clari-

fied the appointment system customary in the women workers' institutions: "The Women Workers Committee was chosen by the Jaffa Workers Council. After it had been operating for a few months, it found it necessary to add another two women: they propose Bluma [Wichotz, an Ahdut ha-Avodah member]," Women Workers' Committee meeting, 2 August 1926. Labor Archive, IV-2367-1-72-250b. Tova Yaffe of Ha-Po'el ha-Tza'ir opposed this appointment, arguing that Bluma Wichotz was not known by the wider women workers' public. The Mo'etzet ha-Po'alim members did not accept her objections. See ibid. and also Sternhell, *Binyan*, pp. 341–66.

International Struggle, Local Victory (pages 217–228)

1. H. Trager, *Pioneers in Palestine: Stories of the First Settlers in Petach Tikva* (New York, 1923), p. 71.
2. Since this paper is focused on Jewish women only, the terms Eretz Israel and Palestine are being used here interchangeably.
3. *Jus Suffragii* 4, no. 9 (July 1920).
4. In this article, I use the term "feminism" for the activity on behalf of equal rights for women at the beginning of the twentieth century. Use of this concept in English began at the end of the nineteenth century, and it has become common since the 1970s. On the complexity in the use of feminism as a definition for a group or a single idea, see K. Offen, "Defining Feminism: A Comparative Historical Approach," *Signs* 14, no. 1 (1988): 119–57.
5. C. E. Dubois, "Woman Suffrage Around the World: Three Phases of Suffragist Internationalism," in *Suffrage and Beyond: International Feminist Perspectives*, ed. C. Daley and M. Nolan, pp. 252–74 (New York, 1994).
6. Sarah Azaryahu (1873–1962), a teacher and public activist, was involved in issues for the advancement of women and peace, and one of the founders and leaders of the "Union of Hebrew Women for Equal Rights in Eretz Israel." She was elected to the first Asefat ha-Nivharim (the Representative Assembly) as the representative of the "Progressive Party" and also to the second Asefat ha-Nivharim on the Union's list. S. Azaryahu, "*Hit'ahdut Nashim Ivriyyot le-Shivvui Zekhuyyot be-Eretz Yisra'el*" [Union of Hebrew Women for Equal Rights in Eretz Israel] (Haifa, 1977) (hereafter cited as Azaryahu, *Hit'ahdut*).
7. M. Shilo, "*Havvat ha-Po'alot be-Kinneret, 1911–1977*" [The Women's Agricultural Training Farm at Kinneret, 1911–1917], *Cathedra* 14 (1980): 81–112; D. Izraeli, "*Tenu'at ha-Po'alot be-Eretz Israel mi-Reishitah ve-ad 1927*" [The Socialist Zionist Women's Movement in Eretz Israel 1927)], *Cathedra* 32 (1985): 128–30; D. Bernstein, *Ishah be-Eretz Yisra'el* [A Woman in Eretz Israel] (Tel Aviv, 1987).
8. M. Shilo, "*Ha-Ishah — 'Ovedet' o Haverah be-Mifal ha-Tehiyyah? Al*

Mekomah shel ha-Ishah ba-Aliyah ha-Rishonah" [The Woman — 'Laborer' or a Member of the Revival Project? On the Place of the Woman in the First Aliyah (1882–1903)], *Yahadut Zemanenu* 9 (1995): 121–47; S. Bijaoui -Fogiel, "*Ha-Omnam be-Derekh le-Shivyon? Ma'avakan shel ha-Nashim li-Zekhut ha-Behirah ba-Yishuv ha-Yehudi be-Eretz Yisra'el*" [Really on the Way to Equality? The Women's Battle for the Right to Vote in the Jewish *Yishuv* in Eretz Israel: 1917–1926)], *Megamot* 34, no. 2 (January 1992): 262–84; R. Elboim-Dror, "*Nashim ba-Utopiyyah ha-Tziyyonit*" [Women in the Zionist Utopia], *Cathedra* 66 (1993): 111–43; N. Kahana, "*Hishtattefut Nashim be-Politikah, ha-Mikreh shel ha-Ma'avak al Zekhut Hatzba'ah le-Nashim bi-Tekufat ha-Yishuv 1919–1926*" [Women's Participation in Politics, the Case of the Struggle for the Women's Right to Vote in the *Yishuv* Period 1919–1926"] (Master's thesis, Haifa University, 1984).

9. Z. Bozich-Hertzig, "*Ha-Pulmus al Zekhut Behirah le-Nashim le-Mosedot ha-Yishuv be-Reishit Tekufat ha-Mandat*" [The Controversy over Women's Right to Vote for *Yishuv* Institutions during the Mandate Period] (Master's thesis, Bar-Ilan University, 1990) (hereafter cited as Bozich-Hertzig, "*Ha-Pulmus*"); H. Herzog, "*Irgunei Nashim be-Hugim Ezrahiyyim — Perek Nishkah be-Historiyyografia shel ha-Yishuv*" [Women's Organizations in Civilian Circles — a Forgotten Chapter in the Historiography of the *Yishuv*], *Cathedra* 70 (1994): 111–33.

10. In many places in the world, the growth of modern nationalism was connected closely to the place of the woman and the perception of her as part of the underlying myth. K. Jayawardena, *Feminism and Nationalism in the Third World* (London, 1986).

11. D. S. Bernstein, "Daughters of the Nation," in *Jewish Women in Historical Perspective*, ed. J. R. Baskin, pp. 287–311 (Detroit, 1998).

12. A. Maimon, *Hamishim Shenot Tenu'at ha-Po'a lot* [Fifty Years of the Women's Labor Movement] (Tel Aviv, 1955).

13. M. H. McFadden, *Golden Cables of Sympathy: The Transatlantic Sources of Nineteenth-Century Feminism* (Lexington, Ky., 1999).

14. C. Chapman Catt, "The Holy Land," *Jus Suffragii* 6, no. 6 (February 1912).

15. M. Fawcett, "A Glimpse of Egypt and a Journey through Palestine," *Jus Suffragii* 15, no. 6 (June 1921).

16. L. G. Kuzmack, *Women's Cause: The Jewish Women's Movement in England and the United States, 1881–1933* (Columbus, Ohio, 1990).

17. R. Abrams, "Jewish Women in the International Woman Suffrage Alliance 1899–1926" (Ph.D. diss., Brandeis University, 1997).

18. R. Kohut, *My Portion* (New York, 1925).

19. Minutes of the Eretz Israel Council, Central Zionist Archives (CZA), J1/8766.

20. Bozich-Hertzig, "*Ha-Pulmus*," pp. 100–107.

21. "The International Woman Suffrage Alliance, Report of the Ninth

Congress, Rome, Italy, May 12–19, 1923, submitted by Rosa Welt Straus," copy in the National Library of Women, London Guildhall University.

22. Azaryahu, *Hit'ahdut*, pp. 52–53.

23. M. Friedman, *Hevrah ve-Dat: Ha-Ortodoksiyyah ha-Lo Tziyyonit be-Eretz Yisra'el 1918–1936* [Society and Religion: The Non-Zionist Orthodoxy in Eretz Israel 1918–1936] (Jerusalem, 1977), p. 148.

24. Bozich-Hertzig, *"Ha-Pulmus,"* pp. 136–65.

25. Azaryahu, *Hit'ahdut*, p. 27.

26. *Ha-Ishah* 2, no. 6 (1928).

27. Sarah Azaryahu Archive, Yad Tabenkin, Ramat Efal, 15/1/7.

28. *Haaretz*, 16 June 1925; *Do'ar ha-Yom*, 16 June 1925.

29. Minutes of the Third Session, CZA, J1/7205.

30. *Hit'ahdut Nashim Ivriyyot le-Shivvui Zekhuyyot be-Eretz Yisra'el*, condensed review (n.d.), Sarah Azaryahu Archive, Yad Tabenkin, 15/3/3.

31. S. Shvarts, *"Histadrut Nashim lema'an Imahot be-Eretz Yisra'el: Pe'ilutan shel 'Hadassah', 'Histadrut Nashim Ivriyyot', u-'Vitzo' le-Hakamat Tahanot Em ve-Yeled be-Eretz Yisra'el be-Shanim 1918–1948"* [A Women's Union for Mothers in Eretz Israel: The Activity of "Hadassah," "The Women's Zionist Federation," and "WIZO" for the Establishment of Mother and Child Care Stations in the Years 1918–1948], *Bittahon Sotziali* 51 (March 1998): 57–81.

32. R. Thon, *Ha-Ma'avak le-Shivyon bein ha-Minim: Sippur Hayyeha shel Sara Thon* [The Struggle for Equality of the Sexes: The Life Story of Sarah Thon] (Israel, 1996), Sarah Azaryahu Archive, Yad Tabenkin, Ramat Efal, 15/1/4.

33. Azaryahu, *Hit'ahdut*.

34. Azaryahu, *Pirkei Hayyim* [Biography] (Tel Aviv, 1957), p. 171.

35. *Jus Suffragii* 33, no. 5 (February 1939); for more about this organization and the connection it had with the Union of Hebrew Women owing to Welt Straus's connections, see Azaryahu, *Hit'ahdut*, n. 6.

36. Minutes of the WIZO Founding Convention, 11 July 1920, CZA, F49/2778.

37. *Ha-Ishah* 3, no. 3 (Jerusalem, 1929).

38. In 1922, the World League for Peace and Freedom (WILPF) refused to accept as members a group of Jewish women from Eretz Israel; see also L. J. Rupp, *Worlds of Women: The Making of an International Women's Movement* (Princeton, N.J., 1997), p. 59. In 1930, Sarah Azaryahu again applied to the World League, and the group was accepted in 1933. Women's International League for Peace and Freedom Collection, Microfilm 78:799.

39. S. Kussey, *Newark Evening News*, 25 January 1923; Hadassah Archives, New York, RG = 4, Box = 2, Folder = 20.

40. J. Antler, *The Journey Home* (New York, 1997).

41. M. Brown, *Henrietta Szold's Progressive American Vision of the Yishuv: Envisioning Israel* (Jerusalem, 1996), p. 61.

42. M. Berkowitz, *Western Jewry and the Zionist Project, 1914–1933* (Cambridge, Mass., 1997); M. Brown, *The Israeli-American Connection: Its Roots in the Yishuv, 1914–1948* (Detroit, 1996).

Nehama Puhachewsky (pages 231–243)

1. Although the family spelling of the name is Pohatcevsky, references in English sources are usually to Puhachewsky (Pukhachewsky is also found), so that spelling was retained throughout this article.

2. Yaffa Berlovitz, *Lehamtzi Eretz, Lehamtzi Am: Tashtiyyot Sifrut ve-Tarbut bi-Yetzirah shel ha-Aliyah ha-Rishonah* [Inventing a Land, Inventing a People: Literary and Cultural Patterns in the Writings of the First Aliyah] (Tel Aviv, 1996); Nurit Govrin, *Devash mi-Sela* [Honey from a Stone: Studies in Eretz Israel Literature] (Tel Aviv, 1989).

3. Gershon Shaked, *Ha-Sipporet ha-Ivrit 1880–1980* [Hebrew Narrative Fiction 1880–1980], vol. 2: *Ba-Aretz u-ba-Tefutzah* [In the Land of Israel and the Dispersion] (Tel Aviv and Jerusalem, 1983), p. 47.

4. Nehama Puhachewsky, *Bil'adeah* (1913), p. 58. Page numbers in this text refer to a later edition: Yaffa Berlovitz (editor), 1984.

5. Govrin, *Devash mi-Sela*, p. 149.

6. Yaffa Berlovitz, "*Kol ha-Melankholiyyah ke-Kol ha-Meha'ah: Iyyun bi-Yziratah shel Nehama Puhatshevski*" [The Voice of Melancholy as the Voice of Protest: A Study of the Works of Nehamam Puhachewsky], in *Eshnav le-Hayyeihen shel Nashim be-Hevrot Yehudiyyot* [A View into the Lives of Women in Jewish Societies], ed. Y. Atzmon, p. 333 (Jerusalem: 1995).

7. Ibid., 328.

8. There is here an irresistible invitation to construct a sexual analogy between Yehudit and the flowers that will not bloom, and between Weinholz and the missing pipes, without which the flowers cannot be watered. The question "Why don't they have children?" is never answered in the story, despite the centrality of this lack in Weinholz's existence. Even if the answer may be self-evident—they might be too young, or Yehudit's illness may keep her from conceiving—the description of the flowers and the absence of the necessary watering pipes invite a reading based on Freudian symbolism, which compares the lack of pipes with a lack of procreating ability on Weinholz's part.

The Growing Silence of the Poetess Rachel (pages 244–256)

1. D. Miron, *Imahot Meyassedot, Ahayot Horgot* [Founding Mothers, Stepsisters] (Tel Aviv, 1991), pp. 160–77.

2. J. Krammer, "The Art of Silence and the Forms of Women's Poetry," in *Shakespeare's Sisters*, ed. Sandra M. Gilbert and Susan Gubar (Bloomington, Ind., 1979), p. 153.

3. Rachel is portrayed as one of the figures representing the Second Aliyah. She put the ideological principles of this Aliyah into practice by joining a communal group and working in agriculture, but in reality the process of her spiritual-artistic crystallization occurred against the backdrop of the Third Aliyah (Meron, *Imahot Meyassedot*, p. 15). Rachel became infused with an intellectual-literary charge in the years of her absence from Eretz Israel, and it was this cultural exposure that filled the depths from which she drew poetically after her return. While studying agronomy in Toulouse, Rachel was exposed to French culture and literature, and later she was influenced by Russian Modernism and its members. B. Hakhlili, *Lakh ve-Alayikh* [To You and About You] (Tel Aviv, 1987), p. 100.

4. The Russian scholar Mikhail Bakhtin dealt with the link between time and space, and termed this association "chronotope," borrowed from physics. When the chronotype is applied as part of structural analysis of a single textual unit, then it is a means for understanding specific revelations of a combination of time and space in narrative forms, as a compositional element in a literary text. Bakhtin focused on the functioning of the chronotype as an essential part in the genre morphology of the novel in its various types and along it developmental continuum. In the study of historical poetics, the chronotype may serve as a means for understanding the relations between any text and its period. M. Holquist, *Dialogism, Bakhtin and His World* (London, 1990), pp. 109, 110, 113.

5. L. Sela, "*Resisim*" (Shards), in *Rahel ve-Shiratah* [Rachel and Her Poetry] (Tel Aviv, 1971), p. 64.

6. Ilana Pardes, "*Le-Damyen et ha-Eretz ha-Muvtahat*" [To Imagine the Promised Land], *Theory and Criticism* 6–7 (1995): 113.

7. Rachel was involved in the publication of her poetry collections and made sure that they looked simple and minimalist — in total contrast to the luxurious printing of recent years. Her first book of poetry was indeed white and small.

8. M. Bakhtin, *Ha-Dibber ba-Roman* [Discourse in the Novel] (Tel Aviv, 1989), p. 134

9. J. Kammer, "The Art of Silence and the Forms of Women's Poetry," in *Shakespeare's Sisters*, p. 154.

10. Milstein, *Rahel — Shirim*, pp. 325–26.

11. M. Buber, *Moses* (in Hebrew) (Jerusalem, 1946), p. 47.

12. R. Kritz, *Al Shirat Rahel* [On Rachel's Poetry] (Tel Aviv, 1987), p. 23.

13. Y. Lichtenbaum, in *Rahel ve-Shiratah* (Tel Aviv, 1971), pp. 240–41.

14. Rachel's drawing on the biblical source charmed readers and was depicted as the linchpin that would stabilize the people's hold on their heritage:

"Rachel . . . lived the Bible. . . . The images and metaphors with which she expressed her spirit are ancient, Hebrew images and metaphors that she saw through the eyes of contemporary Hebrew man. . . . The thread of the generations was not cut off." Habas, *Rahel ve-Shiratah* (Tel Aviv, 1971), 161. Rachel served to reinforce the connection between the people and its land in the period during which her poems were published as well as for years after her death. Simultaneously with the strengthening of the pioneering mythos, stress was placed on the link one feels in her poems to the world of the Patriarchs and the situating of figures from the biblical past in contexts of time and place taken from present reality: "Rachel's life became for her the tragic experience of the fate of Nebo. But now that the poetess has reached her pinnacle, the height of sorrow and suffering, she has extricated herself from them through recourse to the army of old—namely, the Book of books. . . . From the way of the righteous, suffering, tormented forefathers she learned 'to accept the bad as one accepts the good.'" (Y. Tolkes, "*Shiratah shel Rahel*," in *Rahel ve-Shiratah*, p. 119). The feeling was that Rachel's poetry served to renew the connection with the world of the Patriachs and that this link was capable of providing strength and willingness to the young settlers in their Zionist endeavor." "The nature, labor, and love poems were for us like an internal echo, like turning a tune into the voices of the Judean shepherds from the Song of Songs while they merge with the song of our lives." Z. Katznelson, "*Ve-Yom Yagi'a ve-Hayyinu Mishbatz Zahav*" [The Day Will Come and We Will Be a Setting of Gold], in *Rahel ve-Shiratah*, p. 110.

15. In many poems, Rachel intersperses verses from the Song of Songs and clashes with them ("*Ivriyyia*," [Hebrew Woman], "*Sefatayyim Nitzmadot*," [Tight Lips], "*Goral*" [Fate]). In drafts found after her death, a poem was found that relates to Ecclesiastes.

16. For generations, the topic of barrenness recurring as an echo hovered over Rachel's poetry—her depressed soul had a bit of happiness, a feeling of maternal joy: "If I only had a son, a little boy." This natural desire is heart-wrenching in her spare, modest diction. This very intimate, personal poem, with its hidden strong yearning for a child, for the giving of the fruit of life, becomes, therefore, by virtue of its truth, the heritage of many. A. Broides, "*Bi-Mehitzata*" [In Her Presence], in *Rahel ve-Shiratah*, p. 103).

At the same time, it is interesting to see that few poems deal with the issue of barrenness. The most popular poem (its popularity was assisted by its being set to song numerous times) in this context—"*Akarah*" [Barren Woman]—is the only one that treats the desire for the experience of motherhood directly and powerfully, from both a personal and pan-feminine aspect ("like the matriarch Rachel," "like Hannah at Shiloh"). Another mention of a maternal stance comes as a question in the poem "*Edna*," and another poem in which the experience of a child reverberates is "*Ve-Lu*" ["And If"].

It seems that the woman in Rachel was identified with stereotypical feminine roles: the abandoned lover who here calls the beloved and the women who aspires to realize her maternal instincts. These elements are, of course, in her poetry, but the female partner that the speaker constitutes in some of the poems is not exactly the submissive one depicted in the criticism, and her yearning for motherhood gained a resonance that bears no straight relation to the place it occupied in her work. These fixations in Rachel's image as a creative person and in characterizing her emotional world tell us more about the readers than the poetess.

17. Intertexuality is a concept referring to the way a given text is related to a previous (or contemporary) text by the same author.

Anda Amir's Me-Olam, Demuyot mi-Kedem *(pages 257–267)*

1. See Dan Miron, *Immahot Meyassedot, Ahayot Horgot, al Shetei Hathalot be-Shirah ha-Artziyisra'elit* [Founding Mothers, Stepsisters, the Emergence of the First Hebrew Poetesses and Other Essays] (Tel Aviv, 1991), pp. 148–50, 163–71.

2. D. Sadan, *"Ishah ve-Hi Meshoreret"* [A Woman and She Is a Poet], *Hadoar* 36 (1972): 603–604.

3. I. Yaoz-Kest, *"Im Anda Monolog bi-Shnayyim"* [With Anda a Monologue for Two], in *Anda*, a collection of articles, sketches, and other literary items with a bibliographical appendix, ed. Z. Beilin (Tel Aviv, 1977), pp. 131–36.

4. Following the three-stage process of feminism according to Kristeva. See also J. Kristeva, "Women's Time," in *The Kristeva Reader*, ed. T. Moi (London, 1986), pp. 187–211 .

5. B. Y. Michali, *"Me-Olam"* [From Time Immemorial], *Moznayim* 6 (August–September 1942): 326–27; S. Ridnick, *"Pulhan ha-Ishah shel Anda Pinkerfeld"* [Anda Pinkerfeld's Ritual of the Woman"], *Ha-Hevrah* 54 (September 1944): 768–70; N. Govrin, *"Keni'ah zorekh kibbush"* [Surrender for Purposes of Conquest] (1972), in *Anda* (note 3), pp. 114–15.

6. S. Shahar, *Ha-Ishah be-Hevrat Yemei ha-Beinayim* [The Fourth Order, a History of Women in the Middle Ages] (Tel Aviv, 1983), p. 246.

7. R. Radhakrishnan, "Nationalism, Gender, and the Narrative of Identity," in *Nationalisms and Sexualities*, ed. A. Parker, M. Russo, D. Sommer, and P. Yaeger (New York and London, 1992), pp. 81–82.

8. A. Pinkerfeld-Amir, *"Havah"* [Eve], in *Gaddish* (Tel Aviv, 1949), p. 11.

9. D. Hershman, ed., *Elilot Mekomiyyot: Me-Elot Kadmoniyyot ad La-Nashim Ha-Mythologioth shel Ha-Yom* [Local Goddesses: From Ancient Goddesses to Contemporary Mythological Women] (Jerusalem, 1994), pp. 6–33,

36–43; see also studies on this topic, such as T. Frymer Kensky, *In the Wake of Goddesses* (New York, 1992); C. Spretnak, ed., *The Politics of Women's Spirituality* (New York, 1982).

10. Pinkerfeld-Amir, "*Ashtoret*," in *Gaddish*, pp. 82–83.

11. C. Gilligan, *In a Different Voice: Psychological Theory and Women's Development* [Hebrew edition] (Tel Aviv, 1995), pp. 9, 44, 34.

12. Pinkerfeld-Amir, "*Eshet Lot*" [Lot's Wife], in *Gaddish*, pp. 17–19.

13. Ibid., "*Ya'el*" [Jael], pp. 53, 54.

14. See discussion on establishing mutuality in the Song of Songs in A. Pardes, "*'Ani Homah v-Shadai ke-Migdalot'*" ["I Am a Wall, My Breasts Are Like Towers": Song of Songs and the Question of Canonization], in *Ha-Beri'ah lefi Hava, Gishah Sifrtutit Feministit la-Mikra* [Countertraditions in the Bible: A Feminist Approach] (Tel Aviv, 1996), p. 93.

15. Pinkerfeld-Amir, "*Yael*" (Jael), "*Ve-Eleh shirei Hagar ad ha-Yom ha-Zeh*" [And These Are the Poems of Hagar to This Very Day], "*Leah*," "*Delilah*," "*Avishag*" (all in Hebrew), in *Gaddish*, pp. 48–55, 24–35, 41–47, 59–68, 69–74.

16. L. Ratok, "*Deyukan ha-Ishah ke-Meshoreret Yisra'elit*" [Portrait of the Woman as an Israeli Poet], *Moznayim*, nos. 2–3 (May–June 1988): 59.

17. H. Hever, "*Shirat ha-Guf ha-Le'ummi: Nashim Meshorerot be-Milhemet ha-Shihrur* [Poetry of the National Body: Female Poets in the War of Independence], *Theory and Criticism* 7 (1995): 99–123.

18. J. Olney, *Metaphors of Self* (New Jersey, 1981), pp. 2–50; A. Pinkerfeld-Amir, "*Anahnu ha-Nashim Holkhot ba-Olam*" [We the Women Go Forth in the World], and "*Anahnu ha-Galmudot la-Ad*" [We Who Are Lonely Forever], *Yuval* (1932), pp. 81 and 83.

19. I. Even-Zohar, "*Ha-Tzemihah ve-ha-Hitgabeshut shel Tarbut Ivrit Mekomit ve-Yelidit be-Eretz Yisra'el* [The Emergence and Crystallization of Local and Native Hebrew Culture in Eretz-Israel], *Cathedra* 17 (July 1980): 165–89; Y. Berlovitz, "*Hatza'ot le-Antropologiyyah Tziyyonit*" [Suggestions for Zionist Anthropology], in *Le-Hamtzi Eretz le-Hamtzi Am, Tashtiyyot Tarbut ve-Sifrut ba-Yetzirah shel ha-Aliyah ha-Rishonah* [Inventing a Land, Inventing a People: Cultural and Literary Substructures in the Writings of the Aliyah Rishonah] (Tel Aviv, 1996), pp. 15–46; hereafter cited as *Le-Hamtzi*.

20. B. Even Zohar, "*Tzemihat ha-Degem ha-Sifruti shel 'Ha-Ivri he-Hadash' be-Sifrut Ivrit 1880–1930*" [The Emergence of the Model of "The New Hebrew" in Modern Hebrew Literature 1880–1930] (Master's thesis, Tel Aviv University, 1988), pp. 103–104.

21. Y. Berlovitz, "*'Higi'a Sha'ateinu'—Zehut Nashit, Ketiva Nashit*" ["Our Time Has Come"—Feminine Identity, Feminine Writing"], in Berlovitz, *Le-Hamtzi*, n. 18, pp. 47–49; N. Puhachewsky, "*Od al Devar She'elot ha-Banot* [More about the Girls' Questions], *Ha-Melitz*, no. 21 (23 January 1889): 2–3; H. Trager, "*Zekhut Behirah la-Nashim*" [Votes for Women], in *Sippurei*

Nashim Benot ha-Aliyah ha-Rishonah [Women's Stories: Members of the First Aliyah], ed. Y. Berlovitz (Tel Aviv, 1984), pp. 132–35; H. Ben-Yehuda, *"Higi'a Sha'ateinu"* [Our Time Has Come], *Do'Ar ha-Yom*, no. 2 (30 September 1919): 2.

22. D. S. Bernstein, ed., *Pioneers and Homemakers, Jewish Women in Pre-State Israel* (New York, 1992).

23. Y. Berlovitz, *"Sifrut ha-Nashim bi-Tkufat ha-Yishuv: Re'organizaziyyah shel Tarbut Muderet"* [Women's Literature in the Yishuv Period: Reorganization of Excluded Culture], in *Harimi be-Ko'ah Kolekh, al Kolot Nashiyyim u-Parshanut Feministit be-Limmudei ha-Yahadut* [Lift Up Your Voice: Women's Voices and Feminist Interpretation in Jewish Studies], ed. R. Levin Melammed (Tel Aviv, 2001), pp. 97–121, 197–99.

Poems to the Ghetto *(pages 268–276)*

1. Dan Miron, *"Kanfot ha-Artetz (He'arot le-Shirat Yocheved Bat-Miryam)"* [Corners of the Earth (Comments on the Poetry of Yocheved Bat-Miriam)], *Gazit* 16, nos. 7–8, 187–88 (1958–1959): 14–17 (hereafter cited as Miron, "Kanfot"); R. Kartun-Blum, *Ba-Merhak ha-Ne'elam: Iyyunim be-Shiratah shel Yocheved Bat-Miryam* [In the Hidden Distance: Studies on the Poetry of Yocheved Bat-Miriam] (Ramat Gan, 1977), pp. 33–38, 47–70.

2. Benedict Anderson, *Imagined Communities* (London, 1991).

3. Dina Porath, *Hanhagah be-Milkud* [Leadership in a Trap] (Tel Aviv, 1987), pp. 59–100.

4. Hannan Hever, *Pitom Mar'eh ba-Milhamah* [Suddenly, the Sight of War: Nationalism and Violence in Hebrew Poetry of the 1940s] (Tel Aviv, 2001), pp. 64–113.

5. Bat-Miryam, 1943 — *Shirim la-Geto*, p. 15.

6. Ibid., p. 5.

7. Walter Benjamin, *The Origin of German Tragic Drama*, tr. John Osborne (London, 1977), p. 166.

8. Dan Miron has indicated the images illustrating the experience of taking off that stand at the center of Bat-Miryam's poetry: "The most legitimate picture, that permeates into every section of the poem with the power of this experience, is the image of the wing, which is obviously both an expression for taking off as well as for falling . . . a comprehensive examination of Bat-Miryam's poems shows, in reality, that the image of the wing serves here as a basic tool for capturing the experience of the landscape wherever it may be." Yet, in his statements about *Shirim la-Geto* he points out that in them, too, one can discern "that same permanent stance of distance between "I" and "you" (f.) or "you" (m.), but this time under discussion is "my generation," or more precisely the Jewish ghetto . . . we are again dealing with a poem of the path,

of walking, and of persecution." Miron, "*Kanfot*," p. 16. Miron indicates the blurring of the dividing line between (historical) time and (geographic) space and states "that the space through which this path passes is not the geographical space but historical space ('above us will pass the strength of vision and flow to the *wing of the generations* that is turning blue')." But with that Miron subjugated space to historical time while stressing Bat-Miryam's national commitment and suppressing the undermining and plundering of the national order that enables the reverse process — the displacement of the representations of time to representations of space.

9. Ibid., pp. 6, 7.

10. Ibid., p. 6.

11. Ibid., p. 13.

12. Yitzhak Tabenkin, "*Be-Yom Mifkad*" [On the Day of Assembly], *Mi-Bifnim* 9, no. 2 (June 1943): 227–28.

13. Bat-Miriam, *1943 — Shirim la-Geto*, p. 29.

14. Ibid., p. 30.

15. Ibid., p. 40.

16. Ibid., p. 42.

17. Ibid.

18. Ibid.

19. Ibid., p. 43.

20. Ibid., p. 44.

21. Ibid., p. 45.

22. R. Radhakrishnan, "Nationalism, Gender and the Narrative of Identity," *Diasporic Mediation, Between Home and Location* (Minneapolis & London, 1996), pp. 185–202.

Women and Music in Jewish Society (pages 277–282)

1. The role of women in creative popular music in Israel is significant. Notable, for example, are the contributions by Bracha Zefira, Shoshana Damari, Naomi Shemer, and Zipi Fleischer. A discussion on their unique contribution is beyond the scope of the present study.

2. Many researchers have addressed the characteristics of the developing Israeli society. One of the leading scholars in this area since the 1950s has been S. N. Eisenstadt; see, for example, his book *He'arot le-Ba'ayat ha-Hemshekhiyyut shel ha-Defusim ha-Historiyyim ha-Yehudiyyim ba-Hevrah ha-Yehudit* [On the Problem of Continuity of Jewish Historical Patterns in Jewish Society] (Jerusalem, 1977), pp. 156–58; another book is his *Edot be-Yisr'ael u-Mikuman ha-Hevrati* [Communities in Israel and Their Social Role] (Jerusalem, 1993), pp. 21–24. See also D. Silvera, *Tzomet Mizrah u-Ma'arav* [East and West] (Tel Aviv, 1989), p. 135.

3. Y. Atzmon, ed., *Eshnav le-Hayyehen shel Nashim be-Hevrot Yehudiyyot* [A View into the Lives of Women in Jewish Societies] (Jerusalem, 1995), pp. 19–20. On this subject, see also L. Green, *Music, Gender, Education* (Cambridge, Mass., 1997), p. 27.

4. M. Shilo, "*Nashim be-Hevrot Yehudiyyot — al ha-Sefer Eshnav le-Hayyehen shel Nashim be-Hevrot Yehudiyyot*" [Women in Jewish societies — On the Book A *View into the Lives of Women in Jewish Societies*], *Jewish Studies* 36 (1996): 263–66.

5. Studies as early as the 1970s already indicated this change; see, for example, those of A. Abraham and Sh. Tsharni.

6. See also E. Parker, *Nationalisms and Sexualities* (New York, 1992), p. 7.

7. See, among others, J. Blacking, "Some Problems of Theory and Method in the Study of Musical Change," *Yearbook of the International Folk Music Council* 9 (1977): 12–14; J. Blacking, "Identifying Processes of Musical Change," *The World of Music* 28, no. 1 (1986): 5–7; A. P. Merriam, *The Anthropology of Music* (Evanston, Ill., 1964), pp. 32–35; B. Nettl, *The Study of Ethnomusicology: Twenty-Nine Issues and Concepts* (Urbana, Ill., 1983), pp. 131–46; B. Nettl, "Recent Directions in Ethnomusicology," in *Ethnomusicology: An Introduction*, ed. H. Myers, pp. 375–79 (New York, 1992).

8. A. Shiloah and E. Cohen, "*Dinamikat ha-Shinui ba-Musikah shel Edot Yisra'el*" [The Dynamics of Change in the Music of the Jewish Communities], *Peamim* 12 (1982): 3–25; A. Shiloah, "*Ha-Shinui ba-Mesorot ha-Musikaliyyot ha-Yehudiyyot*" [The Change in the Jewish Musical Traditions], *Duchan* 14 (1996): 24–29; U. Sharvit, "*Ha-Mesorot ha-Musikaliyyot She-Be'al-Peh be-Kerev Kehllot Yisra'el*" [The Oral Musical Traditions of the Jewish Communities], *Peamim* 31 (1987): 132–35; U. Sharvit, "*Al ha-Bitui ha-Musikali shel Yehudei ha-Mizrah ha-Sefardim be-Yisra'el*" [On the Musical Expression of the Eastern Jews in Israel], in *Mahatzit ha-Ummah: Iyyunim be-Tarbut u-ve-Ma'amad shel Yotze'Eretz Israel ha-Mizrah be-Yisra'el* (Half of the Nation: On the Culture and Status of the Eastern Jews in Israel), ed. S. Deshen, pp. 131–42 (Ramat-Gan, 1986).

9. Y. Shai, "*Tahalikhei Shinnui be-Repertu'ar ha-Musikali ha-Masorti shel ha-Hatunah be-Kerev Yehude Haban*" [Processes of Change in the Traditional Musical Repertoire of the Haban Jewish Wedding] (Ph.D. diss., Bar-Ilan University, 1977), pp. 283–84, 168–69, 289–90; N. B. Gamlieli, *Ahavat Teiman: Shirat ha-Nashim* [Yemen Love: Women Singing], third edition (Tel Aviv, 1996), pp. 154, 159.

10. Notable is that the women in both communities have not developed an independent status. Moreover, they have no intention of creating equality between the sexes.

11. The present article briefly surveys the main musical elements, which undoubtedly call for further investigation.

12. Notable are Koskoff's words: "It is not surprising that the majority of existing descriptions of women's musical activities and rationales for their behavior focus on their primary social roles, for these roles are central to women's
gender identity in many societies." E. Koskoff, ed., *Women and Music in Cross-
Cultural Perspectives* (Urbana, Ill., 1987), p. 4.

13. See Y. Kazir, "*Nashim Yotze'ot Teiman ke-Sokhenot Shinnui ba-
Moshav*" [Yemen Women as Agents of Change in the Settlement], in *Yehudei
ha-Mizrah: Iyyunim Antropologiyyim shel he-Avar ve-ha-Hoveh* (Eastern Jews:
Anthropological Studies of Past and Present), ed. S. Deshen and M. Shoked
(Jerusalem, 1984), pp. 221–22. The author claims that women show greater in-
clination toward adopting changes than men.

The Legend of Sarah (pages 285–320)

1. The quotation is from Renan's lecture at the Sorbonne, 1 March 1882,
"Qu'est-ce qu'une nation?" *Oeuvres completes*, vol. 1 (Paris, 1947–1961),
pp. 887–907, translated in *Nation and Narration*, ed. Homi K. Bhabha, p. 11
(London, 1990).

2. Charles S. Maier, "A Surfeit of Memory? Reflections on History, Melancholy and Denial," *History & Memory* 5, no. 2 (Fall/Winter 1993): 136–37.

3. Marcel Proust, *Du côté de chez Swann* (Paris, 1954), p. 57.

4. See, for example, Pierre Nora, ed., *Les Lieux de mémoire* (Paris, 1984–
92; hereafter Nora, *Lieux de mémoire*); Paul Connerton, *How Societies Remember* (New York, 1989); John R. Gillis, ed., *Commemorations: The Politics of Na-
tional Identity* (Princeton, 1994) (hereafter cited as Gillis, *Commemorations*);
Raphael Samuel, *Past and Present in Contemporary Culture*, vol. 1, *Theatres of
Memory* (London, 1994); Frances A. Yates, *The Art of Memory* (London, 1984,
reprint); Jay M. Winter, *Sites of Memory, Sites of Mourning* (London, 1996);
George L. Mosse, *Fallen Soldiers: Reshaping the Memory of the World Wars*
(New York, 1990); Natalie Zemon Davis and Randolph Starn, "Introduction,"
Representations 26 (Spring 1989), special issue on collective memory and
counter-memory.

5. Emmanuel Sivan, *Dor Tashah: Mitos, Dyukan ve-Zikkaron* [The Gener-
ation of 1948: Myth, Profile, and Memory] (Tel Aviv, 1991), especially pp. 169–
231 (hereafter Sivan, *Dor Tashah*); Yael Zerubavel, "*Mot ha-Zikaron ve-
Zikkaron ha-Mavet*" [The Death of Memory and the Memory of Death],
Alpayim 10 (1994): 42–68 (hereafter Zerubavel, *Mot ha-Zikaron*); Anita Shapira,
"*Historiografyah ve-Zikkaron: Mikreh Latrun Tashah*" [Historiography and
Memory: The Case of Latroun, 1948], *Alpayim* 10 (1994): 9–42; David Ohana
and Robert S. Wistrich, *Mitos ve-Zikkaron: Gilguleiha shel ha-Toda'ah ha-
Yisre'elit* [Myth and Memory: Transfigurations of Israeli Consciousness] (Jeru-

salem, 1996) (hereafter Ohana and Wistrich, *Mitos ve-Zikkaron*); Yael
Zerubavel, *Recovered Roots: Collective Memory and the Making of Israeli National Tradition* (Chicago, 1995); Yael Zerubavel, "The Historic, the Leg-
endary, and the Incredible in Invented Tradition and Collective Memory in Israel," in Gillis, *Commemorations*, pp. 105–25; David N. Myers, *Reinventing
the Jewish Past in Israel* (New York, 1995); Nachman Ben Yehuda, *The Mas-
sada Myth: Collective Memory and Mythmaking in Israel* (Madison, Wisc.,
1995). See also Idith Zertal, *"Ha-Me'unim ve-ha-Kedoshim: Kinunah shel
Martirologyah Le'ummit"* [The Tortured and the Sanctified: Loss and Commemoration, the Creation of National Martyrology], *Zmanim* 48 (1994): 26–
45; Eliezer Witztum and Rut Malkinson, *"Shekhol ve-Hantzahah: Ha-Panim
ha-Kefulot shel ha-Mitos ha-Le'ummi"* [Bereavement and Commemoration: The Dual Face of the National Myth], in *Ovdan u-Shekhol ba-Hevrah
ha-Yisre'elit* [Loss and Bereavement in Israeli Society], ed. Ruth Malkinson,
Shimshon Rubin, and Eliezer Witztum, pp. 231–58 (Tel Aviv, 1993).

6. Conversations with Natalie Zemon Davis, 17–19 March 1998.

7. Zerubavel, *"Mot ha-Zikkaron"*; Ohana and Wistrich, *Mitos ve-Zikkaron.*
On *The Yizkor Book*, see Jonathan Frankel's important study, *"The Yizkor Book
of 1911 —A Note on National Myth in the Second Aliya,"* in *Religion, Ideology
and Nationalism in Europe and America: Essays in Honor of Yehoshua Arieli*,
ed. Hedva Ben Israel et al., pp. 355–84 (Jerusalem, 1986).

8. For the state of the research see the Hebrew version of this volume; see
Margalit Shilo, Ruth Kark, and Galit Hasan-Rokem, eds., *Nashim ba-Yishuv
u-va-Medinah be-Reishit Darkah* [Jewish Women in the *Yishuv* and Zionism]
(Jerusalem, 2001), especially Deborah S. Bernstein, *"Heker Nashim ba-Histo-
riografyah ha-Yisre'elit: Nekudot Motza, Kavvanot Hadashot ve-Kavvanot she-
ba-Derekh"* [The Study of Women in Israeli Historiography: Starting Points,
New Directions, and Emerging Insights], pp. 7–25 (in this volume pp. 7–17);
Billie Melman, *"Min ha-Shulayim el ha-Historiyah shel ha-Yishuv: Migdar ve-
Eretz Yisre'eliyut (1890–1920)"* [From the Periphery to the Center of *Yishuv*
History: Gender and Nationalism in Eretz Israel (1890–1920)], *Zion* 62, no. 3
(1997), 243–79 (hereafter cited as Melman, *"Min ha-Shulayim"*). See also Ju-
dith T. Baumel, *"'In Everlasting Memory': Individual and Communal Holo-
caust Commemoration in Israel,"* in *The Shaping of Israeli Identity: Myth,
Memory, and Trauma*, ed. Robert Wistrich and David Ohana, pp. 146–70
(London, 1995); Orly Lubin, *"Ha-Eemet she-bein Misgerot ha-Emet: Otobi-
ografiyah, Edut, Guf ve-Atar"* [The Truth between the Frameworks of Truth:
Autobiography, Testimony, Body, and Site], in *Aderet le-Vinyamin: Sefer ha-
Yovel le-Binyamin Harshav* [Jubilee Book for Binyamin Harshav] (Tel Aviv,
1999), 1:133–49; Hannah Naveh, *Be-Shevi ha-Evel: Ha-Evel bi-Re'i ha-Sifrut
ha-Ivrit ha-Hadashah* [In the Thrall of Mourning: Mourning in the Mirror of
the New Israeli Literature] (Tel Aviv, 1993). For more on the definition of the

areas of the history of memory, see Jay Winter and Emmanuel Sivan, eds., *War and Remembrance in the Twentieth Century* (Cambridge, U.K., 1996), pp. 6–40 (hereafter cited as Winter and Sivan, *War and Remembrance*).

9. Alon Confino, "Collective Memory and Cultural History: Problems of Method," *American Historical Review* 102, no. 5 (1997): 1386–403.

10. See Confino's critique of Zerubavel in ibid.; see also Emmanuel Sivan, "Private Pain and Public Remembrance in Israel," in Winter and Sivan, *War and Remembrance*, pp. 177–205.

11. See, for example, Ilan Pappé, "*Seder Yom Hadash le-Historiyah Hadashah*" [A New Agenda for a New History], *Theory and Criticism* 8 (1996): 130–31.

12. See Gillis, *Commemorations*; Maurice Halbwachs, *Les Cadres sociaux de la mémoire* (Paris, 1925); English translation with Foreword by L. A. Ciser, *On Collective Memory* (Chicago, 1992).

13. On polyphony as the proliferation of independent voices and consciousness, see M. M. Bakhtin, *Problems of Dostoevsky's Poetics* [1929], trans. R. W. Rotsel (Ann Arbor, Mich., 1973); Sivan, *Dor Tashah*, especially p. 138.

14. Avigdor Hameiri, "Sarah Aaronsohn," *Do'ar ha-Yom*, 10 October 1923 (in Hebrew); "Sarah Aaronsohn," in *Sarah ve-Aharon Aronson li-Melot 15 Shanah le-Motah Mot Gibborim* [Sarah and Aaron Aaronsohn, in Honor of Fifteen Years since Her Death as a Hero] (Tel Aviv, 1932) (hereafter Hameiri, "Sarah Aaronsohn"). This is the first official commemorative book whose revenues were dedicated to the construction of a memorial for Sarah Aaronsohn. Beit Aaronsohn Archives, Zikhron Yaakov (hereafter BAA), newspaper clippings files, numbering unclear.

15. See Melman, "*Min ha-shulayim*," pp. 243–79.

16. See ibid., pp. 275–77; Billie Melman, "Introduction," in *Borderlines: Genders and Identities in War and Peace, 1870–1930*, ed. Billie Melman (London, 1998), pp. 1–25 (hereafter cited as Melman, *Borderlines*); Rajeswari Sunder Rajan, *Real and Imagined Woman: Gender, Culture, and Postcolonialism* (London, 1993); Gayatri C. Spivak, *In Other Worlds: Essays in Cultural Politics* (New York, 1988), pp. 241–69; and Beth Baron, "The Politics of Female Notables in Postwar Egypt," in Melman, *Borderlines*, pp. 329–51.

17. On the immediate impact of the events at Tel Hai on the public memory, see, for example, the works of Zerubavel and others cited in note 5. For references to her death in the 1920s, see Hameiri, "Sarah Aaronsohn"; Peretz Pascal, "Sarah Aaronsohn," *Do'ar ha-Yom*, 27 October 1920; Zipora Chon, "A Hero of the New Zion," *Jewish Tribune*, 22 May 1922; Benjamin Yablons, "New Palestine's Jean d'Arc," *Jewish Daily Bulletin*, 27 January 1925; Yirmiyahu Jaffe, "*Yoman* Zikhron Yaakov, April 1917–April 1918" [Zikhron Yaakov diary, April 1917–April 1918], BAA. See also Aharon Ever-Hadani's play *Shomerim* [Guards], in which Nili's espionage is condemned in Act 3, Scenes 4–9. The

play opened in the Habimah Theater on 24 August 1937, but was promptly removed because of strong public protest. See A. Ever-Hadani, *Kitvei ne'urim* [Juvenile Writings] (Tel Aviv, 1944), p. 320.

18. Eric Hobsbawm, "Introduction: Inventing Traditions," in *The Invention of Tradition*, ed. Eric Hobsbawm and Terence Ranger (Cambridge, U.K., 1983), pp. 1–15.

19. Clifford Geertz, *The Interpretation of Cultures* (New York, 1973), especially his analysis of the Balinese cock-fight, pp. 412–55; James Clifford, *The Predicament of Culture: Twentieth-Century Ethnography, Literature, and Art* (Cambridge, Mass., 1988), pp. 31–32.

20. *"Ha-aliyah el kever Sarah Aaronson zal"* [The Pilgrimage to the Grave of Sarah Aaronsohn of Blessed Memory], 10 October 1933, BAA, Sarah, Box 2.

21 Melman, *"Min ha-shulayim,"* pp. 243–79; Rachel Elboim-Dror, *"'Hu holekh u-va be-kirbenu ha-ivri he-hadash': Al Tarbut ha-No'ar shel ha-Aliyot ha-Rishonot"* ["He Is Come, from Amongst Us He Is Come, the First Hebrew": On the Youth Culture of the First Waves of Immigration], *Alpayim* 12 (1996): 104–35 (hereafter cited as Elboim-Dror, *"Hu holekh u-Va"*).

22. Y. Drori, *"Reshitam shel Irgunim Kalkaliyyim be-Eretz Yisrael bi-Shnot ha-Esrim"* [The Beginning of Economic Organizations in Eretz Yisrael in the 1920s)], *Cathedra* 25 (1983): 99–112 (hereafter cited as Drori, *"Reshitam shel Irgunim Kalkaliim"*); idem, *"Ha-Hugim ha-Ezrahiyyim ba-Yishuv ha-Eretzyisre'eli bi-Shnot ha-Esrim"* ["Ha-Hugim Ha'ezrahyyiim" in the Jewish "Yishuv" in Eretz Israel, 1920–29] (Ph.D. diss., Tel Aviv University, 1981); see also Amir Ben-Porat, *Heikhan Hem ha-Burganim ha-Hem? Toledot ha-Burganut ha-Yisre'elit* [Where Are Those Bourgeoisie: The History of the Israeli Bourgeois] (Jerusalem, 1999), especially pp. 72–80, for the distinction between the urban and rural bourgeoisie (hereafter Ben-Porat, *Heikhan*). See also Yaacov Shavit, *"Ha-Roved ha-Tarbuti he-Haser u-Milu'av: Bein 'Tarbut Amamit Rishmit' le-'Tarbut Amamit Lo Rishmit' ba-Tarbut ha-Ivrit ha-Le'ummit be-Eretz Yisrael"* [Supplying a Missing System: Between "Official" and "Unofficial" Culture" in Hebrew National Culture in Eretz Yisrael], in *Ha-Tarbut ha-Amamit* [Studies in the History of Popular Culture], ed. B. Z. Kedar, pp. 327–45 (Jerusalem, 1996).

23. *Sarah ve-Aharon Aaronson, li-melot 15 shanah* (1932), p. 7.

24. *"Ha-aliyah al kever Sarah,"* BAA, Sarah, Box 2, pp. 3–5; 18th Anniversary Ceremony (1935), BAA, Sarah, Box 2, p. 1.

25. *Sarah ve-Aharon Aaronson li-melot 15 shanah*, first page (unnumbered).

26. Hayden White, *Metahistory: The Historical Imagination in Nineteenth-Century Europe* (Baltimore, 1973).

27. Elboim-Dror, *"Hu holekh u-va"*; Drori, *"Reshitam shel Irgunim Kalkaliyyim."*

28. A. Zilber, on behalf of the Bnei Binyamin Federation, description of the 18th Memorial Day, 1935 (no exact date), BAA, Sarah, Box 2 (no pagination).

29. "*Yom ha-aliyah le-kever Sarah, 14.10.41*" [Day of the Pilgrimage to Sarah's Grave, 14 October 1941], BAA, Sarah, Box 2.

30. On the juvenile press, see Zohar Shavit, ed., *Toledot ha-Yishuv ha-Yehudi be-Eretz Yisrael me'az ha-Aliyah ha-Rishonah: Beniyatah shel Tarbut Ivrit be-Eretz Yisrael* [The History of the Jewish Community in Eretz Yisrael since 1882: The Construction of Hebrew Culture in Eretz Israel], Part 1 (Jerusalem, 1989); for the children's press, see pp. 455–61. For a discussion of Sarah's depiction and representation in the children's press, see below, pp. 296–97. For plays and stories, see the play by Moshe Smilansky, *Rohele*, in *Kitvei Moshe Smilansky* [The Writings of Moshe Smilansky], vol. 4, *Sippurim* [Stories] (Tel Aviv, 1934), pp. 155–92 (hereafter Smilansky, *Rohele*); Ever-Hadani's play *Shomerim* (n. 17 above); Aharon Avraham Kabak, "*Ha-Meraggelet*" [The Spy], in *Bein ha-midbar u-vein ha-yam* [Between the Desert and the Sea] (Tel Aviv, 1959); the prose poem by Y. Cohen, *Megillat Avshalom ve-Sarah* [The Scroll of Avshalom and Sarah], (Tel Aviv, 1948), pp. 29–50; "Sarah Aharonson: *Arba'im shanah le-motah*" [Sarah Aaronsohn: Forty Years since Her Death] was broadcast on Kol Yisrael radio station on Saturday, 26 October 1957, with Hannah Rovina as Sarah.

31. Samuel, *Past and Present in Contemporary Culture*, vol. 1, *Theatres of Memory*, pp. 1–40.

32. "*Ha-aliyah el kever Sarah Aharonson*," 10 October 1932, BAA, Sarah, Box 2, pp. 3–5.

33. Itamar Even-Zohar, "*Ha-Tzemihah ve-ha-Hitgabbeshut shel Tarbut Ivrit Mekomit u-Yelidit be-Eretz Yisrael, 1882–1948*" [The Emergence and Formation of Local and Native Hebrew Culture in Eretz Yisrael, 1882–1948], *Cathedra* 16 (July 1980): 165–89.

34. Y. Heller, *Lehi, 1940–1949* (in Hebrew; Jerusalem, 1989), vol. 1, pp. 25–26, 61, 81–88, 99, 101, 121–22, 131, 154–55, 172.

35. *Ha-Boker li-Yeladim* [*Ha-Boker* children's newspaper], no. 161–62, 9 October 1946, pp. 10–11; see also ibid., no. 107–108, 20 September 1945, p. 27. A sample of elementary school primers between 1950 and 1960 indicates that the story of Nili was not included in the school curriculum or in the organized collective memory. This, of course, is in contrast to the story of Tel Hai. See also Aviezer Yellin Archives of Jewish Education in Israel and the Diaspora, Tel Aviv University; and Keren Kayemet Archives, Tel Aviv, the Leah and Dov Aloni collections.

36. See, for example, n. 14 above, *Sarah ve-Aharon Aaronsohn li-Melot*, p. 30.

37. See n. 4 above.

38. Melman, "*Min ha-Shulayim*," pp. 255–60; A. Bar-Adon, "'*Ha-Imahot*

ha-Meyassedot' u-Menat Helkan be-Tehiyat ha-Ivrit be-Hithavvutah, 1882–1914" ["The Founding Mothers" and Their Role in the Hebrew Language Revival, 1882–1914], *Lashon ve-Ivrit* 3 (1990): 5–27.

39. Melman, "*Min ha-Shulayim*," pp. 255–60.

40. Pat Thane and Gisela Bock, eds., *Maternity and Gender Politics* (London, 1991); Seth Koven and Sonia Michel, eds., *Mothers of a New World: Maternalist Politics and the Origins of the Welfare State* (New York, 1993); Melman, "Introduction," in *Borderlines*; Fatma Müge Göçek, "From Empire to Nation: Images of Women and War in Ottoman Political Cartoons, 1908–1923," in *Borderlines*, pp. 47–73; Beth Baron, "Mothers, Morality, and Nationalism in Pre-1917 Egypt," in *The Origins of Arab Nationalism*, ed. Rashid Khalidi, pp. 271–88 (New York, 1991).

41. Billie Melman, "Re-Generation: Nation and the Construction of Gender in Peace and War—Palestine Jews, 1900–1918," in *Borderlines*, pp. 121–41.

42. Yaakov Yaari-Polskin, *Nili, Sarah be-Hayeha u-ve-Motah* [Nili, Sarah in Life and Death] (Tel Aviv, 1951), pp. 57–59.

43. Hameiri, "Sarah Aronson."

44. Melman, "*Min ha-shulayim*," pp. 260–67, 274–76.

45. Yaari-Polskin, "*Mi-hayei Sarah Aharonson (Biografiyah ve-epizod)*" [From the Life of Sarah Aaronsohn (Biography and Episode)]," in *Sarah ve-Aharon Aaronsohn*, p. 18.

46. Joseph Klausner, "Sarah Aharonson: *Ha-giborah ha-le'ummit*" [Sarah Aaronsohn: The National Heroine], *Ha-Mashkif*, September 1942; see also his eulogy on the forty-fifth anniversary of her death in 1962, BAA, Sarah, Box 2, undated and unpaginated.

47. Melman, "*Min ha-shulayim*."

48. Smilansky, *Rohele*, p. 181.

49. Ibid., p. 191.

50. Moshe Smilansky, "*Ha-ishah: Ner le-Nishmat* Sarah Aharonson" [The Woman: A Candle for the Soul of Sarah Aaronsohn], in *Kitvei Moshe Smilansky*, vol. 8 (Tel Aviv, 1935), p. 22.

51. See below, pp. 306–7. On Aaronsohn as "the Jewish Edith Cavell," see, for example, "A Tribute to Sarah Aaronsohn," *Jewish Daily Bulletin*, 27 January 1925.

52. On the images of Joan of Arc and on memory, see M. Winock, "Jeanne d'Arc," in Nora, *Lieux de mémoire*, vol. 3, *Les France* (Paris, 1997), pp. 4427–73. On evangelicalism and the suffragette movement in Protestant countries, see Martha Vicinus, *Independent Women: Work and Community for Single Women, 1850–1920* (London, 1985), pp. 20, 266, 270.

53. BAA, Sarah, Box 2, 10 October 1933.

54. BAA, Sarah, Box 2, 14 October 1941; BAA, Sarah, Box 2, 15 October 1946.

55. Ludmila Jordanova, *Sexual Visions: Images of Gender in Science and Medicine between the Eighteenth and Twentieth Centuries* (Madison, Wisc., 1989), pp. 81–111.

56. Ceremony, 1935, BAA, Sarah, Box 2.

57. Ceremony, 1941: "Every Betar club is a temple for your teachings, Commander Sarah! We stand at attention before you — our Commander"; Pilgrimage Ceremony, 1942. BAA, Sarah, Box 2.

58. Pilgrimage Ceremony, 1958, "Professor Klausner," unnumbered, BAA, Sarah, Box 2.

59. Melman, "Introduction," in *Borderlines*.

60. Reports on the activities of Bnei Binyamin in late 1927 and early 1928 record 1,500 "young men" as members of the organization. The English-language report emphasizes "a fine spirit of brotherhood." See *"Doh al Pe'ilut Bnei Binyamin be-Palestinah"* [Report on the Activities of Bnei Binyamin in Palestine], BAA, Alexander Aaronsohn Box, Bnei Binyamin 213. According to the Regulations of the Bnei Binyamin Federation, "The purpose of the organization [is] to unite and to organize the youth of the moshavah." A similar point is made in the 1927 report, in connection with the organization's athletic activities, whose purpose is to "attract our young men" (ibid.).

61. On the organizations, see Rachel Elboim-Dror, *Ha-hinukh ha-Ivri be-Eretz Yisrael* [Hebrew Education in Eretz Israel], vol. 1 (Jerusalem, 1986); Melman, *"Min ha-shulayim,"* p. 266.

62. "Essentialism" refers to the perception of femininity — and of gender in general — not in social-historical terms, but as a natural, unchanging essence. On "androgynous" images, see Mary L. Roberts, *Civilization without Sexes: Reconstructing Gender in France, 1917–1927* (Chicago, 1994); Billie Melman, *Women and the Popular Imagination in the Twenties: Flappers and Nymphs* (London, 1986); Sunder Rajan, *Real and Imagined Women*. It is clear that in cultures like these the worship of women, especially of women leaders as mothers of the nation, can also develop.

63. I am grateful to Sasha Weitman who permitted me to use his data. On the choice of Hebrew national names, see Sasha Weitman, "Prénoms et orientations nationales en Israël, 1882–1890," *Annales ESC* 42, no. 4 (1987): 879–901; Weitman, *"Shemot Pratiyyim ke-Madadim Hevratiyyim: Megamot bi-Zehutam ha-Le'ummit shel Yisre'elim, 1882–1980"* [First Names as Social Indicators: Trends in Israelis' National Identity, 1882–1980], in *Nekudot Tatzpit al Tarbut ve-Hevrah be-Eretz Yisrael* [Perspectives on Culture and Society in Israel], ed. Nurith Gertz, pp. 141–51 (Tel Aviv, 1988).

64. Conversations with Yaffah Berlovitz and Nili Friedland, June 1998.

65. R. Tkhelet, *"Kapitan Lelo Kokhavim"* [Captain without Stars], *La-Ishah*, 2 October 1947. See also *"She'oteha ha-Aharonot shel Sarah"* [Sarah's Last Hours], *Olam ha-Ishah*, 16 October 1947, p. 5. For a different version, see

"*Shtei Nesikhot Ra'ah Avshalom be-Neshef ha-Masekhot*" [Avshalom Saw Two Princesses at the Masked Ball], *Shiva Yamim, Yediot Aharonot* weekend supplement, 5 November 1954; "*Ka-Zeh Hayah Sofam shel Sarah ve-Avshalom*" [Such Was the End of Sarah and Avshalom]," ibid., 12 November 1954.

66. Ohana and Wistrich, *Mitos ve-Zikkaron*, pp. 21–27. These authors locate the "fracture in the collective Israeli experience" in 1973, and point out that the mythology of the "Sabra" and Israeliness, which had already collapsed at the end of the 1960s, was finally buried. See Ben-Porat, "*Heikhan hem ha-burganim ha-hem?*" pp. 130–31.

67. For this information, I thank the staff of Aaronsohn House, and especially the acting director Esther Cohen, as well as David Shoham.

68. Rahel Katzenelson, "*Giborat Nili: Sarah le-Veit Aharonson*" [Heroine of Nili: Sarah of the Aaronsohn family]," *Dvar ha-Po'elet*, 11 November 1967, p. 359 (hereafter Katzenelson, "*Giborat Nili*").

69. Yehudah Slutsky, "*Nishmatah shel Nili: Hamishim Shanah le-Motah shel Sarah Aharonson*" [The Soul of Nili: Fifty Years since the Death of Sarah Aaronsohn], *Davar*, 27 October 1967.

70. Y. Manor, "*Ha-Aggadah ve-ha-Metzi'ut shel Nili: Ha-Reka Hu ha-Noten Partzuf Emet le-Historiyah*" [The Legend and Reality of Nili: The Background Is What Shows the True Face of History], *Davar*, 1 December 1967.

71. Katzenelson, "*Giborat Nili*," p. 361.

72. Shimshon Kirshenbaum, *Toledot Yisrael ba-Dorot ha-Aharonim* [History of Israel in Recent Generations] (Tel Aviv, 1968), p. 78. See also Moshe Lifshitz, *Toledot am Yisrael ba-Dorot ha-Aharonim* [History of the People of Israel in Recent Generations], vol. 1, *Ha-Tenu'ah ha-Le'ummit* (The National Movement) (Tel Aviv, 1985), pp. 75–76.

73. Yisrael Pazi, *Me-Emantzipatziyah le-Tziyonut: Migvan Darkhei Hora'ah le-Kitot 10–11* [From Emancipation to Zionism: A Variety of Teaching Methods for the 10th and 11th Grades] (Tel Aviv, 1975), pp. 255–58.

74. I wish to thank Sreberk Publishers, which made its archives available to me; my special thanks go to Ze'ev Namir.

75. Conversation with Devorah Omer, 1 August 1999.

76. Ibid.

77. Ibid.; conversation with Ze'ev Namir, 1 August 1999.

78. Conversation with Devorah Omer, 1 August 1999.

79. Sreberk Publishers Archives; conversation with Ze'ev Namir, 1 August 1999.

80. BAA; conversations with Esther Cohen, acting director, Aaronsohn House, the Nili Museum, April 1998.

81. Conversation with Devorah Omer, 1 August 1999.

82. Devorah Omer, *Sarah Giborat Nili* (Tel Aviv, 1990), pp. 37–40.

83. Ibid., pp. 21–22.
84. Ibid., p. 33.
85. Ibid., p. 35.
86. Ibid., p. 198.
87. Joan W. Scott, *Only Paradoxes to Offer: French Feminists and the Rights of Man* (Cambridge, Mass., 1996), pp. 1–19.
88. *Sarah*, directed by Orna Ben-Dor, produced by Orna Landau.
89. Melman, "*Min ha-shulayim.*"

"We Were There Too" (pages 321–337)

1. In the past few years, a number of books and studies on this topic have appeared, but little has been written on the reflection of this connection in Israeli society in general and in the field of commemoration in particular. See N. Yuval-Davis and F. Anthias, *Woman-Nation-State* (Houndmills, 1989) (hereafter cited as Yuval-Davis and Anthias, *Woman-Nation-State*); C. Nash, "Men Again: Irish Masculinity, Nature, and Nationhood in the Early Twentieth Century," *Ecumene* 3, no. 4 (1966): 253–427; L. Dowler, "And They Think I'm Just a Nice Old Lady": Women and War in Belfast, Northern Ireland," *Gender Place and Culture* 5, no. 2 (1998): 159–76 (hereafter cited as Dowler, "And They Think"); G. Zwerman, "Mothering on the Lam: Politics, Gender Fantasies and Maternal Thinking in Women Associated with Armed, Clandestine Organizations in the United States," *Feminist Review* 47 (1994): 33–56 (hereafter cited as Zwerman, "Mothering"); J. Elshtain, *Woman and War* (New York, 1987); A. McClintock, "Family Feuds: Gender, Nationalism and the Family," *Feminist Review* 44 (1993): 61–80; K. Jayawardena, *Feminism and Nationalism in the Third World* (London, 1986); D. Kandiyoti, "Identity and its Discontents: Women and the Nation," *Millennium: Journal of International Studies* 20, no. 3 (1991): 229–43; T. Mayer, ed., *Women and the Israeli Occupation: The Politics of Change* (London, 1994) (hereafter cited as Mayer, *Women*).
2. C. Geertz, ed., *Myth, Symbol and Culture* (New York, 1971).
3. O. Almog, "*Andartot le-Halelei Milhamah be-Yisrael: Nitu'ah Semiyologi*" [Memorials to the Fallen in Battle in Israel: A Semiological Analysis], *Megamot* 34, no. 2 (1991): 182. Three books on this issue, published in the past years (*Andartot la-nofelim be-yisra'el* [Monuments to the Fallen in Israel] by Esther Levinger, *Hantzahah ve-Zikkaron* [Commemoration and Memory], and *Gal'ed: Andartot la-Nofelim be-Ma'arakhot Yisra'el* [Monument: Memorials to the Those Who Fell in Israel's Battles], both by Ilana Shamir), deal with a listing and partial analysis of some one thousand memorials scattered throughout the country, but they devoted a scant few lines to the image of the

woman in plastic commemoration. E. Levinger, *Andartot la-Nofelim be-Yisra'el* (Tel Aviv, 1993) (hereafter cited as Levinger, *Andartot*); I. Shamir, *Hantzahah ve-Zikkaron* (Tel Aviv, 1996); see also I. Shamir, ed., *Gal'ed: Andartot la-nofelim be-ma'arakhot yisra'el* (Tel Aviv, 1989).

4. I wish to thank the Division for Soldier Commemoration and the statistical department of the Israeli Ministry of Defense, which provided me with the relevant statistical data. Emmanuel Sivan points out in his book *Dor Tashah, Mitos, Deyukan ve-Zikkaron* [The Generation of 1948, Myth, Portrait and Memory] (Tel Aviv, 1991), pp. 35–39, that 108 women in service were killed in 1948 and the number of female victims, soldiers, and civilians, totaled 469 (hereafter Sivan, *Dor*).

5. S. Reinharz, "Manya Wilbushewitz-Shohat and the Winding Road to Sejera," in *Pioneers and Homemakers: Jewish Women in Pre-State Israel*, ed. D. Bernstein, pp. 69–73 (Albany, 1992).

6. H. Ironi-Avrahami, *Almoniyyot bi-Khaki: Sippuran shel Haverot ha-'Haganah' be-Tel Aviv* [Anonymous Women in Khaki: The Story of the Female Members of the Haganah in Tel Aviv] (Tel Aviv, 1989); A. Gozes-Savorai, *Sapperi Li Sapperi Li — Haverot ha-Palmah Mesapperot* [Tell Me, Tell Me — Female Members of the Palmah Tell Their Tale] (Efal: The Center for the History of the Defense Force, 1993); K. Muir, *Arms and the Woman* (London, 1992), pp. 69–73.

7. Regarding the paratroopers mission, see my article "'Ha-Tzonehim el Amam' — Mivtza ha-Tzanhanim-Shelihim be-Milhemet ha-Olam ha-Sheniyyah be-Perspektiva Historit" ["Parachuting to Their People" — The Paratroopers-Emissaries' Campaign in World War II in Historical Perspective," *Kovetz Yad Vashem* 25 (1996): 103–34.

8. Activities of the Female Member in the Palmah, Report of a symposium held by the Center for the History of the Defense Force — the Haganah, at Yad Tabenkin, 22 December 1986, Tel Aviv, 1988.

9. Women and IDF Service: Reality, Aspiration and Vision, Proceedings of a study-day held on 21 February 1995, Jerusalem, 1995.

10. Zwerman, "Mothering," p. 42.

11. Dowler, "And They Think," p. 16.

12. Yuval-Davis and Anthias, *Woman-Nation-State*, p. 7.

13. N. Ben-Yehudah, *1948: Bein ha-Sefirot* [1948: Between Calendars] (Jerusalem, 1981); Ben-Yehudah, *Ke-she-Partza ha-Medinah* [When the State Broke Out] (Jerusalem, 1991); T. Avidar, *Ke-she-ha-Gerev Hayah Kova* [When the Stocking Was a Cap] (Tel Aviv, 1988).

14. Levinger, *Andartot*, p. 29; interview by R. Porat with Eliahu Amitzur, *Kefar Yehoshua*, 22 March 1998; telephone conversation with the director of the kibbutz Tel Yosef archive, 18 March 1998.

15. A. Priver, "*Ha-Tavlit al Kir ha-Zikkaron le-yad 'Beit Trumpeldor'*" [The

Relief on the Memorial Wall next to "Bet Trumpeldor"], *Mi-Hayyenu* 1002 (18 April 1952): 1 (hereafter Priver, *"Ha-Tavlit"*; C. McIntyre, *Monuments of War: How to Read a War Memorial* (London, 1990), p. 144.

16. J. B. Elshtain, *Women and War* (New York, 1987), p. 11.

17. Memorial to the 44 Slain in the Battle for Negbah and Its Surroundings, Tel Aviv (the Committee for the Commemoration of Those Slain in the Battle for Negbah), n.d.

18. Sivan, *Dor*, pp. 37–39.

19. Telephone conversation of the author with Mordecai Kafri, 30 March 1998.

20. See Sivan, *Dor*, pp. 73–101.

21. I. Eschebach, "Geschlechtsspezifische Symbolisierungen im Gedenken. Zur: Geschichte der Mahn- und Gendenkstaette Ravensbrueck," *Metis: Zeitschrift für historische Frauenforschung und feministische Praxis* 8 Jf., H. 15 (1999): 12–27.

22. Priver, *"Ha-Tavlit,"* n. 15; *"Hinneh Hi Notzevet"* [Behold It Has Been Placed], *Kol Negbah: Bamah le-Bittu'i ve-Informatziyyah* 5 (103), 20 October 1953.

23. The story of this memorial is presented at length in the Hebrew version of this article.

24. J. Young, *The Texture of Memory: Holocaust Memorials and Meaning* (New Haven, Conn., 1993), p. 15.

25. S. Schama, *Landscape and Memory* (New York, 1995), p. 61.

26. D. N. Israeli, "The Women Workers' Movement: First Wave Feminism in Pre-State Israel," in *Pioneers and Homemakers: Jewish Women in Pre-State Israel*, ed. D. Bernstein, pp. 183–210 (Albany, 1992); S. Fogiel-Bijaoui, "From Revolution to Motherhood: The Case of Women in the Kibbutz, 1910–1948," in ibid., pp. 211–34.

27. G. Waylen, "Analysing Women in the Politics of the Third World," in *Women and Politics in the Third World*, ed. H. Afshar (London, 1996), p. 15.

28. Quoted from H. McQueen, *Social Sketches of Australia 1888–1975* (Harmondsworth, 1978), p. 158.

29. *"Ha-Yeshivah ha-Rishonah shel Mo'etzet ha-Am"* [The First Meeting of the National Council], Tel Aviv Jewish National Fund House, 28 Nisan 5708 (4 May 1948), in D. Ben-Gurion, *Be-Hilahem Yisra'el* [When Israel Fought] (Tel Aviv, 1957), p. 98; *"Al ha-Banim she-Naflu"* [On the Fallen Sons], 25 March 1950, ibid., p. 357 (hereafter Ben-Gurion, *"Al ha-Banim"*).

30. N. Gertz, *Sippur me-ha-Seratim* [A Tale from the Movies: Israeli Narrative and Its Cinematic Adaptations] (Tel Aviv 1993).

31. Ben-Gurion, *"Al ha-Banim,"* pp. 357–58.

32. T. Mayer, *Women*, p. 123.

33. At the time of the writing of these statements, research into the history

of the erection the memorial for the Women's Corps is being carried out as part of an extensive research project on the commemoration of fallen female soldiers. Interview by the author of one of the initiators of the memorial, Itzhak Pundak, Kefar Yonah, 9 May 1999.

34. J. Baumel, "Rachel Laments Her Children: Representation of Women in Israeli Holocaust Memorials," *Israel Studies* 1 (1996): 100–26.

Aftermath (pages 338–339)

1. Hannah Trager, *Pioneers in Palestine* (London, 2003).

2. Yehudit Harari, *Bein ha-Keramim* [Between the Vineyards] (Tel Aviv, 1947).

3. Henya M. Pekelman, *Hayyei Po'elet ba-Aretz* [The Life of a Worker in her Homeland], (Or Yehuda, 2007).

Glossary

Ahdut ha-Avodah, Zionist Socialist Labor Party in Eretz Israel, founded in 1919

aliyah (pl. *aliyot*) ["ascent"], immigration to Eretz Israel

Aliyah, waves of immigration to Palestine/Eretz Israel:

> **First Aliyah,** 1882–1903, consisted of individuals and small groups, mostly from Eastern Europe, but also from Yemen and other Middle Eastern and North African countries; the period of the establishment of the early *moshavot* and semi-modern urban neighborhoods.

> **Second Aliyah,** 1904–1914, consisted mainly of immigrants from Eastern Europe, which numbered about 40,000 people. Some were pioneers (*halutzim*) who worked as hired laborers in the *moshavot* and in the cities; most of them were middle-class people who settled in the towns, including the new Jaffa neighborhood (later city) of Tel-Aviv.

> **Third Aliyah,** 1919–1923, included many *halutzim* from Zionist movements. Veteran immigrants of the Second Aliyah and the *halutzim* of the Third founded the Histadrut. More *kevutzot* and kibbutzim were established as were the first *moshavim*; more than 35,000 persons arrived during this period.

> **Fourth Aliyah,** 1924–1928, contained many middle-class immigrants, over half coming from Poland. Some 80 percent of this Aliyah's 67,000 *olim* settled in cities. The rest were pioneers. Thus it was presented as a bourgeois Aliyah with negative connotation.

> **Fifth Aliyah,** 1929–1939, numbered over 250,000, with a prominent role played by refugees from Nazi Germany.

Ashkenazi (pl. Ashkenazim), Jews from Central or Eastern Europe, especially Germany (versus Sephardi, Jew of Spanish stock)

Bilu, acronym—Beit Ya'akov lekhu ve-nelkhah [House of Jacob, go you and

let us go]; established in Russia in 1882, first modern movement for pioneering and agricultural settlement in the Land of Israel

Davar, newspaper of the Israel Labor Movement, founded 1925

Devar ha-Po'elet, founded 1934, women's magazine of the Histadrut, central
journal of the women's movement

Eretz Israel, Hebrew for Land of Israel; the official Hebrew term for the area
governed by British Mandate (1922–1948)

gar'in (pl. *gar'inim*), ["nucleus"], a group of people who train to settle together
in Eretz Israel, either forming a new settlement or reinforcing an existing one

Gidonim, est. 1913, short-lived semi-clandestine group for sons of farmers; one
of its aims was to defend the settlement Zikhron Ya'akov

Golah, voluntary dispersion of Jews outside of Israel

Haganah, underground Jewish organization in Eretz Israel for armed self-
defense under the British Mandate that eventually became the basis for the
Israel Defense Forces

hakhsharah (pl. *hakhsharot*) ["preparation"], training farms in the Diaspora to
prepare pioneers for agricultural settlement in Eretz Israel

halakhah, the body of rabbinic law

halutz (m.), *halutza* (f.) (pl. *halutzim* [m.]; *halutzot* [f.]), pioneers in Eretz Israel, especially in agriculture

halutziyyut, pioneering

Ha-Po'el ha-Tza'ir ["The Young Worker"], Eretz Israel Labor Party, founded
1905

Ha-Po'el ha-Tza'ir ["The Young Worker"], the Ha-Po'el ha-Tza'ir movement's first newspaper; first two issues appeared in 1907, a weekly from 1912
(ceased publication in 1970)

Hashomer ["The Watchman"], association of Jewish watchmen in Eretz Israel, active between 1909 and 1920

Haskalah ["Enlightenment"], movement for the dissemination of modern European culture and education among Jews active from about 1750 to 1880

Hebrew [adj.], used to describe Zionist-Jewish endeavors, representing the attempt to establish a new Eretz Israel culture

hevrat no'ar, an educational unit of Youth Aliyah whose members formed a
self-contained social group with a considerable measure of in-group auton-
omy. The units resided on a kibbutz or in a youth village or other educational institution operated by Youth Aliyah. Within this framework, in addition to group activities, the members usually spent four hours working in
agriculture or in a workshop and four hours in study. *See also* "Youth
Aliyah."

Histadrut (full Heb. name, Ha-Histradrut ha-Kelalit shel ha-Ovedim ha-
Ivriyyim be-Eretz Israel), Eretz Israel Jewish Labor Federation, founded in
1920

Hovevei Zion, an early Zionist movement in Russia pre-dating Herzl that established settlements in Ottoman Palestine

Jewish Colonization Association, founded 1891, philanthropic association to aid needy or persecuted Jews to emigrate and settle where they would be employed productively, among locations for settlement were Argentina and Eretz Israel

kevutzah (pl. *kevutzot*), smaller-size voluntary collective community constituting an agricultural settlement in Eretz Israel; with growth it evolved into the kibbutz

kibbutz (pl. kibbutzim), larger-size voluntary collective community constituting a settlement in Eretz Israel, originally based mainly on agricultural; today also engaged in various industries. *See also "kevutzah"*

kibbush ha-avodah ["the conquest of labor"], preparation of Jews, spiritually and educationally, to work in all the occupations required in a national economy. The concept was linked to the ideal of *halutziyyut.*

Lehi, acronym from Heb. Lohamei Herut Israel ("Fighters for the Freedom of Israel"), a radical anti-British armed underground organization founded in 1940 in Eretz Israel by breakaways from Etzel (Irgun Zeva'i Le'ummi, "National Military Organization," commonly called the Irgun)

ma'barah, temporary settlement for housing newcomers in Israel during the period of mass immigration following 1948

Mapai (acronym—Mifleget Po'alei Eretz Israel), the Israel (previously Palestine) Labor Party, a Zionist-Socialist party founded 1930 through a union of Ahdut ha-Avodah and Ha-Po'el ha-Tza'ir; Mapai was the leading party from pre-State years until the 1970s.

Mizrachi, religious Zionist movement founded in 1902

Mizrahi, Jews from most Islamic and Arab countries

Mo'etzet ha-Po'alim, a local labor council

Mo'etzet ha-Po'alot, Women Workers Council, founded in 1922 as part of the Histadrut

moshav, smallholders' cooperative agricultural settlement.

moshav ovdim ("workers' *moshav*"), smallholders' cooperative agricultural settlement in Palestine and in Israel established on national land. It is based on family farms and individual working of the land, together with mutual liability and aid.

moshavah (pl. *moshavot*), Jewish independent, smallholders' agricultural settlement in Palestine. The earliest type of Jewish agricultural village in modern Eretz Israel; farming was carried out on individual farms, generally on privately owned land.

oleh (m.), *olim* (pl. m), *olah* (f.), *olot* (pl. f.), immigrant(s) to Eretz Israel

Palmah, mobilized striking force of the Haganah, established 1941. When ordered to dismantle by the British in 1943, it became an underground. Mil-

itary training was combined with agricultural work in the kibbutzim and
Zionist education. Considered to encompass a way of life, the Palmah
made a prominent contribution to Israeli culture and ethos.

po'alot, women workers

Sephardim, Jews from Spain and Portugal and their descendants wherever
they reside; today broadly applied to Jews of most Islamic and Arab countries as well

shiv'ah, the period of seven days of mourning following burial of a relative

Tisha b'Av (the Ninth of Av), a traditional day of mourning and fast over the
destruction of the First and Second Temples in Jerusalem

sabra (Heb. *tzabar* [m.], *tzabarit* [f.], "prickly pear"), person born in modern
Eretz Israel, referring metaphorically to prickly exterior and tender heart

tzumud (Arabic), a close, relentless attachment to land and home

Va'ad Leummi, the national council of the *Yishuv* during the British Mandate
period

WIZO (Women's International Zionist Organization), women's Zionist organization founded in London in July 1920

Yishuv, the Jewish Community ("settlement") in Palestine:

    Old *yishuv,* the traditional, religious Jewish community in Palestine

    New *yishuv,* the modernizing, Zionist Jewish community in Palestine
(from 1882 to 1948)

Youth Aliyah, a branch of the Zionist movement whose goal, when founded,
was to rescue Jewish children and young people from difficult situations
abroad and bring them to Eretz Israel to care for them and provide their education. In time, it also focused on children in Israel

Index